Local Government
in Ireland

Desmond Roche

Institute of Public Administration

First published 1982

by the Institute of Public Administration
59 Lansdowne Road Dublin Ireland

© D. Roche 1982

Reprinted 1983.

British Library Cataloguing in Publication Data

Roche, D.
Local Government in Ireland
1. Local government - Ireland
I. Title
352.0415   JS4320
ISBN 0 906980 06 2

Set in Press Roman by Healyset and printed by Mount Salus Press.

Contents

Appendices

Foreword

This book began as a revised and updated version of *Local Government* by John Collins, the second edition of which appeared in 1963. Collins was a former Secretary of the Department of Local Government (now the Environment) whose long and distinguished career in local administration ended with his death in 1954. When preparation of a third edition of his book was belatedly taken in hand, the changes in the system since then involved such a degree of re-writing that the work could no longer be ascribed to Collins. It was therefore thought best to let this version stand on its own. Although portions of the original text have carried over into the new, it is perhaps questionable whether Collins would recognise or approve this version as a development of his own. Any blame will lie solely with the present author.

It is with considerable regret that Collins's name no longer adorns this text, since many of those who knew him, including the writer, owe their interest in local government to his ability to invest the topic with interest, intellectual curiosity, enthusiasm, even passion. Though far from blind to the infirmities of Irish local government, he was always ready to defend its values and undoubted achievements. We in a later day may feel a similar respect, though we may possibly view with trepidation certain of the vicissitudes through which the system has passed since Collins's time.

This revision has attempted to widen the framework in which one might judge, or speculate on, the possibilities of further change in the Irish system. In some ways, of course, our domination by English reform thinking is more pervasive than ever. But entry into the European Communities poses certain questions, or at least reminds us of the existence of alternative systems, whose merits and demerits could repay closer inspection.

Collins took his intellectual stand on English local government, and judged the Irish and other systems from that base line. Circumstances have altered greatly since his day, and if we were in a position to consult him now about our present-day problems, his attitude might be different. Putting aside these pleasing if fruitless speculations, the fact that the 1937 constitution has come again under scrutiny offers an opportunity to include a statement of local rights and responsibilities of the kind that many newer constitutions have: a locality should look after its own affairs, of whatever kind, unless the state says otherwise. The flexibility thus bestowed nust generate self-reliance, perhaps enterprise, and, with luck, creativity. But if the essence of local government is the territorial distribution of power, what is one to say to the abolition of the domestic rate and its consequences? It is not quite true that our system suffered a mortal wound in 1978. Certainly some freedom was yielded up, but much remains. Local authorities can exercise crucially decisive power over physical development; zoning and re-zoning of land; and in general the quality of the environment we live in. Indeed, valid cause of complaint may be found not in lack of power, but in dubious competence and sometimes questionable performance. Does local government measure up?

Criticism from the sidelines is seductively easy. For those in the game it is a struggle to sustain high standards in the rough and tumble of local politics and its open, often wind-blown administration. Management, when first imported from America, carried the promise of transforming local administration into a simulacrum of good business practice — clean, economic, quick and efficient. But despite the heart transplant and other surgery, local government is still far from the business ideal. The 'county manager's hat' once a symbol of managerial power and leadership has faded from the municipal scene. Celebrated in the 1940's by Myles na gCopaleen, it has followed its inventor into the shadows. The conditions under which local administration is conducted are vastly different from the business setting. To the uncertainties of politics must be added the Kafkaesque impenetrable quality of remote controls operated by often mysterious arbiters of local destinies. Things would doubtless improve if one could find some way out of the perennial dilemma between the political elements — local democracy — and the bureaucratic, which is management. But so far the escape route remains hidden.

The intense localism of Irish politics does not, paradoxically, seem to have engendered an equally lively sense of civic involvement, at least in terms of local self-government and self-reliance. The shackles on freedom of taxation imposed by the Financial Provisions Act of 1978 were resisted, almost formally, in the Oireachtas, but there was little popular feeling against the Bill. One explanation of the apathy may be the ease and speed with which local issues can be brought to national level and ventilated to greater effect in Dáil or Seanad. Both ministers and departments are prepared to cope with detailed local affairs, and most Parliamentary Questions concern matters of parochial or personal interest. Hence perhaps the equanimity with which, since 1922, local electorates in town and country have accepted the supersession of their councils by commissioners appointed by ministers.

Local government is currently going through a phase of lowered esteem. Interest has cooled since the early 1970's, when a brisk exchange took place following the White Paper of 1971. The blanketing of community politics by national issues, noted by historians of the 19th century in the cases of O'Connell and Parnell, can be seen in the advance of the Northern, followed by economic, problems to the centre of the stage. But the intrinsic importance and value of local democracy have not declined, and will reassert their claim to attention when national problems, as in good time they may, cease to knock so loudly and insistently on the door.

My thanks for help in compiling this long-delayed book have been earned by so many colleagues and others that I am bound to omit the names of some who deserve mention in any list of acknowledgements. But the list must be attempted, at whatever risk. At its head, let me put Jim O'Donnell, who laboured so long to get the thing started, and to maintain its sluggish momentum. After him, Tony Farmar took up the running, if that is the right term, and whipped it into a smart canter. And as I am on the topic of the Publications Unit, let me cite those other members of the team with whom I found it so pleasant to work: Colette Cullen, Kathleen Harte, Brigid Pike, Sarah O'Hara, and finally and particularly, Elaine Farrell. To all of them my thanks for their inexhaustible patience and good humour.

The book and its author owe a special debt (unlikely, I imagine, to be repaid) to Tom Barrington, whose encouragement and support were forthcoming in so generous measure: to Michael Flannery, Brendan Kiernan, Dr. John Garvin, Frank Litton, Liam Ó Ceallaigh agus a bhean Caitlín, Dick Haslam, Donal Murphy (who kindly contributed appendix IX on the two Tipperaries); and to the staff of the Department of the Environment on whom I called so heavily – Michael Murphy, Brendan O'Donoghue, Tony Keegan, P. J. Tighe, John McGrath, Tim Sexton, Paddy Duffy, Eileen McArdle, John Cullen and Joe Harrington.

Among the libraries and librarians whose services were so readily supplied were the National Library of Ireland, the library of TCD and the UCD Archives Department; Máirín O'Byrne of the Dublin City and County Libraries; Pat Johnston, Curator of the Dublin Civic Museum; Joe Hayes, Wicklow County Librarian and finally, and most notably, Mary Prendergast and her helpers in the IPA library, a never failing source of books, periodicals and documentation of all kinds, of resource in difficulty, of help in all contingencies. Deirdre Shortall, formerly of the IPA library, did the index.

Finally, a word to my wife, Peig, without whose untiring vigilance the book would have taken twice the time. The partners of amateur scribblers are apt to be impatient of living too long with an uncongenial (to them) subject, but their failure to relish its niceties has the precious advantage of saving time all round, including the readers'.

Late Changes

As the book was being printed an agreement of 8 March 1982 between the Taoiseach and Mr Tony Gregory, TD, regarding Dublin's inner city problems had a number of local government implications, the most significant of which was the projected establishment of a new Inner City Authority on SFADCo lines – an authority within an authority, underlining the poverty and restricted scope of local administration.

Soon after this Mr Ray Burke TD, Minister for the Environment, informed local authorities, in a circular letter of 25 March 1982, that he intended to bring forward legislation at an early date (1) authorising a scale of fees for planning applications processed by local authorities and (2) giving local authorities general powers enabling them to charge for services. No specific services were mentioned.

These ideas are not new. They were put forward in the third report (1968) of the Inter-departmental Committee on Local Finance and Taxation, which also recommended public library charges for works of fiction. The suggestions were taken up by the government of the day whose White Paper (1972) on *Local Finance and Taxation* proposed to confer on local authorities a general power to make charges for services and to undertake trading services ancillary to their normal functions. Others dealt with library charges, planning applications, economic charges for sanitary services and with getting adequate returns from local properties.

These proposals were overtaken by the idea, which emerged early in 1973, of 'abolishing' domestic rates by shifting their incidence from householders and flatdwellers to the state. But commuting domestic rate into state grant, while solving one problem, created another in the form of a chronic shortage of cash for local services. Hence the decision to introduce now the long-deferred proposals about payments for beneficial services.

While no definite proposals have emerged so far about particular services (apart from planning applications) certain ideas have gained currency. The main source has been a paper prepared by the County and City Managers' Association for the General Council of County Councils in June 1980. The document *'Local Government Finance – a review'* suggested that in addition to planning applications, charges should be made for licences and investigations under the Water Pollution Act, with a graduated scale of payments for such essential services as water supply, refuse collection, burial ground facilities, and others.

The Inter-departmental Committee thought (para 85) that service charges would not yield more than 'a modest contribution'. But even a modest contribution will not be popular. The proposals are already being viewed with suspicion as the re-introduction of rates by another name.

1

Nature and Purpose of Local Government

Local government, as we know it today, is a modern creation. It carries reminders of a remote past: municipal corporations created before the first Irish parliament still survive, and counties formed in the Middle Ages for judicial purposes have given their names to the administrative counties of today. But there is otherwise little in common between the system now operating, and its earlier forms. Local government as we now know it emerged in the nineteenth century. The term itself was unknown before 1835.

Local government is commonly defined as a system of administration in political sub-divisions of a state, by elected bodies having substantial control of local affairs, including the power to impose taxes. These elected bodies are called local authorities and, if the definition is accepted as valid, a local authority must (a) operate in a restricted geographical area within a nation or state; (b) be elected or selected locally; and (c) enjoy a measure of discretion or autonomy. Powers of taxation are generally regarded as necessary conditions of that degree of independence which is required to qualify an administrative unit as a local authority.

There is no inherent reason why local government should be carried on by locally elected bodies, and in fact many local services are administered by agents of the central government. It would be a more precise use of language to refer to 'local self-government' or to 'local representative government', with the words 'general-purpose' implied in each case, since local government in its wider meaning includes some special-purpose units. But, as the standard work on *The Structure of Local Government* (Humes and Martin, 1969) puts it: 'Generally, local governments are either general-purpose, or representative, or both.'

Local authorities, despite varying degrees of independence, function in most countries as agencies of central government. That role clearly shaped the thinking of the Public Services Organisation Review Group in their comments on local government (PSORG Report 1969, 4.3.2; 5.3.23; 13.6.3; and 25.3.1). But the White Paper on Local Government Reorganisation (1971) dissented sharply from the review group's view of local authorities as 'executive agencies, with elected boards reporting to the Minister for Local Government.' Local government, the White Paper emphasised, was more than mere local administration.

'Local authorities have a considerable degree of independence and freedom of choice in the discharge of their functions and in determining the level and pattern of their expenditure. In addition, they have independent sources of revenue (rates and miscellaneous receipts) which meet about 50% of their expenditure. Even where central control is exercised, due weight must be given to the wishes of the local authority, both for reasons of principle and because of practical considerations.' (para. 2.2.2.).

While the position of local authorities has altered since the White Paper was issued, in particular as regards their financial freedom, this statement of their place in the government structure retains much of its validity. The most explicit statement of the agency theory is to be found in the constitution of the USSR which refers to 'local organs of State power', never to local self-government. This formula has been exported to a number of satellite countries.

Any large bureaucratic machine has certain characteristics: remoteness, inflexibility, insensitivity to feeling and information, with a consequent propensity to error. The injection of locally recruited and elected elements tempers the remoteness of central government and helps to avoid the grosser blunders to which organisations (big and small, but mostly big) are prone. Efficiency may thus be enhanced by democracy, though it must be admitted that somewhat the same effect may be achieved by non-democratic devices such as the nominated executive boards which were part of the structure of the National Health Service in Britain at its introduction in 1947.

The Right to Local Autonomy

A view of the nature of local government which is gaining support in recent years sees local self-government as an expression of democratic 'natural rights'. People have, according to this theory, a right to say how they shall be governed. In national affairs this right is bound to be of rather limited application, but local government multiplies the opportunities of participation and thus converts what must for most people be a notional right into something of a reality. The United Nations Declaration of Human Rights (Article 21) says: 'Everyone has the right to take part in the government of his country, directly or through freely chosen representatives.' This may be cited as a general statement of civic right, but is not directly related to local government. The European Convention on Human Rights does not mention local autonomy, but a resolution of the Council of Europe (14 May 1969) sets out a series of *desiderata* which include the following:

1. The autonomy of a local community is the right of that community to manage under its own responsibility its own affairs with a freely elected assembly.

2. The principle of local autonomy shall be embodied in the constitution of each state.

The full text of the resolution was printed as Appendix II to the report *More Local Government* (Chubb, 1971).

Anyone who has the time and inclination to pursue this fascinating by-way will find most of the references in Mackenzie (1961). To go back a little farther than his starting point, Rousseau held that in a true democracy, if the general will were to find expression, there should be no partial societies — groups, associations, corporations — within the state. This doctrine was translated in Benthamite terms into the notion of national sovereignty centralised in a single repository and source of authority, with ramifications where necessary to all parts of the realm. This is the structure of the reformed English Poor Law of 1834, and its Irish copy of 1838. Jeremy Bentham (1748-1832), a founder of philosophic radicalism, was precursor and prophet of the age of reform. His apostle and missionary, the centraliser Edwin Chadwick, waged a twenty years war against local self-government, condemning it as the enemy both of democracy and efficient administration. The centralists were in turn vigorously opposed by the historicist J. Toulmin Smith, who reached back into the misty Saxon past for arguments based, somewhat shakily, on the ancient English constitution. If the two parties represented thesis and antithesis in the Hegelian dialectic, the synthesis was supplied by John Stuart Mill whose new utilitarianism expounded in his *On Liberty* (1859) and *Representative Government* (1867) provided the intellectual basis for local government as it developed in the later part of the 19th century.

In America something of the same struggle took place between the Jeffersonian believers in the rights of localities to self-government, and subsequent political sceptics. The battles in this case were fought and won in the law courts, where judges Thomas Cooley and John Dillon delivered resounding judgments — Cooley for local self-government as an absolute right, and Dillon against — ending in victory for Dillon. The Dillon Rule, which says that local authorities are mere creatures of a state legislature, is now the accepted American law, confirmed many times by the United States Supreme Court.

Local government in the Constitution

There is no positive provision for local government in Bunreacht na hÉireann. Local institutions are mentioned, but only incidentally. Article 12.4.2, dealing with the Presidency, stipulates that a candidate for office should be nominated by twenty or more Dáil Deputies or Senators or by the Councils of not less than four administrative Counties (including County Boroughs) as defined by law. No presidential candidate has yet been nominated by local bodies. In the 1966 election campaign the late

Eoin O'Mahony sought nomination by these means, but failed to get the measure of support he needed.

Article 15 deals with subordinate legislatures and 'functional or vocational councils', but local government does not fit readily within these categories. Article 22 on the subject of Money Bills excludes from their ambit any taxation, money or loan raised by local authorities or bodies for local purposes. This meagreness of reference to what, after all, constitutes an important component of the political and administrative system calls for some comment. It is curious that both Irish constitutions, those of 1922 and 1937, have been so silent on the subject of local autonomy. Examples are not wanting of constitutions with explicit and sometimes elaborate provisions for local government. The Belgian constitution (1831) contains, in Article 108, a series of provisions on provincial and municipal institutions, including the assignment to local councils of matters of provincial or municipal concern. The constitution (1919) of Finland says in Article 50 that:

> For the purposes of general administration Finland shall remain divided into provinces, circuits and communes. . . . The administration of the communes shall rest on the principle of local self-government as prescribed by special laws.

The Weimar constitution (1919) of Germany contained in Article 127 a statement to the effect that 'Communes and associations of communes have the right to administer their own affairs within the limits of the laws.' In Denmark Article 89 of the constitution (1915 and 1920) says that 'The right of the communes to the free administration of their affairs under State supervision shall be determined by law.' The French constitution of 1958 stipulates in Article 72 that territorial units such as departments and communes 'shall be free to govern themselves through elected councils and under the conditions ordered by law.' The most recent example is the 1979 constitution of Spain, Article 140 of which guarantees municipal or communal autonomy, exercised through elected mayors and councillors.

The Irish constitution of 1922 derived very largely from British practice, and took local government for granted. The constitution committee considered three drafts, only one of which thought it worth while to deal with local institutions. This was Draft C, produced by Professor Alfred O'Rahilly of UCC with the support of Justice Murnaghan, Article 27 of which reads:

> The Irish Free State shall foster the ideal of decentralisation and regional autonomy within the unity Ireland. It shall therefore be within the competence of Congress (Parliament) to transmit to local representative assemblies such derivative authority in legislative, administrative, cultural and economic affairs as is compatible with the unity and integrity

of Ireland, without derogating from essential national services and rights. Congress may delegate to local parliaments the right to make ordinances within the ambit of the Constitution in relation to matters comprised in the following classes of subjects: local administration of justice and maintenance of order, direct taxation for local revenue, borrowing of money on local credit, education other than higher, local institutions and councils, works and undertakings not extending beyond the local borders.

This intriguing vision of a new Ireland was regrettably still-born. Draft C 'was not seriously considered by the Provisional Government or its advisers' (Brian Farrell, *Irish Jurist,* Vol VI, p. 111).

Local Democracy

If it is true that the virtual silence about local government in the Irish constitutions owed much to British influence, it is ironical that it has become accepted in recent years that 'in some sense or other local self-government is now part of the English constitution' (Mackenzie, 1961). That this idea has become part of official doctrine may be inferred from a number of documents of the 1960s and 1970s. An example is the Labour government White Paper (1970) on *Reform of Local Government in England* one of whose aims was expressed as ensuring that local democracy 'should resume its place as a major part of our democratic system.'

Something of the same kind may be found in our 1971 White Paper on *Local Government Reorganisation* which says:

> The real argument . . . for the provision of local services by local authorities . . . is that a system of local self government is one of the essential elements of democracy. Under such a system, local affairs can be settled by the local citizens themselves or their representatives, local services can be locally controlled and local communities can participate in the process and responsibilities of government (2.1.1.).

When therefore we read in Bunreacht na hÉireann (Art 5) that 'Ireland is a sovereign, independent, democratic State', we may, if the White Paper is to be believed, infer that local government is an indispensable item in our heritage. As already noted the White Paper explicitly contradicts the Report of the Public Service Organisation Review Group which pronounced that 'Local authorities should be regarded as Executive Agencies, with elected boards, reporting to the Minister for Local Government.'

The White Paper plainly echoes, in this portion of its argument, an English view of local government in which

representative government properly so called seeks to give outward form to the inward unity of a living community. Local government is with us an instance of democracy at work, and no amount of potential administrative efficiency could make up for the loss of active participation in the work by capable, public-spirited people elected by, responsible to, and in touch with those who elect them. (Royal Commission on Local Government in Greater London (1957–1960) par. 220.)

Popular participation in the business and in some at least of the decisions of government serves moreover as an education in working democracy. This aspect of the system was eloquently described by John Collins in the concluding lines of his book on *Local Government* (1952 and 1963):

It is the part of government that is most accessible to the average citizen, that most closely touches him and presents the most opportunities for public service. It is a school of citizenship. It associates many citizens with the actual business of government and has a peculiar function as the arena in which men and women can graduate as public representatives. It fulfils a higher purpose in a democratic State than that of a mere provider of roads, water, sewers, hospitals and all the rest and its success must be judged by the manner in which it fulfils its dual role.

There is a slight tinge of overstatement in this admirable eulogy. More people gain more experience in public affairs from residents' associations, trade unions, conservation societies and voluntary bodies of all kinds than in local government. Community councils, which have no statutory basis to speak of, are especially attractive to the civic-minded who may be reluctant to engage in the political process. But this does not detract from the function of local government as a gateway giving access to the labyrinth of government.

It is also possible to exaggerate the prevalence of the desire to participate in government. The number of political activists is still, by any standards, a small fraction of the adult population. The total of candidates in the 1974 local elections was some 5000 – a respectable enough figure of aspirants to about 1500 council seats, but small nevertheless when measured against an electorate of more than a million.

Purpose

Two of the principal functions of local government have already been touched on: the administration of a range of important services, and serving as a vitally necessary part of the political system. Local authority services are now concerned, in the main, with the development and concern of the physical environment. With the transfer elsewhere of health and welfare (public assistance) services, the only major social service remaining with local government is housing, which has a substantial environmental content. The trimming process has been accompanied by an expansion in the scope and importance of environmental concerns, so that apart from the logic of confining local government to a compact, reasonably homogeneous body of services, that body has enough weight and size to constitute a full-time job for Minister, Department and local authorities.

Nevertheless local authorities in Ireland have, if we take an international view, a relatively narrow range of functions. It is common to find local authorities elsewhere involved in police, public transport, primary and second-level education, social welfare, public utilities, and municipal undertakings of various kinds. The Irish scene is not, of course, as neat and well ordered as I may have conveyed above, and as the 1971 White Paper admits, there is still a string of bits and pieces of services which local authorities could well be relieved of. These are mostly relics of earlier legislation and different circumstances. Many services handled by present-day local government were assigned under the influence of a combination of history, accident and attachment to tradition. But there are some services which are obviously local in character. They include refuse collection and disposal, street cleaning, urban drainage, public conveniences, parks, swimming pools and recreational facilities of various kinds. A number of such aids to the good life were identified as district services by the Macrory Review Body and assigned to the district councils established in Northern Ireland in 1972. But this rational arrangement has not given universal satisfaction, and there is palpable discontent with the insignificance of the humble though no doubt useful functions to which local elected bodies have been reduced. Demands are emerging for the restoration to local government of some at least of its former glories, eclipsed by the transfer elsewhere of such vital services as education and housing.

On the point of principle, the Macrory Review Body (1970) wrestled with the problem of distinguishing between the types of work appropriate to central departments, statutory boards, and elected local authorities. They concluded that a broad distinction could be drawn between technical services such as electricity, harbours, or fire-fighting which were best looked after by independent nominated boards – and social services whose intimate involvement in human life and welfare made them matters of close, continuous concern to public representatives.

As Dr J. A. Oliver (1978) remarked: 'The fact that we departed radically from that analysis in Ulster in relation to health, personal social services, education and housing is a measure of the unusual conditions that obtained in 1972 and 1973.' In the event the elected local representatives were left with a collection of tasks whose unifying feature was their non-political character.

On this side of the Border the question was discussed briefly in the 1971 White Paper (2.3.1).Local authority services were sorted into (1) purely local services and (2) those which are national in scope, but call for local discretion in their application. It is perhaps worth noting that in 1973 the government decided that housing and health were national social concerns. Although they continued to be administered locally and regionally, their cost became almost wholly a charge on the Exchequer. Certain further purposes may be discerned in the system, though on examination they may prove to be little more than explicitly stated aspects of one or other of the two main objects cited above.

The first of these is the voicing of the opinions, needs and aspirations of the local people in matters of public concern. This seems a trite enough expression of an elected council's role, but in fact local authorities in Ireland have frequently been criticised for passing resolutions about issues not strictly within their competence. This is sometimes justified, or at least explained, as a relic of the period when popular views could not find a native parliamentary outlet, but there is a perfectly reasonable case for allowing a certain latitude to local bodies in voicing public opinion. Critics of this form of by-play are motivated either by the conviction that politics, in the sense of party politics, has no place in local government, or by some extension of the doctrine of ultra vires, which limits the purview of local authorities to a well-defined circle of legally appointed tasks.

There is another purpose in local government, largely unacknowledged in our system. This is the function of providing a political counterpoise to central authority and power. Local government should be able, in the words of the Redcliffe-Maud Commission on Local Government in England, 'to develop enough inherent strength to deal with national authorities in a valid partnership'. This point will not be pursued here, but some facets of it are referred to later (Chapter 7).

2

Comparative Local Government

Irish local government has been dealt with in the preceding chapter mainly in an English context, but there are other systems which aim at much the same results, with different forms of organisation. Some of them though, the French prefectoral pattern for example, would hardly qualify as local government at all in the terms we have been using. But substantial areas of the globe are administered, with more or less satisfaction to governors and governed, under such a system, or some derivative of it.

Typologies of local government are few and not very satisfying. Very little work has been done on comparative local government. But it is nevertheless useful to examine our system with the aid of perspectives supplied by others. The earliest labourer in this vineyard (Harris, 1948) made little inroad into the problem of theory, despite a first chapter entitled 'Underlying Principles'. Three orders of local government (using the term in its widest significance) were distinguished: (1) local self-government (2) local self-administration and (3) local state government. The first order tended to be dominated by English local government and its derivatives, the second by systems with weak legislatures and strong executives, and the third (administration by state agents) hardly qualified at all.

The best known of the more recent attempts at classification is that of Harold Alderfer (1963) who identifies four basic patterns into which most systems can be fitted. These are:

The French pattern: characterised by centralisation, a direct chain of command through a hierarchy of authorities; executive dominance and legislative subordination. These distinguishing marks may be detected in the majority of continental European local governments, but centralism is relatively weak in German and Scandinavian systems.

The English pattern: sometimes called the Anglo-Saxon, it is decentralised, with legislative dominance and independence between authorities. Generally operates through a co-optive committee system, but the use of appointed chief executives (city and county managers, for example) is spreading. Local government in the United Kingdom, Ireland, Australia, Canada and the USA follow this pattern.

The Communist model: characterised by party control under the name of democratic centralism, single candidate elections, a hierarchical chain

9

of command, and a broad range of government powers operating through local councils. According to a recent work, local communist councils

> belong totally to the *unified State administration*. There is no formal division between central government and noncentral governments, which are supposedly self-governing. . . . Each council represents the local population and, at the same time, is the *only* organ of the central government. The local officials elected by and representing the locality are also the officials of the central government (Piekalkiewiez, 1975).

Democratic centralism is a principle combining a necessary degree of centralism with 'true democracy' – mass participation of workers through communes. The structure of the new socialist state is a pyramid of councils, which constitute the basis on which the communist claim to true democracy rests. While mass participation is hardly a reality in, say, the Swiss sense, the figures are nevertheless impressive enough. In a population (1970) of about 33 million in Poland there were 134,000 councillors at various levels – rural, village, county, provincial and city. The Moscow and Leningrad city councils are enormous bodies of up to 1,000 members and the whole of Russia, with a population of 240 million is reported to have 50,000 local Soviets with over 2 million councillors.

Traditional: These survivals from earlier times include 'non-western' governments at village and community levels.

These categories have been accepted with some reservations by other writers on the subject. Not all local governments fit neatly into the scheme: many systems incorporate bits and pieces drawn from at least two of the general patterns described. Japanese local government exhibits signs of English influence as well as of French and German modes. In Ghana the English system prevails in urban areas, but there are characteristics of other patterns to be found elsewhere.

Irish local government was English in origin, and retains much of the general structure, as well as of the details, law and language of its proto-type. There have been major departures from the English model, but the introduction of management did not negate Anglo-Saxon influence, insofar as city and county management evolved in the USA. The modifications made in adapting the device to Irish conditions, nevertheless, were not American in spirit. Other innovations, moreover, such as staff recruitment and control methods, the creation of the Local Appointments Commission, and a general tightening of central controls, derive from sources other than Anglo-Saxon. The Irish system must therefore be characterised as an English design heavily overlaid by lines either of home manufacture or imported from non-English sources.

The French prefectoral system is sometimes included among these sources, mainly on the score of a superficial resemblance between county manager and departmental prefect. But the similarity, if any exists, is only skin deep. The county manager is in no sense a local embodiment of central government, as the prefect is. There is no hierarchy of subsidiary units, as in the French system, extending from *départements* through *arrondissements* and *cantons* to communes. There is nothing in the Irish system corresponding to the communal *maire* in France, who combines the functions of local executive and state official. But there is perhaps more substance to the comparison than may be furnished by a fancied likeness between two basically dissimilar structures. There are, firstly, strong elements of central direction in both systems; and the introduction and spread of management, it can be argued, gave to Irish local government something like the executive strength, if not predominance, which is a distinguishing mark of European systems.

The European Dimension

Most local governments in Europe differ radically from those which have developed in Ireland, North and South of the Border. The differences can be summarised as follows:

1. There is usually a large number of small local bodies (communes or municipalities) at the bottom level. The process of reform has drastically reduced the numbers in some countries. Denmark, which formerly had over 1,000 communes, now has 270; in Germany the number has fallen in recent years from 24,000 to about 3,261. Other countries have followed, e.g. Sweden where 278 municipalities have replaced the earlier 2,500; but France still has more than 30,000 communes, some of them very small. Switzerland also had over 3,000 communes in 1970, the majority of them quite small.
2. Although the overall structure is highly stratified, municipalities or communes generally have the same range of powers, whether urban or rural, and irrespective of size. Continental countries exercise a general competence, and often have a constitutional right to manage local affairs, unless a particular service or power is disposed elsewhere by law.
3. Continental countries usually have no equivalents of our Department of the Environment, or special ministries of local government. Local administration is usually dealt with at the highest level by a Ministry of the Interior. In Germany such central authorities are found at state, not federal level.
4. State control of local administration is usually decentralised to, as in France, prefects and sub-prefects, at *département* and *arrondissement* levels. Thus a hierarchy of authorities has been built up extending from a basic communal stratum through the county or province, to

EUROPEAN LOCAL GOVERNMENT STRUCTURES

Comparisons between modes of government, particularly local government, are difficult to present clearly. The names for different units are often peculiar to the country which uses them or the same words (e.g. mayor, municipality, province) may mean different things in different states. Comparative local government may therefore fail to enlighten, and more often confuse, and even mislead the reader. The following table is an attempt to present a number of European structures in skeletonic and one hopes, simplified form. The figures in brackets indicate the approximate number of organs at each level.

LEVEL	BELGIUM	DENMARK	FRANCE	FEDERAL GERMANY	IRELAND	ITALY
4. Region	(3) Regional Council		(22) Regional Council Regional Prefect	(29) Provincial (State Governor)	(9) Regional Development Organisation	(20) Regional Council Executive Board President
3. County Department Province	(9) Provincial Council State Governor	(16) Provincial or County Council County Mayor Assistant Mayor	(96) Departmental Council Prefect	(316) County Borough with Burgomaster County Council with Chief Executive	(31) County Council County Manager Co. Borough Council City Manager	(91) Provincial Council Prefect
2. District	(44) Arrondissement State Commissioner		(313) Arrondissement Sub-prefect		(84) Borough and Urban District Council Town	
1. Basic	(590) Communal or Municipal Council Executive Board Mayor	(273) Municipal Council Mayor	(36,500) Communal or Municipal Council Mayor Assistant Mayors	(3,261) Municipal Council Burgomaster or Executive Board or Mayor and Director		(8,000) Communal Council Executive Board Mayor

LEVEL	LUXEMBOURG	NETHERLANDS	SWEDEN	SWITZERLAND	ENGLAND & WALES	SCOTLAND	NORTHERN IRELAND
4. Region						(9) Regional Council	(9) Area Board (Mainly Non-Elected)
3. County Department Province	(3) District(State) Commissioner = Departmental Prefect	(11) Provincial Council Royal Commissioner	(23) County Council State Governor	(25) Cantonal Government	(53) County Council		
2. District				District Prefect or Commissioner (in some Cantons)	(369) District Council (in London, Borough Council)	(53) District Council	(26) District Council
1. Basic	(126) Communal Council Executive Board Mayor	(844) Communal Council Executive Board Mayor	(278) Municipal Council Executive Board	(3,000) Communal Assembly or Council Executive Board Mayor	(10,000) Parish or Community Council		

central government ministries. Regional layers have emerged (Italy, France) or are emerging (Belgium, Netherlands).

5. A wide variety of local taxes tends to be levied in Continental countries. Reliance on a single tax (rates) is confined to Ireland and Britain.

The significance of local government in the national economy was measured by J. Copeland and Professor B. M. Walsh for countries in the EEC (ESRI, 1975). The proportions of general government expenditure accounted for by local authorities were assessed for a number of countries in the Community. They found that local governments in the Netherlands, United Kingdom and Ireland generally ranked high.

	Current Local Expenditure as percentage of:	
	General Government Current Expenditure	GNP
	%	%
Germany	14.3	5.5
France	12.7	4.7
Italy	19.2	6.6
Netherlands	29.8	14.1
Belgium	14.1	5.4
UK	29.1	11.3
Ireland	27.0	9.0
Denmark*	(51.9)	(14.3)

*Some services included are more 'agency' than genuinely local.

These figures show Denmark and Netherlands as the most 'decentralised' countries in the Community with Britain and Ireland not too far behind. But there was no evaluation of the extent of local autonomy and local democracy operating in the various countries.

Belgium

Belgian local government follows the continental pattern of a hierarchy of local units, with state authority radiating outwards from the Ministry of the Interior to nine provinces, forty-four districts or *arrondissements* and some 590 communes. The number of communes was reduced by a process of amalgamation which began in 1961, from the earlier total of about 2,400.

Belgium has recently interposed a regional level of government between the central authority and the rest of the administrative apparatus. Three regions have been formed, with three regional councils: a Walloon council for the French speaking region, a Dutch council for the Flemish speaking region, and a Brussels regional council. These councils have advisory functions, their areas of concern being economic development, housing, family planning and population growth, public health, tourism, water supply, physical planning and a few others. The intention is to devolve a large number of central government functions to the regions which, with their sub-regions, will then replace the nine provinces.

Provinces correspond in large measure to the French departments. A Crown-appointed governor acts as agent of the state, responsible for the execution of national laws and regulations. He has the guidance and help of an elected provincial council of from fifty to ninety members, with a four-year term of office. The council chooses an executive board called the 'permanent deputation' to share the administration with the governor. Provincial functions are comprehensive, but they have certain special responsibilities for services such as vocational education and welfare. The 'permanent deputation' has a strong tutelary role in relation to municipal activities.

The provinces are sub-divided into *arrondissements* or districts administered by state commissioners whose principal function is to supervise the activities of the municipalities or communes in their areas. The communes have councils of from seven to forty-five members elected every six years. The chief executive or mayor (*bourgmestre*) is a state appointee, chosen by the council, usually from its own membership. The council also elects from two to nine councillors to form, with the mayor, a board of management (*collège de bourgmestre et échevins*).

The mayor and *collège* see to the execution of council decisions, and the general administration of communal affairs. The mayor has, in addition, certain responsibilities as a state official, mainly concerned with law and order, security and police.

Although closely supervised, the municipalities have a tradition of substantial autonomy derived from the express rights of local liberty included in the Belgian constitution of 1831. They possess a general competence to cater for the needs of their inhabitants, and many provide public utilities such as water supply, sewerage, gas, and engage in municipal trading. Their discretionary powers may embrace a wide range of services and amenities, environmental and personal, such as libraries, museums, swimming facilities and some public assistance and care of the mentally ill.

Local finances comprise, on the income side, a combination of general or support grant, and grants for specific services. The general grant is distributed from a municipal fund (*Fonds des communes*) according to formula. The fund, formerly recruited by means of local property and income taxes, now receives a settled proportion of total tax yield. Local authorities take an effective part in the administration of the fund through an advisory board made up wholly of representatives of the municipalities. The new regional governments will in future determine the basis of sharing their regional allocations among the municipalities.

Additional local taxes may be imposed by the communes as needed to supplement grants from the municipal fund. Under a recent (1971) amendment to the constitution five municipal federations have been formed in the following urban areas: Antwerp, Brussels, Charleroi, Ghent and Liege. In the Brussels area, as an example, nineteen municipalities have been placed under a metropolitan council having eighty-three members, with a nine-man Executive Committee under a President. The councils are mainly coordinating bodies, but certain functions may be transferred to them from the municipalities. Where this is done the councils can levy taxes to meet their expenses.

Denmark

Denmark was up to recently divided for local administrative purposes into twenty-five provinces or counties, and over 1,200 municipalities. The counties were territorial units corresponding to the department in France and the province in Belgium, Italy and elsewhere. They had a dual function, serving on the one hand as administrative divisions for a corps of state officers with some resemblance to French prefects; and as a unit of local representative government. The governor or *amtmand* was charged with general responsibility for state administration in his area, and kept an eye on the activities of the municipalities. This latter function he shared with a five-member board nominated by the county council, a body of from eleven to twenty-five members elected for a four-year term. The council was responsible in addition for certain services — secondary education, county roads, hospitals and physical planning.

This local administrative structure was re-shaped in 1970. Counties were enlarged to regional dimensions, and reduced in number to fourteen. Municipalities were drastically pruned and now number 273. The county organisation has also been placed on a wholly elected basis: councils have increased slightly in size, and must have between thirteen and thirty-one members; and the chief executive, the county mayor or *amtsborgmester,* is now chosen by the council from among its members. He replaces the former county governor, and gets a salary appropriate to full time employment. He holds office for the four-year term of the council, and may have two assistant mayors. The new system is described as one of democratically elected political management which, at county level, is an innovation in Denmark.

In addition to the fourteen counties there are two city areas which rank both as counties and communes, and would thus correspond to county boroughs. These are Copenhagen and Frederiksborg, both of which form part of the metropolitan area of Copenhagen. A Metropolitan Council was created in 1974 to cope with problems affecting three counties — Copenhagen, Frederiksborg and Roskilde — and the two boroughs of Copenhagen and Frederiksborg, all of them compressed into a relatively small and built-up corner of Zealand island. The council deals with physical planning, traffic, water supply, hospitals, and transport in the region.

There are now 273 communes, in each of which an elected council (average membership seventeen) looks after municipal affairs. The council chooses a mayor or *borgmester* as chief executive and chairman. In most urban municipalities there is in addition an appointed chief administrator or manager. There are over 5,000 local representatives in Denmark: 370 county councillors and 4,735 municipal councillors.

Local government functions are comprehensive. At county level they include secondary education, social welfare and health services, county roads and bridges, physical planning and hospitals. An important and growing element is cultural affairs — theatres, orchestras, museums, etc. Municipalities, in addition to a general competence in local matters, have specific powers in primary education, social services, homes for the aged, public works, road construction, housing and town planning.

Following the 1970 local government reforms enlarging the size of local units, a large-scale devolution of central government functions has been carried through. Both county councils and municipalities have gained additional functions. A further aspect of reform has been the alignment of police districts and other state administrative divisions with the new county and municipal boundaries.

Both county and communal authorities can levy income and real property taxes, and these taxes, especially local income tax, produce over half their income. The great bulk of the remainder comes from the new subsidy system.

A restructuring of local finances in 1971 substituted two new general or block grants for a large number of grants for specific services and projects. The new grants are (1) an equalisation grant, to bring tax revenues up to a national average and (2) a grant in aid of expenditure, based on needs: total population; children under seven years; education requirements, etc.

France

French local government, which is the model for most European systems, contains a large element of central administration through a hierarchy of local institutions. In contrast to the British system of mutually independent councils, each in direct relationship with central government, France is characterised by a chain of command extending downwards through successive strata: from the Ministry of the Interior through 96 *départements* or provinces, and 313 *arrondissements* to some 36,500 communes. Down to *arrondissement* level the system is largely one of localised state administration, with elements of representative government. In the communes the emphasis shifts towards local popular government of communal affairs. *Départements* are managed by state officials called prefects, who are heads and co-ordinators of all government activities in their departments. Each *département* has an elected general council of from twenty to sixty-eight members for which the prefect acts as chief executive.

A regional level, between *département* and commune, was introduced in 1964. *Départements* were grouped in twenty-two regions for planning and development purposes, the senior prefect acting as regional prefect. He carries responsibility for co-ordination and promoting regional development. He acts also as executive to the regional council, a body composed of all deputies and senators in the region, together with representatives of departmental and communal councils. Regional councils are not local authorities in the full sense: their primary function is co-ordination. With the limited funds at their disposal they can carry out studies, and participate in state investment projects. The regional structure was given a statutory basis in July 1972. The departmental apparatus, in addition to administering government services, exercises close supervision over the activities of all communal governments in its area.

Each commune elects, for a six-yearly term, a council of from nine to thirty-seven members. The council chooses its own chief executive or mayor, and, if the size of the commune warrants it, from one to twelve assistant mayors. Communal councils and their executives are invested by law with a general competence to deal with the affairs and needs of the commune. In addition, they must provide funds for police services, education, the fire service, some environmental health services, and minor roads. The larger communes have certain housing responsibilities. Communes may also provide parks, swimming pools, libraries, hospitals and childcare services, transport and other public utilities. Municipal trading is common, in the form of shops, savings banks and the like.

Income for local purposes is obtained mainly from (1) a resources or wealth tax and (2) real estate taxes. Over a quarter of current income comes from a block grant introduced to replace a pay-roll tax which was abolished in 1968 for reasons of administrative convenience.

Socialist election victories in 1981 have led to plans for decentralisation, including the decline of prefectoral power.

Federal Republic of Germany

As under other federal constitutions, the governments of the states or *länder* are not regarded as part of the local government system. The position is complicated in Germany by the fact that the cities of Hamburg, Bremen, and West Berlin rank as *länder* and their governments have therefore something of a municipal character. But in general the State governments, through the various Ministers of the Interior, play the role of central authorities in relation to local government.

Local government proper, as in most Continental systems, begins at the provincial level. The *Länder,* with some exceptions, are divided into provinces or districts, each of them under a *Land* official, the *Regierungs-Präsident,* who in addition to his duties as provincial governor has a supervisory function in relation to certain municipalities. At the next level, local authorities are of two main kinds. The county borough system operates in eighty-six of the larger towns, where the municipalities are responsible for all local services in their areas. Elsewhere there is a two-tier system, having an upper tier of 230 *landkreise* or counties, and a basic tier of 3261 enlarged *gemeinde* or communes. These figures (1976) represent a sharp reduction in numbers from the 1966 position, when there were 141 county boroughs; 425 counties; and 24,444 communes. County governments consist of elected councils having twenty-one to forty-seven members and, in common with other German local authorities, a four-year life; a board of management, and a chief executive carrying the title of *Landrat, Kreisrat* or *Oberkreisdirektor.* The *Landkreis* has no general competence, but its functions, conferred specifically by law, may include housing, highways, hospitals, secondary and vocational education, and public utilities such as gas, water and electricity.

There are four types of government at commune or *Gemeinde* level, depending on location. In Rhineland and Palatinate the elected council appoints a chief executive (*Burgermeister*) who will act also as council chairman. In Bavaria and Baden Wurtemberg, where there is another version of the 'strong mayor', the chief executive is elected directly by the voters. In Hesse and Schleswig-Holstein the council may choose a board of management or *Magistrat,* and designate one of its members to be board chairman and mayor to the municipality. The chairman of the council is called president. In the States of North Rhine-Westphalia and Lower Saxony, the Council selects a mayor as political head of the municipality and appoints a director or manager as chief executive.

The last-mentioned area came under British control for a period after 1945. The strong mayor system, which was traditional there as elsewhere in Germany (except Prussia, where the *Magistrat* ruled) was 'a form of local government opposed to the British belief in the vesting of all duties — legislative, deliberative and executive — in the council' (Marshall, 1967). Hence the non-political director, 'a person intended to carry out broadly the duties of an English town clerk.'

The functions of German local authorities are numerous and extensive. County governments generally take on tasks too great for communes, such as hospitals, roads, housing for the aged, and schools. They also exercise considerable supervisory powers over the smaller municipalities. The communes, large and smaller, have a general competence to undertake all local functions not assigned by law to other agencies. These may take the form of providing theatres, libraries, museums, hospitals; public utilities such as electricity and transport; savings banks, sports facilities and many other amenities. Communes also have mandatory functions in relation to schools, youth welfare, roads, housing and fire prevention. Functions may also be delegated to communes by the federal or state government, in relation to public security, civil defence and the regulation of traffic and trade.

Local authorities obtain a substantial proportion of needs from (1) local income tax and (2) taxes on real estate. A tax on business profits also yields a large contribution. Municipalities receive a fixed proportion of State taxes.

Italy

Italian local government operates through a hierarchy of local units comprising twenty regions subdivided into ninety-one provinces and a basic stratum of some 8,000 communes.

Although the 1948 Constitution envisaged a government decentralised through twenty regions, it was not until 1970 that the task of full implementation was finally faced. Regional councils were elected in 1972, but even then the original intentions were only partially realised. However, following a shift of power to the left in the general election of 1976, the process of devolution was accelerated, and co-ordination at regional level of services and administration became more of a reality. Three main areas were concerned: social and community services such as welfare, health, local transport, libraries and museums; environmental matters, mainly land-use planning and urban development; and regional economic development.

The regional governments consist of an elected council, executive board, and a president. Each region is supervised by a regional commissioner, a state appointee, and, through a Committee of Control, exercises supervision over the provinces and communes in the region. This Committee is made up of three administrative experts nominated by the regional president, a judge from the region's administrative tribunal, and a nominee of the Regional Commissioner.

Provinces serve a two-fold purpose. They are at the same time units of local representative government and of decentralised state administration. In this they correspond to French *départements*, having prefects who are appointed by and responsible to the Ministry of the Interior, and elected councils. The provincial council consists of twenty-four to forty-five members elected every five years; it appoints a board of management and a chairman, who share with the prefect the administration of the province. Provincial functions are however tightly limited and include local roads and bridges, maintenance of secondary school buildings, certain social services and public order and security. The province formerly kept a close watch over the activities of communal governments, but this function has been taken over by the regions. The need for continued existence of the provinces is coming into question since regional administration has emerged. Communal councils may have from fifteen to eighty members, elected for five-year terms. The council selects a board of management of from four to fifteen members, and a mayor who acts as head of the executive. Much of the business of the executive is however in the hands of a secretary-general appointed by the central government who supervises and co-ordinates the day-to-day administration of the commune.

The functions of the municipalities include in addition to responsibility for urban development, sanitary or public health services, public lighting and parks, roads, regulation of traffic, education, social welfare services, certain public enterprises and municipal police. The mayor, in addition, carries responsibilities in relation to law and order, vital statistics, the electoral register, and certain other matters delegated to him by the central government.

Local taxes are numerous: they include rates on dwellings, other buildings, and land. There is also a tax on agricultural profits, and taxes on businesses and occupations; entertainment taxes, a tax on hotels and restaurants, and a motor tax. The Ministry of the Interior distributes a general grant to augment local revenues where resources are insufficient to support local needs. Special grants are paid for education, culture, social welfare and health.

Grand Duchy of Luxembourg

Local government in Luxembourg exhibits the same features as other continental systems, particularly the Belgian, but on a smaller scale. The country is divided into three districts (Luxembourg, Diekirch, Grevenmacher), each under a district commissioner, a state official who acts as agent of the central government and, in addition, supervises municipal government in his area.

There are 126 communes or municipalities with elected councils of varying size. The life of the council is six years. The day-to-day management of communal affairs is in the hands of a board or college whose members are appointed by the central government from among the councillors. The mayor (*bourgmestre*) is also appointed by the central government, either from the council or outside it.

The functions of the municipalities follow the Belgian pattern. The communes possess a general power to manage local affairs and meet the collective needs and wishes of the inhabitants. Specific powers relate to such matters as education, water supply, fire prevention, the regulation of building, sanitation, traffic, health, security and public order.

The principal source is a local income tax, followed by a profits tax on business. There are also real estate and pay-roll taxes. General and some specific grants are paid by the central government.

Netherlands

Netherlands local government follows the continental pattern of a hierarchy of local units under the Ministry of the Interior, with a line of authority leading through eleven provincial governments to 844 communes. The provinces are units for the administration of all central government services, under the general control of Royal Commissioners. These are Crown-appointed officers with much of the status and functions of French prefects. Each province also elects a provincial council with from thirty-nine to eighty-three members holding office for four years. The council in turn chooses a board of six members to work, under the chairmanship of the Royal Commissioner, in the day-to-day administration of the province. Provincial governments are concerned with physical planning, the control of water boards, main roads and bridges, and with the supervision of local government at communal level.

The 844 communes elect councils of from seven to forty-five members for four-year terms. The councils choose boards of management of from two to six councillors, and the mayor. The mayor or *burgemester* is appointed by the Crown on the recommendation of the Royal Commissioner of the province, who takes account of, inter alia, the wishes of the commune. He acts as chief executive of the communal council, presides over the board of management, and discharges certain duties as a state official, notably concerned with fire protection, public order and police and civil defence.

Netherlands local authorities possess a general competence to administer the affairs of the commune and meet the collective wishes and needs of its inhabitants. Specific functions include the construction of roads, bridges, tramways, and airports; the regulation of buildings; and housing, schools, cultural and recreational services.

The Netherlands has the lowest proportion of any Community country in local tax yield as a percentage of total local revenue. The figure is 3.2 per cent, as compared with 78.6 per cent from central taxation (1972). The central contribution is channelled through a Municipal Fund in accordance with a formula, and some degree of local autonomy is preserved.

Sweden

A series of structural reforms has, as in many other countries, concentrated local resources into a smaller number of local units. Up to 1952 the basic level comprised 2,500 primary communes. In that year a process of amalgamation began which, in several stages, succeeded in reducing the number to 278. There are now twenty-three secondary authorities (formerly twenty-five), usually called county councils. These are elected bodies, subject to the general law of local government, but the continental pattern is evident in that each 'county' coincides with the province of a state-appointed governor. There are three all-purpose 'county boroughs': the cities of Stockholm, Gothenburg and Malmo.

A Municipal Administration Act of 1977 liberalised the system by empowering the municipalities themselves to determine their forms of internal organisation. The municipalities were also authorised to conduct opinion polls on certain municipal issues.

Municipal councils are elected every three years, and membership varies from thirty-one to sixty-one according to population. Stockholm has 101 members. Sweden has a total of about 30,000 councillors. Employees number some 700,000. Executive authority is exercised by a municipal board chosen by the council. It generally has eleven to seventeen members, although a small municipality may have as little as five board members.

Local authorities can exercise a general capability in the conduct of local business, but in addition have been assigned a growing number of formerly central services and responsibilities. Central controls have also been gradually withdrawn. The proportion of Gross National Product accounted for by the municipalities (it increased from 15 per cent to 20 per cent in the decade 1960–70) is expanding at an accelerating pace.

Education is a principal concern of the municipalities – virtually the entire public education system is municipally administered. Municipal welfare – child care, care of the aged, services for the handicapped, etc. – is a major feature of their advanced social welfare. Municipalities also handle physical planning, housing, roads and streets, the fire services, parks, recreational facilities, and libraries. The county councils look after medical and dental care and personal health services in general.

A major source of strength and independence in Swedish local government is the municipal income tax, which supplies most local financial needs. This tax is levied on the same basis as the national income tax, but at a rate fixed by the municipal council. In addition, however, state grants are paid for education, some forms of social welfare, and the fire service. Income is also derived from municipal gas and electricity undertakings, as well as from housing.

Switzerland

Each of the twenty-five cantonal administrations in Switzerland (nineteen cantons and six demi-cantons) has a distinct system of local government. While there is no national system (the Federal government has no authority in local administrative affairs) there is a strong family likeness running through Swiss local government. Communes, most of which are quite small (two-thirds with less than 1,000 inhabitants), exercise an extraordinary degree of autonomy, subject only to cantonal supervision of a very general nature. This is done in a minority of cantons through prefects or commissioners appointed by the cantons to look after districts called *Bezirke* or *Kreise;* but mostly it is done directly by the cantonal governments.

There are over 3,000 communes, some of them minuscule in size, but all prepared by law and tradition to take on an impressive array of responsibilities: public order, education, roads, social welfare, public buildings, museums, theatres, and so on.

The smallness of most communes may be gauged by the fact that it is still possible to dispense with elected councils. In the great majority of communes the general business (municipal legislation, budgets, borrowing, and such major issues) is transacted at assemblies of all the electors in periodic meetings. Where the commune is densely populated, a council is elected. In either case a municipal board or college is appointed, with three to nine members, for executive functions. The chairman may be styled *stadt-präsident, maire,* or *sindico,* according to the vernacular.

Important communal affairs are often referred for decision by plebiscite. There is much use of the referendum and popular initiative in policy matters.

The bulk of taxation is levied by the cantons and communes. Federal taxation yielded up to recently less than one third of total taxes, although its share is tending to grow. The principal local taxes are: income tax; real estate tax; a land tax on capital gains from sales of land; poll taxes; and entertainment tax. Income tax is primarily a cantonal tax, but the communes (which are the collecting agencies) may levy an additional percentage for local purposes. Equalisation and specific taxes are paid by the cantonal and federal governments to the communes.

United Kingdom

The British system of local government has a number of features which distinguish it sharply from continental local government. There is little or no hierarchy of local units, no line of state authority running through several strata to a basic tier of small councils. Local authorities are, in the main, mutually independent, and deal directly with central government principally with the Departments of the Environment, and Education and Science, in matters of legislation, finance, policy and administrative controls. There are no regional authorities as such, although eight regional planning areas have been defined.

A new structure for local government in England and Wales (outside Greater London) came into effect on 1 April 1974. The reorganisation forms part of a complete reform of local government structure throughout Britain. In Greater London the present structure (which is unique in the country) came into being in 1965; changes in the organisation and functions of local authorities were made in Northern Ireland in 1973 and a reorganisation in Scotland – on a pattern broadly similar to that in England and Wales – took place in May 1975.

Under the Local Government Act 1972 existing local authorities in England and Wales (outside of London) have been replaced by fifty-three large county authorities, within which there are 369 smaller district authorities. Both types of authority have independent, locally-elected councils, and have separate functions to perform. County authorities normally provide the large-scale local government services, while the districts are responsible for the more local ones (see below). In the six heavily populated 'metropolitan' counties in England, however, responsibility for certain large-scale services rests with the district authorities.

There is no specific legal provision for a separate executive, extensive use being made of the committee system. The concept of the chief executive is however gradually gaining ground. In rural areas of England some 10,000 parish councils or meetings — the great majority representing fewer than 5,000 people although some range up to and exceed 20,000 — are largely unaffected by the new structure, and continue to serve as focuses for local opinion with powers for the provision of services of essentially local interest.

The main local authority functions are exercised by the county and district authorities, but as far as possible their responsibilities are mutually independent. Broadly speaking, county authorities are responsible for planning, transport co-ordination, education, most highways, consumer protection and (in England) refuse disposal. Police and fire services are operated at county level, though in some cases counties are grouped together to provide these services.

District authorities have responsibility for most housing functions, local plans and development control, building regulations, refuse collection (and, in Wales, refuse disposal) and many other environmental health functions including, in certain instances, sewerage. They are education authorities in the metropolitan counties.

In Scotland the two-tier structure has also been preserved, in a very altered shape. Nine regional authorities constitute the upper level, with fifty-three district councils in second place. There are, in addition, three all-purpose councils for the islands of Orkney, Shetland and the Western Isles. Regional councils administer the major services: education, police, fire, highways, water, sewerage, consumer protection, public transport and strategic planning. District councils handle housing, environmental health, libraries, museums and local planning.

In Northern Ireland the local government system has been radically altered by the substitution of twenty-six district councils, with limited powers, for the former two-tier system comprising six county councils, two county borough councils and some sixty urban and rural district councils. Outside the new local government structure there are nine area boards, mainly non-elected. Four of these boards carry responsibility for health and social services; five deal with education and libraries. Housing, planning, roads, water, sewerage and the fire service have been centralised in Belfast.

Local taxation is limited to a single tax — the rate on houses, buildings and certain other kinds of immovable properties. Agricultural land has been wholly de-rated since 1929. The main source of local revenues is the Exchequer, but efforts have been made to moderate central intervention in local affairs by resort to the block grant system. The principal grant is the Rate Support Grant, calculated on a formula taking account of local resources and needs. The Land and Planning (No. 2) Act, 1980 marked a departure from the Rate Support Grant and a return to a form of block grant containing a penal element designed to curb local over-spending.

Greece is the latest adherent to the EEC. See Appendix VII for an account of its local government.

3

Origins of Irish Local Government

It is commonly said that our political system owes nothing to native sources, but local government provides a few minor exceptions to the universality of the proposition. There are one or two elements pointing to links with a remoter past than the advent of the Anglo-Normans. The native Irish society was almost wholly rural, pastoral if not exactly arcadian. The earliest unit exhibiting anything like urban characteristics was the monastic settlement, itself an imported accompaniment of Christianity. Cities and walled towns were introduced in the ninth century by the Norsemen. The type of municipal institutions we recognise today — the corporation, the mayor or chief citizen, and the council — began to appear in the twelfth century, with the hesitant progress of the Anglo-Norman invasion.

The native Irish territorial unit was the *tuath* an area corresponding, sometimes, with the barony under the rule of a king. His rule was direct and personal: there were no intermediate bodies between king and people. There was a public tribal assembly at fixed intervals, where ordinances could be promulgated; there were judges and certain other officers (such as *rechtaire* or steward) and a professional class or *aes dana*. Order was maintained — with remarkable success in the absence of a state system of enforcement — by an intricate body of law administered by a prestigious learned profession, their decisions buttressed by sureties. But there was little resemblance in all this to the administration of the modern state.

The interesting aspect is that the district of the *tuath*, insofar as it co-incided with the barony, formed the basic unit from which counties were put together. The process is described in the Act of 1556, creating King's and Queen's Counties from the 'countries of Leix, Slewmargy, Irry, Glenmarily and Offaly.'

It is impossible to say with certainty that all the counties were so formed, but such evidence as there is points in that direction, and leaves us with the probability that the baronies and counties were formed of pre-existing organisms. Baronies corresponded to the English hundred, and were delineated finally in the early part of the seventeenth century.

Counties

The origins and development of the county system cannot be traced with absolute certainty, but the outlines of the story are clear enough. From the conquest to the end of the thirteenth century the machinery of county administration through sheriffs and itinerant justices was extended to about half the island. Thereafter, for upwards of two centuries, the area of effective control contracted until it survived only in Dublin and three contiguous counties. Elsewhere county government did not altogether cease, but took the form of liberties or counties palatine, virtually independent of central control. With the sixteenth century began a dual process of reasserting royal authority in the palatine counties, and creating new counties in areas hitherto under Irish rule, or where English authority was merely nominal.

The first essay in county creation was credited by early historians to King John, who was said to have carved out a dozen in 1210 (*A Discoverie of the State of Ireland*, Sir John Davies, 1613). They were named as Dublin, Kildare, Meath, Louth (Uriel), Carlow, Kilkenny, Wexford, Waterford, Cork, Kerry, Limerick and Tipperary. But the formation of counties on this scale, and at that time, is hardly possible. While Dublin certainly existed as a county in the 1190s, such evidence as there is does not support King John's or any earlier claim to system-building. The facts seem to be that in the course of the thirteenth century a chain of counties was gradually built up, mainly on the East, South and West coasts. When John died in 1216 three counties had definitely taken shape: Dublin, Waterford and Cork.

By the early part of the fourteenth century a further eight had emerged: Kildare, Louth, Meath, Limerick, Kerry, Tipperary, Connacht and Roscommon. This was the highest point reached by English authority in the four centuries following the conquest; thereafter followed a long period of decay and withdrawal marked by the re-emergence of liberties or counties palatine outside the contracting circle of direct royal authority. In 1328 Edward III granted palatine powers in North Kerry to the Earl of Ormond, while liberties also existed about this time in Carlow, Kildare, Kilkenny, Meath, Ulster and Wexford.

The evolution of Kerry is, like almost everything else in the county, individual. The North Kerry palatinate endured from 1328 until about 1571, when the Presidency of Munster was established. At that time a new county of Desmond was formed of South Kerry and West Cork. This lasted until 1606 when Cork and Kerry took on their present boundaries.

Counties palatine gradually ceased to exist with the growth of royal authority. All except North Kerry and Tipperary had been absorbed by the time Henry VIII reached the throne in 1509. Tipperary survived as a palatinate until the time of James I. Henry VIII, although notably effective in extending English control in Ireland, added only one new county to the list, and that by division of an existing shire. By 34 Henry VIII c.I (1543), Westmeath was detached from Meath to form a county on its own. King's and Queen's counties followed in 1556; and the Connaught counties about 1570 — Galway, Mayo, Roscommon and Sligo. To these were added Thomond or Clare; it was separated from Connaught in 1576, and became part of Munster. Leitrim became a county in 1583, followed by Longford and Cavan.

Ulster remained mostly undivided until late in Elizabeth I's reign (1558–1603). Antrim and Down seem to have had earlier if shadowy histories, but the shiring of the province is generally assigned to 1584, with the creation of Armagh, Tyrone, Monaghan, Fermanagh, Derry (Londonderry), Donegal, Antrim and Down. Cavan was of earlier formation, as part of Leinster. Wicklow was the last county to emerge, in 1606. It had been delineated somewhat earlier, in 1578, but the troubles of the times prevented the commission being carried into effect.

County Administration

At the centre of local or county administration was the sheriff, a royal officer, appointed either by the King, or by the Irish treasurer or justiciar. The sheriff's administrative duties, apart from tax collection, included repair of royal castles and gaols, arrangements for court sessions (he had his own court of sheriff's tourn, for minor cases) and policing the county. He also had to attend to the election of a coroner, and of knights of the shire; and to the construction of a variety of public works.

The county staff included a subsheriff, clerks and record-keepers, and serjeants who acted as general assistants to the sheriffs in the baronies, although the chief serjeant was usually responsible for the whole county. There were also the coroner, escheator (whose job was to oversee the feudal rights of the crown) and sub-escheators; together with a kind of police force composed of keepers of the peace. Clerks of the market who investigated weights and measures seem to have been less county officers than inspectors despatched by the central government. The baronies served as subdivisions of the county for administrative purposes. Collectors of subsidies for example were appointed two to each barony.

Mention above of knights of the shire calls for some brief comment on the role of counties and boroughs in parliamentary representation. Each county as it emerged, and each borough as created, sent two members to parliament: knights of the shire from counties, and burgesses from the boroughs. The multiplication of boroughs by James I in the early part of the seventeenth century was mainly for the purpose of packing the parliament of 1615. A vestigial survival of the parliamentary function may perhaps be detected in the role played by county councils in elections to the Senate and Presidency.

The organisation of a liberty or county palatine was a somewhat different affair. It was, in the words of Professor D. Quinn 'a microcosm of royal government. This was, I suppose, the apotheosis of local government: rather too exalted to last. The optimum of feudal state was only less than that of a king.' *(Irish Historical Studies,* Vol. 1 page 362).

Apart from their function in parliamentary representation, counties were formed principally as units for the territorial administration of justice. The King's judges visited each county (including counties of cities and towns) twice yearly and held assizes for the hearing and adjudication of cases, with the assistance of grand juries. These were chosen, twenty-three in number, by the High sheriffs, from among property owners – the biggest landholders in counties, and the higher bourgeoisie in cities and towns. From the seventeenth century onwards this piece of judicial machinery began to accumulate certain administrative functions, which came to be known as the fiscal business of the grand juries.

The first statute giving a clue to the course of the fiscal business was an Act of 1634, 'An Act concerning the repairing and amending of Bridges, Causeways and Toghers in the Highways', authorising the justices of assize, with the consent of the grand jury, to levy the cost of road and bridge works on the county or barony, according to the importance, one assumes, of the road or bridge affected. The levy came to be known as the county cess. The names of those liable, by ownership or occupation of land or other property, were inscribed in a roll, and collectors were appointed for each barony and parish.

The system took little hold until settled conditions, of a sort, began to appear towards the end of the seventeenth century with the total victory of the Protestant cause. An Act of 1705 authorised the grand juries to take the initiative in making presentments, or proposing works for financing by the county cess-payers. The types of work gradually expanded, and services began to be included, until the grand juries were dealing with a large body of miscellaneous tasks. These included roads, paths and bridges, the maintenance of lunatic asylums, cost of extra police, courthouses, conveyance of prisoners, salaries of county officers (secretary, surveyor, etc.) contributions to county infirmaries and fever hospitals, dispensaries, loan repayments, and compensation for malicious injuries. Two assizes were held each year, in spring and summer.

By the early part of the nineteenth century the volume of law dealing with the fiscal work of grand juries had greatly increased, and the reformers, in addition to clarifying and consolidating the law, made an attempt to curb the grosser malpractices which had grown up. Inefficiency and corruption were widespread: grand jurors exerted themselves to secure presentments for works of benefit to themselves and their friends. As early as 1816 a parliamentary select committee recommended the separation of civil from criminal business, and an Act of 1817 established the office of County Surveyor with the aim of bringing some control into the disorderly business of making presentments for roads and other works. Valiant efforts were made also to cope with the centuries-old problem of equitable valuations for cess-payers, and a Valuation Act of 1826 began the process of rectifying anomalies. An Act of 1833, soon to be incorporated in the Grand Jury Act of 1836, democratised the system in some small degree, by requiring the High Sheriff to include at presentment sessions one resident £50 freeholder or £100 leaseholder from each barony, the remainder to be chosen from men of like qualifications in any part of the county. Catholics were eligible to become grand jurors since the Catholic Relief Act of 1793. The Act of 1836 instituted a system of presentment sessions in counties and baronies. The baronial presentment sessions (dealing with expenditure for the benefit of the barony) were conducted by juries composed of justices of the peace and cess-payers – the latter numbering from five to twelve chosen by a complicated formula. Cess-payers were in practice slow to attend because they could not be sure of selection, and the business of the session tended to be left in the hands of the justices.

County at large presentment sessions dealt with expenses of benefit to the whole county (they also handled baronial presentments for the barony where the courthouse was situated). In addition to the justices of the peace, one cess-payer nominated by each baronial session figured on the county body. The function of county and baronial presentment sessions was to take over the initiation of expenditure from the grand jury. The initiatory role, that vital step in the local administrative process, was thus transferred to a somewhat more representative body.

The Act of 1836 had little real effect, and dissatisfaction with the fiscal operations of the grand juries persisted. The system was fully investigated by a Royal Commission in 1840–2, but no action ensued, and twenty years later Isaac Butt and other members of parliament were still trying by means of private Bills to reform the grand jury. But reform eluded them, and the system stayed as it was until it was abolished in 1898.

The pressure – it was never an agitation – for better county government was a low-key affair; it had little popular support. O'Connell was more or less indifferent. The torch was carried by Whig reformers like Lord Monteagle, an Irish landlord whose family name of Spring Rice recurs from time to time in our history. A note of passionate denunciation may however be detected in Carleton's little-known novel *Valentine McClutchy*, Ch. 22.

The counties have remained substantially as delimited in the sixteenth and seventeenth centuries. The principal departure, in the local government context, was the division of Tipperary into North and South ridings in December 1838, (see Appendix IX). The two grand juries so created each dealt with fiscal business under general grand jury law. And the grand juries, in their fiscal capacities, became the two county councils which operate in Tipperary to the present day.

Cork county was divided into ridings in 1823, but for Quarter Sessions only, and thus retained its single grand jury, and in due course its single county council. Galway county had an east and west riding in the nineteenth century for certain administrative purposes – the appointment of county surveyors, and police management.

The term county is now generally applied to territorial divisions of considerable extent, with a rural or urban-rural character. There are however four urban counties, styled county boroughs or, in certain contexts, cities: Cork, Dublin, Limerick and Waterford. There were formerly eight counties of cities and towns, including in addition to the four cities mentioned above, the boroughs of Carrickfergus, Drogheda and Kilkenny, and the urban district of Galway. But the four last-mentioned were merged in their counties by the Local Government (Ireland) Act, 1898. Belfast and Londonderry became county boroughs under the same Act.

Municipal Government

Ireland had towns before the Normans came, some of Irish origins but most of them Danish creations. Dublin, Cork, Limerick, Wexford and Waterford were among those of pre-Norman source; others emerged shortly after the invasion. All of these were given charters by Henry II, his son John, or by their barons, and became boroughs on the Norman pattern with their own courts (principal among them the hundred court), chief executive officers (generally titled mayors) and councils. The charters vested the land on which the town was built in the general body of citizens or burgesses; and the grant of land might also include additional acreage in the adjacent territory. The idea of creating bodies corporate, by incorporating the mayor, burgesses and commonalty of citizens, which land-holding on this scale would seem to necessitate, did not in fact emerge until the Tudor period, when clauses to this effect began to appear in the charters.

The mayor, portreeve, sovereign or other chief executive was an early type of city manager, but with wide powers, more authority and even greater prestige. He was chosen by his fellow citizens through the hundred court and held office for a year. The numerous band of similarly selected officers – recorder, coroner, town or city clerk, treasurer, town serjeant and so forth – made up the management team which conducted the military, judicial and much of the economic affairs of the town. The town council, a universal feature of the municipal structure, exhibited a tendency to evolve into two forms of organisation: a small inner council consisting in the main of former officers who, with the mayor, ran the town; and an assembly or common council, with some representative character, whose powers were mainly legislative. Revenue required for the expenses of defending and managing the town came from customs, tolls and rents charged for municipal properties. Local taxes in the modern sense were not levied.

The larger towns enjoyed freedom from the supervision of county authorities, had their own courts to administer justice, and regulated their markets and trade. Towns also asserted a large measure of independence of the crown in civic affairs from the twelfth to the sixteenth centuries. With the recovery and growth of royal authority the central government took advantage of grants of incorporation to confer municipal powers not on the general body of the townspeople, but on close corporations. In the many new boroughs created during the seventeenth century, civic authority was centralised in small self-perpetuating oligarchies. This practice opened the way to the corruption and decay which infected virtually all boroughs in the eighteenth and early nineteenth century both in Britain and Ireland.

During this period the corporations, while flagrantly neglecting town services, concentrated on the important political function of returning members of the right colour to parliament. But even before the tide of reform finally overtook them, thirty boroughs were wiped out by the Act of Union, twenty of them close corporations of Stuart creation.

Lighting of Towns Act, 1828

A further sign of the coming reform was the growth of bodies of commissioners in many towns who undertook such matters as public lighting, street-cleaning, paving, water supply, drainage and police in the latter half of the eighteenth century. These services, demanded by rising urban standards, underlined the inadequacy and failure of the old municipal system. A series of Acts creating bodies of locally elected commissioners culminated in the Lighting of Towns Act, 1828, a general adoptive statute under which sixty-five towns either bypassed their inactive corporations or attained new municipal status. The Act introduced a modified form of local democracy which limited both liability to the new rate and the privilege of voting to householders occupying houses of annual value of £5 or upwards. Eligibility to stand for election as commissioner required occupation of property of £20 valuation at least. Commissioners held office for three years, and could run for re-election.

Municipal Reform

With the Reform Act of 1832 the political usefulness of the corporations diminished sharply. In 1833 a royal commission was established to examine the municipal corporations of England and Wales, and similar inquiries were set going for Scotland and Ireland. The English report was presented in 1835, and a Bill to reform and restructure the whole system was introduced in Parliament and passed without much difficulty or delay: the Municipal Corporations Act, 1835. The report for Ireland was also presented in 1835, and a Bill on English lines was also introduced with commendable speed. But the Irish Bill had a much rougher, and slower, passage. It took five years to reach the statute book, and despite the pressure for reform, the Benthamite ideal of household suffrage (embodied in the English Act) was severely modified to require a £10 valuation for Irish householders aspiring to the municipal franchise. In Ireland also the appointment of sheriffs and resident magistrates, and control of the police (under the English Act vested in the municipalities) were reserved to the Lord Lieutenant.

The Act of Union, which had wiped out thirty decayed corporations left sixty-eight still standing, in varying conditions of maladministration and civic distemper. Sir Robert Peel, in opposition in 1835, urged the total extinction of the Irish corporations, to be replaced by town commissioners under the Act of 1828, although the Irish corporations were not shown by the investigators to be notably worse, on the whole, than their English counterparts. But in the end the Irish Bill followed the lines of the 1835 Act for England and Wales. Of the sixty-eight surviving corporations fifty-eight were dissolved by the Municipal Corporations (Ireland) Act, 1840. Only ten — two of which, Belfast and Londonderry, are now in Northern Ireland — were continued but under a new constitution and name. Their charters were annulled so far as they were inconsistent with the new Act; and corporate property, over which the old corporations had absolute control, was diverted to public use. The new councils, which were elective, were restrained by Treasury control in the disposal of this property. The new borough fund had to be used for the public benefit, and the councils were empowered to raise a limited borough rate. The councils were also given the powers of the Act of 1828, but only so far as related to public lighting.

The powers conferred on the new councils were, in fact, curiously restricted. They amounted to little more than a power to make byelaws for the good rule and government of the borough, and the abatement of nuisances; with limited powers of sale and leasing the corporate estate and rating. The reason appears to have been that the corporations had inspired such distrust that even in their reformed state Parliament was unwilling to give them a wide range of duties. And, besides, improvement commissioners under either private legislation or the Act of 1828 were already operating in the boroughs and elsewhere.

Thirty-eight of the fifty-eight boroughs that had lost their status, and any town with a population of three thousand, were given the right to petition the Crown for a new charter. Only one town, Wexford, applied for and obtained (in 1845) a fresh charter in this way.

Although the Municipal Corporations (Ireland) Act was passed two years after the Poor Relief (Ireland) Act of 1838 it did not follow the same principle. The Benthamites had hoped to see all local government organised on the same lines as poor relief; but this hope was not realised. The new Poor Law was detested in England and Ireland and the urge for reform had slackened. Governments were not prepared to incur the unpopularity which they foresaw the extension of Bentham's ideas would involve and, therefore, no root and branch reform was attempted. The old system was patched up piecemeal, and the old historical areas of county and borough preserved. Under the Act of 1840, the accounts of the corporations were to be audited by locally elected auditors, whereas the auditors of poor relief expenditure were appointed by the Poor Law Commissioners. The borough councils had, as already noted, very few powers or duties; and the borough rate was limited to one shilling, or, if the Lighting of Towns Act of 1828 was in force in the town, to threepence. In course of time, by means of private legislation which they promoted in parliament, the borough corporations did obtain new powers, including power to strike improvement and other rates. This private legislation dealt with water supply, drainage, markets, rates and other matters that became increasingly the subjects of general legislation.

Clauses Acts

The outburst of private or local legislation in the early part of the nineteenth century inspired a series of reformist measures which went some way to span the gap between local initiatives and general legislation. These were the Clauses Acts, notably the Towns Improvement Clauses Act and the Commissioners Clauses Act both of 1847. The Clauses Act was a device, invented by a noted Benthamite, Joseph Hume MP, for helping local legislators with a package of ideas from which they could pick or choose; and at the same time for saving parliamentary time. The clauses were drawn from private legislation, and brought together in an Act which could be incorporated wholly or partly in subsequent legislation. There was a wide variety of Clauses Acts. In addition to the Towns Improvement Clauses Act which was a collection of provisions found in earlier private Acts dealing with paving, draining, cleansing, lighting, and so on; and the Commissioners Clauses Act which dealt with the constitution and regulation of public bodies, there were Clauses Acts on such subjects as land acquisition, waterworks, markets, harbours, electric lighting, and railways.

Towns Improvement (Ireland) Act, 1854

Various sections of the Towns Improvement Clauses and Commissioners Clauses Acts were incorporated in the Act of 1854 which was in essence an expanded and updated version of the Lighting of Towns Act, 1828. It had much the same procedure for local option in putting the Act into force in the town, or leaving it alone. The public health provisions (later replaced by the Public Health (Ireland) Act, 1878) reflected a substantial advance on the somewhat rudimentary enactment of 1828. And there were more elaborate and, one supposes, more effective police clauses. It is curious perhaps that despite these improvements a number of towns where the 1828 Act had been adopted did not take advantage of the opportunity of changing over to the Act of 1854, and remained unreconstructed until the 1898 Local Government Act forcibly placed them all under the later code. The Towns Improvement (Ireland) Act 1854, although antiquated and now in large degree ineffective, is still operative in over twenty towns, and there are proceedings afoot to put the creaking machinery of adoption into arthritic motion in some new towns.

Urban Districts

The somewhat haphazard emergence of municipal towns took a small step forward with the Public Health (Ireland) Act, 1874, which was one of the first measures following the establishment in 1872 of the Local Government Board for Ireland. The Act of 1874 set up a nationwide network of urban and rural sanitary authorities – but no new bodies were called into being. The Act made use of the bodies already there, and gave them new titles. Borough corporations and commissioners of towns with populations over 6,000 became urban sanitary authorities. Commissioners in smaller towns could apply to the Local Government Board for sanitary powers. Poor Law guardians became rural sanitary authorities (for areas not covered by an urban authority). This Act conferred no new powers, but four years later under the Public Health (Ireland) Act, 1878, the new authorities were given a comprehensive and (for the time) updated code of sanitary law.

The work of system-building culminated with the Local Government (Ireland) Act, 1898, which converted urban and rural sanitary districts into a second tier of local government under the new county councils. Urban and rural district councils endured as a complete second level covering the whole of the country until the re-structuring of the 1920s.

Poor Relief

Poor relief in Ireland hardly existed as a system before the nineteenth century. There were some institutions, and a few general enactments with more intention than achievement. An Act of 1635 projected a scheme of county houses of correction for the 'keeping, and correcting and setting to work of rogues, vagabonds, sturdy beggars and other idle and disorderly persons'. The purpose was punitive rather than philanthropic, and in fact the first effort of the Irish parliament to care for the poor was the establishment, by Act of 1703, of a workhouse in Dublin. This institution gradually evolved into a foundling hospital, and a similar venture in Cork launched by Act of 1735, developed on the same lines.

There was nothing in Ireland comparable with the Elizabethan poor law: the national system of parish relief and rating which had operated in England from 1601 onwards. And as the Irish poor were numerous and clamant (Dean Swift wrote repeatedly about 'the prodigious number of beggars throughout this kingdom in proportion to so small a number of people') opinions began to gather during the eighteenth century in favour of action of some kind. The County Infirmaries Act of 1765 grappled fairly effectively with a very important aspect of poor relief. Richard Woodward, an immigrant Englishman who eventually became Bishop of Cloyne, published (1766) a pamphlet outlining *A Scheme for establishing County Poorhouses in the Kingdom of Ireland* followed two years later by *An Argument in Support of the Right of the Poor of the Kingdom of Ireland to a National Provision*. These admonitions fired an outburst of legislative activity in 1771–2 of which the most notable product was an Act for the provision of houses of industry or workhouses in counties for maintaining the helpless poor. But Dr Woodward's modest successes fell a good deal short of that general measure of poor relief which most thoughtful observers regarded as essential in the Irish situation.

The Union of 1800 brought Irish social and economic problems directly to England's door, and by the 1830s the Irish poor law had become a national question in the United Kingdom. Malthus, Ricardo and other classical economists joined in rejecting the case for poor relief, arguing that a public provison would aggravate Ireland's traditional failings — improvidence, idleness, pauperism and lack of enterprise. But influential opinion in the radical and other elements of the Whig party was beginning to move powerfully against the experts. The pressure was generated mainly by a widespread conviction that the absence of a poor law in Ireland caused Irish paupers to descend in droves onto the backs of English ratepayers.

Opinion in Ireland was more fragmented than in England: the bulk of landowners were antagonistic, but there were exceptions, notably Lord Cloncurry and William Smith O'Brien. Daniel O'Connell was opposed to any kind of compulsory rate, on the moral ground that a poor law would dry up the wells of private charity. In this he was at odds with most of the Catholic clergy, led forcefully on this issue by Bishop James Doyle of Kildare and Leighlin. But in the main it was English opinion which counted and the gradual progress towards some kind of decision was marked by the number of inquiries and committees set up to collect information about the state of the Irish poor. These culminated in 1833 with the appointment of a royal commission under Archbishop Whately of Dublin, which everyone assumed would settle the matter one way or another. The commission worked assiduously for three years, assembled an immense array of facts and figures, and reported finally in 1836. Their recommendations ranged widely outside the problems of poor relief in the narrow sense and focused on the theme of economic development which they rightly discerned as the real, the paramount issue. They rejected the new reformed English poor law of 1834 as designed for a totally different situation; they also rejected any form of poor relief, indoor or outdoor, for the able-bodied or their families. State institutions, supported by a national rate or land tax, should be provided for the insane, mentally defective, deaf, dumb and blind; as well as hospitals for the physically ill. Apart from these, relief should be available, they thought, only to the aged and infirm, deserted children, orphans and widows — and this through voluntary bodies, with some state aid. For the able-bodied poor, estimated (with their dependants) at two million or more, they recommended a scheme of assisted emigration, and a national programme of public works under a Board of Improvement: a vast complex of land reclamation, drainage, and other forms of productive investment.

It looked good, but the government hesitated, for two reasons. In the first place, orthodox economic theory ran counter to direct measures of land improvement by government. And in the second, the Commission had not supplied what the government were really looking for, a workable, practical system of poor relief; an answer, in short, to the persistent demand for an Irish poor law. The Whately Report, too, had certain shortcomings. It is an exaggeration to say, as George O'Brien (1921) does, that the Report 'embraced a complete scheme for the industrial regeneration of the country' (p. 181). The proposals for a form of outdoor relief for the aged, children, widows, etc., in which the initiative would be taken by voluntary agencies, were visionary. A minority of three members were strongly opposed to fund-raising on a voluntary basis, and urged the imposition of a local tax, or poor rate.

In addition, Lord John Russell, who was then Prime Minister, had given hints in favour of the new English workhouse system even before the Commission reported. It was he who in August 1836 instructed George Nicholls, one of the English poor law commissioners, to visit Ireland and report on the relative merits of the Irish Commission's plan and a workhouse system. Nicholls was a former ship's captain who became a successful banker, and an expert on canals. He had spent some time as a workhouse master, was a firm believer in the system, an energetic administrator and a quick worker. He went to Ireland with his mind as near to made up as it could well be, and nothing he saw there (and he saw much on his six weeks tour) succeeded in shaking his preconvictions. He reported in November 1836, rejecting Dr Whately's plan in favour of a not greatly modified version of the English reformed poor law, and a Bill was introduced on these lines on 13 February 1837. Its passage through parliament was interrupted by the death of William IV, but it was reintroduced in December 1837, and despite O'Connell's opposition – he argued that Ireland was too poor for a poor law – the bill became law on 31 July, 1838.

Nicholls was chosen to carry the new scheme into effect. There was to be no separate body of Irish commissioners; the English commission would supervise the work. Nicholls set to work energetically with the aid of four assistant commissioners. By 1841 the machinery was in operation: 130 unions had been defined and poor law guardians elected. Design and construction of the workhouses were kept in the hands of the central commission, which worked through Nicholls. He drove ahead to such purpose that 118 workhouses were ready for occupation in 1845, and about 40,000 paupers were getting 'indoor relief'. There was no outdoor relief under the Irish scheme.

The expenses of poor relief were entirely a local charge, assessed originally on District Electoral Divisions according to the numbers of paupers originating in each – on the absurd reasoning that the sin of poverty could best be expiated by the unfortunate reprobate's neighbours. The rate was payable by the occupiers of the houses, lands or other rateable property, but tenants could deduct half of the rates from their rents.

Boards of guardians were the first representative local bodies in Ireland, but they were only part elected: after 1847 a major proportion, up to half, were *ex officio* members, justices of the peace. The electors were owners and occupiers of property liable to pay the new poor rate, and a system of plural voting ensured that property had its rights as well as its duties.

The unions were formed from aggregations of townlands, but with small regard to any other historic local boundaries which then existed: counties, baronies, boroughs and parishes. The underlying principle was utility: geographical and administrative convenience. An area averaging about 250 sq. miles was centred on a market town containing the workhouse with its boardroom, offices etc., the idea being that the guardians could attend both meeting and market on the same day without overmuch trouble or loss of time. It was the first and, as it turned out, the last attempt to settle local government areas on some rational foundation. The guardians of the poor were invested with wide statutory powers, acted through paid officers and were under the direction and control of a central department for which at first no minister was directly responsible to Parliament. The Act was a version for Ireland of the reformed English Poor Law of 1834 and its origins are, therefore, to be found in England.

The administration was under the control of the three Poor Law Commissioners sitting in London, and remained under their control until 1847, when their powers were transferred to commissioners appointed for Ireland. The purpose of granting this control was to secure uniformity in administration and prevent laxity. The commissioners had power to lay down the lines the guardians were to follow and to deal with recalcitrant boards by dissolving them and appointing paid officers in their place. They were, however, precluded from ordering relief in individual cases. Through the eyes of their assistant commissioners or inspectors they watched the proceedings of the guardians, and appointed auditors to examine the accounts and disallow illegal and unfounded payments.

The English Act of 1834 and the Irish Act of 1838 were the legislative outcome of the report of a Royal Commission of Inquiry into the working of the poor law in England. According to the recommendations of the Commission the able-bodied man looking for relief should be compelled to earn it in a workhouse where his condition should be made less desirable than that of the lowest labourer outside. This was the 'workhouse test'. The scheme of organisation and control of the new guardians of the poor was devised under the influence of the writings of Jeremy Bentham.

The secretary of the Commission of 1832, Edwin Chadwick, had been at one time Bentham's literary secretary. The report of the Commission, and consequently the Acts of 1834 and 1838 based on it, are permeated by Bentham's ideas of local government organisation. Under his plan the country would be divided into districts each of which would have a popularly elected assembly. These assemblies would have salaried officers, and both the assemblies and their officers would be subject to government departments, to be newly created.

It has been argued that Bentham's notion of local government was not local government at all, at least in the English sense. It was a continental concept, with adaptations. His centralism, promoted with tireless energy by disciples like Chadwick, and, at another remove, Nicholls, was anathema to English traditionalists. But Ireland was not England, had no tradition of local self-government and was in a smouldering condition of sporadic disorder and anti-government feeling. All things considered, the introduction of local administration on the scale described was a brave experiment in local decentralised administration — firmly directed and controlled it is true, but with a fairly strong, while not dominant, admixture of local democracy.

The impact of the Great Famine on the new system was crushing: famine and disease on the appalling scale which developed after 1845 were burdens which the service was simply not designed to carry. Parliament reacted in somewhat arthritic fashion with a trio of Acts, one of which, the Poor Law Administration Act, 1847, set up a separate central authority for Ireland — an Irish Poor Law Commission. The Poor Relief Extension Act, 1847, conceded a restricted form of outdoor relief as a countermeasure to gross overcrowding of the workhouses, which had over 135,000 inmates in the spring of 1848. The numbers on outdoor relief amounted to about 700,000. By 1849 these figures had risen to 215,000 and 769,000 respectively. The third measure of 1847 was a Vagrants Act for the punishment and repression of vagrancy, begging and wife-desertion.

These were not of course the sole measures taken by the government to alleviate distress. A Special Relief Commission was set up as early as 1845 to promote and co-ordinate relief measures, but the heavy hand of the Treasury (guided by Charles Trevelyan, creator of the modern civil service in these islands) and a change of government which brought the Whigs to power in June 1846, combined to curb the Commission's efforts. Public works programmes, mostly ineffective, were put in hand. For a brief period public supplies of food were organised as an emergency move. Private charities both at home and abroad gave assistance. But all these measures taken together fell so far short of what the calamity called for, that the question of deliberate inaction and planned depopulation has sometimes been raised. It was however inability to grasp and then to cope with the magnitude of the disaster that paralysed the will to action. The government, themselves governed by the contemporary principles of political economy, followed that commandment in A. H. Clough's updated decalogue:

> Thou shalt not kill but needst not strive
> Officiously to keep alive

Such were the combined effects of famine, fever and emigration in the three years after 1846, that more than two million people perished or fled the country.

Shortly after the worst of the famine was over the Medical Charities Act, 1851, expanded the work of poor law authorities by transferring responsibility for the dispensary system to boards of guardians. Two members were added to the three man Poor Law Commission, one of them a medical commissioner.

Health and Sanitary Administration

A writer on English local government has described the development of the system in the nineteenth century as primarily a response to the problems of urban growth following the Industrial Revolution. Ireland had, outside Belfast, no industrial revolution. It did have, partly in consequence, a formidable problem of poverty both urban and rural, and the efforts to cope with it stamped our system of local administration with an indelible mark of Benthamite centralism, and gave it a strong bias towards the alleviation of distress, and various other aspects of poverty.

But Ireland was not without its urban problems, since endemic diseases — typhus or famine fever, cholera and other water-borne infections, with various other contagious diseases — ravaged both town and country. When therefore the Royal Sanitary Commision of 1866–69 resulted in the formation of the Local Government Board in 1871, a similar body for Ireland was set up in the following year. The Local Government Board for Ireland absorbed the Poor Law Commission and took in certain other public health and local government functions. But while some emphasis was laid on the public health aspects of its work, the predominance of the poor relief side was not threatened in any appreciable way.

Extension of Guardians' Functions

The guardians of the poor were not long in existence when Parliament began to extend their functions beyond poor relief. In 1846 they were required on the requisition of the commissioners of health, a temporary body appointed by the government, to provide and equip hospitals and dispensaries for the sick poor. Sanitary administration was becoming intimately bound up with the administration of the poor law. In 1851 the Poor Law Commissioners were given the central administration of the Nuisances Removal and the Diseases Prevention Acts (an early form of environmental legislation) and in the same year under their direction the dispensary system of medical relief for the poor was organised as part of the administration of the guardians. In 1856 the guardians became the burial ground board for the rural parts of the union.

In 1863 when the civil registration of births and deaths was introduced the poor law unions were utilised as registration areas. Every union was made a superintendent registrar's district and every dispensary district a registrar's district. The Births and Deaths Registration Act, 1863, required that in registering the death the cause and the duration of illness should be stated. This provision enabled statistics of mortality to be compiled, a necessary preliminary to the organisation of the public health service.

It was inevitable that the boards of guardians should be used for health purposes. They had an organisation of officers and institutions in every part of the country. Unlike the grand juries they were permanent bodies holding frequent meetings. Their dispensary medical officers were well placed to observe outbreaks of disease and suggest remedies for prevention. Under the Sanitary Act of 1866 the guardians became the sewer authorities in rural areas and the Poor Law Commissioners were authorised to issue regulations under the Act.

The first of the Public Health Acts was the Act of 1874, but this was repealed four years later when the Public Health (Ireland) Act of 1878 was passed. It was modelled closely on an English statute of 1875. The Act of 1878, which is still for the most part in operation, consolidated and amended the provisions with regard to sanitary matters to be found in twenty earlier statutes, eighteen of which were wholly repealed. This Act was drafted under the influence of the theories of the causes of disease current at the time. Its remedy against the spread of infectious diseases was the creation of clean surroundings by eliminating nuisances, cleansing infected premises, providing water supplies, drainage and proper burial grounds, reducing overcrowding in houses, destroying unsound food, regulating slaughter houses and dealing with infectious diseases in hospitals.

The Act made use of existing areas, and gave greater discretion to the sanitary authorities than the Act of 1838 had given to the poor law authorities. Although the association of the guardians with public health measures may have had administrative advantages it probably had a retarding effect on the development of an adequate public health service. Health administration was subordinated to poor relief. The remuneration of the dispensary doctor in his capacity of medical officer of health was about one-sixth of the remuneration he received for his dispensary work.

Local Taxation

The first of the annual summaries of local taxation was made for the year 1865. These returns show that the principal local taxes at the time were the grand jury cess, the poor rate and various rates raised in boroughs and other towns. The grand juries in all Ireland raised a million pounds and spent the money principally on roads and lunatic asylums. The boards of guardians spent less than three-quarters of a million on poor relief, and town taxation for paving, lighting, cleansing, water supply and drainage did not in the aggregate reach half a million. The grand jury cess remained until the grand juries were relieved of their powers as county fiscal authorities by the Act of 1898. It was then merged in the new poor rate which has since been renamed county rate. Rates in towns were assessed under various names. The boroughs had a borough rate and other towns a town rate, and, in addition, separate rates were raised for many purposes such as, water supply, bridges and general improvement.

State Financial Aid

Before 1865 the government had not come to the view that the taxpayer as such was under any obligation to help the ratepayer by giving regular financial assistance. The Irish parliament had given help to the county infirmaries and annual grants to hospitals in Dublin. These had been continued after the Union. Money had been advanced to build lunatic asylums but it had to be paid back by the grand juries. The workhouses had been built by the poor law commissioners in whom they were vested and the loans, for the most part, had to be written off. From 1822 to 1846 half the cost of the constabulary (then a local charge) came out of government funds, and from 1846 the entire cost, an arrangement which according to Sir Robert Peel was intended to compensate Ireland for the effects of the repeal of the Corn Laws. Local police and the watch lingered on in a few places, and ultimately disappeared. The government controlled the para-military Royal Irish Constabulary that took over police duties. Local prisons passed to the government in 1877.

The first of the annual grants in aid of poor law expenditure was voted in 1867 for half the salaries of medical officers in workhouses and dispensaries and the whole of the salaries of workhouse school teachers, but there was no general system of grants in aid of poor law or public health expenditure. It was not until 1898 that a general grant in relief of rate-payers was introduced, confined to those liable for rates on a particular kind of property — agricultural land.

4

Old Regime: the Final Decades

For twenty years after the passing of the Public Health (Ireland) Act of 1878 no major change was made in the structure of local government. Parliament had since 1840 been giving new functions to local authorities, and many towns were themselves obtaining new powers. In the 1880s the guardians of the poor, as the rural sanitary authority, were made responsible – by the Labourers (Ireland) Act, 1883– for housing agricultural labourers where existing housing was unhealthy or deficient. In 1890 all earlier housing legislation for towns was consolidated and amended by the Housing of the Working Classes Act, since replaced by the Housing Act, 1966.

As yet parliament had not produced a comprehensive system of local government. It had adopted expedients to meet difficulties as they arose or as the political complexion of parliament changed. There was no unifying conception running through its local legislation. The principle of representative institutions had been applied in the towns but not in the counties, although some efforts had been made during the nineteenth century to reform county government. The grand jury system had little to recommend it, but nationalist opinion, though officially favouring reform, conserved its energy and passion for the Home Rule struggle. The two issues became entangled in 1884 when Joseph Chamberlain, under the mistaken impression that Parnell would accept local administration under an Irish Council as a substitute for Home Rule, brought his local government scheme to the cabinet. It was rejected. This confused episode, in which Parnell, O'Shea, Cardinal Manning, Dilke and Gladstone took part, had a decisive influence on the fate of Gladstone's first Home Rule Bill in 1886.

There were other attempts at reform, none of them successful, and the century drew towards its close with local administration still in a chaotic condition. The principle of suitable areas was adopted for poor law and public health purposes and the principle of strict central control had only limited application. The picture that local government presented was of independent authorities operating in overlapping areas. In the counties were the grand juries assisted by presentment sessions, in the boroughs the town councils, in the smaller towns the town commissioners, some of which were urban sanitary authorities. In the poor law unions which covered counties, cities and towns the board is of guardians acted as poor law authorities and in the rural part of the unions as sanitary authorities. In asylum districts, which were either single counties or combinations of counties, boards of governors nominated by the government and bound by the rules of the Privy Council managed the district asylums. Besides these authorities there were trustees for drainage districts and navigation, harbour and pier authorities, burial boards and governors of the eighteenth century system of county infirmaries. Some of the authorities were subject to control by the central authorities and some were not.

Local Government (Ireland) Act, 1898

The first step in reducing this jumble of authorities to order was taken in 1898, when the Local Government (Ireland) Act was passed. The key to rationalisation of local bodies lay in solving the problem of county government, which meant overcoming or bypassing the reluctance of landowners to abandon the virtual monopoly of local power which they exercised under the grand jury system. In England the Local Government Act, 1888, had transferred to county councils the administrative functions of justices of the peace in Quarter Sessions, but reform in Ireland was delayed for a further decade by unionist fears of nationalist ambitions and spendthrift councils. The stalemate was eventually resolved by extending the new Agricultural Grant to Ireland — which meant that the Exchequer paid half of the rates on agricultural land — and at the same time relieving landlords of their liability for half of the poor rate. As a result of this piece of legerdemain, for which Tim Healy claimed the credit, the occupiers of land — in effect the nationalist farmers — remained financially more or less as they had been, but with vastly enhanced political power, at least in local affairs.

The primary purpose of the Local Government Act of 1898 was to put county government on a representative basis. It transferred to elected councils that business of the grand juries and presentment sessions unconnected with the administration of justice. Here again, as in 1838, 1840 and 1878, legislation for Ireland followed, after a time lag and with some variation to meet Irish conditions, what had already been enacted for England. Administrative counties with county councils were created. Six of the cities (two in Northern Ireland) were made county boroughs in which the corporations had almost all the functions of a county council as well as the functions of a borough corporation. Kilkenny, Drogheda and the town of Galway, which for grand jury purposes had ranked as counties, ceased to exist as such and were merged in the administrative counties. In Tipperary, which had two grand juries, two administrative counties were formed, one for each riding. Elsewhere each county was one administrative county.

The administrative county was divided into county districts, which in a few counties were all rural districts and in the rest rural or urban. The part of a rural sanitary district formed under the 1878 Act within a county became a rural district with a rural district council, and the urban sanitary district became an urban district with an urban district council. The district councils took over the business of the baronial presentment sessions, and the business of the grand juries in relation to roads and public works, the cost of which was borne by the district. The rural district councils were assigned the sanitary functions of guardians. The towns under town commissioners that were not urban sanitary authorities remained part of the rural district.

The boards of guardians were confined to poor (including medical) relief, but their power to levy the poor rate was transferred to the county council. The district asylums were handed over to the county councils, which were required to appoint committees of management for these institutions. The financial relations between the counties and the Exchequer were revised and a grant — the Agricultural Grant referred to above — was given in relief of rates on land outside the county boroughs, boroughs and other urban districts.

Political Aspects

Democratic local government, of which county councils were the central example, was a virtually unwanted gift from the Conservative government to the Irish people. There was no agitation in its favour. The Irish Party's feelings about county government were soured by the belief, widely held, that the English Local Government Act of 1888 which was the model used for the Irish Act, was a reward to Chamberlain and the other Liberal Unionists for their help in defeating Gladstone's (and Parnell's) first Home Rule Bill in 1886.

The new Act was met therefore with suspicion and grudging acceptance. The Irish Party looked on it as no substitute for national self-government, and as another Conservative attempt to kill home rule with kindness. But once the Bill was passed, nationalist opinion quickly adjusted itself to the new situation, and made the most of it — particularly in political terms.

There was indeed a small minority who favoured the use of local councils as a foundation on which to build up a substitute for Westminister. The idea was developed by Sir Thomas Esmonde MP a member of Wexford County Council, in conjunction with John Sweetman, vice-chairman of Meath County Council, and second president of Sinn Féin. The immediate result was the emergence in 1899 of the General Council of County Councils, but the more ambitious plan of a Council of Three Hundred, despite strong backing by Arthur Griffith and adoption as an item of Sinn Féin policy, was never realised. Its attractions faded with the revival of the parliamentary party after 1900, and the brightening prospects of home rule.

Extension of Franchise

Up to 1899 the right to vote in local elections was confined to those who were ratepaying occupiers or owners. The qualification varied. In the boroughs it was £10 yearly value; in other towns it was £4 in some and £5 in others. In the poor law unions the guardians were elected by rate-payers on a system of plural voting. The more property occupied the greater the number of votes. One vote was allowed up to £20 valuation. The number of votes increased by stages to six at £200 valuation, and if the occupier paying the rate was not entitled to deduct any part of it from his rent the number of his votes was doubled. Voting by proxy was allowed.

The Local Government (Ireland) Act of 1898 made the parliamentary electorate (plus peers and qualified women) the local government elec-torate. Householders and persons occupying part of a house then had the vote. Multiple votes proportionate to the amount of rateable property were abolished. Women, incidentally, could become guardians and district councillors but were debarred from county and borough councils until 1911, when they were admitted by the Local Authorities (Ireland) (Quali-fication of Women) Act of that year. The next stage in enfranchisement was reached in 1918 when married women of thirty years of age and over got the vote. Proportional representation was first introduced in Sligo Borough in 1918 by a local Act and was applied generally to local elec-tions by the Local Government (Ireland) Act, 1919.

Effects of the 1898 Act

The Act of 1898 made the last major change in local government before it came under the control of an Irish government. Except for the merging of the rural districts within a county into one enlarged county health district, and the abolition of the poor law unions, the areas still remain as formed by that Act, with some adjustments of boundaries. The historical counties were retained notwithstanding great disparities in size, population and topography. The Act did not deal with the poor law except in some minor matters such as the removal of the ex officio justices of the peace from the boards of guardians and widening the area of the expenses of relief by spreading them over the union.

The councils that began to function in 1899 brought new men into local government. In the counties the landlords, from whom the grand juries were mainly drawn, virtually disappeared from local bodies. In the towns the councils became more fully representative of all classes owing to the broadening of the franchise. The county councils did not at first have much to do other than maintain roads and mental hospitals and collect rates. The main business was carried on by the district councils, the guardians and the mental hospital committees. In the towns there was a moderately progressive spirit; water and sewerage schemes were undertaken, a beginning was made with technical instruction, some houses were built for the working classes and in a few towns public libraries were provided.

The Twentieth Century

In the new century mechanically propelled cars came on to the roads in increasing numbers and raised a problem of road improvement, the solution of which was beyond the resources of local authorities. The motor car had direct effects on the roads and remote effects on other branches of the administration. When motor buses began to operate in the twenties the small administrative rural areas were already disappearing. The union was the first to go and the rural district followed. It was not alone on the ground of convenience that they were no longer needed; larger areas were required to give scope for the proper organisation of services, particularly hospitals and homes, and to secure adequate financial resources.

After 1900 the idea of the state as the promoter of social welfare began to manifest itself in numerous statutes. The first Old Age Pensions Act and the first Tuberculosis Prevention Act were passed in 1908, the National Insurance Act in 1911. They were followed by the first School Meals Act in 1914, and the Notification of Births (Extension) Act, 1915, under which mother and child welfare schemes were put into operation. The Public Health (Medical Treatment of Children) Act came in 1919 under which provision was made for attending to the health of school children. Under the Blind Persons Act, 1920, arrangements could be made for looking after the blind. Local authorities were concerned in some way with the administration of all these Acts.

In the first decade of the present century the working of the poor law was twice submitted to investigation by government commissions. The first commission was confined to the investigation of its working in Ireland; the terms of reference of the second covered Britain as well as Ireland. The Irish study by a three-man Vice-Regal Commission (1906) recommended the abolition of the workhouse system and segregation of the various classes of inmates in separate institutions. The larger Royal Commission on the Poor Law (1909) proposed the abolition of the boards of guardians and the transfer of their powers to the county councils. The system of relief that had sprung from the Acts of 1834 and 1838 was now universally condemned. The trend was away from the idea of a deterrent poor law with its workhouse test. But before anything was done the war of 1914—18 broke out and the question of legislation was shelved.

Local Government (Ireland) Act, 1919

The last piece of British legislation on general aspects of local administration reflects the unsettled post-war condition of Ireland. The Local Government (Ireland) Bill became law in June 1919. It made universal in local elections the system of proportional representation inaugurated in Sligo the year before, mainly in the hope that it would preserve the interest of minorities. The Act also attempted to protect local officers from vindictive action on the part of nationalist councils by guaranteeing their pensions against dismissal, or refusal to vote allowances. The Bill, incidentally, included a provision empowering the Local Government Board to get rid of recalcitrant local bodies, but the clause was dropped in deference to protests by Sir Edward Carson, who thought that action of this kind would be undemocratic.

The situation, as viewed from the Custom House, (still intact — it was not burnt until May 1921) must have made Carson's high-mindedness and the government's restraint seem quixotic. Sir Henry Robinson, last Vice-President of the Local Government Board, had no strain of idealism in his make-up, but even he was at pains, in *Memories Wise and Otherwise* (1923) to deny authorship of the retaliatory plan to withhold loans and local taxation grants from disloyal councils.

The impression of gathering storm-clouds, of slow retreat broken by last-ditch stands, is conveyed vividly by a brief succession of legislative blows aimed at recalcitrant ratepayers and rating authorities: the Criminal Injuries (Ireland) Act, 1919, the Restoration of Order (Ireland) Act, 1920 and the Criminal Injuries (Ireland) Act, 1920. These strokes were met by Dáil countermeasures in circular letters outlining a defensive strategy, all of which may be found in the introduction to the First Report of the Department of Local Government and Public Health (1922-25).

5

The new State: first decades

In 1920 the underground Dáil Éireann, which had been elected in 1919, set up a local government department which assumed the functions of a central authority, while the Local Government Board for Ireland was still active and, nominally at least, in control of affairs. A majority of the local authorities recognised the control of the new department and broke with the Local Government Board. For a time there were two central authorities in Ireland. The vigour and leadership which marked the Dáil attack was the distinctive contribution of Kevin O'Higgins, who was Assistant Minister in the Dáil Department of Local Government — a Department ably led by W. T. Cosgrave, its first Minister.

The conflict between the Dáil department and the Local Government Board was the occasion of the Dáil setting up, in June 1920, a Commission of Inquiry into local government. The chairman was Kevin O'Higgins, and the Commission was required to report, not on general aspects of local government — that would have been impossible in the time allowed (four weeks!) — but on the problem of survival without the sanction and countenance of the Local Government Board. Its report therefore was limited mainly to the severe economy measures necessary for the system's continued existence. A few general policy initiatives were also recommended, such as the pooling of contracts under a scheme of combined purchase, and the sale of labourers' cottages to occupants.

As the *comitats* did in Hungary in the preceding century — Arthur Griffith's *Resurrection of Hungary* was then a Sinn Féin manual — local authorities in Ireland played a valuable part in resisting central government, and both councillors and property suffered from British terrorist attacks. In Cork, for example, the City Hall was burned and two of its Lord Mayors died in the struggle for independence. But once the battle was won, local autonomy began to lose its attractions. The concept of a tightly centralised modern state took hold, and governed the shaping of the new state. One of the first symptoms of the trend was the direction taken by the Constitution Committee in 1922. Of the three drafts submitted to government by the committee, only one (a minority document drafted by Alfred O'Rahilly) recommended a decentralised administration with regional autonomy. It sank with hardly a trace.

In April 1922 the Ministry of Local Government, acting under the

Provisional Government, took over the central administration which passed in 1924 to the Department of Local Government and Public Health, established by the Ministers and Secretaries Act, 1924.

The Irish Free State started life under a constitution lacking all but incidental mention of local government. Nothing new in this perhaps, since most earlier constitutions (e.g. the American Constitution) overlooked this aspect of administration. But the newer note struck by the Weimar constitution and some other post-war constitutions found no echo in the Irish document.

As the Devlin Report put it: 'One of the first acts of the new Government was to extend to all local authorities the fullest of the central controls exercised by the Local Government Board although the local government system was maintained with some degree of autonomy. In the same way as the central administration, the local administration was brought unambiguously under the control of the new Government. Thus was established a highly centralised system of both central and local government.' (PSORG 1969 3.3.5)

Public administration under the new state exhibited marked differences of approach and treatment in different sectors. The civil service was handled with diffidence and caution and there was no attempt at innovation. Michael Collins's determination to replace 'an alien and cumbersome administration' with 'fresh, Gaelic' instruments died with him, insofar as it had the civil service in mind. Originality began, however, to show itself in creating the earliest of the state-sponsored bodies. The attitude to local government was bold and confident from the start, and a diverse programme of reform emerged almost at once. It included:

(1) reform of the poor law;
(2) abolition of boards of guardians and rural district councils;
(3) strict control of local authorities and staffs;
(4) formation of unified local service; Local Appointments Commission;
(5) introduction of city management;
(6) centralised purchasing;
(7) joint local insurance.

Adapting the old system

The first enactment of the Oireachtas relating to local government was the Local Government (Temporary Provisions) Act of 1923, an interim measure to confirm the work already done by the Dáil in placing public assistance on a county basis. The Act also removed the statutory restrictions on relief being granted to certain classes outside the workhouse. Four years earlier, in January 1919, the First Dáil had, following the declaration of an independent Irish republic, adopted a Democratic Programme which called for, as part of its objectives, the abolition of the 'odious, degrading and foreign poor law system, substituting therefor a sympathetic native scheme for the care of the nation's aged and infirm, who shall no longer be regarded as a burden, but rather entitled to the nation's gratitude and consideration.'

These ideals were not easily realised, but the new republicans set to work at once on the task of demolishing the old system and assembling the pieces in the order sketched by the Vice-Regal Commission. In 1923, schemes which had been hurriedly adopted for placing poor relief on a county basis were reviewed and redrawn on a uniform pattern with some local variations. County boards were appointed to administer relief, except in a few areas in Dublin where the old union areas remained in being. The principal institutions under the new arrangement were normally the county home, which received the old and infirm and classes other than the sick that were formerly in the workhouse, and the county hospital.

For the rest, the government set up a commission in March 1925, to inquire into and make recommendations on the relief of the sick and destitute poor. The commission reported in 1927.

Abolition of Boards of Guardians and Rural Councils

Sinn Féin policy on local government, from which much of the reform thinking of this time derives, was aimed at clearing away most if not all of the undergrowth of small local bodies at sub-county level. Boards of guardians were the first to go — a clean sweep (outside Dublin) was made by the county schemes to which the Act of 1923 gave statutory effect.

Rural district councils set up under the Act of 1898 were abolished by the Local Government Act, 1925 and a new and enlarged rural sanitary district was created which generally extended over the whole county excluding the urban districts. The functions of the abolished rural district councils, which related mainly to road maintenance and sanitary matters, were transferred to the county councils which were required to discharge the new sanitary duties through boards of health. These boards, except where there were joint arrangements for the administration of public assistance, had the same membership (ten) as the body entrusted with the administration of poor relief.

The county boards of health and public assistance survived until August 1942, when the administration of public assistance (except in a few districts) and sanitary matters came under the direct control of the county council acting through the new county managers. The changes of 1925 did not apply immediately to Dublin City and County as the future government of these areas was at the time under examination by the Greater Dublin Commission (1924–6). It was dealt with eventually in the Local Government (Dublin) Act of 1930. Every county council was required to appoint a medical officer of health who would be responsible in the county at large for the effective administration of the enactments for safeguarding the public health.

Dissolution of Councils

The heavily reinforced apparatus of control over local bodies which was a feature of the new government had (apart from the ideological reasons cited above) two impelling forces behind it. One was a general feeling, amounting almost to a tradition, that local councils could not be trusted to fill jobs fairly; the other was the administrative disorder caused by the Civil War. Hostilities between Republicans and the Free State government broke out in June 1922, and local government, already badly shaken by four years of war, deteriorated in some places to near disaster. A number of local bodies ceased to hold meetings and rate collection lapsed. It was essential to resore the situation, and for the task it was decided to call in aid the drastic armoury of poor law powers designed originally for use against recalcitrant Irish guardians.

The principles of 1838 were given extended application in two directions: the Minister was given the same power over other local officers and employees as he had over poor law officers and he was empowered to dissolve bodies that were not duly and effectually discharging their duties or were neglecting to obey lawful orders, or not complying with judgements of the Courts. This power of dissolution appeared first in the Act of 1838. The Public Health Acts following the Sanitary Act of 1866 also provided a means, although rarely if ever used, of enforcing the performance of certain duties by a defaulting sanitary authority; a mandamus could be sought from the High Court, or a person could be appointed to perform the duty in default.

The power of dissolution was used freely at first, and with a breathtaking disregard of the antiquity and prestige of the victims. The corporations of Cork and Dublin were among the first to fall – Dublin, (May 1924) the oldest public body in Ireland, and Cork (October 1924) not far behind. Whether dissolution was a deserved or appropriate fate is debatable, but the surprising thing was the quiet acquiescence of the citizens in these violent assaults on their civic privileges, such as they were. A number of ex-councillors (eleven, including Sean T. Ó Ceallaigh later Tánaiste, Minister for Local Government and Public Health, and President) published *A Vindication of the Municipal Council of the City of Dublin,* but it drew little notice. President Cosgrave offered the chairmanship of the three Dublin Commissioners (P. J. Hernon, Dr W. Dwyer and S. Murphy) to the dismissed Lord Mayor, Laurence O'Neill, who refused out of loyalty to his colleagues. O'Neill became a Senator and at least once (28 May 1930) vigorously defended the old city council.

Dublin and Cork were, however, not the first to go. Kerry and Leitrim County Councils led the roster of dismissals as early as May 1923, and Dublin Board of Guardians followed later in that year. A total of twenty bodies were replaced by commissioners in the first three years of the new regime.

The original intention was that the powers of dissolution should be a temporary device for use only while the emergency lasted. But the powers in section 12 of the 1923 Act were found so useful that they were renewed in permanent form by Section 72 of the Local Government Act, 1925, and eventually re-enacted more elaborately in Local Government Act, 1941 (S. 44).

Local Appointments Commission

When Arthur Griffith talked about his ideal of a national civil service he did not mean a regiment of officials recruited by the imperial civil service commissioners. He dreamt of welding together in a single service 'all the employees of the county councils, rural councils, poor law boards, harbour boards and other bodies responsible to the Irish people, by the institution of a common national qualifying examination and a local competitive examination'. This aim was achieved by two principal means, neither of which included the 'common national qualifying examination' envisaged in the Sinn Féin programme. The first was the comprehensive superannuation code for local officers contained in the Local Government Act, 1925. Its effect was to facilitate mobility from one local authority to another, and to remove all restrictions on free movement within the local service.

Another significant departure from the traditional role of the central authority took place in 1926. The Minister's powers over the appointment, continuance in office and removal of local officers had been extended in 1923 but the benefits of this extension were negative rather than positive. Whilst he could refuse to sanction unsuitable nominees he could do little to provide suitable candidates for appointment. There was no power to require a special examination except in an appointment to the office of county surveyor. The earliest solution, for which there was a respectable body of support, was to extend the scope of the new Civil Service Commission to include the local service. This idea was put forward in 1923 by Professor Eoin MacNeill, then Minister for Education. But the Commissioners were reluctant to take on both tasks and the novel alternative of a separate local commission emerged in 1926 and was quickly put into legislative form. The Local Authorities (Officers and Employees) Act, 1926 established a three-man Commission which had the duty of selecting and recommending to the local authorities persons for appointment to the principal offices.

The categories specified in the Act were: chief executive offices, professional and technical offices; to these could be added any other offices to which the Minister applied the Act. The commissioners are not tied to any one method of selection. They can use competitive written examinations or selection by oral examination or interview, or a combination of both or any other method. The local authority is bound to appoint the candidate recommended or one of the candidates if more than one is recommended. This mode of selection has now become part of the normal machinery of local administration and the local authorities recoup the government any expenses incurred in working it.

City and County Management

Perhaps the most eye-catching item in the whole reform package was city management, an idea imported from America and adapted to Irish conditions. Professor Basil Chubb thought that the adaptation was 'perhaps Ireland's major invention in the field of government' (*Source Book* p. 261). An overstatement? Perhaps, until you contemplate the flatness of the surrounding countryside. In any event, management has become the most interesting feature of Irish local government to outside observers and students. Management, with the Local Appointments Commission, are the elements which distinguish the Irish system most clearly from all others – particularly the British.

The idea of city management spread from the business-dominated culture of the USA in the early years of the present century, and was eagerly pounced on by reformist-minded people in the prevailing climate of dissatisfaction with Irish local councils. The committee system which then operated was open, as all such systems are, to dilatory procedures, pressures, self-interest, corrupting 'influence', evasion of personal responsibility and to what was thought of as a peculiarly Irish weakness – garrulity as a substitute for action. The attractions of a one-man executive, a man of action who would replace the talking shop where decisions were lost in a mist of verbiage, were overwhelming. And although this picture of Irish local government was grossly overdrawn, the popular preference was made crystal clear by the seemingly glad acceptance of three commissioners in place of the eighty-four member Dublin city council, a single commissioner in Cork, and other examples of brisk, business-like, no-nonsense administration.

The movement towards management was probably helped by the fact that parliamentary democracy was then·entering a period of eclipse and lowered esteem. Developments in Europe – particularly in Italy – threw a shadow over any form of government by discussion, and the ideological assault on parliamentary procedures was felt in the humble institutions of local government. Catholic Italy exercised a specially potent influence in Ireland, particularly since Pius XI was known to favour some form of Italian corporatism.

The first application of the city management concept was in Cork, with the passing of the Cork City Management Act, 1929. Dublin followed a year later, and management was then extended in stages to the whole of local government (see Chapter 9).

Combined Purchasing

In the period 1921–2, the new government did not feel constrained to confine themselves altogether to the then-understood role of the central authority in local government. Broadly this role was one of general superintendence – administration was the local authority's business. The Dáil decided, on the advice of the 1920 Commission on Local Government, that the system by which every authority obtained separately the commodities they required could be improved. A system of combined purchasing was introduced on a non-statutory basis in December 1921. By this system the central authority invites tenders and appoints official contractors at the prices in the accepted tenders. An official list of contractors and prices is prepared and circulated to local authorities who can then order what they require. There is no central purchase or storing. In connection with the scheme standards and specifications were introduced. In 1925 legal sanction was given to the scheme by a temporary Act – The Local Authorities (Combined Purchasing) Act, 1925 – which was continued from year to year after its expiry. In 1939 a permanent Act was passed, but it was not possible to put it into operation at once owing to the abnormal conditions that existed during and immediately after the Emergency. It was brought into operation in 1961.

The scheme had two main objects: firstly, that search for economy with improved quality which was the hallmark of the 1920s. The system of contracts made with 'Official Contractors' succeeded in bringing prices down and achieving a degree of uniformity in purchase terms for local authorities. The Trade Section of the Department of Local Government was also in a strong negotiating position to press for standards of excellence in the goods supplied. Secondly, the Trade Section worked to promote the maximum possible use of Irish manufacturers by local bodies. The scheme was operated from 1925 onwards in co-operation with a small committee of local authority and business representatives: the Local Supplies Advisory Committee. Central administrative expenses were levied under the 1925 Act on counties and county boroughs.

Mutual Assurance

The success of combined purchasing prompted a corresponding effort in property insurance. The General Council of County Councils was convinced that the premiums charged for fire and other insurance cover were excessive, and thought that a remedy would be found in some kind of co-operative venture. Something of this kind had been working in England since the early years of the century. Under the Local Authorities (Mutual Assurance) Act, 1926, a company was established under the sponsorship of the General Council. This was the Irish Public Bodies Mutual Insurances Ltd. It was moderately effective in gaining its objectives.

Tourist Trade

Another form of combined effort was the promotion of tourism through the Irish Tourist Association, a body approved for the purpose by the Minister for Industry and Commerce. Local interest in tourism went back to the Health Resorts and Watering Places (Ireland) Act, 1909, an expanded version of which was included in the Local Government Act, 1925. The 1925 legislation enabled local authorities to contribute towards the expenses of an approved company. The idea was continued by the Tourist Traffic (Development) Act, 1931, but the national body was replaced in 1964 by a network of regional companies set up by Bord Fáilte with the aim of restoring a degree of local involvement in the promotion of tourism.

Hospitals Trust Fund

A break with departmental procedure arose out of the disposition of surpluses that became available from sweepstakes for hospitals and other institutions for the sick and disabled. A hospitals trust fund was established in 1933 to receive these funds and the Minister for Local Government and Public Health could out of this fund make grants to any hospital or nursing organisation.

A Hospitals Commission of not less than three members was set up under the Public Hospitals Act, 1933 with the function of giving expert advice on the best disposition of the resources of the Fund. The Commission published a number of reports on hospital and nursing facilities.

The Hospitals Commission ceased to exist in 1971 when the Health Act, 1970 came into operation. It was replaced by a new hospitals body with wider powers and functions: Comhairle na n-Ospidéal.

In 1945 the Minister was empowered to establish a new sanatorium in any area in which he considered it necessary, the cost to be met out of the fund. These sanatoria would when built be handed over to the local authorities to maintain and manage. The erection of the buildings became the direct responsibility of the Minister, who established in his Department a special organisation for the planning of the new institutions.

Local Government Legislation after 1925

The general fabric of local government in the era of independence was shaped by 1925: the Local Government Act of that year had settled the structures which endured for the next forty years and in large measure are still with us. The Local Government Act, 1927 made a few amendments in the 1925 system, none of them of major significance. The Local Government (Amendment) (No. 2) Act, 1934 deserves mention because it authorised the creation of two or more county health districts in a county. Cork was the only instance of this power being used, where three districts were created: north, south and west.

The Local Government Act, 1941 embodies the very considerable changes which followed the County Management Act, 1940. It is a curious fact that although the 1940 Act completed the process of professionalisation over the whole range of local administration (with the exception of vocational education committees and county committees of agriculture), there was little evidence of heightened confidence in local institutions on the part of the government. There was, on the contrary, a substantial increase in the already formidable powers of central authorities in relation to local authorities, their staffs, and services. The principal features of the Act of 1941 were (Part II) a clarification of the position of various 'appropriate' Ministers vis-à-vis local offices and employments, the inauguration of a new code of law and regulations for personnel, and (Part III) a set of provisions on the constitution and procedure of local authorities. The latter included a reduction in the size of county councils by about a third, and empowered the Minister for Local Government and Public Health to fix the number of members of local authorities. Part IV re-enacted in more elaborate form the Minister's ultimate power to 'dissolve' local authorities by removing the members from office and appointing commissioners. Part V contained some miscellaneous material about rates and rating, but nothing of a reforming nature. Part VII of the Act had the merit of novelty: it furnished a procedure for establishing some kind of relationship between county councils and the numerous voluntary self-help bodies then springing up under the spur of Emergency conditions. Parish councils and the like became 'approved local councils'. The relationship between official local government and the bodies remained however, an uneasy one, and the wartime movement tended to fade out with the return of peace.

The next Act, the Local Government Act, 1946 contained, in Part II, some elements of reform but they were confined to financial measures, and concerned solely with the machinery of local authority expenses. Rating was tidied up — the poor rate became the only rate leviable in counties where it took the new name of county rate; or in urban areas where it became the municipal rate. Apart from genuine improvement, the new names sounded better. Town commissioners took one more step towards what seemed inevitable liquidation by losing their old rating powers. They were to be funded by way of demand on county councils, which recovered their outlay in the form of a charge on the towns. This Part contained, incidentally, a new provision (s. 30) for dealing with 'insufficiency of rates', by adding it to the growing catalogue of crimes for which a local authority could be suspended by the Minister. A different aspect of expanding ministerial authority gave rise to great controversy in Dáil and Senate. This was an extension of central control to minor employments and servants of local authorities (s. 42).

The recital of general statutes dealing with local authorities may be closed with the Local Government Act, 1955. Though its size and intricacies are evidence of great industry, the Act is little more than a rag-bag of minor improvements and reinforcements to a system which, in spite of the brief rejuvenation effected by the county management injection, was already showing signs of age. The 1955 Act did not continue any of the lines of reform sketched, however tentatively, by the Acts of 1941 and 1946. Nor did it break any new ground or hint at any novelties of attitude or thought.

Local Government Franchise

The extension of universal suffrage to local government did not take effect until 1935. The Electoral Act, 1923 legalised adult suffrage for parliamentary elections thus removing the thirty-year age qualification for women voters enacted in the Representation of the People Act, 1918. The thirty-year age minimum was retained however for women local electors, as was the requirement that voters (male or female) should have occupied, as owners or tenants, land or premises in the electoral area for a period of at least six months. The wives of local electors were also entitled to the local vote, provided they had reached the thirty-year age limit.

The Local Government (Extension of Franchise) Act, 1935 gave a vote in local elections to every Irish citizen over twenty-one who was not subject to legal incapacity. Registration could be claimed either at place of residence, or in respect of property occupied elsewhere, but only one vote was allowable. There was considerable opposition to the Bill, despite the seemingly compelling arguments advanced in support – that, for example, a person entrusted with a vote in Dáil elections should be able to shoulder the added responsibility; and that, in any event, some 50 per cent of local expenditure was met by central taxpayers. Introduced in May 1933, the Bill took some two years to pass through the Oireachtas. It was rejected by the Senate in June 1933, partly on grounds of principle, and partly with the local elections in mind. These were held in 1934, with disappointing results for the opposition. The Bill was sent again to the Senate after the constitutional delay of eighteen months, and passed finally in March 1935.

An attempt in 1947 to change the electoral system for county councils is perhaps worthy of mention. The Local Elections Bill, 1947 proposed to substitute single-member constituencies for the multi-member electoral areas created by the Local Government Act, 1919. The object was 'to reimpose upon the members of county councils that peculiar personal obligation which attaches to a single individual who does not share with others the responsibility of representing a particular district (Dáil Debates, 26 November 1947). The single transferable vote was to be retained, and would operate in the reduced constituencies. The Bill lapsed with the dissolution of Dáil and Senad early in 1948, and was not subsequently reintroduced.

Vocational Education

Local authorities are not directly concerned in the provision of primary or secondary education but they have ancillary powers in regard to scholarships and, in the county boroughs and Dun Laoghaire, enforcing school attendance through school attendance committees. They are, however, indirectly responsible for the provision of vocational schools.

In 1889 urban and rural sanitary authorities had been empowered to supply or aid the supply of technical or manual instruction and to raise a rate for this purpose. A few urban authorities availed of this power but generally the rate, being limited, was too small to be of use. Very little progress was made until the Local Government Act of 1898 came into operation and the Department of Agriculture and Technical Instruction was set up in Ireland to take over the administration of the grant in aid of technical instruction. Committees of county and urban councils were appointed and schemes for the provision of technical instruction were put into operation. A commission of inquiry appointed in 1926 surveyed the progress made up to that time and as a result of their recommendations fresh legislation in 1930 provided for the appointment of vocational education committees in the counties, county boroughs and seven urban districts. It is the duty of these committees to supply vocational instruction and establish a suitable system of continuation education. The committees come under the general supervision of the Minister for Education.

Agriculture

In 1899 county councils were empowered to raise a limited rate for the purposes of agriculture and appoint a committee to administer it. These committees have been succeeded by county committees of agriculture which the councils were bound to appoint under the Agriculture Act of 1931, to carry out schemes in relation to agriculture and rural industries. County committees of agriculture come under the supervision of the Minister for Agriculture.

These two committees, the vocational education committee and the county committee of agriculture, were not brought within the county management system and therefore the county manager has no functions in relation to them.

Health Services

In 1922 the new government inherited a tangle of authorities — county councils, urban and rural councils, and boards of guardians — each with powers in relation to health. By the cumulative effect of a series of statutes the county council became by 1942 the public assistance authority for the county and the sanitary authority for the rural area of the county and was then dealing with health services in three capacities, as public assistance authority, as sanitary authority and simply as county council. In urban county districts the urban councils were also administering health services.

The Health Act of 1947 made the county councils and county borough corporations health authorities for their respective areas. The effect of this was to take from sanitary authorities as such, including urban district councils, responsibility for health administration. This change did not remove from the public assistance authorities responsibility for the county and district hospitals and dispensaries. That change was made by the Health Act of 1953 which transferred the county and district hospitals and other district institutions to the health authorities and thus detached from the public assistance system the treatment of the sick. In four areas, that is, Dublin, Cork, Limerick and Waterford, each of which includes a county borough, special joint health authorities were established in 1960.

Greater Dublin Tribunal

The Greater Dublin Commission of 1924–26 led eventually, in a round-about way, to the Local Government (Dublin) Act, 1930, which brought the benefits of city management to the capital. But that was not its only sequel. It also enlarged the old city area by absorbing the urban districts of Rathmines, Rathgar, Pembroke, and a considerable part of the county. In addition it created the coastal borough of Dun Laoghaire by amalgamating the urban districts of Blackrock, Kingstown, Dalkey and Killiney-Ballybrack. Further, provision was made (s. 101) for two tribunals to assess the results of the 1930 arrangement and recommend possible changes, the first tribunal within five years, and the second after a further three years. The new government which took over in 1932 set up the first tribunal on 17 July, 1935, just as the time limit expired. It had as chairman a judge of the High Court, George Gavan Duffy, and the other members were two departmental experts, an engineer and an auditor. Their report, submitted in 1938, recommended a single metropolitan government for Dublin city and county, including Dun Laoghaire and the urban district of Howth. The metropolitan corporation, with a council of not more than 40 and a manager, would carry out local administration in the whole area, urban and rural.

The report does not seem to have been welcomed by the government, though it led to certain changes – unification of Dublin city and county management; and, in 1940, the addition of Howth to the city. A second tribunal was not appointed.

THE ADMINISTRATIVE COUNTY

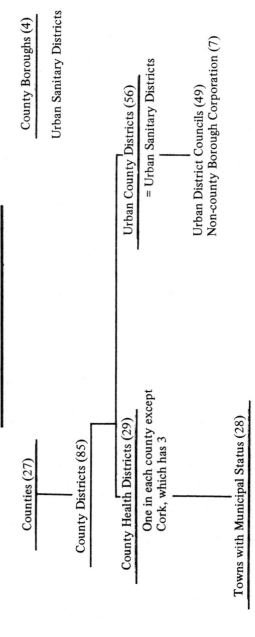

Counties (27)

County Districts (85)

County Health Districts (29)
One in each county except
Cork, which has 3

Urban County Districts (56)
= Urban Sanitary Districts

Urban District Councils (49)
Non-county Borough Corporation (7)

County Boroughs (4)
Urban Sanitary Districts

Towns with Municipal Status (28)

Towns with elected commissioners (23)
Towns administered by county councils (5)

Towns are part of County Health Districts

6

Local Government Areas

Administrative Counties

The administrative county, which is either a county for which a county council is elected or a county borough, is the principal area of local government. Administrative counties covering the whole country were formed in 1898 from pre-existing judicial counties, that is the counties as bounded for grand jury purposes. In thirteen counties the boundaries as they had been for judicial purposes were not altered. The area of every administrative county other than a county borough is as laid down in the Order of the Local Government Board of 1 November 1898, with such changes as have since been made by statute or provisional order confirmed by statute. The geographical county of Tipperary forms two administrative counties; it was divided in 1838 into two ridings north and south, each being made a separate county.

County Boroughs

County boroughs are areas which rank both as counties and as boroughs. There are four in the Republic: Cork, Dublin, Limerick and Waterford. Before 1922 there were in addition two in Northern Ireland: Belfast and Londonderry. County boroughs were created by the Local Government (Ireland) Act, 1898, which borrowed the idea and the term from the English Local Government Act of 1888. The notion has however an earlier ancestry, and one nearer home. In the eighteenth and nineteenth centuries (to go back no farther) a number of cities and boroughs were counties and had their own grand juries. Cork, Dublin, Limerick and Waterford figured in that group. The county of the city of Kilkenny and the counties of the towns of Drogheda, Carrickfergus and Galway ceased to be counties in 1898 and were merged in the adjoining administrative counties.

County Districts

Every administrative county for which a county council is elected consists of one or more county districts. A county district may be either an urban county district or a county health district. The urban county district is an urban sanitary district and the county health district a rural sanitary district. In 1925 the rural districts formed in 1898 within every county were combined to form one enlarged rural sanitary district which was given the name county health district. In a county that has no urban district the county health district coincides with the administrative county. A county health district may be divided by an order of the Minister for the Environment on the application of the county council: Local Government (Amendment) (No. 2) Act, 1934. The area of county Cork that is not included in urban county districts has been divided into three county health districts. Cork is the only county that has been so divided up to the present. The urban county districts include the non-county boroughs and every town other than the county boroughs that has become an urban sanitary district under the Public Health Act, 1878.

Boroughs

The boroughs are areas to which the Municipal Corporations Acts apply. They number eleven, of which four are county boroughs. Ten boroughs (two of them now in Northern Ireland) survived the dissolutions of 1840. In these the municipal corporations owed their origin to charters. Three have come into existence since 1840; one, Wexford, by the grant of a charter in 1845 and, two others, Dun Laoghaire (1930) and Galway (1937), by Acts of the Oireachtas. The power to grant a charter, which may now rest with the government, has not been repealed. The Municipal Corporations Act, 1840, defined the boundaries of the boroughs in which the corporations were not dissolved. As regards boroughs created since 1840, the boundaries of Wexford were delimited by the Wexford charter, Dun Laoghaire consists of four pre-existing urban districts in county Dublin, and Galway has the same area as the urban district which was the area of the town as defined in the Galway Town Improvement Act, 1853.

Urban Districts

Besides the boroughs, seventy-seven towns have municipal government. These towns fall into two categories: urban county districts, and towns that are not urban county districts. Originally town, township or improvement commissioners were constituted in these seventy-seven towns either under the Lighting of Towns Act, 1828, the Towns Improvement (Ireland) Act, 1854, or in one case, Bray, under a special Act of 1866. Most of these acquired public health or sanitary powers under the Public Health (Ireland) Act 1878 and became urban sanitary authorities. The residue remained as towns with attenuated functions under boards of town commissioners. In five towns commissioners are no longer elected.

Boroughs, towns with a population of 6,000 and having town commissioners, towns under local Acts having commissioners and towns separated from the rural sanitary district by provisional order became urban sanitary districts under the Public Health Act, 1878. Under the Local Government Act, 1898 these towns became urban districts and where they were under town commissioners the commissioners became the urban district council for the town. That Act repealed the Lighting of Towns Act, 1828, and replaced it in the towns in which it was in force by the Towns Improvement (Ireland) Act, 1854.

A town that is not an urban district may petition the Minister for Local Government to separate it from the rural sanitary district. This separation may be effected by means of a provisional order which, if the town has a population over 1,500 and at least one fourth of the electors do not petition against it, takes effect without confirmation by the Oireachtas (1898 Act s. 42). There is a reverse process, introduced by the Local Government Act, 1925 s. 74, by which an urban district not being a borough may relinquish urban status by applying to the Minister to be added to the rural sanitary district. If this is done, the council ceases to be an urban council and the members become town commissioners. This transition has taken place in recent years in four towns; Belturbet (1950), Cootehill (1950), Granard (1944) and Passage West (1942).

Towns

Of the seventy-seven municipal towns mentioned in the preceding section, twenty-eight have remained at, or opted to return to, the basic level of towns under commissioners. Twenty-three were constituted as towns before 1922, but did not proceed any farther up the municipal ladder. Four urban districts chose to revert to town status under the 1925 Act. One town, Tramore, has been constituted since 1922. Tramore became a town in 1948. Shannon, Co Clare is in the process of becoming a town.

When a market town or any town having a population of 1,500 and upwards desires to have a form of municipal government the electors to the number of at least twenty-one may apply to the Minister for the Environment for authority to carry the Towns Improvement (Ireland) Act, 1854 into execution in the town. The proposed boundaries must be specified in the application and prescribed notices published. If the Minister approves of the boundaries he directs the county manager to convene a meeting of the electors of the town to decide whether or not the Act will be adopted. If it is adopted in whole or in part and the Minister approves, arrangements are made for an election of town commissioners. Such commissioners when constituted have not only powers under the Towns Improvement Act, 1854, but all other powers that have been conferred on town commissioners since the Act of 1854 was passed.

A board of town commissioners can be dissolved by the Minister for the Environment under the Local Government Act, 1925 s. 74, and its powers, property and functions transferred to the county council. Five boards have been so dealt with: Callan (1940), Fethard (1936), Newcastle West (1941), Rathkeale (1926) and Roscommon (1927). These areas continue, however, to exist as towns. Another town, Tullow, appears periodically in the Census reports, but never in the annual Returns of Local Taxation. After successfully applying for constitution as a town it changed its mind and decided to go no farther. No candidates went for election as commissioners, and the town has remained dormant since 1902.

Regionalism and Localism

The preceding pages dealt with the traditional areas of local administration and politics, but counties, boroughs, urban districts and towns do not exhaust the rollcall of local divisions, which has in recent years begun to fill up with new forms of collective action, with new areas of operation. The most notable of these are various kinds of regional agency, and community councils.

Regions

The word 'region' has many meanings. Used in a general sense it means a tract of country having, usually, some distinctive character. In the political and administrative contexts its meaning depends on the point of observation. Seen from Washington D.C. a region may include several States of the Union; viewed from Brussels a regional problem may span the whole of Ireland, taking in both sides of the Border. But in the national perspective, our regions are usually groupings of counties varying from two to seven. In exceptional cases a single county or county borough may be given regional status: Dublin city for tourism; and Donegal for planning.

Regional organisation was largely a development of the period after World War Two. But there were a few earlier manifestations — the Circuit Court system created in 1924, and a rather ineffective walk-on part in the Town and Regional Planning Act, 1934, for example. During the war eight regional commissioners for all-purpose administration were appointed and assigned, but were never called on to act.

The Local Government (Planning and Development) Act, 1963 is, curiously, silent on the subject of regional planning, although, as the 1971 White Paper on Local Government Reorganisation says (7.2.1) 'the importance of a regional framework was recognised from the outset of the physical planning programme undertaken under the . . . Act.' A series of regional studies was commenced about 1964 on the provisional basis of nine regions. About the same time Bord Fáilte decided to replace the old Irish Tourist Association with eight regional tourism companies. In 1966 the Minister for Health projected reorganising the health services on a regional basis. Technical education, industrial development, and the new National Manpower Service followed.

There was some agreement between the various categories of region, but there were also serious discrepancies. The boundaries determined for the purposes of regional planning could claim the widest measure of adherence. After some chopping and changing they finally settled down at nine regions, with Donegal county serving as one of them. The Regional Development Organisations, which emerged in the late 1960s, operated therefore in the following regions; the Industrial Development Authority and the National Manpower service adopted the same pattern:

Region	Counties and County Boroughs	Population (1971) Thousands
East	Dublin City and County, Kildare, Meath, Wicklow	1062.2
South-East	Carlow, Kilkenny, Tipperary SR, Waterford City & County, Wexford	328.6
South-West	Cork City and County, Kerry	465.7
Mid-West	Clare, Limerick City and County Tipperary NR	269.8
West	Galway, Mayo	258.7
Midlands	Roscommon, Westmeath, Longford, Offaly, Laois	232.4
North-East	Cavan, Louth, Monaghan	173.9
North-West	Sligo, Leitrim	78.6
North	Donegal	108.3

Bord Fáilte's scheme of tourism companies had eight regions, some of them very different from the planning regions:

Region	Counties and County Boroughs	Population (1971) Thousands
Dublin	Dublin City	567.9
East	Dublin County, Meath, Louth, Kildare Wicklow	569.3
South-East	Carlow, Kilkenny, Tipperary SR, Waterford City & County, Wexford	328.6
South	Cork City and County, Kerry	465.7
Mid-West	Clare, Limerick City and County, Tipperary NR	269.8
West	Galway, Mayo	258.7
Midlands	Roscommon, Westmeath, Longford Offaly, Laois, Cavan, Monaghan	331.3
North West	Donegal, Leitrim, Sligo	187.0

Of these eight, only four are the same as the planning regions: South-East, South, Mid-West and West.

The health services regions, which emerged in 1970, showed a number of variations from the planning matrix; only three of their regions (the total had been fixed at eight) were similar:

Region	Counties and County Boroughs	Population (1971) Thousands
East	Dublin City and County, Kildare, Wicklow	990.5
South-East	Carlow, Kilkenny, Tipperary SR, Waterford City and County, Wexford	328.6
South-West	Cork City and County, Kerry	465.7
Mid-West	Clare, Limerick City & County, Tipperary NR	269.8
West	Galway, Mayo, Roscommon	312.3
Midlands	Longford, Westmeath, Laois, Offaly	178.9
North-East	Louth, Meath, Cavan, Monaghan	245.5
North-West	Donegal, Leitrim, Sligo	187.0

The Regional Technical Colleges were planned to serve ten regions, all showing divergences from the patterns set out above.

The PSORG Report (1969) commented at some length on the regional organisation of numerous government services, central and local (6.4.1-7), as well as those of many state-sponsored bodies. In view of the growing number of regionally managed activities in the public service, and the absence of any special co-ordinating agency, the Group recommended that the scope of the Department of Local Government should be extended to include the co-ordination of all aspects of regional development, and that its name should be altered to become the 'Department of Regional Development' (25.4.1-3). This proposal has not been accepted by the government. The Department became the Department of the Environment after the General Election of 1977.

The Gaeltacht is in some sense a region, although it does not fit readily within the ordinary definitions of the word. A new authority, mainly elective, has been created under the Udaras na Gaeltachta Act, 1979 with responsibility for the linguistic, cultural, social, physical and economic development of the Gaeltacht.

Sub-County Units

The White Paper on *Local Government Reorganisation* (1971) sketched a scheme of area committees to be organised in county electoral areas. There are about 130 of these areas in all, an average of five to a county. The idea of area committees to be made up of councillors and representatives of voluntary groups was unwelcome to elected members and has not been proceeded with. The White Paper went on (11.6.1-3) to discuss the merits of community councils. Although the role and functions of such councils were clearly set out, no specific areas could be assigned to them. Such councils have been formed in recent years by purely voluntary action, and the people involved have made their own decisions about areas of operation. A multitude of local improvement groups has emerged under a variety of names — local development associations, residents' associations, parish councils and the like — and with varying territories. Some operate in parishes or parts of parishes, others have wider concerns. The community council movement has tended in recent years to aim at groups of parishes.

Public Assistance and Registration Districts

The public assistance district was formerly, for the purpose of the civil registration of births, deaths and marriages, the district of the superintendent registrar. Since the replacement of public assistance by other means of welfare, the old registration areas are being rearranged by the Department of Health. The aim is to concentrate the work in centres large enough to warrant the engagement of full time registrars.

Vocational Education Areas

Vocational education areas consist of borough, urban district and county vocational areas. Every county borough is a borough vocational area, the boroughs of Drogheda, Dun Laoghaire, Galway, Sligo and Wexford and the urban districts of Bray and Tralee are urban district vocational areas and every county, exclusive of the urban vocational areas, is a county vocational area.

School Attendance Areas

School attendance areas, as determined by the School Attendance Act, 1926, are the county boroughs, the borough of Dun Laoghaire and areas into which the Minister for Education in consultation with the Minister for Justice has divided the rest of the country for the purpose of enforcing the attendance of children at primary schools.

Other Areas

United sanitary districts are districts that have been combined for any purpose of the Local Government (Sanitary Services) Acts 1878 to 1964. Seven united districts have been formed and six joint burial boards and one joint committee constituted for them.

Drainage districts were originally constituted under Drainage Acts of 1842 and 1863. These districts were under the control of trustees or drainage boards who had the care and management of the drainage works. After 1898 some districts were transferred to the county councils (1898 Act, s. 20). In 1925 provision was made in the Arterial Drainage Act of that year for the formation of new drainage districts. Existing districts may be taken over by the Commissioners of Public Works but until they are taken over they remain with the existing drainage authorities.

Navigations made in connection with drainage were vested in trustees on behalf of the counties and other areas affected. Galway and Mayo county councils and the borough corporation of Galway are empowered to appoint trustees for the Corrib.

Boards of conservators are elected for fishery districts, of which there were seventeen. Under the Fisheries Act 1980, seven regions replaced the old fishery districts, and the new system will function under a Central Board appointed by the Minister for Fisheries and Forestry.

Townlands

Townlands are ancient areas that were used under the Act of 1838 to form electoral divisions into which the poor law unions were divided. A comprehensive index to the townlands was published in 1901. The poor law union electoral divisions became district electoral divisions under the Local Government Act, 1898. They ceased to be used for electoral purposes in 1919 but are, however, still retained for purposes incidental to parliamentary and local elections and for administrative convenience. The populations of the district electoral divisions are shown in the Census.

Parishes

The civil parish is now obsolete as a local government area. In the seventeenth century an unsuccessful attempt was made (Highways Act, 1612) to persuade the parishes to maintain highways. Damages for malicious injuries were sometimes assessed on parishes and for the collection of county cess the parish was part of the barony, which was a sub-division of the county that ceased to be used for administration purposes after the Local Government Act, 1898 came into operation.

In England the Parish and District Councils Act of 1894 filled in the local administrative framework at sub-county levels. This was part of the Liberal programme for democratising rural society. The Tory government gave Ireland district councils in the 1898 package, but balked at the parish. Apart from possible religious difficulties, there was no strong tradition of parish administration in Ireland.

Alteration of Boundaries

The boundaries of counties, urban districts and towns under town commissioners may be altered. The procedure in the case of a county is for the county council to represent to the Minister for the Environment that the alteration is desirable (Application of Enactments Order, 1898, art. 20). The Minister, if he thinks the application ought to be entertained, causes a local inquiry to be held and may then make a provisional order and submit it to the Oireachtas for confirmation. The boundary of a borough may be altered by a similar procedure. The Local Government (Dublin) Act, 1930 authorised the inclusion in boundary alteration orders under that Act, of certain provisions in relation to added rural areas. These provisions may be included in orders extending the boundaries of any county borough.

A county council could also change the boundaries of an urban district other than a borough by means of an order (Application of Enactments Order, 1898, art. 26). This provision was replaced by the Local Authorities (Miscellaneous Provision) Act 1936, s. 10 of which enabled the urban council to take the initiative.

An urban district council that is not a borough may apply to the county council to have the boundaries of the urban district altered. The county council, after inquiry, may alter the boundaries. In case of refusal the urban council may appeal to the Minister for the Environment who can make the alteration with or without modifications or refuse to make it. The order when made is laid on the table of both Houses of the Oireachtas, but does not require confirmation. The boundaries of a town under town commissioners may be altered by the commissioners with the consent of the Minister for the Environment (Towns Improvement (Ireland) Act, 1854, s. 5).

On the application of an urban district council or the commissioners of a town the Government may change the name of the district or town (Local Government Act, 1946, s. 76). The county council's consent to the application being made is required. There is also a prescribed procedure (s. 77) for changing the names of non-municipal towns, townlands, streets and localities. In all proposals to change names of areas mentioned above there must be prior consultations with the ratepayers, four-sevenths of whom at least must consent to the change. The names of district electoral divisions can be altered by the Minister for the Environment.

Abolition of domestic rates has not affected the rights of former ratepayers in the matter of name changes: Local Government (Financial Provisions) Act, 1978, S.17.

7

Structure

Incorporation

All boroughs have municipal corporations. The corporation of a borough consists of the inhabitants who in their corporate capacity are as a rule styled the mayor (or the Right Honourable the Lord Mayor as the case may be), aldermen and burgesses. The local government electors are the burgesses. In Dun Laoghaire the corporation is styled simply The Corporation of Dun Laoghaire. Although borough councils are sometimes referred to as corporations, the council is an entity distinct from the corporation. The municipal corporation is a continuing body whose identity is not affected by changes in the persons composing it. It has perpetual succession, can hold property, sue, and be sued. The common seal of the corporation (which must, under the Management Acts, be affixed to documents in the presence of the mayor or chairman) is used as evidence of its more formal acts.

The position as regards incorporation is somewhat different in the counties and urban districts that are not boroughs. The body corporate in these cases is the council (Application of Enactments Order, 1898, art 13). The commissioners of towns were incorporated in 1955 as 'the . . . Town Commissioners' (the name of the town being inserted). They can sue or be sued in their corporate name (Local Government Act, 1955, s.65).

Corporations are somewhat abstract legal entities. In local government law they function usually through the agency of councils. Under the Municipal Corporations Acts the council was, and is, separate and distinct from the corporation. Thus the Local Government Act 1898, s. 21 says 'The mayor, aldermen and burgesses of each county borough acting by the council . . .' In the case of county councils the council was both the corporate body and the agency, and separation of the two was difficult to grasp, especially for laymen. Indeed, the confusion was fairly general in the early years of the state, when the Acts of 1923 and 1925 spoke of 'dissolving' local authorities. But the legal position was clarified by the Local Government Act, 1941, s. 44 of which substituted a Ministerial power to remove the members of a local authority from office. The object was to preserve the corporate character or *persona* of the local authority. The same Act, s. 51, restored the position of local authorities which had been

72

dissolved under earlier legislation. The point is discussed at some length in H.A. Street, *Local Government,* 1955, pp 283-4.

The effect of introducing city and county management was to add another agency through which the corporate bodies could perform the executive part of their function. The manager was thus not only an officer but a statutory part of the corporation, on the same level in law as the council. This proved to be too refined a concept for most councillors, and gave rise to such misunderstanding, especially in county councils during the early years of management.

County Councils

The council of an administrative county for which a county council is elected consists of a chairman and councillors. The total number of members of the council and the number to be elected from every county electoral area have been fixed under statute by orders of the Minister for the Environment (Local Government Act, 1941, s. 33). Cork county council has forty-six and other county councils currently vary in number of members from twenty to thirty-six. The number of members for each electoral area in a county and the number for the whole country are shown in Appendix II.

The functions of county councils span the full range of services now covered by the term 'local government'. A wider view may be taken of the scope of local administration, and the PSORG in fact took this view, but a strict interpretation would exclude a number of the agencies and services which they (rightly of course) classed as local.

The services have (since 1976) been arranged in eight programme groups:

(1) Housing and Building
(2) Road Transportation and Safety
(3) Water Supply and Sewerage
(4) Development Incentives and Controls
(5) Environmental Protection
(6) Recreation and Amenity
(7) Agriculture, Education, Health and Welfare
(8) Miscellaneous.

These programmes, and the numerous sub-programmes which go to make them up, are dealt with in Chapters 14 to 21 below.

County Borough Corporations

The county boroughs at Cork and Dublin have Lord Mayors: Cork's is a recent creation (1900 — when Belfast also got a Lord Mayor); the Dublin dignitary dates from 1665 and after London is the second oldest in these islands. Limerick and Waterford have mayors simply. Representative local government is in the hands of the city council whose membership ranges from forty-five in Dublin through thirty-one in Cork, seventeen in Limerick to fifteen in Waterford. Each county borough has a city manager.

Candidates who top the poll in their electoral areas become aldermen: Dublin has eleven, Cork six, Limerick four and Waterford five. The county borough corporations have practically all the functions of county, borough and district councils except such as are not appropriate to a city (e.g. the setting up of a committee of agriculture). Where functions are assigned to joint or regional authorities, as in the case of health these functions are not of course exercised directly by the corporations, but the councils of the county boroughs appoint their representatives on the regional boards. They may, therefore, deal with the following matters: roads, sanitary services (sewers, water supply, cleansing, pollution control, baths and swimming pools, burial grounds, abbattoirs, public lighting, etc.); housing; public museums and art galleries; weights and measures; parks; fire brigades; school meals; diseases of animals; municipal buildings; motor registration; registration of voters; preparation of jurors' lists; valuation expenses; maintenance of courthouses; vocational education (through statutory committees); town planning; open spaces; play centres; protection from dangerous buildings; public libraries; allotments; markets and civil defence.

Borough Corporations

The council of a borough consists of a mayor, aldermen and councillors except in Dun Laoghaire where the council consists of councillors only. The number of members of each council is fixed by or under statute (1941 Act, s. 34). Dun Laoghaire has fifteen and the other boroughs twelve each.

Dun Laoghaire has no aldermen while all other boroughs have four. The mayor, or in Dun Laoghaire the chairman, may be paid such salary or allowance as the council fixes.

The corporations of the seven non-county boroughs have the powers of urban district councils: housing, roads, water supply and sewerage, planning and development, and some others. In addition they have such powers as are vested in borough corporations and councils by the Municipal Corporation Acts and any Private Act relating to the town. These additional powers are not extensive, the difference between the non-county boroughs and the urban councils being in the main a difference of status rather than powers. Borough councils can make byelaws for the good rule and government of the borough and can vote a salary to the mayor.

Urban District Councils

The council of every urban district not a borough consists of a chairman and councillors. In Bray, Dundalk and Tralee the number of members is twelve, elsewhere nine (1941 Act, s. 34).

When a town is detached from the county health district and becomes an urban sanitary district the town commissioners become an urban district council. They retain all their powers as commissioners and in addition obtain the functions and powers of the urban council. They then become the road authority, sanitary authority, library authority and rating authority for the urban district.

As road authority they are responsible for urban roads that are not main roads, the county council being the authority for main roads, but the urban council can accept responsibility for all roads or transfer responsibility for urban roads to the county council without altering the incidence of the charge. All but three urban district councils have availed of a provision which enables them to relinquish their library powers to the county council. In non-county boroughs, which are all urban county districts, the Sale of Food and Drugs Acts are administered by the corporations.

The principal functions of urban district councils are planning and development, paving, repairing, cleansing, watering and lighting streets; supplying water, making sewers and drains; dealing with derelict sites, housing, the provision of market houses and weighbridges, fire brigades, gas supply where authorised by provisional order (Clonmel is the only urban authority left in this business, apart from Limerick City); school meals, allotments, levying and collecting the municipal rate, meeting the demand of the county council for their share of the county expenses, contributing to tourist development, acquiring and maintaining recreation grounds and public walks, and in the case of seven urban districts, including five non-county boroughs, making provision for vocational education.

Town Commissioners

The number of commissioners in every town that is not an urban district is nine. In five towns the commissioners have been permanently removed from office and their functions transferred to the county council. See above pp.65-6.

When the electors in a town first constitute a body of town commissioners their ostensible purpose is to put the Towns Improvement Act, 1854 or part of it into operation in the town. The Act of 1854 and the two Clauses Acts incorporated with it covered a great variety of matters, particularly paving, lighting, draining, cleansing, water supply and public order. It was both a sanitary Act and a police Act. When sanitary administration was reorganised by the Public Health Act, 1878 the commissioners of the larger towns became sanitary authorities with extended power. The municipal towns that did not become urban sanitary districts became part of the rural sanitary district and the commissioners of these towns lost some of their powers by the repeal of the provisions of the Act relating to water, sewers, drainage, cleansing of streets, prevention of nuisances, registration of lodging houses, sale of unwholesome food and adulteration of food. Since 1878 the Act has been further amended by the repeal of provisions relating to paving, fire prevention, assessments to rates, prevention of obstruction in streets, fire engines and the increase of the police force. These amendments have diminished further the powers of town commissioners that have not become sanitary authorities.

On the other hand whilst many important functions have been withdrawn from town commissioners and given to the sanitary authority for the town, which is now the county council, some new functions were added. These added functions included the provision of houses, allotments, meals for school children, parks, granting licences to store petroleum, promotion of or opposition to local legislation, and the prosecution or defence of legal proceedings in the interests of the inhabitants. Also included were advertising the amenities of the town as a health resort, licensing cinemas and providing and improving markets. A survey reported in the White Paper of 1971 demonstrated that town commissioners had ceased to build houses since 1953, and made little use of their statutory power for fairs and markets, tourist development and school meals.

The powers given by the Act of 1854 which still rest with the commissioners relate to numbering houses, removal of obstructions and dangerous buildings, precautions during construction of sewers, streets and houses, public lighting, ventilation of places where people assemble, control of offensive trades, prohibition of cellar dwellings, erection of public clocks, impounding stray cattle, control of sale and keeping of gunpowder, licensing powers, building a town hall and maintaining it, making application to have the town constituted an urban district and making of byelaws with regard to parks and boats plying for hire. The provisions of the Act in regard to the licensing of horse-drawn hackney carriages still apply but motor vehicles are now dealt with under the Road Traffic Act of 1961. The 1854 Act specified thirty offences against good order in the streets which rendered the offender liable to arrest and possible conviction with a fine. The administration of this part of the Act rests with the Garda Siochána.

Town commissioners now get from the county council the money they require by means of an annual demand and the council levy it off the town with the county rate. They are no longer rating authorities.

Committees

County, borough and district councils and town commissioners have power to appoint committees for any purpose which would be better regulated and managed by committees (Local Government Act, 1925, s. 58; CM Act 1940, s. 18; MC Act 1840, s. 102 and CC Act 1847, s. 49). Before the introduction of the management system, the system of working through committees had been developed by the larger urban authorities and to some extent by the county councils and other elective bodies. Where there was much to be done and executive functions could not be delegated to an officer, work was divided among committees. A large council is not a suitable body for the prompt discharge of routine work or for close supervision. The committee system enabled business to be dispatched without making excessive demands on the time of members of the parent body. Area Committees operate in many counties for road programmes and other purposes. Three District Committees have been set up in Dublin County to deal with matters of special local concern in the North County, Mid-West and South County.

Discussion in committee is usually less formal and freer than in council and by referring matters to committees in the first instance the local authority ensured that hasty decisions were not taken. Under the management system which placed the responsibility for the discharge of executive functions on a whole-time paid manager there was not the same necessity for committees as executive bodies but some authorities, notably Dublin city council, have continued committees in an advisory capacity. Under the County Management Act, 1940 committees can still be set up but the power to delegate executive functions may be exercised only by the manager with the consent of the Minister.

Committees are of two kinds, optional and obligatory. Examples of the former are library committees and national monuments advisory committees. Obligatory or statutory committees include vocational education committees, county committees of agriculture, consultative health committees, old age pensions committees and school attendance committees. There are other bodies which although called boards are in their nature committees. These boards include six burial boards and a cemetery joint committee.

Local authorities generally were given power by the Local Government Act, 1955 s. 60 to set up advisory committees of not less than three members. These committees, while they must include some local authority members, may also include non-members. Under the City and County Management (Amendment) Act, 1955 s. 7 a local authority may also appoint an estimates committee consisting of, in the case of a county council, two members from each electoral area, and, in other cases, not more than one-third of the total membership.

Vocational Education Committees

These are statutory (i.e. obligatory) committees under the Vocational Education Act, 1930. Vocational education committees are bodies corporate and consist, in the county boroughs and the seven urban county districts that have been made vocational education areas, of fourteen members of whom not less than five nor more than eight must be members of the council of the borough or urban district. In the county areas the number is fourteen together with representatives of the urban districts where such districts are not vocational education areas. Not less than five nor more than eight must be members of the county council and the urban district councils of the county may appoint to the committee members of their own body or persons who are not members of the council.

In electing members to the committee the council must have regard to the interest and experience in education of persons proposed and to recommendations made to them by bodies interested in manufactures or trades. The committee is elected in every election year and holds an annual meeting before 1 December each year and monthly meetings at least once a month except in July and September. The quorum is one-fourth of the members. The Minister for Education may make regulations respecting procedure. An inspector of the Department of Education is entitled to be present at and address meetings. Sub-committees may be appointed and must be appointed if the Minister for Education so requires for any part of the vocational education area.

Each committee employs a Chief Executive Officer and other staff.

Committees of Agriculture

Under the Agriculture Act, 1931 a county committee of agriculture consisting of persons who have a knowledge of or an estate in land or persons with special local knowledge of agricultural matters must be appointed by every county council. The size of the committee depends on the number of county electoral areas. At least one member must come from every electoral area and the total number must not be less than three nor more than four times the number of electoral areas. Persons who are not members of the council may be appointed to the committee. The Minister for Agriculture may regulate the proceedings of the committee. The quorum is four. These committees are now corporate bodies with power to hold land and borrow money. Each committee employs a Chief Agricultural Officer and other staff.

Under the National Agricultural Advisory, Education and Research Authority Act, 1977, as amended by the Agriculture (An Chomhairle Oiliúna Talmhaíochta) Act, 1979, responsibility for the agricultural advisory service has been transferred to a new state-sponsored body called ACOT.

County committees of agriculture will continue with new duties and new membership. Two-fifths of the members will be elected by farming and agricultural organisations – the Irish Farmers Association, Irish Creamery Milk Suppliers Association, the Irish Countrywomen's Association and Macra na Feirme.

County Development Teams

The teams are small high-level groups which operate in thirteen western counties, under the aegis of the Department of Finance. The idea originated with the Inter-Departmental Committee on the Problems of Small Western Farms (1963) which saw a need in each county for some focus of information, ideas, and local enterprise. As initially composed the Teams were not notably successful. They were re-organised in 1965 at the instance of the Department of Finance (Development Division) and now consist of: County Manager as chairman, Chairman of the county council, County Engineer, Chief Agricultural Officer, CEO of the Vocational Education Committee, and the IDA Regional Manager.

Each Team has a small staff headed by a County Development officer, who is an officer of the Department of Finance. The work of the Teams is co-ordinated by the Central Development Committee, a body made up of six County Managers, with officials of the Departments of Finance, Agriculture, Environment, Education, Fisheries, Gaeltacht, Industry and Energy, Trade, Commerce and Tourism, Transport and Labour; and the IDA The counties or parts of counties for which the Teams function are: Cavan, Clare, Donegal, Galway, Kerry, Leitrim, Longford, Mayo, Monaghan, Roscommon, Sligo, West Cork and West Limerick.

The Teams' objectives are (1) to foster economic development by ensuring maximum use of State grants, incentives, and services; (2) co-ordination of public service activities in each county, and (3) stimulating entrepreneurial ideas and attitudes. Special attention is given to the needs and problems of the Gaeltacht areas.

Pension Committees

Old age pensions commitees are appointed for every county and for borough and urban districts over ten thousand in population. The members need not be members of the council that appoints them. The pensions officer who sends his reports on claims for the consideration of the committee may attend meetings, raise questions or may apply for revocation of provisional allowances. An appeal by the pensions officer or any person aggrieved lies to the Minister for Social Welfare. A pensions committee may appoint sub-committees and delegate powers to them.

School Attendance Committees

School attendance committees are appointed only in the county boroughs of Cork, Dublin and Waterford and the borough of Dun Laoghaire, and these boroughs may each be divided into two or more areas with a committee for each. The number of members is ten, or if there is a juvenile advisory committee, eleven. The Minister for Education appoints five members and the council of the borough the remaining five or six. Provision is made for the representation on the committees of school managers and teachers and also of the juvenile advisory committees where they exist. The Minister for Education regulates the time of meeting, quorum, conduct of business and keeping of acccounts.

Diseases of Animals Committees

The county council as the local authority under the Diseases of Animals Acts are required to form a committee to administer the Acts. The committee may consist wholly of members of the council or partly of members and partly of rated occupiers. To this committee the council may delegate any or all of their powers under the Acts.

Local Health Committees

These are generally county committees operating under the Health Act, 1970 as local contact groups between the public and the regional boards which are felt to be somewhat remote. The committees have no executive functions and act only in an advisory role, transmitting local feelings, aspirations and reactions to the health boards.

The committees comprise:
  (1) councillors – three from each electoral area
  (2) county manager (or his nominee)
  (3) county medical officer or equivalent
  (4) RMS of district mental hospital
  (5) a group of doctors, nurses, dentist, pharmacist
  (6) two voluntary representatives of voluntary organisations in social service work.
Committee meetings are attended either by the regional CEO or other senior officer.

Visiting Committees

The Mental Treatment Act, 1945 placed an obligation on mental hospital authorities to appoint visiting committees, not more than half of the members of which might not be members of the authority. The business of the committee was to visit the mental hospital, hear complaints, inspect the building and report any matter to the authorities which they think expedient. Although the legal requirement has been repealed, committees have been continued under a more general provision of the Health Act 1970, s. 8.

Joint Bodies

Burial boards are formed for united districts. Ordinarily the sanitary authority is the burial board but under a general power to form united districts and constitute governing bodies of such districts and also a power to appoint joint committees six joint boards and one committee have been set up. These boards are bodies corporate. The provisional order forming a united district made under the Local Government (Sanitary Services)

Acts defines the scope of the board's powers and contains regulations as to elections, continuance in office, meetings and other matters. A joint committee is appointed under article 38 of the Schedule to the Local Government (Application of Enactments) Order, 1898.

The Minister for Health has power under the Health Act 1970, s. 11 to authorise two or more regional boards to act jointly and establish a joint board. The power was exercised to create the General Medical Services (Payments) Board in 1972. This Board is a co-operative undertaking involving all eight health boards. It plays a major part in assessing and paying claims from doctors and pharmacists under the choice-of-doctor scheme.

Community Councils

In recent years a multitude of local bodies have sprung up, mostly without benefit of approved status under the general label of community councils or associations. These are voluntary groups of various kinds, from expanded versions of urban and suburban residents' associations to, in country districts, a developed form of Muintir na Tíre parish guilds. Some originated as development associations, others as Tidy Towns committees. And many, of course, had no previous incarnation, and emerged in response to impulses such as industrialisation or the need of it, or growing population, or a determination to get more and better amenities, or just a desire for communal self expression. The last-mentioned often takes the form of organising pressure on the official agencies, central and local, with the aim of improving services, or countering unpopular official action, or the remedy of grievances.

Community councils or associations enjoy considerable freedom of action, and most if not all such bodies and their promoters seem very reluctant to give up their independence of the weighty shackles which afflict statutory bodies. Their situation naturally carries certain disabilities: no powers of taxation or regular recourse to funds, no clearly defined role, functions or duties, and no certainty of continuance. But community activists display few regrets and seem to have no wish to enjoy the settled if unexciting way of life of an English parish council or meeting, or a Welsh community council as exhibited in the Local Government Act 1972.

Parish councils in Ireland have played no part in formal local government, and although added as a lowest tier in 1894 to the English local government structure, they were omitted from the Irish 1898 package. The reason was the presence in Ireland of two sets of parishes: Catholic parishes and 'civil' parishes. During the debates on the Local Government Bill, 1924, the possibility of parish or community councils was suggested as a means of filling the vacuum left by the disappearance of rural district councils, but the idea was not taken up. It came to life again with the outbreak of the 1939 war, and the Local Government Bill, 1940, included a cluster of provisions (Part VIII, ss. 72 to 75 in the 1941 Act) on what were described as Approved Local Councils.

County councils, if they accepted a body set up for the furtherance of the general social and economic interests of a locality, could assist the council or committee in various ways, and even devolve some functions to it. The process was confined to county health districts, reflecting in this the major thrust behind the movement, which came from Muintir na Tíre, a community development (although the term was not then in use) organisation with a marked rural bias. Muintir na Tíre influence also showed itself in the legislature's decision to leave initiative in setting up local councils and follow-up action, to the people themselves. There was some opinion in favour of giving the councils a more formalised status in the system (Senate Debates 25, 2137-2173, 31 July 1941). But the passion for liberty prevailed. There was a fair degree of activity and enthusiasm during the Emergency, although only a minority of parish councils became approved local councils. But with the return of peace much of the sense of purpose tended to evaporate, and with it the spontaneity and ardour which had characterised the movement. Muintir na Tíre worked hard to keep the spirit alive, but in the early 1950s only fifty-four approved local councils were active, thirty-five of them in County Limerick. There were signs that growth had shifted from the country to the cities and in response to pressure the Local Government Act, 1955, extended the powers of approving and helping local councils to the corporations of county boroughs (1955 Act, Part V, ss. 51-54). Grants could now be given for community halls, a power which remained, however, limited to county councils.

The 1971 plan for local government reorganisation contained a modest set of proposals for establishing local councils, particularly in counties and major cities where identifiable communities existed with their own interests, needs and aspirations. These ideas were especially relevant in towns and urban districts where it was intended to abolish commissioners and urban councils. The question of establishing statutory local councils was considered briefly and dismissed, on the ground that statutory councils would necessarily take on the inflexibility of the local government system, with its controls, safeguards and procedures. The government decided therefore to follow the line laid down in 1941:

11.3.2 Development in all its forms, and at all levels, requires the active participation of all sections of the community; if economic and social development is to be advanced in all areas of the country, the initiative, skill and energy of every community must be harnessed. This can best be done through voluntary bodies. But there must be a partnership between these bodies and the statutory local authorities.

The suggestions put forward were twofold: (1) area committees of county councils, and (2) encouragement of local community councils of the statutory local authorities (11.6.1).

The proposals in the 1971 White Paper were not pursued, but a considerable number of Community Councils have been formed and are in operation. Their activities are multifarious. Some are more imaginative and energetic than others. The Ballyfermot Community Association in Dublin has pioneered work in urban planning, facilities for recreation and athletics, and operated a local television transmitter. A number of community councils have taken a hand in educational matters, have surveyed community opinion and channelled demands to the authorities.

A notable feature of the community movement is a distrust of party politics and politicians. The 1974 local elections were marked by the success in the Dublin area of a number of community candidates, and there is a prospect of political action being carried from local to national levels, towards what is described as community government. Local councillors associated with the traditional parties, it must be said, reciprocate these feelings and expressions of antagonism towards community councils and their political manifestation are sometimes heard.

Harbour Authorities

Harbour authorities are not amongst the authorities defined as 'local authorities' for the purposes of the Local Government Acts but nevertheless they must be regarded as part of the local government system inasmuch as they are subordinate representative bodies exercising in defined areas powers (including a power to levy rates on tonnage and goods) assigned to them by the Oireachtas and operating under the general supervision of a Minister of State.

Harbour authorities have been constituted under the Harbours Act, 1946 for the control, operation and development of the harbours. The Act of 1946 does not affect the state harbours of Howth, Dun Laoghaire and Dunmore East which are under the Commissioners of Public Works, or numerous small harbours, piers and quays which are under the control of the county councils.

Harbour authorities are bodies corporate and consist of representatives appointed by local bodies named in the First Schedule to the Act of 1946 and by the interests directly concerned in the use of the harbour. The local bodies that appoint representatives include the county borough corporations and certain county, borough and urban district councils. The central authority for the supervision of harbour authorities is the Minister for Transport who has powers corresponding broadly to those of the Minister for the Environment in relation to the local bodies that come within his cognisance. He can authorise harbour works, the compulsory acquisition of land, transfer a harbour to a local authority and alter the limits of a harbour. He appoints the auditors who audit the accounts. He may remove the members of an authority that do not discharge their duties effectually and replace them by a commissioner, declare qualifications for offices, amalgamate offices and fix age limits for retirement. The four principal harbour authorities in the county boroughs must appoint a general manager whose position in relation to the authority is much the same as that of a manager to a city or county council.

The function of a harbour authority is to provide facilities for vessels that come to the port and for discharging and loading cargoes. Their current revenues are derived from rates levied in respect of tonnage, goods and services. They have a general power to borrow but a limit placed on loans cannot be exceeded without the consent of the Minister for Finance. A local authority may guarantee a loan or contribute to the interest of a loan or borrow in order to advance money to a harbour authority.

The White Paper of 1971 proposed a measure of rationalisation of the system of harbour management. Ten of the smaller out of the twenty-four harbours managed under the Harbours Act, 1946 would be, it was intended, transferred to county councils, and their special authorities abolished. This proposal has not been proceeded with. The most recent development has in fact been in the opposite direction. The Harbour Act, 1976 authorised the establishment of separate harbour commissioners for Bantry Bay following local agitation for greater powers of control of an oil terminal sited in the area.

Regional Fisheries Boards

Seven regional fisheries boards have replaced the seventeen boards of fisheries conservators constituted under a series of Fisheries Acts running back to 1849. The former boards consisted of elected members, ex officio members and representatives of holders of certain licences. The conservators issued fishing licences and struck rates on rateable fisheries within their district. Persons rated for fisheries are exempt from local rates on the fishery levied by local authorities. Where this exemption has the effect of increasing the local rate by more than a penny in the pound a grant is made to the local authority out of voted moneys to meet the excess.

A new Central Fisheries Board, established under the Fisheries Act, 1980, replaces the Inland Fisheries Trust, and will function as a supervisory and co-ordinating agency under the Minister for Fisheries and Forestry. The new structure follows generally the recommendations of the Inland Fisheries Commission which reported in 1975.

Regional Development Organisations

Regional Development Organisations (RDOs) are non-statutory bodies representing planning authorities and other development interests in the region — tourism, industry, harbours and the like. Membership includes both elected and appointed office-holders. The RDOs were a product of the impetus towards regional planning and development which followed the Local Government (Planning and Development) Act, 1963. Commissioned by the Minister for the Environment (then Local Government), UN consultants Colin Buchanan and Partners carried out a national survey of the regions. Their report of May 1969 *'Regional Studies in Ireland'* recommended the appointment in each region of a joint planning authority with statutory responsibility for major or strategic planning. But the government rejected the proposal and announced in May 1969 their decision that co-ordinating groups of planning authorities and other interests should be established in all regions. The pattern chosen as a model had emerged from local initiative in the Mid-West region in 1968: it combined elective and official representatives of the planning authorities, the Shannon Free Airport Development Co., the Regional Tourism Organisation and the harbour authorities in Limerick and Foynes, IDA, ESB, CIE and Aer Rianta. In addition three government departments are represented — Agriculture, Environment and Labour.

The non-statutory character of the RDOs gives them the advantage of flexibility both in organisation and operation. The prototype RDO in the Mid-West has a two-tier structure — a large representative board with over forty members, and a smaller executive committee.

Functions equally allow for local initiative. The RDOs have a general co-ordinating and advisory role in regional planning. They carry out surveys and studies of regional resources, and organise seminars, conferences and other activities bearing on regional development. Each RDO has a director (usually a seconded local officer) and secretarial staff. Expenses are shared by the planning authorities concerned, and annual grants are made by the Department of the Environment. The necessary legal substructure is supplied by Application of Enactments Order, 1898, Act 38 (joint committees), Local Government Act, 1925, s. 58 (committees of county councils) and Local Government Act, 1955, s. 60 (advisory committees): RDOs are not corporate bodies.

Regional Health Boards

These Boards, presaged in the White Paper *The Health Services and their Further Development* (1966), emerged in statutory form from the Health Act, 1970. The Boards were intended to be the expression of 'a partnership between local government, central government and the vocational organisations.' This was a new concept in local administration. Local government had developed through the 19th and 20th centuries on the principle of representation, with an ever-broadening electorate. It could not readily accommodate the new composite boards, and the health services accordingly moved away from local government, breaking a tie which had endured for almost a century and a half.

The decision to opt for regionalism was influenced by the belief that the county was too small a unit for modern hospital and specialist services, and that the new type of general medical service projected would be better organised in regions. The move also involved a break with city and county management. The new health boards have their own manager-equivalent in their chief executive officer (CEO). There were two main reasons: the expanding health services were a growing burden on the time and energies of managers (the proportions of local authority work absorbed by health before the split were 41 per cent in terms of expenditure and 38 per cent in personnel); and, secondly, local work in planning, housing, roads, etc. also claimed an increasing amount of attention. The break may also have owed something to the unconscious tendency of central Departments to work towards an arrangement giving them undivided control of their own local systems. On this line of argument the decision to achieve separate agencies followed inevitably from the establishment of the Department of Health in 1947.

Membership of the health boards ranges from twenty-seven to thirty-five. The majority of members in every board must be local councillors, nominated by city or county councils. The balance is made up of medical doctors, dentists, pharmacists, and nurses, with three Ministerial nominees. Numbers are as follows:

Health Board	Councillors	Doctors	Other*	Total
Eastern	19	9	7	35
South Eastern	16	8	7	31
Southern	18	8	7	33
Mid Western	15	6	7	28
Western	15	7	7	29
North Western	14	6	7	27
North Eastern	16	7	7	30
Midland	16	7	7	30

*One dentist, pharmacist, general nurse and psychiatric nurse; and three nominees of the Minister.

Each regional board is required to have a CEO. In contrast with the local government management system, the reserved powers and functions are those of the CEO and comprise a limited range of decisions, mainly relating to eligibility of individuals for services, and personnel matters. All other business rests with the board, but in practice virtually the whole of the day to day management has been delegated to the CEO and his aides. On the advice of management consultants McKinsey and Co. the work of the boards has been broken down into three broad programmes: (1) community care (2) general hospital services and (3) special hospital services. These were put in the charge of three, sometimes two programme managers in each region. Each board also has functional officers to take care of finance, personnel and planning.

Regional Tourism Organisations

These are public companies set on foot by Bord Fáilte in 1964 to promote tourism, by involving local interests, in the eight regions defined by the Board. Participation is sought from local authorities, clubs, associations and others with tourist interests. The companies are financed by Bord Fáilte, local authorities, and subscribing members. The regional programmes include encouragement and help to local development associations, angling clubs and game councils. The Organisations also arrange for tourist information bureaux, room reservation systems, guides, itineraries and other publicity material. Each Organisation has the task of preparing a tourism development plan for the region. The staff is headed by a regional tourist manager.

Regional Game Councils

Not regional bodies in the currently accepted sense. They are, broadly, federations of sporting clubs and other rural or agricultural organisations in counties. They work for the improvement of game and wildlife resources by restocking, improving habitats, and the provision of refuges and sanctuaries. They get financial and technical assistance from the Forest and Wildlife Service of the Department of Fisheries and Forestry.

Central Authorities

Departments and offices of central government are an important, even a predominant part of the structure of local administration. They play a crucial role in the formation of policy, the preparation of legislation and statutory instruments, the provision of finance for local services and in the stimulation and control of local authorities in their various operations. Central departments may also themselves provide services for local bodies, or directly for the public.

Central intervention in local affairs has a long history. Government settled the county systems, created city and borough administration, and kept an intermittent eye on the way things were going in the outlying territories. There was no systematic oversight. At the beginning of the nineteenth century 'there was no government department specially responsible for local affairs' (McDowell, 1964). The Irish Poor Law Commission of 1847 was the first central agency which could lay some claim to this position but its scope was restricted to boards of guardians. It did not concern itself with county or town government. But when, in 1872, the

Poor Law Commissioners gave place to the Local Government Board for Ireland, the new Board's powers were extended to cover virtually the whole range of local affairs.

The Local Government Board was superseded formally in 1922 by the Department of Local Government, a creation of the Provisional Government, which gave way in turn in 1924 to the Department of Local Government and Public Health. The Ministers and Secretaries Act, 1924 expanded the Department so that it embraced, in addition to the Local Government Board, the following: Inspectors of Lunatic Asylums in Ireland, National Health Insurance Commission, Registrar-General of Births, Deaths and Marriages in Ireland, Roads Department (this had been with the Ministry of Transport), Clerk of the Crown and Hanaper as far as concerned Elections, General Nursing Council, and Central Midwives Board.

The Department of Local Government and Public Health occupied the centre of the stage until 1947 when, under the pressure of demands for central re-organisation and improved health and social welfare services, it split into three parts. A new Department of Health took over, in 1947, the supervision and direction of local and other services relating to personal health. Certain supervisory functions in connection with milk and meat were transferred to the Department of Agriculture early in 1948. And the Department of Social Welfare took over national health insurance, old age pensions appeals, widows' and orphans' pensions, school meals and a few other local services of a welfare nature.

The Department of Local Government was left with a reasonably homogeneous group of environmental services — roads and road traffic, housing, physical planning, water supply, sewerage, fire services, libraries, swimming pools, parks and playing fields. The Department also exercised a general oversight on local structures and finances — rating, audit, elections (including Dáil, Seanad and Presidential elections) and combined purchasing. The name of the Department was changed in 1977 to Department of the Environment.

The Departments of Local Government, Health and Social Welfare do not exhaust the list of those concerned with local administration. Virtually every department has some local function or is geared into some aspect of local or regional activity. The following statement gives some idea of the spread of interaction:

Central Departments	*Local Responsibilities*
1. Agriculture	Committees of Agriculture, diseases of animals
2. Defence	Civil Defence
3. Education	Vocational Education Committees, School Attendance Committees, higher education grants

4. Environment	Local Authorities: organisation, services and finance, Local and parliamentary (including European Parliament) elections
5. Finance	Agricultural Grant, regional planning, County Development Teams
— Office of Public Works	Local Loans Fund, coast erosion, drainage, national monuments
— Valuation Office	Valuation for rating
6. Fisheries & Forestry	Regional Fisheries Boards
7. Gaeltacht	Gaeltacht housing, water and sewerage
8. Health	Regional Health Boards: organisation, services and finance, general and special hospitals, voluntary hospitals, Hospital Sweeps Fund
9. Industry and Energy	Gas production plants
10. Justice	Coroners, courthouses, pounds, traffic control
11. Labour	Factories Act, Office Premises Act, Labour Court
12. Public Service	Local Appointments Commission, remuneration in higher public service, Inter-Departmental Committee on Sub-National Systems
13. Social Welfare	Fuel and footwear scheme, blind welfare, Unemployment Assistance Fund
14. Trade, Commerce & Tourism	Consumer protection, weights and measures, Regional Tourism Organisations
15. Transport	Harbours

State Sponsored Bodies

A small group of State-sponsored bodies are concerned with local government, and may legitimately be regarded as part of the structure. They include An Foras Forbartha, An Chomhairle Leabharlanna, and a few more.

The National Institute for Physical Planning and Construction Research (An Foras Forbartha) was established in 1964, on the initiative of the then Minister for Local Government, with the aid of grants from the United Nations. The objects were to provide research, training and information services in

(1) Physical planning and development,
(2) building and construction,
(3) roads, and
(4) water resources (added later).

The Institute has a Board of Directors whose members are appointed for three year terms by the Minister for the Environment. It has a Chief Executive Officer, and the staff is organised in four divisions: planning, water resources, construction and roads. Foras Forbartha acts as national focal point for the United Nations Environment Programme Referral Service; and is linked with such international information networks as the Environment Protection Agency, and the Highway Research Information Service in USA.

The Library Council, An Chomhairle Leabharlanna, under the Public Libraries Act, 1947, took over the Irish Central Library for Students which had been established in 1923 by the Carnegie United Kingdom Trust. The Council also functions as an expert advisory body to the Minister for the Environment in library matters and gives subsidies for library buildings and improvements in the services. The Council is financed by a state grant and a levy on local authorities.

Members are appointed for five year terms by the Minister for the Environment. The choice of chairman rests with the Minister (in consultation with the Minister for Education), but other appointments are made on the nomination of:

Trinity College Dublin	2 Members
University College Dublin	1 Member
University College Cork	1 Member
University College Galway	1 Member
National Library of Ireland	1 Member
General Council of County Councils	3 Members
Association of Municipal Authorities	2 Members
Library Association of Ireland	1 Member

The National Building Agency Ltd was set up in 1960 by the Minister for the Environment to supplement local and state housing operations. It acts as agent for the Industrial Development Authority in housing key workers, and builds houses by arrangement with departments of state for their employees. It may also build on behalf of local housing authorities. The Agency is a private company financed by the state. Directors are appointed by the Minister for the Environment.

An Bord Pleanála was established in 1977 under the Local Government (Planning and Development) Act, 1976, and in March 1977 took over from the Minister the function of adjudicating on appeals and references under the Planning Acts of 1963 and 1976. The Board has also been assigned the duty of deciding appeals under the Local Government (Water Pollution) Act, 1977. Members are appointed by the Minister for the Environment. The chairman is a former judge of the High Court. The five other members are professional and administrative people drawn from the Department of the Environment, local authorities and the private sector.

The Local Government Computer Services Board was established in 1975 by the Minister for the Environment, under the Local Government (Corporate Bodies) Act, 1971. The Board includes representatives of City and County Managers, and the Departments of the Environment and the Public Service.

Local Government Associations

The two principal associations of local authorities are the General Council of County Councils and the Association of Municipal Authorities of Ireland.

The General Council of County Councils was established in 1899, soon after the Local Government (Ireland) Act, 1898 began to operate. According to its constitution the object of the General Council is to safeguard the interests, rights and privileges of county councils, and take action on matters arising under the Local Government Acts or affecting the public welfare.

The General Council, originally a purely voluntary body, was given statutory recognition by the Local Government (Ireland) (Amendment) Act, 1902. County and county borough councils were authorised to pay affiliation fees, and to allow travelling expenses to delegates attending meetings. The Act of 1902 limited subscriptions to £10 a year – raised to £20 by the Local Government Act, 1925 s. 78. Under the Local Government (No. 2) Act, 1960 s. 14, the limit can be fixed by Ministerial orders: it stands currently at £150 a year. All county councils and one county borough council are members, and may each nominate up to three members to the general Council. The General Council meets four times a year and its business is managed by an Executive Committee. A part-time Secretary is employed.

The main work of the Council is considering resolutions submitted for debate by member authorities. Matters affecting ministers are transmitted to them for action as appropriate. Sometimes, but not often, the Minister for the Environment consults the General Council – an instance was the White Paper of 1971 on Local Government Reorganisation. He entertains the Council to lunch every year and takes the opportunity of addressing the members on local authority topics.

The Association of Municipal Authorities of Ireland is the corresponding body for urban authorities: although the General Council is not by any means confined to rural affairs, the special interests of urban district councils and non-county boroughs are catered for by the Association, which was formed in 1912. Membership includes the four city corporations, together with a majority of boroughs, urban district and town authorities. Members meet in annual conference at various centres, and resolutions submitted by members are debated, and rejected or adopted. A president is elected for the year, and an executive committee which meets quarterly. There are two joint part-time secretaries.

The Public Health and Local Government Conferences Act, 1885 authorised urban and rural sanitary authorities to pay the expenses of members and officials attending conferences. County councils were not covered by that Act, and had to be specially dealt with by s. 59 of the 1925 Act. The Local Government Act, 1941 s. 88 clarified the position of urban authorities in the matter of affiliation fees.

In the first decade of the present century, Sinn Féin assigned to the General Council of County Councils a most important central role in its plan for a new Ireland. Total disenchantment with the Irish Parliamentary Party created the problem of how to find a practical by-path towards Home Rule: the General Council was part of the answer. Apart from furnishing the basis of a National Assembly of a para-parliamentary character, it was given certain immediate and practical tasks. In the Sinn Féin plan for A National Civil Service, for example, the Council would appoint an Examining Board to issue certificates to qualified applicants for employment by county councils, urban and rural district councils and other local authorities. And it would take the lead in other developments of an economic and financial kind. But these visions came to nothing, at least so far as they concerned the General Council.

Both the General Council of County Councils and the Association of Municipal Authorities have, in fact, remained more or less at the same stage of development reached by them half a century and more ago, doing much the same things, and maintaining the same modest organisations. The incomes of both are insufficient to support any more elaborate structure – the principal reason being, possibly, the flat rate system of contributions which in effect pegs the rate at the level acceptable to the least affluent authority. There is no move to relate affiliation fees to resources, and it is possible that such a move would be resisted by some if not all contributors.

There has, however, been some evidence of dissatisfaction with the present position. A proposition to break new ground emerged in the 1970s in the form of a plan for a new body to be called the Convention of Local Authorities of Ireland. The main impulse came from the General Council of County Councils. The Association of Municipal Authorities and – a novel feature – the City and County Managers Association, were to be involved. The intention was to provide a single strong voice for local government which would offer some counter-weight to the ever-growing dominance of central authorities in local affairs. The Convention would also mobilise local resources, both of talent and cash, for collecting information, developing ideas and generally taking a more momentous part in the process of local government change. The plan for a Convention was not favoured by Mr Tully, then Minister for Local Government, especially the projected inclusion of managers. It has fallen into abeyance.

8

Local Elections

The councils of counties, county boroughs, boroughs and urban districts and commissioners of towns are elected by the local government electors. The local government electors are the persons whose names are in the register of local government electors. The duty of compiling the register of electors was by the Electoral Act, 1963 transferred from county registrars to county councils and county borough corporations, subject to adjudication by county registrars of claims for and objections to the entry of names in the register. The cost of compilation is shared about equally by the state and local authorities.

The law governing local elections has been tidied up and simplified in recent years, and is now contained mainly in Parts III and IV of the Local Government Act, 1941 and Parts II and VI of the Electoral Act, 1963. These statutes have been supplemented by regulations, the principal being the Local Elections Regulations, 1965. Every person is entitled to be registered in the area in which he or she was ordinarily resident on 15 September in any year if he or she is eighteen years of age or over on the following 15 April. The Electoral Act, 1963 extended entitlement to registration as a local government elector to any person, whether or not an Irish citizen, subject to the age and residence conditions referred to. A person may not vote more than once at a local election.

Local government is essentially an open system. Every citizen, virtually without exception, can go forward for election, and the business of candidature has been greatly simplified.

It is no longer necessary to be registered as a local government elector in the area one wishes to represent, nor is it necessary to have property there. The Electoral Act, 1963, removed these and some other requirements for eligibility as candidate. Candidates must be nominated, but a candidate may nominate himself or herself, or may have the nomination paper signed by a local government elector for the area concerned. Nomination forms are available at the offices of the local authority or in specified places elsewhere. When local elections are announced, public notices are issued giving this information, and indicating the dead-line for lodging nominations with the returning officer (usually the county secretary or town clerk). A deposit must accompany the nomination: £10 in the case of county or county borough councils, and £5 for the others. Deposits are forfeited if the candidate does not get more than one third of the quota of votes required for election.

The Local Elections (Petitions and Disqualifications) Act, 1974 removed the disqualification for membership of a local authority from (1) aliens, (2) persons in holy orders or ministers of religious denominations and (3) the great majority of local officers and employees, who may now contest local elections while retaining their employment in the local service. Large numbers of civil servants (generally speaking, all those of clerical and lower grades) have also become eligible for membership of local bodies.

This Act also introduced a mechanism of petitions, by which a local election may be questioned either by the Attorney General or any person over eighteen years of age. A petition may be lodged with the Circuit Court generally within twenty-eight days of the declaration of the result of the election. The court may order a recount of votes, if mistake or irregularity is alleged; or state a case for the Supreme Court on a point of law.

Disqualifications

Many of the disqualifications for membership of a county council, county borough or borough corporation, urban district council or town commissioners have been abolished, but a number remain:

(1) Being under eighteen years of age.

(2) Having been convicted within five years before the election or since election of a crime and sentenced to imprisonment with hard labour without the option of a fine, or to any greater punishment, and not having received a free pardon: Application of Enactments Order, 1898 art. 12.

(3) Conviction of having knowingly acted as a member when disqualified, disqualifies for ten years: Local Government Act, 1925 s. 60.

(4) Being a member of the Defence Forces on the active list: Defence Act, 1954 s. 104.

(5) Failing to pay a local government auditor's surcharge: 1925 Act s. 62.

(6) Failing to pay rates before the end of the financial year for which they are due: Local Government Act 1941 s. 57.

(7) Being absent from meetings for a disqualifying period unless absence is due to illness or a reason approved by the council or town commissioners. The disqualifying period of absence is twelve months in the case of a county council and six months in the case of a district council: 1898 Order art. 12.

Disfranchisement or disqualification for membership of the Dáil, Seanad and local authorities, which were part of the penalties for certain offences (e.g. corrupt practices at elections) do not under the Electoral Act, 1963, now follow conviction. They have been replaced by heavier fines or larger sentences, where appropriate.

Electoral Areas

Counties for which county councils are elected and cities and towns may be divided into electoral areas. With the exception of Drogheda, Dun Laoghaire, Galway and Sligo all boroughs are each one electoral area at present. Urban districts (except Bray and Dundalk) and towns under town commissioners are also single electoral areas. In effect, all areas with less than 12,000 inhabitants are undivided.

The Local Government (Dublin) Act, 1930 s. 33, required the Minister to divide the city into electoral areas without initiative on the part of the council. The Electoral Act, 1963, enabled the Minister to divide Cork, Limerick and Waterford County Boroughs into local electoral areas without formal request from the local authority.

Dublin City now has eleven electoral areas, Cork six, Limerick four and Waterford three. The borough of Dun Laoghaire has been divided into three areas as have Galway, Sligo and Drogheda. Dundalk Urban District has four divisions, and Bray three. There are about 240 local electoral areas in all including 125 county electoral areas.

Elections

Local elections are held every five years. Formerly the term of office of councillors and town commissioners was three years, but on several occasions elections were postponed and the term extended. In 1953 the normal term was changed from three to five years: Local Elections Act, 1953. Up to 1973 postponement demanded the passage of a Bill by the Oireachtas, but the Local Elections Act, 1973 s. 2, enables the Minister to postpone elections by order, which must be laid in draft before each House of the Oireachtas, and passed by resolution before coming into effect.

The Local Elections Regulations, 1965 provide that candidates in local elections must lodge deposits and, if not self-nominated, must give their consent to nomination. Nomination may be made by a single local government elector. Local authorities are empowered to issue polling cards. The names of the political parties, if any, which the candidates represent appear on the ballot papers. Polling takes place on the same day throughout the country, but a returning officer may arrange for advance polling on islands if the need arises. Postal voting is permitted, and conditions governing admission were eased by the Local Elections (Amendment) Order, 1974.

The polls at contested elections are conducted on the principle of proportional representation, each elector having one transferable vote. The single transferable vote is defined as a vote capable of being given so as to indicate the voter's preference of the candidates in order. It is thus capable of being transferred to the next choice if not required to give a prior choice the necessary quota of votes, or when, owing to the deficiency in the number of votes given for a prior choice, that choice is eliminated from the list of candidates.

Every elector can express the order of his preference by marking the ballot paper 1, 2, 3 and so on. At the beginning of the count all ballot papers are arranged in bundles showing the first preference for each candidate. Invalid papers are rejected. The first preferences are counted and the quota is ascertained. The quota is the minimum number of votes sufficient to secure election and is ascertained by dividing the number of valid papers by the number of vacancies plus one and increasing the result (disregarding any fraction) by one. When a candidate has a number of votes equal to or greater than the quota he is deemed to be elected and his surplus votes (if any) are transferred to the continuing candidates proportionately to the next preferences shown on his papers. If after these transfers there is still a vacancy the candidate with the lowest number of votes is excluded and his votes transferred according to the next available preference.

Acceptance and Tenure of Office

Successful candidates were formerly required to make a declaration accepting office before they could act but this requirement was abolished by the Electoral Act, 1963. If they are new members they take up duty when the former councillors retire. He or she remains in office until the day fixed for the retirement of members after the next election. Unless of course he or she resigns or becomes disqualified in the meantime. When a new election is held the old councillors retire — in the case of the county council on the seventh day after election, and in the case of borough and urban district councils and town commissioners on the fifth day — and the newly elected councillors then come into office.

Casual Vacancies

Vacancies caused by death, resignation or disqualification of members called casual vacancies, are not filled by the local government electors but by co-option by the body affected. The co-opted member retires in due course with the other members. Co-option was introduced by the Local Government (Ireland) Act, 1898 s. 94, as a time-and-trouble saving substitute for the earlier bye-election procedure. Co-option was adopted subsequently in the City Management Acts and became general under the

Local Government Act, 1941 s. 42. A convention has grown up in some areas that the appointee to a casual vacancy should be of the same political colour as the departed councillor.

Political Aspects

Local government is an important part of the Irish political system, and elections are keenly contested. Candidates outnumber places by more than two to one (there were 3,265 candidates in the 1979 local elections), in contrast with Britain, and a number of other countries, where a high proportion of seats are uncontested. The turnout of voters is high in Ireland by international standards, and interest has been well maintained in recent decades. Some increase is observable in Dublin and other county boroughs. The table below gives the percentage votes since 1950 in counties and urban areas.

Turnout of Voters in Local Elections

AREA	Election					
	1950 %	1953 %	1960 %	1967 %	1974 %	1979 %
Dublin Co. Borough	39	39	29	31	40	48
Other Co. Boroughs	57	65	55	66	57	59
Urban Dis. Council (incl. boroughs)	62	62	59	67	65	64
Towns	67	68	60	71	70	70
Counties	62	65	60	70	68	67
Average for all areas	58	60	54	67	63	64

Taken (with updating) from Basic Chubb *Government and Politics of Ireland*, London 1970, Table 11.7.

Apart from national comparisons, the main conclusion to be drawn from the figures is the obvious and hardly surprising one that local affairs and personalities attract more attention in rural and small town settings than in metropolitan conditions. The relatively high turnout for local elections has been ascribed to the relatively strong political element in Irish local government. Before independence, local councils served as a platform for the voicing of political aspirations, grievances and demands. The civil war which followed the 1922 settlement had the inevitable result that local as well as parliamentary elections were fought on political party lines. It has so continued to the present day. Dáil elections, of course, attract a larger turnout: 76 per cent of the electorate voted in 1977.

Although Marshall (1965) considered that there were no fundamental differences in local government policies between the parties, some divergences are nevertheless observable. The Labour Party, for instance, has been traditionally cool on management, and strong on the powers and privileges of elected members. Fine Gael led the way with the 1920's reform package which included management and have traditionally been more concerned with efficiency than local democracy. Fianna Fáil have applied their energies more on expanding services – housing, roads, health and planning – than on structures, and displayed little interest in the theoretical aspects of local government. Their major structural change – regionalising the health services – could be justified on practical grounds. These broad descriptive strokes do not sort the parties into sharply distinctive categories, but they serve to lend a recognisable coloration to each party, with of course, a good deal of shading at the edges.

Marshall's related assertion that political allegiances do not affect attitudes or decisions in local matters is nearer the mark. Exceptions are elections of mayors or chairmen, and the appointment of members to boards or committees – though even here party lines are sometimes crossed, and inter-party arrangements are not unknown. At council meetings, issues are generally argued on pragmatic or geographical grounds. Irish councillors tend to be, according to political scientists, non-ideological and particularist, not so much legislators or policy-makers as consumer representatives concerned with complaints, grievances, and pleas to mediate between constituents and a somewhat bureaucratic management. The councillor lives and works, in Chubb's expression, 'with the elector literally on his doorstep'. Councillors, in common with other political aspirants, depend on clientele networks, and our multi-member PR system makes them especially sensitive to electorate pressure and opinion shifts.

Local government affords valuable scope for political activity. Nearly two thirds of Deputies and Senators are also councillors. The clear inference is that local government is regarded as something more than a useful recruiting and training ground for higher office. It is seen also as a means of keeping in close touch with constituents, and maintaining the flow of information and 'favours' which constitute the essential small change of the political process.

As local authority service provides the major means of entry to the Dáil and Seanad, the parties naturally take local office very seriously, and party members form the vast majority of councillors. There is of course a sprinkling of independent members, and the 1974 local elections broke new ground by throwing up a group of six community councillors in Dublin city, whose general line was to maintain a non-partisan stance eschewing party politics and acting according to what they felt to be a general or civic good.

Certain occupational groups dominate local councils – farmers on county councils, closely followed by shopkeepers, publicans and other small businessmen (Chubb 288-9). Employers with shops and other minor businesses are prominent also on city and urban councils, with a fair admixture of professional people in the cities. Semi-skilled and unskilled workers are not well represented in point of numbers, but the imbalances do not seem to cause much public concern. This is possibly a tacit admission that the councils are not taken seriously as policy-making bodies. There is more politics than policies in most local bodies.

The aggregate number of elected members is about 1,550, of whom 698 are county councillors and 108 members of county borough councils. The remainder are distributed among the eighty or so towns with municipal government. Nearly six per cent of councillors are women, in contrast with 17 per cent in Britain and 47 per cent (the world's highest) in the USSR. Of thirty-one county and county borough councils, eight have all-male councils. There are only thirty-two women county councillors out of nearly 700; eleven out of 108 county borough councillors; and forty-seven out of 745 borough, urban district and town councillors. Over the years since the 1930s there has been some improvement in numbers, (thirteen women councillors in 1934, twenty in 1967) but no dramatic impact from the entry on the scene of outstanding women politicians.

There will probably be further improvement both on the parliamentary and local fronts but it will be slow. Progress can best be achieved, it is argued, by women

using local government both as a means of improving their local communities and as a training ground and jumping-off ground for higher office. And of all the ways through which progress to equality will be made this last path is likely to prove the most effective. (Maurice Manning (1978)

9

City and County Management

The first city manager, a civil engineer, was appointed in Staunton, Virginia, (birthplace of Woodrow Wilson) in 1908. Some years previously, a new form of city government which became known as the commission plan had emerged in Galveston, Texas. In 1901, following a natural disaster, municipal affairs had been handed over to a five-man group of business executives who were dramatically successful in bringing order out of chaos . When the two ideas were (according to himself), married by an energetic, pushing young advertising man called R. S. Childs, city management proper was born. It was known at first as the commission-manager plan, and Childs was pertinacious and dogmatic in insisting that the commission part was just as essential to the success of the plan as the manager. Both elements were necessary to translate business organisation into municipal terms: the commission flanked by the city manager were a close analogue of the board of directors and general manager which characterised the business corporation.

The rapid spread of city management in America, which soon took on the scale of a national movement, attracted attention and interest abroad. Its first Irish publicist was a Cork solicitor, John J. Horgan, (known as Coroner Horgan in City and County) who published an article 'City Management in America' in *Studies* in 1920. In addition to this and other articles he founded a civic reform body called the Cork Progressive Association which helped to bring about the dissolution of Cork Corporation in 1924, and the appointment of a commissioner in its stead. Horgan followed up this victory with vigorous pressure for the adoption of a commission-manager plan modelled closely on American ideas.

In a small work published in 1929, Horgan staked his claim to be the architect of the Cork scheme — the prototype which gave Irish management its distinctive, even unique character. He was a convinced adherent of the Childs doctrine, and his brief account of the origins of city management starts with Dayton, Ohio, where the commission-manager plan was launched in 1914. Horgan struggled hard to keep the commission idea, and limit the number of councillors. He was only moderately successful in this, but the sharp division in law between the council's reserved and the manager's administrative functions was first clearly enunciated in the Cork Bill. The reserved functions, then few in number, were carefully spelt out;

the manager was in charge of everything else. His were the residual powers. This arrangement has stamped city and county management ever since.

In the meantime the reform movement had been proceeding in Dublin under the influence of a body calling themselves the Greater Dublin Movement. The Dublin Board of Guardians were replaced by commissioners in late 1923 and the Corporation dissolved in May 1924, after a rather perfunctory inquiry. This unprecedented display of force by government against the most ancient form of local self-rule in Ireland was received with equanimity by the citizens who seemed to share the accepted view of the Corporation as a combination of corruption and inefficiency. But the inquiry, such as it was, discovered little evidence to support the indictment, and the suspicion has persisted that the government welcomed the opportunity of denying a platform to their political opponents and critics. Shortly afterwards the government set up (July 1924) the Greater Dublin Commission, under the chairmanship of Professor William Magennis. The Commission was a blend of business, labour, learning and literature (Dr Oliver St. John Gogarty was there) with a stiffening of political experience in the shape of three Dáil Deputies and two Senators. Two members were aldermen.

Magennis was professor of metaphysics in UCD, and had become a Dáil Deputy in 1923. He had an interest in civic affairs, and held strong views on a variety of issues — including the conviction that municipal administration could flourish only in a community with a high level of civic education and spirit. As chairman he had certain defects. He talked too much, monopolised discussion and put witnesses off their stride. Witnesses generally favoured a board of management for Dublin, either with or without a city manager — the American commission system, or its variant the commission-manager. There were few advocates of the city manager as a one man show — Professor Alton of TCD thought it 'hopelessly undemocratic'. There was much support for the ideas canvassed by Monsignor Michael Cronin, Professor of Ethics and Politics at UCD, in an article on 'City Administration in Ireland' in *Studies* (September 1923) in which he urged instead of the Dayton system of the small elected commission working on the legislative side with a city manager on the administrative, a large elected council for legislation and financial appropriation, and a small commission elected for the whole work of administration. Coroner Horgan condemned the plan; nevertheless it had many adherents. The influential Greater Dublin Movement favoured it. It was this body's plan for a Greater Dublin Authority which was the basis for that part of the Commission's report.

Oliver Gogarty took little part in the proceedings. He was, it appears, averse to local elected bodies, and would have abolished the lot. Other members of the Commission gradually ceased to attend. The report, when it appeared in 1926, was said to have been written by Magennis, working mainly on a submission put in by the Greater Dublin Movement. It proposed a thorough modernisation of the city government: Lord Mayor, Swordbearer, Macebearer and City Marshal were to be swept away, and the redundant Mansion House would become a municipal art gallery. The city council would be restricted to matters of civic policy, budget, rating, adoptive legislation, and general supervision. Civic administration would be in the hands of a city manager and board of directors.

> The scheme of city management under an elective council accords with the best experience of the United States, Germany, and the more progressive cantons of Switzerland. Civic administration is a business; accordingly the Commission recommends the entrusting of the civic management of Greater Dublin to the business conduct of a body of Directors.

But the scheme was poorly worked out, and the board turned out to be an advisory board of department heads, subordinate to the city manager who had sole executive authority.

The report was, according to Seán Lemass who was then (1928) an Opposition T.D. 'treated by government as a sort of joke'. It was remitted by the Minister for Local Government and Public Health (by then General Richard Mulcahy, who had replaced Séamus de Burca in June 1927) to a Departmental Committee for further study. General Mulcahy said later in the Dáil (26 February 1930) that 'the Commission's proposals . . . were not satisfactory and . . . did not provide effectively for the carrying out of the business of the people'.

The committee 'to inquire into the practicability of the Greater Dublin Commission's proposals included Dr Dwyer and P. J. Hernon, who were carrying on the administration of the city in place of the Council; Nicholas O'Dwyer, Chief Engineering Adviser, Sam Hastings, Assistant Legal Adviser and J. J. McAsey, who had been secretary to the Greater Dublin Commission. John Garvin was secretary to the committee. It reported in less than a year, drastically revising the Commission's plans for a Greater Dublin Council and recommending that, in lieu of a direct transition to the city management, the new city council should act through a Board of Management with collective responsibility. This Board would consist initially of the three Dublin commissioners, to be appointed by the Minister for a period of five years. The Council would then take over, and make appointments for seven year terms.

By the middle of 1928, however, the drafting of the Cork City Management Bill had been completed. It was introduced in the Dáil in June, 1928, about the time when the Departmental Committee finished their examination, and as the Bill had a fully drawn scheme of city management, the Committee's plan for a management board for Dublin was put into abeyance until the Oireachtas had decided on the Cork scheme. The outcome was that the government's intention to use Dublin as a model was frustrated by the delay, and Cork slipped in ahead. Its problems were less complex, and its proposals better presented, and more tenaciously urged. And so Cork, against the odds, carried the banner of city management into Irish local government.

The Cork City Management Act, 1929 was a considerable modification of the original plan imported by Horgan from the National Municipal League of America, and owed much to E. P. McCarron, the first and arguably the greatest Secretary of the Department of Local Government and Public Health. The Bill, introduced in the Dáil in June 1928, was cautiously accepted in principle and despite sustained Labour opposition and criticism by the new Fianna Fáil party, survived the parliamentary process with few changes. The most significant was an increase in the size of the city council from fifteen (in the Bill) to twenty-one. The old Cork City Council had fifty-six members.

The Cork prototype had virtually all the ingredients which characterise Irish city and county management. The reserved powers (an expression said to have been borrowed from the Bombay Corporation Act, 1889, but in fact derived from the Home Rule Bills) of the elected members were precisely set out, and included rating, borrowing, legislation, elections and a few others. The City Manager did the rest, acting by way of signed orders, a register of which was kept for inspection by the members. He had the right of attendance at meetings, could take part in discussions but not vote. He prepared the city budget. It was his duty to advise and assist the council in getting through the reserved business.

The city manager was an officer of the corporation. He was to be appointed by the council but his selection was not in their hands. The first manager was named in the Act: he was the former secondary teacher and mayor of Drogheda, Philip Monahan, who had been commissioner in Cork since 1924, and as supremo had developed that autocratic manner characteristic of some early managers. Thereafter selection was to be made by the Local Appointments Commission. Salary was fixed by the Minister. The office of town clerk was (until 1941) a separate job. In the Dublin and subsequent city management Acts, the town clerkship was merged with that of city manager.

Dublin's turn came next. The Local Government (Dublin) Bill was introduced in December 1929. A long, complex Bill covering both the city and Dun Laoghaire, it ran immediately into heavy weather, and its progress was not helped by a novel and unpopular proposal to modify the local government franchise in Dublin by instituting a 'commercial register' giving special representation to business on the new city council. The council was to be cut down from an impressive eighty-four to twenty-five members. The triumvirate of commissioners (P. J. Hernon, Dr W. Dwyer and Seamas Murphy) was passed over for nomination as first city manager in favour of the well-liked and respected Town Clerk, Gerald Sherlock. The borough manager for Dun Laoghaire was to be chosen by the Local Appointments Commissioners. The job went to Hernon.

The demarcation lines between councils and managers followed the Cork model in its main features, but a number of enlargements of the councils' powers was conceded by government in the course of the debate. The most noteworthy of these was a power — hedged about with discouraging procedural barriers — to direct the manager to do a particular executive act. After a rough passage the Bill passed in July 1930. Council size in Dublin had been raised to thirty-five—thirty ordinary and five commercial members. The coastal borough plan attracted much artillery fire, in the course of which the new Dun Laoghaire lost its mayor and had to make do with a chairman. For some reason the idea of a mayor in rebaptised Kingstown brought out the worst in the Opposition. The realities were preserved (the chairman gets a mayor's stipend) but there was a certain loss of colour.

City management was extended to Limerick in 1934 at the request of the city council. During the early part of the thirties the tide ran strongly in favour of management in urban affairs following the relative success of the Cork and Dublin experiments — though Cork's attitude towards Monahan was always ambivalent: respect for his consummate ability was strongly tempered by resentment at his authoritarian style of action. In Dublin Gerald Sherlock, at the opposite end of the spectrum, won hearts by his reluctance to range outside his old job of town clerk, left decisions to council and their revived committees, and never became city manager in anything but name. A borough manager was seriously considered by the citizens of Galway on the occasion of their private Bill for restoring borough status to the city in 1937. The idea was rejected because, it is said, of the expense. There appeared, however, to be no local demand for city management in Waterford, and it is probable that the Department wished to clear the decks in anticipation of the expected struggle in the counties. The Waterford City Management Act, completed the county borough coverage. The Limerick and Waterford Acts followed the pattern hammered out in Cork and Dublin — a tribute to the suitability of the system to Irish conditions. A comment also on the durability of departmental policies in spite of political change.

County Management

The Poor Relief Commission of 1925–7 recommended that county boards of health should be abolished and replaced by paid officers who would take full charge of the poor law services under the general oversight of county councils 'in the same manner as a general manager of a company under the control of a board of directors'. This would have been the equivalent of a county manager for the home assistance, medical, hospital and other institutional services provided by boards of health. The suggestion was not however put into operation before the government changed in 1932.

In May 1931 Ernest Blythe, then Minister for Finance, announced a radical reform of county government as a condition of adding £750,000 to the Agricultural Grant. Boards of health would be 'drawn into county councils', the councils would be reduced substantially in size, and managers would be appointed in the style of those in Cork and Dublin. An acerbic reference to the need to curb council 'windbags' gave great offence. But the plan was still-born: the government fell a few months later. When Fianna Fáil took over in March 1932, nothing further was heard of county management, at least in public. De Valera had, in 1931, announced his party's opposition to the idea of extending management to counties, but there is reason to believe that opinion in the party was divided. The Minister, Seán T. Ó Ceallaigh favoured reform, and it is possible (but this is mere speculation) that the curious developments which followed were an effort to reconcile the public commitment to oppose county management with the Minister's determination to reform administration in the counties.

The Department had, it appears, plans for an even more fundamental reconstruction of county government than was implied in county management. A scheme of county commissioners was prepared in the Department in 1933. Local elected councils, it was argued, were a relic of British administration. With independence and the advent of a national government, local bodies became an expensive anachronism. Moreover, many services locally administered were national in scope — housing, public health, hospitals, roads and so on. Local finances were becoming increasingly dependent on the state. The criticisms of local administration — the intrusion of irrelevant political issues, inefficiency, etc. — were aimed less at urban than county government, and the scheme visualised the survival of city and a number of large urban councils.

These proposals for the virtual abolition of county councils were submitted by the Minister to the Executive Council early in 1934. They met with powerful opposition and after some months were withdrawn from the cabinet agenda. Later in 1934 the question was remitted to a cabinet sub-committee under P. J. Little, then Chief Whip, and a scheme of county management was gradually worked out. There was no pressure to hurry things up — the Minister's own attitude seemed ambiguous. Eventually, in December 1938, the Government decided to have a Bill drafted and the County Management Bill, 1939 was introduced in the Dáil in July 1939. The Bill became law in June 1940, but did not come into operation until August 1942 because of the volume of preparatory work (selecting managers, etc.) to be done. The abolition of boards of health also gave rise to much consequential re-shuffling. The first managers were mainly existing county secretaries or secretaries of boards of health, but they included four commissioners: P. Bartley who had replaced Laois County Council; P. J. Meghen who had been acting in Tipperary S.R. and moved to Limerick; S. J. Moynihan who took on the linked counties of Waterford-Kilkenny; and D. O'Keefe who became first manager in Clare.

The County Management Act was an expression in county terms of the city management principles worked out in the decade since 1929. Council and manager occupied much the same relative positions in the city and county systems, but county management had a number of special characteristics:

1. Managers were selected by the Local Appointments Commission at the request, not of the council, but the Minister for Local Government and Public Health. The persons selected automatically became managers. This device forestalled possible recalcitrance on the part of the councils.

2. The manager acted not only for his county council, but for all elective local authorities in the county — boroughs, urban councils and towns. The intention was to assert and advance the paramount position of county councils, and at the same time to raise the standard of administration in smaller units by providing well qualified expert staff to augment the efforts of town clerks. The first cycle of managers in particular were pressed by the Department to improve financial management in the many urban councils which needed attention.

3. Certain counties were grouped for management purposes:
Carlow — Kildare
Kilkenny — Waterford
Laois — Offaly
Leitrim — Sligo
Longford — Westmeath
Tipperary North Riding — South Riding

4. Dublin City and county were also grouped. The Dublin City Manager became County Manager. The idea surfaced during the passage of the Bill through the Oireachtas as a concession to the strong movement of opinion in favour of a Dublin Metropolitan Council which emerged from the Report (1938) of the Greater Dublin Tribunal.

5. Assistant Managers were to be appointed: two in Dublin City and County, two in Cork County, one in the two Ridings of Tipperary. Others could be appointed if the Minister made orders to that effect.

6. County rate collectors were to be appointed by county councils, not by managers. This item (it totally traverses the management principle) was so odd, and caused such curious behaviour on the part of local councillors, that it was thought by many people to have been left behind, in deliberate error as a cautionary relic of the bad old pre-management days. But the aberration was not really so Machiavellian

— it first appeared in 1935 in the county management plan drawn up by P. J. Little's Cabinet sub-committee. The explanation is said to have lain in the semi-political nature of the county rate collector's job. The error, if it was an error, was retrieved in 1972 by the County Management (Amendment) Act of that year.

Although the County Management Bill had passed relatively peaceably through the Oireachtas, trouble appeared soon after the Act came into operation in 1942.

A minority of managers, some of them new to county government, took a literal view of their role, as set out plainly, it seemed, in the County Management Act, 1940. A typical statement of this view was expressed by Denis Hegarty, the Sligo-Leitrim Manager in a lecture to the Civics Institute in 1944 (*Public Administration in Ireland,* Vol 1 1944):

"It is important to note that the manager is not selected by the council. The manager is, in fact, responsible for practically all the functions of the local authority, and he is entitled to take decisions on nearly all executive matters without reference to the elected council, though he may keep them informed of his activities. For instance, subject only to the Minister, he may appoint, retire, remove or fix the remuneration of the officers of the local authority, and the elected body may not interfere in the matter. The independent control thus given to the manager distinguishes him from the managing director of a commercial concern who would, of course, be subject to the majority control of his co-directors; or from the American city manager, who is appointed by the council who have delegated functions to him which they may withdraw if the council and the people of the area should so decide."

What seemed to be managerial arrogance in the lecture was probably less obvious in the daily conduct of business, but nevertheless uneasiness about their novel condition began to spread among county councillors. The position, moreover, was not helped by the actions of one or two former commissioners who were slow to adjust to their altered situation.

Disharmony between councils and managers showed in many places, and a large body of local councillors were clearly unhappy under the new system. The Minister issued a series of circular letters in the period 1942–6 underlining the importance and extent of councils' powers. These were amplified by a White Paper (1945) entitled 'The Powers and Functions of Elected Members of Local Bodies', but they met, on the whole, with little success. Councillors remained unconvinced. So it was that when the first Inter-Party government took over in 1948, the new Minister for Local Government (T. J. Murphy, Labour Party) undertook a radical modification of county management. The object of the Local Government

(County Administration) Bill, 1950 was to substitute for management a system of administration by (1) small executive committees and (2) county officers, who would exercise employment, house tenancy and individual health functions. The latter were a new breed of officers, representing an amalgam of county manager and county secretary. The Bill lapsed with the dissolution of the Dáil in May 1951, and was never re-introduced. The need for some kind of readjustment nevertheless remained in the air, and the County Management (Amendment) Bill, 1953 was intended to do the necessary minimum. Its main provision was one strengthening the financial controls exerciseable by councils over managers. It also proposed to de-group counties, giving each county the opportunity of having its own manager. This Bill too did not survive the 1954 change of government.

The second Inter-Party Government (1954 to 1957) were less radical than the first in their approach to the problem, and the relevant part of their twelve-point programme read:

> To restore democratic rights in respect of local government by amending the County Management Acts and giving to local authorities greater autonomy and effective power in local affairs.

This item could be read as a statement of intent to assert local power against central government, but that aspect was speedily lost sight of in the re-opening debate about county management. The Minister entered the fray without pre-conceived notions, and his first step was to visit every county and hear its views and grievances at first hand — a display of impartiality which may have owed something to Fine Gael pride of paternity as the inventors of Irish city management. The eventual outcome was the City and County Management (Amendment) Act, 1955.

This Act restored the position of councils vis-à-vis managers and brought the two into some sort of equipoise. Its provisions were by no means earth-shaking: a power enabling councils to direct their managers to keep them informed of what they were about to do in executive matters (such as house tenancies, contracts, planning decisions and so on), consultation before undertaking new works, and the need for council approval of new posts or changes in levels of salaries. The procedure for directing a manager to act in a particular way in doing an executive function (apart from staff matters) was simplified — rather over-simplified as it turned out, at least in some counties. The Act, which in effect brought the long and acrimonious dispute to a peaceful conclusion, illustrates the fact that the sense of help-lessness which assailed many councillors in the years after 1942 was due as much to lack of information as to lack of power. There was of course a definite accession of power to councils in 1955, but in many cases the new statutory powers remained unused. But one most not lose sight of the fact that most managers adjusted to the new situation and did what was needed without waiting to be ordered to do so.

The Act made no difference to the balance of power, if one can call it that, between central and local interests. There was formal surrender of Ministerial authority in sending requests to the Local Appointments Commission, and in appointing county managers. The 1972 transfer from councils to county managers of the power to appoint rate collectors met with little opposition (County Management (Amendment) Act, 1972). Many councillors, it was said, were glad to be relieved of what had become a contentious and troublesome chore.

City and County Management: Operation

The bodies with which managers are associated are county councils, borough corporations, urban district councils, any joint board or committee established to execute functions of these authorities, town commissioners, and burial boards. Managers are not appointed for vocational education committees, county committees of agriculture, old age pension committees, school attendance committees, or committees under the Diseases of Animal Acts. Where not less than half the members of a joint board or committee (other than a pier or harbour authority or a vocational education committee) are appointed by two or more rating authorities, the appropriate Minister may bring the board or committee within the management system.

Reserved powers: Executive Functions

The powers and functions reserved for direct performance by the elected members have grown in number and significance since 1929, and now constitute a formidable armoury. They fall into five main categories: finance, legislation, political affairs, policy decisions and control of the executive branch.

Financial business, the 'power of the purse' was of paramount importance as a lever in the hands of the council in bringing its weight to bear on a manager. In the early years of management the budgetary function was represented to elected members as, and no doubt actually was, an engine of democratic control and (in relation to the manager at any rate) overriding power. With the expansion of council functions, both in numbers and significance, there has been less emphasis on rates and borrowing as key concerns of elected members, but there was nevertheless considerable opposition to the Local Government (Financial Provisions) Bill, 1977 on the grounds that it diminished local responsibility and freedom in financial matters. The Local Government (Financial Provisions) Act, 1978 s.13, removed 'the making of a rate' from the list of reserved functions, at the head of which it had stood since management was introduced in 1929. The making of the rate was then taken to cover both the determination of a rate in the pound and the application of that decision to a multitude of individual rateable properties, the results being detailed in rate books. This ambiguity was clarified over the years and 'making' of a rate had come to mean assessment subsequent to the 'determination' (Street p. 501). As the work of making out assessments was essentially an executive task it was no longer appropriate to the reserved functions. Section 13 of the 1978 Act assigns it to the manager. Council are generally precluded from involving themselves in staff matters, but they have a few statutory functions: including appointment and superannuation of managers, and, if necessary their suspension. Consent of the council is also required for creation of posts, and any variation (upwards or downwards) in the general levels of pay to classes or grades of staff. Up to 1972 county councils made appointments to offices of rate collector, but that is now done by managers.

The law relating to management recognises only two categories of functions: reserved and executive. But in practice a third has grown up. This is a general supervisory function, or continuing oversight of the managers' conduct of the councils' business. From the outset of the system city and then county managers were required by law to submit to the members at each meeting a register of the orders made by him since the previous meeting. Then provision was made in the Management Acts for intervention by the council in the executive area, by passing a special resolution directing the manager to act in a particular way. This power, now contained in City and County Management (Amendment) Act, 1955 s. 4, applies to all executive functions with the exception of staff control and management; but it cannot be used to dictate a line of action in all cases of a specified kind. Neither can the manager be coerced under s. 4 to do anything of an illegal nature, and this escape hatch was used in 1979 in one of the later episodes of the Wood Quay affair. The newly elected Dublin City Council sought to halt progress on the civic offices project pending clarification of the position vis-à-vis the Viking remains and the archaeological excavation of the site, part of which had been declared by the High Court to be a national monument. The deputy city manager, acting on the Law Agent's unambiguous advice, said it would be illegal for him to do what the Council wanted. The Lord Mayor followed the deputy manager, and ruled the section 4 motion out of order. The Council was supplied with the opinions of the Law Agent and Senior Counsel.

It is the manager's duty to advise and assist the council in the exercise of their reserved powers, and in such other matters as they may require his help. The manager must attend meetings of the council or a committee of the council if requested to do so. On his side, the manager has the right of attendance at council meetings, and may take part in the discussions but not vote.

Managers

In the four county boroughs the city manager is an officer of the corporation. The county manager is an officer of the county council, but he is manager also for each borough corporation, urban district council, board of town commissioners, and every joint body whose functional area is wholly within the county. His salary, fixed by the Minister, is paid by the county council, which recovers portions from the other bodies concerned, either as a county-at-large charge or in the form of contributions fixed by the Minister. A deputy city or county manager must be appointed to function during the manager's absence on vacation, sick leave or otherwise. Deputies may be designated either by the manager, or if circumstances require, by the Lord Mayor or Mayor or chairman of the county council. The Minister's approval is necessary (1955 Act s. 18).

The manager acts formally by way of written orders, signed and dated. The earlier requirement that an order should show the time when made was altered by City and County Management (Amendment) Act, 1955 s. 20, to say that a statement of date was sufficient. A register of orders must be kept, and a record of orders made since the previous meeting must be available to the members at each meeting.

There are twenty-nine managers in local government – four city and twenty-five county managers. Each county has a separate manager, with the exception of Dublin, Laois and Offaly. Dublin county is paired with the city and is managed by two of the five Dublin Assistant City and County Managers; Laois shares a county manager with Offaly. The Laois–Offaly arrangement is the last and only survivor of the six pairs of contiguous counties coupled for management purposes by the County Management Act, 1940.

The City and County Management (Amendment) Act, 1955 responding to local opinion, provided a procedure for paired counties which were not happy to continue sharing a manager. The procedure could also be availed of to separate Dublin county from the city, but it was never so used. Five paired counties did, however, opt to split.

Present System

City managers are officers of the corporations, and county managers of the county councils. Appointments are made only on the recommendations of the Local Appointments Commission. A manager can be suspended by a two-thirds majority of the city or county council; and removed from office with the consent of the Minister. The manager is the chief executive officer for the local authorities in his bailiwick. He organises, controls and if necessary disciplines the staff; enters into contracts, gives or withholds planning permissions, allots house tenancies, and makes a host of other decisions as part of the day-to-day business of the local authorities. A major preoccupation is the budgetary process, in which he has a central role – preparing annual estimates, and seeing them through the councils. Even where an estimates committee has been appointed (the only one is in Monaghan) the responsibility, and burden of work must be shouldered by the manager.

An admirable account of the Irish management system is that by

Dr A. H. Marshall in *Local Government Administration Abroad* (1967), a series of reports on American and European systems commissioned by the Maud Committee on Management of Local Government (Report, Volume 4). Dr Marshall commented on the large measure of acceptance and appreciation of the system he found among the elected members; on relations between managers and technical officers — 'the one unsettled problem of the manager system' — the persistent tendency among members to underrate their collective capabilities; and, in general, despite some objections, the obvious merits of the system. He sums up:

> The undeniable fact is that Ireland having sought for an answer to the problem of reconciling ultimate democratic control with prompt discharge of duties, has found a solution which under Irish conditions is working well. The name 'manager' is perhaps unfortunate. There is no doubt that it is responsible for a good deal of the misunderstanding in the country itself, and certainly outside, where the name 'manager' conveys the impression that the Irish manager is like his American counterpart. This is not so. The Irish manager is a manager neither in the commercial sense nor in the American local government sense. He is in fact more akin to the English official, especially in his relations with the elected members.

Dr. Marshall's assessment has not been controverted in its general findings, and may be accepted as accurate. A subsequent report by McKinsey & Co. 'Strengthening the Local Government Service' (1972) dealt less with the position and performance of managers than with county staff structures, but the recommendations imply a general view that county managers were involved too closely in detailed administration — a position forced on them, perhaps, by their experience with councils — and not enough in planning and organisation. The consultants' recommendations included proposals for:

1. management posts under the county manager for each of the major services, thus integrating technical and administrative responsibility.

2. a Planning and Development Officer in each county both for preparing county plans and for facilitating economic development (in co-operation with IDA).

3. a Personnel and Administration Officer in each county for recruitment and training, and co-ordination of Administrative Services.

4. a county Finance Officer for all financial and management accounting services.

These proposals were based on a projected integration of urban (borough, urban and town) and county staffs, which has not materialised. The staffs of several pairs of smaller counties were to be amalgamated under a single manager: this also has not been adopted. In general, therefore, the proposed re-organisation of staff structures has not occurred as planned.

Assistant Managers

The number of assistant managers has increased in recent years. In addition to five Assistants in Dublin City and County and three in Cork County, there are now nine Assistant managers: one in Clare, Kerry, Limerick County, Mayo, Meath, Wexford; two in Galway; and one in Cork City.

Postscript on Management

In his *Government and Politics of Ireland* (1970) Professor Chubb gives what is probably the definitive verdict on management in Irish local government. He notes two tendencies which should make for conflict but are in fact complementary. One is the emergence of the manager as 'increasingly the major source of initiative in a local authority', and 'the powerhouse of local government' (pp. 286–287). The other is the gradual accretion of power to the council in both the reserved and executive areas. The result has been that 'the roles of councillor and manager have evolved differently from those that were first envisaged and that the original statutes spelled out'. This is tellingly borne out by a quotation (p. 285) from M. Macken, a former Dublin City and County Manager which is worth reproducing here:

> The original intention of the legislators to draw a clear line, both in law and in practice, between the Council's reserved functions and the Manager's executive functions has been lost sight of in some degree in the evolution of the system. Managers find themselves involved in business reserved to the Councils. . . . On the other hand Councillors have gained over the years considerable influence in relation to the Manager's functions.

The Irish Management System, although admittedly successful here, has had no imitators abroad; and has not been extended to vocational education, agricultural instruction, or, most recently, health. Why? And is there some message in the universally acknowledged discrepancy between what we read in the City and County Management Acts and what actually happens? Is the system as the law has it with limited powers 'reserved' to the councils, and residual powers left with managers an outmoded relic of a very different past, the disturbed but often creative 1920s? During the debate on the second reading of the Cork City Management Bill, 1928, Deputy Sean Lemass suggested that the manager's functions should be specified in the Bill, leaving all residual powers to the city council. With the manager exercising a range of functions without formal limit, the councils and the citizens of Cork were buying a pig in a poke. But the Minister and the Department were not to be shaken, and when Lemass repeated his idea in the debate on the Dublin Bill of 1929, he was equally unsuccessful. But there was then and is now much more to be said for the Lemass thesis.

The solution adopted in the Health Bill, 1969 was that of a chief executive officer in each regional health board who would carry on the business of the board in accordance with its decisions and directions − except as regards matters set out specifically in the Bill, which he was empowered to exercise on his own account. These are (1) individual applications for health services and (2) management of staff. The Minister for Health, in his introductory statement on the second reading (16 April 1969) pointed out that the Chief Executive Officer (CEO) while rather similar to, would not be analogous with a city or county manager. The relationship between board and CEO would be different in that 'the different legal status of members of a health board vis-à--vis the board's chief executive officer and the other officers will be significant in giving considerably more weight to the authority of the members.' Whether this is so or not, it is certainly true that the tensions which reached near breaking point during the first decade of the council-manager relationship have not manifested themselves in the health boards.

Managers as Prefects

The Irish county manager (city management does not come into this) has sometimes been discussed in terms of the **French** prefectoral model, but there are too many divergences between the two to make the comparison anyway fruitful. It is said that there was a strand of thinking in the Department in the early forties which saw the prefect as the next step after county management, but if that is true, it never came to anything. The trend has been rather the other way. County managers began as ministerial appointees and, although definitely local officers, with a high degree of legal independence. What with one thing and another their position was modified until they became, as seen by Dr Hedley Marshall in the mid-sixties, not so much managers as team-mates with their councils. And that is still the position. Managers must exercise leadership, and their professional qualities, expertise, and experience places them in a relationship of strength with the councillors, but it is a strength that cannot be displayed too often, or with ostentation.

All this is quite apart from the constitutional structure in Ireland which would make the prefect an uncongenial animal in the home environment. The French prefect is an agent of central government: he is not exactly omni-competent, but his range of authority is very wide, from law and order and economic planning to supervising the lower tiers of local government: he is concerned with government in the round. The powers of even an Irish minister are vastly more circumscribed, and even if one regards local authorities as agents of a minister, that simply means that such local powers as managers may exercise are correspondingly restricted. The county manager's position as chairman of the County Development Team has added considerably to his stature in areas where he so operates, but his actual powers are not thereby expanded. The only indigenous officer with affinity to the prefect was the Regional Commissioner who stood by during the Emergency of 1939—45, ready to take over in the event of invasion and the disruption of normal government. Nothing of this kind happened, and while it may be pleasing to speculate on the peace-time possibilities open to government if decentralisation ever became a burning national issue, the likelihood of a wholesale abdication of power by government as at present constituted is too remote for serious consideration.

10

Process: How the System Operates

Local authorities carry out the business assigned to them in several ways: some business is done by the members of the authority acting as a body at meetings, some through committees, some, where a manager is associated with the authority, through the manager and some through officers who have been given the necessary authority to act. For instance, only the members at a meeting can decide how much is to be raised in taxation in any year, they cannot delegate this duty; vocational education cannot be administered directly by the council, a committee must be appointed for this purpose; the control of officers and the discharge of executive functions are matters for the manager in the case of bodies for which a manager is appointed, and when a particular officer has been assigned a duty by statute the duty must be discharged by that officer.

Meetings and Procedure

The meetings of local authorities have been regulated either by the statutes or by statutory instruments made by the appropriate minister or other authority. Certain meetings must be held at prescribed times, others may be held at the discretion of the local authority; notices must be given for some meetings but are not necessary for all. Decisions are normally taken by the majority of the members present who vote, not necessarily the majority present (1941 Act, s.41).

For the election of mayor or chairman there is a special procedure (1941 Act s.43). All candidates must be proposed at the outset and the candidate getting the least number of votes is eliminated at each stage until the number is reduced to two. If there is a tie in regard to which is to be eliminated or which is to be elected there is no casting vote; the decision is taken by lot. This procedure does not apply to vocational education committees or county committees of agriculture.

For every authority a quorum is fixed; usually one fourth of membership, with a minimum of three (Local Government Act, 1898 s.23 (2); Application of Enactments Order, 1898 art. 36; City Management Acts, and Local Government Act, 1946 s.66). Decisions cannot be questioned on the ground that a vacancy existed or a member was disqualified. Minutes of proceedings must be kept and authenticated by the chairman signing them.

The public have no general or absolute right to be present at local authority meetings: it is a matter for each local authority to decide whether or not to admit them. The intention was, in 1971, to give the public a statutory right of admission to meetings (other than committee meetings) accompanied by a power to local authorities to regulate admissions. This legislation has not materialised, and in the meantime the matter is one of local discretion. The *Citizen's Guides* to local services in Dublin City and County, for example, say that the public can attend meetings 'on an invitation from a Council member.'

A court case in Dun Laoghaire (1972) arising from the ejectment of two people from a Borough Council meeting attracted some public attention (*Irish Times* 2.1.1973). The case for a democratic right of public admission was pressed in view of the upsurge of civic interest in local affairs and the proliferation of community councils and residents' associations, all wanting to know more about what was going on at council meetings.

The press is in a somewhat stronger position than the general public. Rules made by the Local Government Board in 1903 under the Local Government (Ireland) Act, 1902, oblige a county or urban district council, or a board of town commissioners, to admit the press to meetings, unless a resolution to exclude them is sanctioned by the Minister for the Environment. This does not apply to borough councils, and press reporters may be barred from their meetings if the councils so decide.

In practice the press can attend local authority meetings and even (in Dublin City) committee meetings. Proceedings are usually reported at length in the local and sometimes in the national press. There is, on the whole, little demand from the public for admission unless some controversy is on foot, or a question of uncommon local concern is being debated. Meetings of Vocational Educational Committees and Committees of Agriculture are usually open to the press. Dublin City VEC remained an exception until a change of membership following the 1979 local elections led to a change of practice.

In England the question of public right of admission was clarified in 1960 (Public Bodies (Admission to Meetings) Act, 1960). All local authority meetings there are now open to the public unless the council decides to restrict admission in a particular case. The Circuit Court (*Irish Times,* 20 March 1981) decided that local authorities have qualified privilege. The right of a public representative to speak freely at meetings should not be curbed; representatives must be protected.

Public Relations

Dublin Corporation employs a public relations officer; a limited number of county councils have information officers. Not an impressive line-up in terms of numbers, but the arguments in favour of assigning special staff to public relations duties have only comparatively recently been accepted in local government, where councillors supposedly 'carry out their weekly or monthly deliberations in the full blaze of press publicity.' (Garvin 1955)

Participation

Local government supplied, and still supplies, access to decision-making in local affairs to a fair number – but still a minority – of people. In what has been described as a mythical golden age of self-government (Hill, 1970) the numbers involved were greater, local authorities smaller and more numerous, and effective citizen intervention easier. During the last half-century or more local authorities in Ireland and elsewhere have become larger and fewer, and the decision-making process more remote. The movement for modifying local government in some way to make the organisation sensitive to local opinion has therefore found a ready response in most countries.

There are a number of statutory provisions for public consultation: in planning as regards draft development plans, and individual planning permission; and in cases of compulsory acquisition of land. Copies of annual estimates of expenses may be purchased or inspected at local offices. Where the desired change has not taken place at the statutory level, the pressure to participate in or influence decisions has taken the form of non-statutory community councils, development associations, residents' associations and interest groups of various kinds. A further impulse towards the creation of voluntary groups has come from a combination of factors tending to diminish the discretionary scope of local elected members – the bureaucratisation of local authorities, and the growth of professional decision-making; removal of effective powers in most issues to central government; and the strength of party politics in local councils.

Attempts to incorporate voluntary effort in some formal way in the official system have failed on the whole. The machinery in the Local Government Acts, 1941 and 1955 for creating 'approved local councils' has not been operated to any great extent. The suggestion in the White Paper (1971) for county area committees made up of elected councillors and nominees of community councils ran into strong opposition and has not been proceeded with.

There are numerous examples of joint citizen action for local improvements, conservation, and pressure. One of the best known is the emergence of grouped water supplies (and occasionally sewerage schemes) in rural districts. Clubs and local associations have been successful in providing swimming facilities, with the aid of official grants and other forms of help. Tidy Towns Committees have been very effective in raising the standard of communal care and maintenance in villages and small towns. Voluntary activists have also been effective in the settlement of itinerants, anti-pollution campaigns, and controversies about development. A number of national organisations have been based on federations of local voluntary organisations. The National Association of Tenants Organisations (NATO) gave a central focus to agitation by groups of local authority tenants; and the Association of Combined Residents' Associations (ACRA) filled a similar role for private houseowners and tenants. Muintir na Tire and the Irish Countrywomen's Association (ICA) are concerned in different ways with community development and enhancing the quality of rural life.

Irish attitudes to citizen participation were surveyed by Raven and Whelan (1976) and placed in context with findings in the USA, UK, Germany, Italy and Mexico. The percentage of those surveyed who were confident of their ability to influence local decisions was comparatively low, and of these the majority would seek to intervene, not by individual or group action, but by getting in touch with an elected member, or a local officer. But the need for some new method of bringing opinion to bear on public issues seems to be keenly felt.

A vote every four or five years is altogether too blunt an instrument. Somehow the citizenry needs to be much more actively engaged in the initiation, execution and evaluation of policy. New structures for the management of society are urgently needed. Yet, when considering the appropriate form of these structures, it is important to note that the data presented in this paper and elsewhere show that participation itself is not felt to be the key issue. The government and the bureaucracy should be open to *influence,* but the people do not necessarily want to participate actively in managing their society . . . (Raven and Whelan (1976) p.60)

An instructive case study in popular participation, its strengths and weaknesses may be found in the Dublin Wood Quay affair of 1978–9. Here a group, led by a mediaeval historian, were passionately concerned to preserve the site of a Viking settlement, which formed part of a larger area acquired by Dublin Corporation for badly needed municipal offices. All available means were brought into play in an effort to halt progress on the project — legal proceedings, mass meetings, protest marches and petitions. At a critical stage of the struggle the local elections of 1979 gave the citizens an opportunity of expressing their views, and although voting is a crude indicator, there seemed an unambiguous statement by the populace, or a majority of them, that Wood Quay should be preserved. The newly elected City Council sought to reverse or at least substantially alter the plans approved by their predecessors, but decisions taken by large organisations are not easily changed, and the council's impotence to carve out a new line in accord with popular wishes was exposed when it became apparent that the real power to change course rested with the central government.

County Council Meetings

The council is required to hold each year an annual meeting, quarterly meetings and an estimates meeting. The council may be authorised to hold half-yearly meetings instead of quarterly meetings. Meetings may be held wherever the council directs either in or outside the county but meetings on licensed premises are prohibited unless no other suitable room is available free of charge or at reasonable cost, nor can such premises be used as offices or for any purpose incidental to the business of the council (Act 1898 s. 77; Application of Enactments Order, 1898 arts 35 and 36; Local Elections Act 1927 s. 8; City and County Management Act 1955 s. 10).

The chairman may call a meeting at any time, or any five members may call a meeting if the chairman, after requisition by five members to do so, refuses. Except in the case of the annual meeting which is held in the period 23 June — 1 July to elect the chairman and appoint committees, the business to be transacted is that specified in the summons to the meeting. The names of members present are recorded as well as the names of members voting for or against on each question. The chairman presides, or if he is absent the vice-chairman. If both are absent members choose a councillor to take the chair. In the case of equality of votes the chairman has a second or casting vote except in the election of chairman (Local Government Act, 1946 s. 62).

County councils were enabled by article 36 (10) of the Application of Enactments Order, 1898 to regulate their proceedings by means of standing orders. The position in other local authorities was less clear. The Local Government Act, 1955 s. 62 clarified the situation by giving local authorities a general power to make standing orders regulating procedure at meetings. The preceding section (s.61) of the same Act enabled the Minister to make regulations of general application on procedural matters. The intention was to introduce a uniform code regarding the holding and summoning of meetings, quorums and so on.

Borough Council Meetings

A borough council must hold quarterly meetings and an estimates meeting each year. It is not necessary to give notice of the business to be transacted at the quarterly meetings. The mayor may call a meeting at any time, or five members can requisition him to call a meeting and if he refuses call it themselves. The business to be transacted at these special meetings must be specified in a summons left at the member's residence three clear days before the meeting.

The quorum in Cork is ten, in Dublin twelve, in Limerick and Waterford seven, in Dun Laoghaire six, in Galway four and in other boroughs one-fourth of the total number of members. Up to 1955 the councils had no express power to make standing orders but municipal corporations appear to have had a common law right to make byelaws or standing orders for the transaction of their business.

Urban Council and Town Commissioners' Meetings

Urban councils that are not borough councils hold each year an annual meeting in the period 23 June – 1 July, monthly meetings, an estimates meeting, and such other meetings as may be necessary. The meetings must be held within the district. The same prohibition applies to meeting on licensed premises or using such premises for the business of the council as in the case of county councils. The time of meeting is the first Monday in each month at noon, but the day and hour of meeting may be altered by the Minister for the Environment at the request of the council. The quorum is one-fourth of the total number of members. The chairman or, in his absence, the vice-chairman or, in the absence of both, a councillor chosen by the members presides at meetings. The chairman has a casting vote in case of equality of votes, except in the election of the chairman.

Monthly meetings for the transaction of ordinary business may be held without notice but no extraordinary business can be transacted at meetings unless notice is given. Resolutions cannot be revoked except after notice and by a two-thirds majority of members present, or by a majority if the number of members present be greater than the number at the former meeting (Commissioners Clauses Act, 1847 s. 44). Special meetings may be held and five members may require such a meeting to be called. Two days' notice is required and no business can be transacted at special meetings except that stated in the notice.

Meetings of town commissioners are subject to much the same code as applies to urban councils. The quorum is three. There is no prohibition against meeting on licensed premises but in practice meetings are not held on such premises.

Travelling Expenses and Allowances

Payment of expenses to councillors was introduced by the Local Government Act, 1925 s. 63, and extended by the Local Government Act, 1941, s. 80. Subsistence allowances were added by the Act of 1946 s. 67. Travelling expenses are payable to a member of a county council attending meetings at a place more than five miles from his residence. Where a county councillor attends a meeting at a place not less than one mile away and is obliged to remain from home for more than three hours an allowance in the nature of subsistence allowance has been given to cover expenses in attending meetings. A county councillor residing less than five miles from the meeting place may also, if the council passes a resolution under section 67 of the Local Government Act, 1955, be paid an inclusive allowance in respect of travelling and subsistence expenses, if he is kept more than three hours from home. Certain other authorities such as vocational education committees, county committees of agriculture and health boards also pay travelling expenses and allowances. The principle in English local government law of reimbursing members for loss of earnings caused by attendance has not been carried into Irish law. In most other countries some form of compensation is paid to members for time spent at meetings in addition to travel and subsistence costs.

Entertainment allowances are not expressly authorised by local government law, but are usually met in county boroughs and boroughs out of the annual salary payable to the Lord Mayor, Mayor or (in Dun Laoghaire) Chairman. It was proposed in 1971 to legislate for local authorities generally, allowing a limited payment from rates towards expenses incurred on the reception of distinguished visitors. The Harbours Act, 1946, has a provision on these lines.

Conflict of Interest

Conflict of interest may arise where a councillor (or, for that matter a local officer or employee) finds himself dealing, in his public capacity, with an issue in which he has a personal interest. Some years ago a question involving a councillor arose on a planning case and there was some public controversy. The councillor had done public relations work on behalf of a developer. The decisions involved in that case were not a reserved function, and the councillor was not directly involved. The councillor also quoted in his defence a council standing order, which he had observed:

> No member of the council shall attend a meeting of a committee or sub-committee or section of sub-committee during consideration of any matter in which he is pecuniarily or professionally interested.

The position is that the legal safeguards as they affected councillors were removed with the introduction of management. Thus the disqualifying clause in article 12(4) and the prohibition in article 36(6) of the Local Government (Application of Enactments) Order, 1898, together with s.2 of the Municipal Corporations (Ireland) Act 1842 were repealed by the Local Government Act, 1941. The reason was that the decisions involved were executive functions in which councillors could not intervene, but the position is not now so clear-cut as it then appeared. The prohibitions against taking part in decision-taking where councillors have a personal interest have been revived by the Housing Act, 1966 s. 115, and the Local Government (Planning and Development) Act, 1976 s. 32–4. The planning provisions apply not only to councillors but to prescribed classes of officers and employees, as well as members and employees of An Bord Pleanála.

Central government controls

The principal Departments of State concerned with local administration are enumerated in Chapter 7. Some fifteen out of eighteen departments have local involvements of one kind or another. Posts and Telegraphs has, of course, its own highly developed local organisations, but is omitted from the list for reasons which do not require elaboration.

The methods by which control is exercised from central government are laid down in the statutes. The commonest is to require the sanction, approval or concurrence by the Minister to or in a decision before it can take effect. It is now the normal practice for the Oireachtas where complete legislation would burden statutes with excessive detail to authorise the Minister concerned to make regulations to fill in these details. Such regulations are usually laid before the Oireachtas which can annul them within a specified time. The Minister in making regulations may, therefore, be said to legislate for the local authorities and to guide them in implementing the law with the tacit approval of the Oireachtas.

Removal of Members from Office

The most drastic of all the numerous forms of discipline available to Ministers is sacking the elected members and putting in a commissioner to perform the reserved functions. This device is now rarely used. It was last called into play in 1969 when the Dublin City Council deliberately struck a rate less than the full amount required to meet the demand for health services.

The Minister for the Environment may remove the members of county, borough and district councils and town commissioners from office for any of the following reasons: (1) if he is satisfied after a local inquiry that the local authority is not effectually discharging its duty or (2) if the local authority refuses to obey an order of any court or (3) neglects to comply with an express requirement of any enactment (such for instance as the requirement that a sufficient rate shall be made to maintain the public services for which the local authority is responsible), or (4) refuses to allow their accounts to be audited or (5) if the number of members are insufficient to form a quorum for meetings.

It is not necessary to order a new election immediately. Five years may be allowed to elapse, or even longer if the next following statutory election is to be held within a year of the expiry of five years. The Minister has full power to do whatever is necessary to ensure that all subsidiary bodies continue to function when the removal of members of a parent body deprives the subsidiary body of members: Local Government Act 1941, Part IV and Local Government Act 1946, ss. 30 and 64.

Control of Officers

Although the appointment of officers still rests with the local authority, the local authority can only exercise this power in certain ways laid down in the Acts and statutory instruments. In the case of vacancies that must be referred in the first instance to the Local Appointments Commissioners for their recommendation, the law makes the act of appointment by the local authority a matter of form, and in the case of other appointments prescribes either competitive examinations or some other impartial method of selection. Qualifications have been prescribed for almost all offices and where that is done no further qualifications can be prescribed by local authorities without the sanction of the Minister.

Remuneration is subject to the control of the central authority. The Minister may require an officer to resign for unfitness and suspend or remove an officer who is unsatisfactory. The central authority may, therefore, be said to be predominant in the general control of local officers. The remuneration of minor officers and servants cannot be increased without Ministerial approval (Local Government Acts, 1941, Part II, 1946, Part III).

In lieu of giving numerous individual sanctions in local establishment matters, the appropriate Minister may exercise his powers of control by specifying general conditions to be observed by local authorities (Local Government Act 1955, Part II). The County and City Management (Amendment) Act, 1955, requires the consent of the local authority, by resolution, to the submission by the manager, for Ministerial approval, of any proposals for varying (1) the numbers of permanent officers; or (2) the rate of remuneration of any class or grade of officers or employees.

Courts

Local administration, in common with central government, operates subject to judicial review. This process comes into play where exception is taken to any local action or decision and redress is sought from a competent court. Whereas a written constitution exists as in Ireland, some decisions or practices may be open to criticism as conflicting with an article of the constitution, particularly in the area of fundamental rights. A current case before the High Court is grounded on the alleged inequities of the valuation system as it affects rating and taxation on land (*Irish Times,* 31 July 1981).

A local authority must be able to adduce legal authority for its actions. If a local authority purports to do something in exercise of its powers but is acting beyond these powers it is said to be acting ultra vires and can be restrained by the High Court. On the other hand, if it fails to carry out a duty imposed by law, the Court may direct it to perform the duty. The Court may review and, if necessary, quash decisions of a judicial character taken by a minister if he exceeds his statutory powers and therefore acts without jurisdiction. The High Court may act by way of the prerogative orders of prohibition, mandamus or certiorari. A rare form of order, quo warranto, has been invoked in disputed elections or appointments to offices. Charges and surcharges made by local government auditors may also be brought before the Court for review. Local authorities can be sued for acts which cause damage to others and be made amenable for the consequence to others of their neglect or default. The members are not, however, liable individually.

Local Ombudsman

The appointment of a parliamentary commissioner to investigate cases of administrative injustice was recommended by an Oireachtas All-Party Informal Committee in 1977. While the Committee favoured a wide ambit for the Ombudsman, setting out the case for scrutinising local administration, the Ombudsman Act, 1980 was, as passed, restricted to civil service misdeeds. In response, however, to pressure during Oireachtas debates on the Bill, the then Government undertook to extend the Ombudsman's brief to cover local authorities and health boards (Dáil Debates, 24.6.1980). The Minister for the Public Service may do this by Order, after consultation with the other Ministers concerned.

Inspection and Audit

An inspector appointed by the appropriate Minister may visit and inspect any premises used by the local authority and may be directed to hold a local inquiry at which he can obtain evidence on oath (L. G. Act 1941 83–6). Auditors appointed by the Minister for the Environment audit the accounts of local authorities and have power to surcharge persons who authorise unfounded or illegal payments (L. G. Act 1941, Part VII. Street, Appendix A).

Loans cannot be raised by local authorities without the sanction of the central authority. This applies even to temporary loans from banks by means of overdrafts. The Oireachtas formerly fixed limits beyond which borrowing for some purposes cannot be effected, but these limits were removed in 1960 (L.G. (No. 2) Act, 1960).

Grants voted by the Oireachtas and other subventions that flow from the Exchequer to local authorities all go through the appropriate departments and final payments are not as a rule made until an examination of the relevant expenditure has been made. The great increase that has taken place in these grants has made local authorities more dependent than formerly on Government financial assistance.

The stream of local legislation promoted by individual authorities which at one time flowed strongly has now almost dried up. Private bills when they are promoted by local authorities (e.g., Local Government (Galway) Act, 1937 or the Limerick Corporation Gas Undertakings (Pensions) Act, 1929) are invariably referred for preliminary examination by the appropriate department.

Central-Local Relations

The relations of central to local authorities have developed according to no general principle. In the period before the reform of parliament in 1832 local authorities were left very much to their own devices. Occasionally there was intervention as in the attempt to regulate the borough corporations in the seventeenth century but such intervention was exceptional. In the nineteenth century there was no consistent policy as regards control. Although in 1838 strict supervision was established over the poor law authorities the borough corporations were in 1840 allowed autonomy except in a few matters such as loans and the disposal of corporate property. It is only since local government has been put on a representative basis and local services have grown that the need was felt for a uniform system of regulation. But the need was slow to impress itself to the point of action on the central government. The dominant thinking during the nineteenth century, in spite of Bentham and Chadwick and the poor-law system they helped to shape was that of J. S. Mill whose *Representative Government* furnished much of the intellectual basis for English local government:

> The Authority which is most conversant with principles should be supreme over principles, while that which is most competent in details should have the details left to it. The principal business of the central authority should be to give instruction, of the local authority to apply it. Power may be localised, but knowledge, to be more useful, must be centralised — (Ch.XV).

The Local Government Board (1871) and its Irish equivalent reflected part at least of this liberal philosophy and although the devolutionary ideas inherent in the Acts of 1888 and 1898 were never fully realised, central intervention in local affairs was, even in Ireland, kept to a decent minimum. Control, however, expanded with the extension of the franchise and the increase of state subsidies. In the case of only one service, public assistance, was there any express power of general direction and control given to the appropriate Minister but in practice the degree of supervision exercised was not appreciably less over certain other services such as roads, health, housing, and technical education.

Observers have repeatedly remarked on the unusually subordinate status of our local authorities. The PSORG Report (1969) said:

> The striking feature of the Irish system of local government, whether it is compared with local government systems abroad *or with other administrative systems within the country*, is the degree and extent of the controls exercised over it. The Maud Committee on the Management of Local Government in Britain (HMSO 1967) made a perceptive study of local government in seven countries including Ireland. They concluded that, in Ireland, 'central control is the most stringent of all' (Volume 1 p. 13).

The White Paper (1971) recognised excessive controls as one of the problems of local government reorganisation and gave a chapter (ch. 13) to the subject. Some improvement had taken place:

> Considerable progress had been made in recent years towards the relaxation of controls. Modern enactments have widened considerably the dis-

cretionary powers of local authorities and Ministerial approvals are increasingly being given in general form. A significant step was the decision not to require central approval of development plans (13.1.5).

But much remained to be done. The White Paper then dealt with the scope for liberalising law and practice in the three major areas of control: statutory, financial and administrative.

It should not of course be overlooked that a central department's major claim to authority does not rest solely on its powers of control, however formidable these may be. A department must justify its existence by other means. It must provide a degree of leadership for the system as a whole by introducing new policies or refurbishing the old. It must gather and, as appropriate, disseminate facts, opinions and information. It must conduct research or at least tap research resources elsewhere. And it must, as far as possible, provide guidance and technical assistance for local authorities who lay on the services which are the end-product of the system and the inducement to the public to continue, however reluctantly, paying for it.

Some examples drawn from the Department of the Environment: the Local Government (Planning and Development) Act, 1963, gave physical planning a much-needed face-lift and local government generally a shot in the arm. The Department, with the aid of its research agency, An Foras Forbartha, brought a regional framework to planning and gave nationwide currency to the idea of Regional Development Organisations which had originated in the Mid-West region. The White Paper of 1971 furnished a volume of information and proposals to the public on local government reorganisation. Neither its plan nor the counter-project in the Discussion Document of 1973 reached statutory fulfilment, but that is not the point. The White Paper (1972) on Local Finance and Taxation was the culmination of a series of reports from an Inter-Departmental Committee. It projected a programme of reform, but came too late. It was trumped almost immediately by a master-card: abolition of rates on domestic and certain other premises. This was a salutary but nevertheless bitter lesson in the dangers of neglecting until the eleventh hour a problem which cried loudly for attention. The Department commissioned the ESRI to research the problem and an excellent report (Copeland, Walsh) on *Economic Aspects of Local Authority Expenditure and Finance* was submitted in December 1975. But the horse had already bolted. Other aspects of the Department's concerns got attention: roads and road traffic, water pollution, the fire services, housing and others. The Department's record, while imperfect, has been creditable enough.

Services

Finally, a Departmental function which calls for mention: provision of services for local authorities. These include the system of combined purchasing; the Local Appointments Commissioners; the Computer Services Board; the Staff Negotiations Board and the local government audit service.

Certain services of local impact are administered directly by the Department. The principal are housing, private water supply, and private sanitation grants, and driver testing. They involve the Department in large-scale executive operations, and are at variance with the main purposes of the Departments, which are advisory, supervisory and directive.

Combined Purchasing

The origins of the system have been dealt with in Chapter 5. Official contractors, chosen by the Minister for the Environment in accordance with procedures under the Combined Purchasing Act, 1939, act generally for twelve months in specified areas. From 1971 there are three areas — Cork, Dublin and the rest of Ireland. In addition to local authorities and health boards, a number of voluntary hospitals participate in the scheme.

A statutory committee, the Local Supplies Advisory Committee representing local authorities and supplies, acts as a consultative body.

A working party set up in 1969 to review the system, reported in 1971 in favour of continuance with some alterations. Central purchase was rejected, as was detachment of the system from the Department of the Environment proposed by PSORG, 1969 which had in mind a Procurement Division in the new Department of the Public Service.

The system should also remain binding on local authorities, and other related bodies should be admitted as participants.

Contractors for medicines were not appointed after 1972; alternative arrangements were made by the Department of Health.

Contract periods were reduced in 1976 from twelve to six months, in an effort to cope with accelerating price changes.

The volume of business done under the scheme averages about £6 million a year.

Powers and Functions

Local authorities derive their powers, functions and duties from Acts of the Oireachtas and also, in the case of boroughs, from charters. British and Irish pre-Union statutes, so far as they were in force in Ireland in 1922, were continued until repealed or amended, and under the Constitution of 1937 the then existing laws were also continued. The law relating to the functions of local authorities is to be found principally in Public Acts but some of it is in Private Acts. It is also to be found in statutory instruments, formerly called statutory rules and orders, made under the authority of the Oireachtas; in provisional orders which with some exceptions have been confirmed by Parliament or the Oireachtas; and in byelaws made by the local authority which may or may not require confirmation by the central authority.

Local authorities are bound by the legal rule which forbids the spending of money other than for objects authorised by statute. This rule of law emerged in the courts during the nineteenth century; it has never been enacted by parliament in these terms, but the general effect of a series of decisions, combined with the scrutiny by local government auditors, has magnified its importance.

The *ultra vires* rule has been criticised because it inhibits local enterprise and experiment. The PSORG Report (1969) gave their views:

Local authorities could . . . be given more general powers to act in the interests of their areas, subject to appropriate safeguards. The current application of the doctrine of *ultra vires,* together with the specific terms in which local government statutes tend to be drawn, encourage rigid control over local authority activities by the Department and deter local authority initiative. In a number of other countries, local authorities operate successfully within a general competence to act for the good of the community.

The White Paper Prl 1572 (1971) noted the grim consequences of contravening the *ultra vires* rule viz, either a High Court declaration or injunction, or a disallowance and surcharge by an auditor. But it also said that the rigidity of the rule had been softened by

(1) the court interpretation which allows a local authority to do anything incidental to, or consequential upon actions for which there is explicit or implied statutory authority; and
(2) recent legislation, particularly the Local Government (Planning and Development) Act, 1963, which is drawn in broad, non-restrictive terms.

The White Paper (at 14.1.3) nevertheless proposed to bring forward legislation restating the permissive powers of local authorities. This would be supplemented by general provision enabling them to spend money on the betterment of their areas or in the interests of the inhabitants. The English Local Government Act 1972 allows a local authority to do just that, subject to a limit of two new pence in the pound. The Maud Committee (1966) suggested giving local authorities a general competence to do whatever they feel to be of worth or benefit to their areas. This is a much wider idea, and has not been taken up, although its attractions in enlivening local government, and releasing local initiative and imagination are well recognised.

Public and Private Acts

In the nineteenth century boroughs and other towns promoted a large volume of legislation relating to their towns and in this way obtained powers to effect improvements. Cork city for instance promoted fifteen Acts in the period 1852–99 and Dublin in the same period twenty Acts. This legislation dealt with improvements, waterworks, markets, drainage, rates, fire brigades, boundary extensions and other matters. As local government developed and general legislation covered a wider field, the necessity for this type of local legislation diminished; moreover some legislation of only local interest has in recent times been dealt with in Public Acts. Conspicuous instances of this are the group of Acts beginning with the Cork City Management Act, 1929, followed by the Local Government (Dublin) Act, 1930, relating to Dublin and Dun Laoghaire. The City Management Acts for Limerick (1934) and Waterford (1939) are in this category. The Act restoring borough stature to Galway in 1937 was, on the other hand, a Private Act.

Provisional Orders

Provisional orders also serve to shorten proceedings in the Oireachtas by allowing matters to be inquired into locally instead of by parliamentary committees. The Public Health Act, 1878, the Local Government Act, 1898, and other statutes gave the central authority power to make provisional orders conferring powers in certain matters on local authorities. The local authority, instead of applying to the Oireachtas for the powers they desire to have, apply to the appropriate Minister. After holding a local inquiry at which objections are heard the Minister may make a provisional order. When made the order is normally submitted by the Minister with other such orders in a Bill for confirmation by the Oireachtas. Not all provisional orders have, however, to be confirmed by the Oireachtas. Provisional orders for the compulsory acquisition of land under the Acts of 1878 and 1898 referred to above were confirmed by the Minister or the Circuit Court in accordance with rules prescribed in 1925; and as already mentioned provisional orders constituting a town an urban sanitary district take effect without the authority of the Oireachtas if one-fourth of the electors do not petition against it.

Orders in Council

The comprehensive scope of the reforms made by the Act of 1898 presented an unusual problem. The intricacies of local government law would have faced Parliament with such a mass of detail that MPs were glad to accept the idea put forward (according to himself) by Timothy Healy for having the work done by civil servants. The result was two monumental Orders in Council, one of them applying English and Scottish enactments to Ireland; and the other adapting the Irish Grand Jury law to the new position. These were the Local Government (Application of Enactments) Order 1898 and the Local Government (Adaptation of Irish Enactments) Order 1899.

Byelaws

Local authorities can themselves, under powers delegated to them, make laws called byelaws enforceable by the Courts. These laws affect a particular area and are only of local interest. They relate to good rule and government (Local Government Act 1898 s. 16 and Municipal Corporations Act 1840 ss. 125–7), the regulation of markets, the suppression of nuisances, disposal of house refuse, buildings, burial grounds, keeping of animals and other matters: mainly Public Health Act of 1878; for burial grounds and open spaces: Open Spaces Act, 1906 s. 15. Some byelaws take effect after a certain time if they are not disallowed by the central authority, but most byelaws must be confirmed by the appropriate Minister. Byelaws must be reasonable, consistent with and not repugnant to the general law, provide something additional to the general law, be certain and free from ambiguity, and be obligatory on everyone in the area without discrimination. It must be within the power of the local authority to make them. When making byelaws the usual practice is for a local authority to follow, with adaptations, model codes issued by the central authority rather than framing their own.

Byelaws may vary from area to area, and some local authorities may opt for not making them. A recent piece of legislation has solved the problem (insofar as it is a problem) by transferring power to the Minister. The Local Government (Planning and Development) Act, 1963 s. 86, empowers the Minister for the Environment to make regulations covering the matters formerly dealt with in building byelaws: Public Health Act, 1878 s. 41; and Public Health Acts Amendment Act, 1890 s. 23. The *National Building Regulations* made by the Minister (and now in draft) would when made supersede all existing local byelaws.

An earlier example of central power to make byelaws: Road Traffic Act, 1933 ss. 118, 148, enabling the Commissioner of the Garda Siochána to sub-legislate — with the consent of the Minister for the Environment.

Functions

It would be possible, if not particularly easy, to work out from first principles what kind of functions should be assigned to local government, and what left with central departments or some other parts of the political or administrative system. But the exercise, though instructive, would certainly not be all that fruitful. This is because any group of people faced with a practical problem must take their stand on things as they exist, and operate, even in matters of reform or change, out of a firm framework of actuality. Thus the Redcliffe-Maud Commission (1969) answered the first big question posed to them in the following terms:

> We conclude then that the purpose of local government is to provide a democratic means both of focusing national attention on local prob-

lems affecting the safety, health and well-being of the people, and of discharging, in relation to these things, all the responsibilities of government which can be discharged at a level below that of the national government.

This language gives us, in masterly summary, a reflection of what English local government actually is and does: a system which, with a very fair degree of local democracy, delivers services ranging from police, fire service, almost all education other than university, to health and welfare of mothers and infants, the old and the sick, children in need of care, public health, housing, sport and recreation, museums, art galleries and libraries, the physical environment and use of land, highways, traffic and transport, and a host of less eye-catching matters.

Local government in Ireland is much less wide-ranging in scope, and if one concedes that the health services and vocational education have moved outside local government proper, it is concerned largely with the care and improvement of the physical environment. The White Paper (1971) says succinctly:

Nowadays Irish local government is mainly concerned with physical planning and development, the provision of infrastructure, environmental services, amenity services and, to a lesser extent, with protective and regulatory services.

But the White Paper does not present the existing position as the best practicable arrangement of functions. There are references to anomalies (3.1.1.) and to the desirability of adding to what seems a too restricted band of local functions: 'the government favour the delegation of as many appropriate functions and duties as possible to local authorities and they propose to review, in the light of the report of the PSORG, the possibility of delegating additional responsibilities to them' (3.1.2).

The Discussion Document on Local Government Reorganisation (1973) which was intended to replace the White Paper proposals endorsed, more or less, this part of the earlier scheme:

Powers of Local Authorities The Minister believes that the powers of local authorities should be widened and that there should be a reduction in the detailed controls exercised by his Department . . . . Apart from the question of devolution, there is also a special need to restate the permissive powers of local authorities on a broader basis and to modify the *ultra vires* rule. This will require legislation at a later stage.

An Inter-Departmental Committee is currently at work on the problems of what are described as Subnational Systems; a vital part of that task is, in the words of PSORG (5.3.23) 'to clarify responsibilities and roles in accordance with some clear-cut principles.'

Does local government do too little or too much? Mention of too much may seem paradoxical in the light of what has gone before, but the arguments deployed in Chapter 3 of the 1971 White Paper point towards the following conclusion: that local government is, despite considerable trimming, burdened with a ragbag of miscellaneous jobs with no logical cohesion. These historical remnants, if jettisoned, would leave the system free to concentrate on tasks for which some respectable principle can be found. This line of argument rested, for one of its ends, on the limited resources at the disposal of local authorities. A great deal has been done since 1971 to relieve local taxation, but local authorities are still a far cry from enjoying freedom of choice and manoeuvre; and the room for manoeuvre is narrowing rather than the reverse.

A recent Council of Europe survey, *A Comparative Analysis of European Towns* (1977) demonstrates the rather meagre range of Irish local services in the European context. Here is the check-list of functions:

Security, police	* Slaughterhouses
* Fire protection	Theatres, Concerts
Justice	* Museums, Art Galleries and
Pre-School education	Libraries
Primary and Secondary	* Parks and Open Spaces
* Vocational and Technical	* Sports and Leisure Pursuits
Training	* Roads
Higher Education	Urban Road Transport
Adult Education	Ports
Hospitals and Convalescent	Airports
Homes	District Heating
Personal Health	* Water Supply
Family Welfare Services	Agriculture, Forestry, Fishing,
Welfare Homes	Hunting
* Housing	Electricity
* Town Planning	Commerce
* Refuse collection and disposal	Tourism

The services operated through local authorities in Ireland (11 out of 30) are marked*.

The reduction process, at least in terms of variety, may be seen in the older categories of services which have now been replaced by programme groups. The previous classification was

1 Roads
2 Housing
3 Sanitary Services
4 Health
5 Public assistance
6 General Purposes

Re-classification has resulted in dropping two major headings, Health and Public Assistance, both of them personal, non-environmental services. The

new categories are however more numerous, and highlight some services
e.g. planning, which were obscured under the heading General Purposes.

The Public Bodies (Amendment) Order 1975 breaks down local services
into eight programme groups:

1. *Housing and Building*
   Management and provision of local authority housing; assistance to persons housing themselves or improving their houses; itinerant rehabilitation; enforcement of housing standards and controls.

2. *Road Transportation and Safety*
   Road upkeep and improvement; public lighting; traffic management
   facilities; safety education and propaganda; collection of motor taxation; licensing of drivers, etc.

3. *Water Supply and Sewerage*
   Public water supply and sewerage schemes; assistance for private water
   and sewerage facilities; public conveniences, etc.

4. *Development Incentives and Controls*
   Physical planning policy; control of new development and building;
   promotion of industrial and other development, etc.

5. *Environmental Protection*
   Waste collection and disposal; burial grounds; safety of structures and
   places; fire protection; pollution control, etc.

6. *Recreation and Amenity*
   Swimming pools; libraries; parks; open spaces; recreation centres; art
   galleries; museums, theatres; conservation and improvement of amenities,
   etc.

7. *Agriculture, Education, Health and Welfare*
   Contributions to County Committees of Agriculture, Vocational Educational Committees, Regional Health Boards, Joint Drainage Committees, and the Unemployment Assistance Fund; public assistance; rates
   waiver schemes; other services of an agricultural education or welfare
   nature, etc.

8. *Miscellaneous Services*
   Financial management and rate collection; elections; courthouses;
   coroners and inquests; consumer protection measures; markets, fairs
   and abattoirs; gasworks; corporate estate; malicious injuries, etc.

This list, although showing a heavy emphasis on the physical aspects
of the environment, is not wholly materialist. Libraries, art galleries and
museums are evidence of concern with the cultural and educational strands
in society. The White Paper (1971) saw a glowing future for local government in these and allied aspects:

> Local authorities can play a vital role in achieving a number of . . . social
> objectives . . . for instance fostering cultural and artistic values, preserv-
> ing and developing the national heritage, improving the environment,
> promoting community development and the better use of leisure. Local

authorities will therefore be encouraged to promote cultural activities; to establish (or help in establishing) local museums and art galleries; to help in the conservation of national monuments and particularly in the provision of access and parking facilities; to provide sporting and recreational facilities, particularly for the young; to encourage and assist in the development of community centres and youth clubs (3.4.5).

Development Corporations

The developmental role of local government was given statutory recognition by the Local Government (Planning and Development) Act, 1963 under which local authorities were 'invested with wide and flexible powers to engage in economic activity and to further the development of their areas'. The White Paper (1971) went further to say 'Local authorities therefore must now regard themselves and be regarded as development corporations for their areas.'

This last may be thought to overstate the case a little. The expression development corporation derives from British legislation on the creation of new towns, and signifies a state body with extensive powers of land acquisition and development: constructing roads, streets and open spaces; houses, flats, shops, offices, factories and all the components of a town; providing services and (at least for a time) managing the properties so created. The project involves very heavy capital investment, supplied by the state. No Irish local authority is in a position to take on and accomplish an undertaking of this magnitude. The only organisation with access to anything like the resources needed, and able to exercise the freedom of initiative essential to the operation, is the Shannon Free Airport Development Company, whose Shannon Town, built as an accessory to its industrial estate, is our only New Town in the sense in which the term is used in Northern Ireland and abroad.

11

Personnel

The appointment of paid officers by local authorities was a cardinal feature of the reform of local government in the thirties of the last century. At that time the limited functions of local authorities did not render large staffs necessary but as the responsibilities of local authorities grew the need for paid officers increased and it has been found necessary to make provision for their proper recruitment and organisation. There are certain officers who *must* be appointed, such as the county and city manager, secretary of the county council, town clerk, and county surveyor. More numerous than these statutory officers are the officers that local authorities appoint under their general powers to appoint such officers as they require. Each service as a rule requires a number of officers peculiar to itself; for public works and roads, engineers and surveyors; for housing and planning, architects, planners and draughtsmen; for libraries, professional librarians.

Recruitment: Local Appointments Commission

Local staffing came under the general supervision of the Minister for Local Government in 1923, but it was not until 1941, in anticipation of the repeal of the Poor Relief Acts by the Public Assistance Act, 1939, which at the time had not been brought into operation, that a general code was enacted. In the meantime, the Local Appointments Commission was set up in 1926 to examine, select and present candidates for appointment to vacancies under local authorities in the chief executive, technical, professional and certain other offices. Local authorities still have power to appoint their own officers and servants but so far as officers are concerned the power is now strictly regulated. If a vacancy occurs in the offices mentioned above (with the exception of certain part-time professional offices, posts of nurse and midwife and technical posts, which were excluded by the Local Government Act, 1955) it cannot be filled until a recommendation is obtained from the Local Appointments Commissioners, unless with the Minister's consent it is filled by promotion. The office of manager, however, cannot be filled simply by promotion. A person recommended by the Commissioners must be appointed. In addition to local offices, the Local Appointments Commission carry out selection functions for the larger harbour authorities, vocational education committees and committees of agriculture.

The position of health boards under the Health Act, 1970 is that the Local Authorities (Offices and Employees) Act, 1926 and the amending Act of 1940 do not apply automatically to offices other than those of chief executive officer. The Minister for Health can apply the procedure to other offices, and has done so for posts of programme manager. Senior medical posts, and those of dental surgeon, analytical chemist, public analyst and pharmacist are also filled through the Commissioners; as are posts of health inspector, matron and assistant matron. Other vacancies are filled either after competitive examination or, if that method is not suitable, by some other procedure, such as a local interview board set up by the county manager.

Dublin Corporation and Dublin County Council are exceptions from the general rule as regards making appointments. Vacancies in many senior (but not top) administrative and professional posts are filled by promotion from among eligible officers serving with these bodies. Competition is confined to City or County staffs, whose numbers, comparable with some civil service departments, are held to justify the departure.

Local Authority Staffs

In 1971, just before the new regional health boards began administering health institutions and services, there were 55,900 local officers and employees. Some 55 per cent of this total, (31,000) continued with local authorities from 1 April 1971. About 25,000 transferred to health boards and ceased to be local authority staffs. There are at present (1980) 34,000 local officers and employees; and 38,000 health board staff members. The local authority figure includes administrative, professional and technical officers; executive and clerical officers; road workers and a variety of miscellaneous workers.

The standard county administrative organisation is:

1. County Manager
2. County Secretary
3. County Accountant, or in a growing number of areas, Finance Officer
4. Administrative Officers
5. Senior Staff Officers
6. Staff Officers
7. Assistant Staff Officers
8. Clerical Officers
9. Clerk Typists
10. Clerical Assistants

The seven grades from 4 to 10 are recruited at the clerical officer, clerk-typist and clerical assistant levels; clerical officers are taken from the results of Leaving Certificate examinations. Appointments to grades 7 to 4 are made by way of promotion competitions held locally. Appointments as County Accountant and upwards involve selection and recommendation by the Local Appointments Commissioners: vacancies are publicly advertised and open to all qualified candidates. Knowledge and experience of local administration are decisive factors.

The bulk of appointments, then, go to people who have spent some years in local government. If there is a fault in the system, it may lie in the few points of entry below county accountant level. Upwards of that level the chances of an entrant from outside the service are slim enough (PSORG Report 5.3.18). There have been certain exceptions, of course. Some county secretaries came, via the Local Appointments Commission, from central departments, notably the Department of the Environment. And, in recent years, a few engineers have successfully competed for county managerships, thus extending the range of experience to be found in the corps of managers. One further example deserves mention: an engineering graduate with a post-graduate qualification in business management, who has become a principal officer — equivalent of a programme manager — in charge of development and engineering services in a large county council.

On the professional side there are:
County Engineer, with Chief Assistant and Assistant Engineers
County Architect
County Librarian and other library staff
County Solicitor
County Coroner
Chief Fire Officer and other fire service staff.

The present (1980) engineering structure is in process of reorganisation. A four tier structure will replace the existing arrangement. Under the County Engineer there will be (1) Senior Executive Engineers (2) Executive Engineers (3) Assistant Engineers. The last-mentioned will be the normal entry grade, open to engineers with at least two years service. There is the possibility of a fifth level — graduate engineer — which would provide an alternative entry point to the service. There may also be County Development Officers, County Checkers for internal audit, and there are instances of social workers, information officers, landscaping advisers and others.

Coroners are appointed by county councils and county borough corporations on the recommendation of the Local Appointments Commissioners. Coroners and deputy coroners must be either registered medical practitioners, or practising barristers or solicitors of at least five years' standing. Each coroner has a district in which he must reside, unless the Minister for Justice permits otherwise. He must appoint a deputy acceptable to the local authority. Although appointed and paid by the local authority he is not a local officer. He can be removed by the Minister for Justice for misconduct, neglect of duty or incapacity by reason of infirmity. His expenses in holding inquests are recouped by the local authority. Courthouse caretakers and pound keepers to the number required by the county registrar are appointed by the local authority, in effect by the manager.

When the Departments of Health and Social Welfare were created the officers of health and, so far as they were dealing with health matters, officers of public assistance authorities came within the cognisance of the Minister for Health, and assistance officers within that of the Minister for Social Welfare.

The Local Government Act, 1941 had in view the making of general regulations by the Minister which would govern the relations between the officer and the local authority. The Minister can under the Act direct the kind and number of officers to be appointed for a particular purpose, decide appeals from local officers aggrieved by a decision of the manager, require an officer in certain circumstances to resign, or suspend or remove him from office. The LG (Officers) Regulations of 1943 govern appointments, promotion, remuneration, annual leave and other matters. Apart from control over the remuneration of servants and certain matters relating to their superannuation, the Minister has no statutory power over local authorities in relation to servants. The regulations of 1943 do not affect officers that were not at that time under the Minister for Local Government and Public Health. Officers of vocational education committees and school attendance committees remained within the supervision of the Minister for Education and officers of county committees of agriculture remained subject to the Minister for Agriculture. The central authority in the cases of coroners, courthouse caretakers and pound keepers is the Minister for Justice.

Women: Marriage Bar

A general amendment of qualifications was made by the Minister for Local Government, with effect from August 1973, removing the marriage bar which had precluded the employment of married women by local authorities. The local position was thus equated to that in the public service generally.

The marriage bar of course affected the extent to which women attained high office in the public service. It may possibly be significant that the local service has fewer examples of successful women than the civil service. The local environment was less congenial, perhaps, than a government department. The first woman Permanent Secretary was appointed in 1958, and many women became assistant secretaries and principal officers.

City and county managers have been exclusively male, and so have assistant managers, county secretaries and county accountants. On the professional side engineers and architects were all male until recent years, but there were outstanding women in the library service, as well as in medicine and nursing, which have a significant local dimension. Local authorities have currently among their women employees a dozen or so city and county librarians and numerous assistants; many administrative officers, staff officers and town clerks; some solicitors and law agents; a few engineers, architects and planning assistants; an art gallery curator and a small group of social workers and civil defence officers. There is at present (1980) a woman acting county secretary.

Staff Relations

Under the Industrial Relations (Amendment) Act, 1955 the following local authority officers and employees were brought within the compass of the Labour Court: servants (including servants of vocational education committees and committees of agriculture); health inspectors; mental nurses and home assistance officers.

Dr Marshall, in the work on local administration in the Republic of Ireland referred to above (p. 112) mentions the practice which had developed of conducting negotiations for pay and conditions between staff associations and unions, and the County and City Managers Association. He also notes certain objections he had heard voiced against the managers' association assuming this role. The practice was, however, formalised by the institution in 1963 of a scheme of conciliation and arbitration for local officers: this was the product of an agreement between the managers' association, trade unions and staff associations. The scheme featured a bilateral conciliation council and a similarly balanced arbitration board, the latter with an independent chairman. Neither the Minister nor the elected members were parties to the scheme, which covered both administrative-clerical and professional officers (engineers, doctors, dentists, etc.).

The County and City Managers' Association continued to represent the employer side for road workers and other local employees: the Association made an agreement in 1969 for such workers with the Public Services Committee of the Irish Congress of Trade Unions. In 1971 the position altered with the establishment of the Local Government Staff Negotiations Board. This was a special agency created by the Minister for the Environment under the new Local Government (Corporate Bodies) Act, 1971 to provide services for conciliation and arbitration as well as Labour Court proceedings. The Board has a Council made up of selected managers or assistant managers as well as of chief executive officers of health boards. In 1975 the Board was augmented with representatives from each of the Departments of the Environment and Health, three from Environment and two from Health. The Board employs a Chief Officer and support staff.

In 1976 the original conciliation and arbitration scheme was replaced by one worked out by a consortium of civil servants from the Departments of Environment and Health, managers, health chief executive officers, and representatives of staff associations. The new scheme has a National Joint Council and an Arbitration Board, and covers, in addition to recommendations and allowances, such matters as overtime rates, subsistence allowances, travelling and removal expenses, hours of attendance, and annual leave and sick leave. Questions about recruitment, promotion, pensions, grading, etc., can be discussed at conciliation level only.

The National Joint Council is a standing body, meeting at regular intervals, and has a permanent chairman. Representatives of Ministers who may be involved can be added to Council or Board as appropriate.

Local Government Manpower Committee

This committee, a standing body, was set up in 1973 by the Minister for the Environment with representatives of his Department together with nominees of the Departments of the Public Service and Health, the County and City Managers Association, the Local Government and Public Services Union, the Institute of Public Administration, Foras Forbartha, and the Institution of Engineers in Ireland. Its purpose is to examine and make suggestions on the manpower needs of local authorities. It has submitted several reports.

Local Authorities Training Committee

This is a standing sub-committee of the Manpower Committee, with the duty of surveying training needs in the local service, and furnishing ideas for staff development.

Certain local authority activities come within the scope of the Construction Industry Training Committee, a body set up by An Chomhairle Oiliúna (AnCO).

Unions and Worker Participation

A high proportion of local authority employees are organised in trade unions. The degree of unionisation is higher than in the country as a whole (Murray 1978). In addition to large general unions like the Irish Transport and General Workers Union and the Workers Union of Ireland, which have many local authority members, there are a number of specialised unions: the Local Government and Public Services Union, Irish Municipal Employees Trades Union, and others. There are also associations of local officers: the County and City Managers Association, the County Secretaries Association, Association of Town Clerks, Association of County and City Accountants and Finance Officers and others.

While there is nothing in local government law corresponding to the Worker Participation (State Enterprise) Act, 1977, a number of local authorities have Works Councils or Committees in operation, while the majority have regular consultation with union representatives on work conditions, etc.

The Health Act, 1970, legislated for a special type of worker participation. Regional Health Boards have a minority – but a strong minority – of members drawn from the health professions: medical, dental, pharmaceutical and nursing. Regional Development Organisations have something of the same kind of structure.

Review Body on Higher Remuneration in the Public Sector

This non-statutory body, set up by the Department of the Public Service, reviewed the salaries of managers and assistant managers and made recommendations in 1972. The Body has also furnished observations on arbitration findings in the case of engineers and county accountants.

Use of Irish Language in Local Government

The White Paper on *Restoration of the Irish Language* (1965) contained a number of recommendations on the wider use of Irish in local administration. The Minister for Local Government (Environment) wrote to every mayor and chairman asking for support and co-operation, and in particular for a greater use of Irish at council meetings. The Department also circularised local authorities drawing attention to the relevant parts of the White Paper. Proposals in the Paper for a revision of the Irish language regulations were carried into effect the following year by the Local Officers (Irish Language) Regulations, 1966, made by the Minister for Local Government conjointly with the Ministers for Health, Social Welfare, Agriculture and Defence. In addition to other changes the new rules introduced an incentive bonus scheme for officers in the Gaeltacht who use the language in their work.

A National Steering Group was established by the Minister for the Environment in July, 1979, under Liam O Murchú, Director of Bórd na Gaeilge. The Group's purpose is to foster the use of Irish in local government.

Superannuation

The general effect of staffing developments has been to assimilate the system of recruitment and conditions of service of local officers to that of the civil service, to lay down the qualifications as to age, education, experience, etc., for the various offices, to promote uniformity in the organisation of staffs under authorities of the same type and to open wider fields of promotion. Officers can pass from one authority to another without losing superannuation rights. These rights were put on a new basis by the Local Government (Superannuation) Act, 1948. Under that Act, since replaced by the Local Government (Superannuation) Acts, 1956 and 1980, annual allowances for pensionable officers are calculated at the rate of one-eightieth of remuneration for each year of service, to a maximum of one-half the remuneration. In addition there is a lump sum payment equivalent to one-thirtieth for each year, the maximum being one and a half times the remuneration. Newly appointed officers pay five per cent of their re-muneration by way of contribution. Gratuities for women on leaving the service after marriage are being phased out. A gratuity is payable to the personal representative of an officer having five years' service in case of death whilst serving.

If the authority adopt Part III of the 1956 Act (or if they have adopted Part III of the 1948 Act) they can superannuate their pensionable servants as well as officers. The annual allowance is in these cases calculated at the higher rate of one-sixtieth for each year of service with a maximum of two-thirds of the employee's pay but there is no lump sum payment. The con-tributions to be made by established servants other than 'existing servants' is four and one-sixth per cent of the annual remuneration. Fire brigade officers and servants and certain mental hospital officers and servants have somewhat better terms than others, service after twenty years being doubled.

The Act of 1956 made a number of innovations: it required local authorities to maintain registers of pensionable officers and servants, pro-vided a new basis for calculation of pensionable remuneration of officers, and enabled officers to arrange for the partial assignment of pensions to wives or other dependants. The Act also introduced a system of compen-sation for injuries received by officers and servants in the actual discharge of their duties. The updated adjustment of pensions to take account of rises in the cost of living developed hesitantly and on limited lines, in the post-war period, and statutory provision for the purpose was made in the Acts of 1948 and 1956. A series of special Pensions (Increase) Acts in 1950, 1956 and 1960 culminated in the Pensions (Increases) Act, 1964, enabling the Minister for Finance to make regulations covering adjust-ments in both civil and local service pensions. Annual adjustments followed, until the Minister for Finance announced in his 1974 Budget speech the Government's intention to maintain, year by year, parity between pen-sions legislation and public service pay.

In March 1971, the Minister for Local Government authorised (in anticipation of legislation) by circular Letter a number of changes in pen-sion practice: reckoning of temporary and broken service, service as prim-ary or secondary teacher in the case of VEC staff, and the like.

The legislation was somewhat slow in coming, and in June 1976 the Minister for the Environment set up a Working Party to examine the local superannuation code, and recommend ways and means of achieving a bal-anced relationship between it and pension arrangements in other sectors of the public service. The local code, incidentally, covers health boards, VE committees, committees of agriculture, school attendance committees, and agencies created under the Health (Corporate Bodies) Act, 1961 and the corresponding local government Act of 1971. In addition to the Departments of Environment and Health the Working Party included representatives of the managers' association, the health CEO's group, the ICTU and the local conciliation and arbitration staff panel.

An Interim Report in 1977 (accepted by the government) contained proposals for equalising superannuation terms of local officers and manual workers, and for approximating both to civil service pensions. The agreed arrangements have been embodied in a Superannuation Revision Scheme, and put into operation. The Local Government (Superannuation) Act, 1980 enables the Minister for the Environment, with the consent of the Minister for the Public Service, to make pension schemes (including lump sums, gratuities and other allowances) by way of statutory instruments.

Widows and Orphans Pension Scheme

A contributory scheme was adopted for civil servants in 1968, and extended to local officers in the following year. It has now been widened to include local manual workers.

Management Services

A working group set up by the Minister in 1969 found considerable scope for computer use in local government at both Departmental and local levels (Report 1979, Prl 1194). The Local Government Computer Services Board was established in 1975 by order under the Corporate Bodies Act of 1971. The Board is made up of representatives of Managers, and Departments of Environment and Public Service. Valuation lists, rating, house purchase statistics, and vehicle registration were areas considered for computerisation. The Board has recruited a Director, together with specialist and other staff.

Removals

Staff management involves occasional suspensions and, more rarely, dismissals, both of which are regulated by law and statutory rules. As regards officers, s.25 of the LG Act, 1941, empowers the appropriate minister to remove from office on 'statutory grounds', while s.26 as extended by Art. 31 of the LG (Officers) Regulations, 1943, vests a power of removal in the local authority, acting through the manager. This procedure was subjected to judicial scrutiny in the case Tadg O'Mahony v. Arklow UDC and the Minister for Local Government, decided by the Supreme Court in 1965.

The LG Act, 1955, s.14(I), intended to replace s.26 of the 1941 Act, but the intention never came to fruition. Health Authorities, it may be noted, operate a different procedure: Health Act, 1970, ss. 23, 24.

Age Limits

The Act of 1941, s.23, enabled the appropriate minister to specify upper age limits for officers of various grades and classes. In addition to general orders, special orders were made for certain offices including city and county managers. Section 24 of the LG Act, 1955, clarified the earlier section and also attempted to deal with officers having life tenure under statute, such as managers. But the refusal of a city manager (Liam Raftis, Waterford) to yield up his statutory right to stay in office made a further piece of legislation necessary, the LG Act, 1958.

12

Local Finance I

Local authorities spend a sizeable proportion of the national income on the various services they provide. In recent years the proportion has been one tenth or somewhat less. Total expenditure (current and capital) in the period 1976 to 1979 rose from about £400 to £613 million (see table on page 149).

Local expenditure for 1976–9 was about 9 per cent of national income. In 1975 the proportion was slightly over 10 per cent. In 1971, the last year before health services were detached from local government, the figure was 10 per cent.

Trends in Local Expenditure

Two series of statistics are used in official publications. Those in the annual *Returns of Local Taxation* are confined to local authorities in the narrow sense of county councils, the corporations of county and other boroughs, urban district councils, towns commissioners, and a few minor bodies: Joint burial boards, joint drainage committees, joint library committees, etc. The *Returns* distinguish between receipts-expenditure on revenue account, which contain a deal of capital outlay; and similar figures for loan and stock account.

The local authority figures included in the annual *National Income and Expenditure* statistics contain in addition to those in the Returns, figures for Vocational Education Committees, Committees of Agriculture, Harbour Boards and (since 1971) Regional Health Boards. But that is not the only difference. The treatment of current and capital transactions is not the same in both sets of statistics: adjustments are made in the *Returns* data for roads and housing to bring them into line with *National Income* concepts. In what follows, however, the *Returns* data are used, and without adjustment, because the purpose is simply to give an idea of trends.

A number of inferences can be drawn from these figures, and still others from comparisons between the proportions of aggregate annual expenditures spent on various services, particularly health, housing and roads. The growth of health expenditure from 1955 onwards (when public assistance services were absorbed in the health programme) is very noticeable. By the time (1970–71) health was taken over by the regional health boards, health

146

Trends in Local Authority Expenditure

Year Starting 1st April	(1) Revenue Expenditure £ million	(2) at 1953 Prices* £ million	(3) Capital Expenditure £ million	(1) as Percentage of GNP	(1) + (3) as Percentage of GNP
1953	40.3	40.3	17.7	7.9	11.4
1955	46.4	45.7	17.0	8.6	11.8
1960	55.9	49.5	12.3	8.5	9.9
1965	86.4	65.6	23.2	8.6	11.0
1970	158.1	96.0	40.6	9.5	11.9
1975†	224.9	70.6	148.0	6.1	10.1

†Calendar year

expenditure had increased from 34.8 per cent of local expenditure to 44.4 per cent. Over the same period housing had maintained its position and roads had lost much ground – the fall was from 26.0 per cent to 16.5 per cent.

Figures taken from the National Income statistics show that the proportion of Gross National Product devoted to all kinds of local expenditure has gone from 13.6 per cent in 1970/71 to 16.7 per cent in 1978. The rise is mainly due to the marked rise in health expenditure.

Local expenditure and GNP (£m)

Year	GNP	Local Expenditure	Local % of GNP
1970/71	1648.5	224.3	13.6
1973/74	2701.7	396.9	14.7
1978	6245.0	1041.8	16.7

The Public Capital Programme includes expenditure by local authorities.

Local Authority share of Public Capital Programme

	1976 £m	1977 £m	1978 £m	1979 £m
Local Housing	69	74	81	88
House Purchase Loans and supplementary grants	31	20	37	46
Water Supply & Sewerage	25	25	29	36
Roads	12	19	23	30
Miscellaneous Environmental	2	3	6	7
Totals	140	141	175	207
Public Capital Programme	547	658	766	1001

Note

There are some discrepancies between the figures in this table and those on p. 149. Provision for roads was included in the PCP for the first time in 1978. Before that year grants for both road improvement and mainten-

ance were made from the Roads Fund, and were shown as a charge on the current budget. The roads figures above for 1976 and subsequent years are grants for roads improvement, and are shown for comparison.

Housing has traditionally been the predominant element in local capital outlay, but in recent years the proportion represented by housing has fallen from 71 to 64 per cent. Local capital expenditure as a whole, has diminished from about a quarter of the PCP to one fifth. Net local indebtedness now stands at about £1000 million.

Sources of Revenue

The current expenses of local authorities are met from rates, government grants, rents from property and other less important sources, such as receipts from tolls, charges for special supplies of water and receipts from gas undertakings. Expenditure on works of a permanent nature, so far as it is not met out of grants, is, as a rule, met by borrowing.

A substantial proportion of current income – about one fifth of the whole – is earned by services. By far the most productive item is housing, in the form of repayments of house loans and rents of dwellings. Important contributions also come from rents and other charges for water supply, payments for connections with water and sewerage schemes, abattoir charges, stallages, and wide variety of other fees.

On the other side of this account the largest item is the contribution which the county borough corporations and the larger urban district councils make towards meeting the cost of unemployment assistance. This contribution is imperative and referred to in Chapter 21 under Social Assistance. Local authorities repay the costs of the Local Appointments Commission, combined purchasing, audit, and sworn inquiries, all of which are primarily met by the Government, and then recovered from local sources. A contribution is made towards portion of the expense of the annual revision of valuation. While there are doubtless good reasons of principle for exacting these charges, their practical value, set against the state's now overwhelming share of local revenue, is negligible.

Local Expenditure and the state

The growing proportion of local expenditure met by the state has been a theme of commentators for many years, but in fact the upward curve has not been unbroken. The state percentage dropped by about 10 per cent in the first half of the 1970s – a result of the transfer to health boards of the heavily state-aided health services. Towards the end of the 1960s the state had been bearing about 50 per cent of local authority expenditure. In 1976 the proportion was less than 40 per cent, not that the taxpayer gained relief thereby: he merely took up the burden in another, weightier form. From 1977 onwards the de-rating of dwellings and certain other rateable properties began to take effect.

LOCAL GOVERNMENT EXPENDITURE 1976—78

Service	1976 Revenue £m	%	Capital £m	%	1977 Revenue £m	%	Capital £m	%	1978 Revenue £m	%	Capital £m	%
Housing and Building	76	29	101	71	94	29	103	71	105	27	117	70
Road Transportation and Safety	69	26	2	1	87	28	2	1	109	28	2	1
Water Supply & Sewerage	32	12	30	21	40	13	27	18	48	12	28	17
Planning & Development	5	2	4	2	6	2	4	3	8	2	6	4
Environmental Protection	21	8	1	1	26	8	1	1	34	9	3	2
Recreation & Amenity	13	5	2	1	17	5	3	2	23	6	3	2
Agriculture, education, health & welfare	26	10	1	1	24	8	1	1	26	7	1	1
Miscellaneous Services	21	8	3	2	23	7	4	3	32	8	6	4
Total	263	100	143	100	317	100	145	100	384	100	166	100
Gross National Product	4508				5340				6245			

*Expenditure less than £0.5 million.

Roche: Local Government

Rates proportion of Local Authority Income

Receipts	1977		1978		1979	
	£	%	£	%	£	%
Rates	107.4	34	81.6	21	89.7	21
State Grants	145.7	46	228.9	59	266.4	61
Other	63.5	20	77.6	20	80.1	18
Total	316.6	100	388.1	100	436.2	100

Local Finance: The Problem

The problem of local authority finance is largely a product of the present century. When local government began to assume its modern lineaments in the nineteenth century, expenditure on the rudimentary services then locally administered — highways, poor relief, sanitation and certain aspects of law and order — was met almost wholly from local resources. The problem began to take shape when the new social legislation imposed heavier burdens on local authorities than unaided local taxation could (or should) bear. Local government felt the onset of that chronic malaise of enforced living beyond one's means, descending ever deeper into the condition of dependance on a rich, parsimonious and tetchy relative.

A further aspect of the local predicament was thrown into relief with the development of the idea of national standards of service. The basic dilemma has been summarised by Copeland-Walsh (ESRI, 1975) as follows:

national standards in the provision of local services are considered desirable, but excessive reliance on purely local financial resources could result in marked regional disparities in the level of services provided.

The practice of augmenting local revenues from central taxation became an accepted feature of public finance from 1850 onwards. Early subsidies were too small to affect the principle that central taxation admitted no liability for local services, but by the 1880s state grants had grown in number and amount to the point where orthodox fiscal doctrine was at hazard. A Conservative government made an effort to preserve the separation of local from central liabilities with the establishment by Mr (later Viscount) Goschen of the Local Taxation Account in 1888. To this Account were assigned certain excise licences, probate duty, and beer and spirit duties. These were designated local taxes, and found their way to the Account without the intervention of Parliament. A Local Taxation (Ireland) Account was set up in the same year, on the same general lines, with a similar object.

The Local Taxation Accounts were designed to keep the balance between local outgoings and local taxation as far ahead could be seen, but the whole plan fell to pieces within a decade. In 1898 a major subsidy in aid of rural ratepayers, both landlords and tenants, was part of the reform package which replaced grand juries (in their administrative role) by county councils. The Agricultural Grant was channelled through the Local Taxation Account, but any idea that the grant was levied by some form of local taxation could not be maintained.

The period 1922 to 1939 witnessed a steady growth in local services, with a corresponding rise in state subvention. The Agricultural Grant was augmented, the Road Fund expanded with the growing use of motor-cars, buses and lorries, housing subsidies enlarged to encourage slum clearance and house building, and public health improvements secured with the aid of state money. The result was a gradual assumption by the state of a higher share of the local financial burden. A comparison of the positions in 1925 and 1939 illustrates this trend.

Local receipts, £ million

	1925	%	1939	%
Rates	5.3	60	6.27	50
State Grants	1.9	21	4.70	37
Other	1.7	19	1.67	13
Total	8.9	100	12.64	100

The Walker Papers
Despite the greatly enlarged state assistance to local authorities, rate levels continued to rise in the post war period. Between 1949 and 1959, the state contribution doubled – from £11m to £22m. But so did the rates levy, from £10m to £20m. During this period there was much criticism both of the rating system and the general structure of local finance. In 1961 the Economic Research Institute (as it then was) began an investigation into the economics of local authority finances. The first fruits of this work, undertaken at the suggestion of the Department of Finance, was Professor David Walker's paper of May 1962 entitled *Local Government Finance in Ireland: A Preliminary Survey*. This was an introductory paper, limited to revenue income and outgoings, and made the following general points:

(1) Local authorities in Ireland have a certain freedom of action, and should not be regarded purely as agencies of the central government.
(2) It is probably best that local authorities should be financed both from resources under their own control and by state grants.
(3) Grants may be of three types: (a) specific, (b) equalisation or redistributive; and (c) general or neutral. In Ireland specific grants are numerous and offer a wide variety of aims and methods. There are, curiously, no examples of the other two categories, but many specific grants are

partly redistributive in design, while the Agricultural Grant has many of the characteristics of a support or general grant.

(4) Valuation for rating purposes is demonstrably in need of revision and up-dating.

(5) Rates are arguably a regressive tax, but clearly there will always be some anomalies and apparent inequities in any tax system which is not composed entirely of income taxes and, perhaps, general sales taxes.

Professor Walker's general conclusion regarding rates was that while a formidable case could be built up against them – particularly where the foundation of the system, valuation, was completely out of date – it would be unrealistic to think of the abolition of local rates or even of drastic changes in their scope.

As regards local revenue and expenditure, the following points emerged:

(1) The levels of services varied considerably from one local authority to another.

(2) The burden of local taxation also varied from area to area.

(3) A high level of services seemed to be associated with low taxation, and vice versa.

(4) The state grants system was not designed to help poorer counties more than the better off.

Professor Walker followed his *Preliminary Survey* with a paper in 1964 on *Local Government Finance and County Incomes.* This essay, based largely on the pioneer work on county incomes by E. A. Attwood and R. C. Geary published in 1963, concluded: 'there is a strong argument for an alteration in the grant structure so as to provide special help for the areas which are relatively poor'.

Inter-Departmental Committee on Local Finance and Taxation

Shortly after Professor Walker's paper appeared, the Minister for Local Government set up an informal committee comprising officials of the Departments of Agriculture and Fisheries, Education, Finance, Health and Local Government to examine and report on the present system of financing the operations of local authorities. The Committee furnished a series of reports, three of which were published. The first dealt with *Valuation for Rating Purposes* (1965). The others were *Exemptions from and Remissions of Rates* (1967) and *Rates and Other Sources of Revenue for Local Authorities,* which appeared in 1968.

The report on valuation rehearsed the case for a general revaluation of rateable property. In the matter of land, the distortion of relativities emerged shortly after the completion of Griffith's monumental effort of 1853–65, and valuations of buildings were also open to question, besides being grossly out of date. The recommendations of the Inter-Departmental Committee in favour of a general revaluation nevertheless excluded from its scope all agricultural land outside the four county boroughs, and the

Borough of Dun Laoghaire. The report on rates exemptions and remissions gave details of the remarkable number and variety of exceptions from the general rateability of real property, and the consequent loss to the productivity of local rates. The committee recommended adherence to the cardinal principle that: 'local rates . . . should be seen to operate fairly, without discrimination in favour of state or semi-state bodies or of particular concerns at the expense of the general body of ratepayers.' Concessions, if any, should be on grounds of principle, e.g., places of worship, burial grounds, air-raid shelters, lighthouses, national, vocational and reformatory schools; local authority property, voluntary hospitals and institutions; and temporary remissions at the discretion of rating authorities. Property occupied by the state should be assessed for rates in the same way as private or commercial holdings. The rating of half rents should be abolished. The system of writing off irrecoverable rates should be continued and given statutory validity.

The third report, on rates and other sources of revenue, discussed the merits of rating as a local tax; charges for local services; and alternative forms of local taxation. It recommended retention of the rating system as an independent source of revenue for local authorities. In the matter of possible additional taxes, the Committee:

(1) rejected site value rating, but recommended that 'a very full investigation should be carried out by an expert body into the question of rating site value as part of the valuation of a tenement';

(2) decided that a local income tax would not be practicable and rejected also such devices as betterment levies, poll taxes, taxes on advertising signs and public lotteries;

(3) recommended introduction of a limited local turnover tax; and local entertainment taxes.

The government's response to the Inter-Departmental Committee's proposals was one of partial and guarded acceptance. No action was taken on the valuation problem, apart from the decisions announced in the White Paper of December 1972, which included the transfer of the central function from the Minister for Finance to the Minister for Local Government. On the topic of rates remissions and exemptions, two moves were made:

(1) rates relief on buildings other than new and reconstructed houses was phased out: Local Government (Temporary Reduction of Valuation) Act, 1970.

(2) the rating of half-rents was abolished: Local Government (Rateability of Rents) (Abolition) Act, 1970.

The Committee's third report, on types and methods of local taxation, included two minor recommendations, on rates relief in cases of hardship, and payment by instalments. Both of these were given statutory recognition in the Local Government (Rates) Act, 1970, but as noted above, were shortly superseded, so far as domestic rates were concerned, by the de-rating of dwellings.

The Inter-Departmental Committee did not publish a report on state grants and other contributions towards local expenditure, although they gave time and consideration to this subject. A major change in the rating situation occurred, however, while the Committee was sitting. This was the total de-rating of agricultural holdings of land up to £20 valuation, which in effect, exempted 320,000 holdings from rates liability on land, or 76 per cent of all agricultural holdings in county health districts. The Rates on Agricultural Land (Relief) Act, 1967, also applied 100 per cent relief to the first £20 of holdings valued up to £33; the occupier was liable for rates only on that portion of his valuation in excess of £20. In the cases of larger holdings the total holding qualified for the following reliefs:

(1) primary allowance of 80 per cent on the first £20 valuation;
(2) supplementary allowance of 30 per cent of the remainder;
(3) employment allowance of £17 for each adult male worker.

The White Paper

In December 1972, the government issued its White Paper *Local Finance and Taxation* (Prl. 2745). The principal proposals it announced were:

(1) valuation to be modernised as a matter of urgency. As a first step the Valuation Office would be transferred to the Department of Local Government;
(2) valuations (based possibly on capital values) to be brought ultimately to full current values;
(3) site values to be considered in determining levels of valuation, especially in the case of development land;
(4) decentralisation of Valuation Office to be pursued, with possible devolution to local authorities;
(5) rates remissions and exemptions to be drastically curtailed;
(6) rates waiver scheme to be reviewed in association with reform of the social assistance services;
(7) local authorities to be given a general power to make charges for their services, and to undertake trading services ancillary to their normal functions.

On certain issues of general policy, the government announced that rates would remain the principal local source of tax revenue available to local authorities. Site value rating, local income taxes, poll tax etc. were dismissed as possible alternatives, as was any prospect of a local value-added tax as successor to the local turnover tax suggested by the Inter-Departmental Committee. The idea of a local entertainment tax was, however, accepted. A full review of the entire financial relationship between the state, local authorities and other local bodies was to be put in hands with a view to a comprehensive reorganisation of state-local financial relations. As a preliminary move in this direction a report of the Inter-Departmental Committee would be published, dealing with the Agritural Grant. The government would consider, in the light of this report, various proposals put forward for changes in the present system of rating land.

Health and Housing

The steep rise in local rate levels in the late 1960s and early 1970s aroused much opposition. There was widespread anti-rates agitation, which focused on health expenditure as (by now) the largest and fastest growing item in the rates bill. Health charges were the point at issue when Dublin City Council (followed by Bray UDC) refused to strike an adequate rate in 1969, and were removed from office.

Although local authorities were relieved in 1971 of direct responsibility for the health services, they remained liable for a substantial proportion of health costs. The White Paper of 1972 rejected the view that health expenditure should be a wholly state charge. The Fine Gael and Labour parties had developed the principle that large-scale social expenditure should be not a local but a national charge. Social expenditure in this context meant health and housing — public assistance, which was still a local service, was relatively inexpensive.

When the National Coalition took office in 1973, they set about putting this principle into practice by phasing out over a four year period the rates contribution to the cost of health services and housing. The phasing-out process was completed in 1977.

The Copeland-Walsh Paper

During the same period the Minister for Local Government referred the rates problem to the Economic and Social Research Institute. Their report *Economic Aspects of Local Authority Expenditure and Finance* (J. Copeland and B. Walsh, 1975) confirmed the international use and general acceptability of rates as a form of local taxation; and pointed out that rates were, with the introduction of rates waiver schemes, no longer regressive, although rates were not proportionate to income in the higher brackets. 'The widely-held view that rates are regressive seems to derive mainly from the fact that many retired persons, living on reduced incomes, own houses bought when their incomes were much higher.' Land valuations were outdated, and the valuation system generally needed reconditioning. Exemptions and reductions should be ended, and other suggestions were made for improving rates as a tax. There was little room for other local taxes on low-income groups. A small local income tax was a possibility, but it would have to be nationally supervised and collected and would hardly be a genuine local tax.

On the general issue of local finance, Copeland-Walsh concluded that by international standards local authorities in Ireland spent a normal proportion of total public expenditure. Most countries had a greater variety of local taxes. General or block grants, rather than grants for specific services, were a common feature of most local support systems. 'There is marked regional variation in the structure of Irish local finances. In most of the poorer counties, rates payable locally contribute relatively little to total receipts.' But it was noted that despite this richer counties spent more on local services than the less well-off. Some system of revenue sharing (between state and local authorities) might be substituted for many of the present specific grants.

During the general election campaign of 1973, the Fianna Fáil (then the government) party undertook to remove rates altogether from houses and other dwellings. The National Coalition parties (Fine Gael and Labour) won the election, however, and as outlined above went ahead with their own ideas, which included the ESRI examination of the rates issues. Despite the, on the whole, favourable verdict of the Copeland-Walsh team on the rates system, the Coalition government decided towards the end of 1976 to phase out domestic rates and in his 1977 Budget the Minister for Finance announced a 25 per cent cut, with a hint of more to follow. In the meantime Fianna Fáil had developed their own plans – immediate abolition of domestic rates, and in addition removal of rates from secondary schools, community halls and such farm buildings as were still subject to rating. With the Fianna Fáil victory in the 1977 election these plans were put into operation, with effect from 1 January 1978. A Bill to give the necessary legislative assent was introduced in December 1977 and became law the following year.

Local Government (Financial Provisions) Act, 1978

The Minister for the Environment, on the second reading of the Bill, gave a brief account of its background:

the need to modify the rating system in its impact on domestic property has thus been frequently admitted in the past. The several investigations and studies of the rating system undertaken in recent years have been prompted more than anything else by a basic dissatisfaction with the way in which rates bore on householders. No fundamental solution to the problem emerged until our proposal to give total relief of domestic rates. Despite the last government's action for example, between 1973 and 1977 in phasing health and housing charges from the rates, the average rate in the pound still rose in this period from £6.70 to £9.00. Our initiative has been bolder and more clearcut. In this Bill we are removing once and for all the burden of rates from over 850,000 householders and other persons benefiting from the new reliefs – *Dáil Debates*, 307, 8 June 1978.

The opposition could not attack the main aims of the Bill, on which all parties were agreed, and confined their criticisms to the methods proposed — particularly the new financial controls. For the first time (unless one counts the statutory requirement to strike a *sufficient* rate) local discretion in fixing rate levels was to be fettered. Section 10 empowers the Minister, with the consent of the Minister for Finance, to issue directions to rating authorities setting limits to their estimates, and the rates struck to meet them. Section 11 extended the Minister's control to decisions of local authorities authorising expenditure over and above the amounts in their estimates.

Section 13 dispensed with the formal 'striking' of the rate on the basis of the estimates adopted by a rating authority. The substantive decision at the estimates meeting would suffice. Section 9 obliged the Minister to recoup local authorities the full amount lost to them by the de-rating of houses, flats, schools and other properties specified in the Bill. The aggregate recoupment for 1978 was over £80 million. The state would pay nearly £2 out of every £3 leviable in rates. A new financial burden of this magnitude justified the Minister, he considered, in tightening the controls over local taxation. Reasonable measures were needed also to protect non-domestic ratepayers — factory owners, hoteliers, shopkeepers and the like.

The main point of principle urged by the opposition was the severe blow to local democracy. They deplored the shackles fastened on elected members in the exercise of their most important function — fixing the level of local taxation. As Deputy T. J. Fitzpatrick put it: 'As a result of this derating local government would become centralised in the Custom House, and the powers of local councils and local representatives would be drastically eroded.'

The control method adopted by the Minister has been to set a percentage limit to rate poundages leviable by rating authorities. Although the Minister is empowered to limit estimates of expenses he has not so far done so, and local authorities are free, within the rate limit, to order their own priorities in revenue-financed services. The rate rises permitted were 11 per cent in 1978 and 10 per cent in 1979 and 1980.

The nagging irritation of domestic rates has been finally cured — by amputation. But other aspects of local finance call for attention. There is still need for some system of rates equalisation, either by way of a block grant based on a resources-needs formula, or otherwise. The unsolved problem of revaluation of rateable property must eventually be faced, unless a substitute is found for the various purposes for which valuation is still a criterion. There is, of course, the chronic shortage of money which local authorities suffer, in common with the rest of the public sector. And finally there is the question of local democracy — the question, present in many minds, whether the government have not laid the rates problems to rest at the cost of altering, fundamentally, the character of local government.

Local Democracy

It is generally conceded that some powers of local taxation are essential to local government — a necessary item in the degree of local autonomy which the term implies. But there are divergent views on the topic. One is the British official line, echoed in our White Paper on Local Finance and Taxation that local taxes 'should be capable of financing a significant proportion of local expenditure, if local democracy, and a sound local government system is to survive'. The contrary view has been maintained by K. J. Davey in *Public Administration*, 49 (1971) who argued that the source of local revenue was not important. Much the same line was taken by Donal de Buitleir in *Problems of Irish Local Finance*, (1974): he dismissed the necessity for local sources as a myth — 'as much a myth as the belief that the earth is flat.'

The problem created by the Local Government (Financial Provisions) Act, 1978 is of a different order. Rates have not been abolished; local taxation is still alive and well, as occupiers of non-domestic properties — land and buildings — are keenly aware. In 1979 the tax yielded some £90 million. The Minister, on behalf of the people of Ireland, paid an additional £90 million or so in relief of domestic rates; and the Minister of Finance paid a further £40 million or so in rates on agricultural land, and government property.

The Agricultural Grant, together with the payment or 'bounty' in lieu of rates, have never been used as a control mechanism over specific local decisions. If the Minister for the Environment follows the same practice, his assurance should be accepted that: 'with the responsible co-operation for all concerned, little if any interference will be caused to the free ordering of priorities by local authorities' (*Dáil Debates* 8 June 1978). There is, however, a snag. The Minister was arguing in defence of a power enabling him to control a sensitive area of operations — the local budgetary process, the most important function reserved under the Management Acts for exercise by the elected members. This new control has not perhaps been as pervasive as that of the Minister for Health over the Regional Health Boards' annual estimates, but its existence and potential are enough to spread alarm and despondency among councillors and officials. Much will depend on the spirit in which the new control is imposed. A number of European systems have such a control, but a good deal of latitude is allowed in their management of local affairs which is denied to Irish local authorities.

But whatever enlightened forbearance the Minister may exercise, local authorities must continue to live under uneasy apprehension, unless they can reconcile themselves — an unlikely prospect — to the idea that it doesn't matter where the money comes from, provided enough of it comes. There is no possibility of domestic rates being restored. The only hope of independence would then be in uncovering some source of buoyant, inflation-proof income – a forlorn hope, if one can judge by the results of searches hitherto for alternatives or supplements to rates. And the government, worried about the inflationary effects of public sector spending, are unlikely to look kindly on any competitor for an abundant source of supply.

Alternative Local Taxes

The two greatest faults (viewed of course from the council or managerial standpoint) of the rates system are (1) it is the only local tax available to local authorities, and (2) the tax base is extraordinarily inelastic. The search for some substitute or supplement to rates has been going on desultorily for many years. For the conditions we now live in a new local tax, to be worthwhile, must be elastic enough to offer some answer to inflation. The only effective alternatives to rates would therefore be a local income or sales tax.

Local Income Tax

A local income tax would be related to ability to pay, and the buoyancy of revenue would be considerable. Local authorities would also receive a contribution towards local revenue from the many individuals who are not, for rating purposes, the occupiers of property, and therefore do not pay rates directly. Local income taxes are levied in many countries. Sweden has a long established system involving local surcharges varying from area to area, as additions to the national income tax. Denmark, Finland and Germany also operate local income taxes. In the USA, although taxes on real property are the mainstay of local revenues, as of virtually all other national systems, local income taxes are imposed in many states of the Union. In England the idea has been investigated several times since the beginning of the century. Fairly recent instances are *New Sources of Local Revenue* (1956) by a study group set up by RIPA, and *Sources of Local Revenue* (1968) by Hindersley and Nottage. The IMTA carried out a separate study, *Local Income Tax as a Source of Local Government Finance* (1968). The most recent examination was that of the Layfield Committee, *Local Government Finance* (HMSO, 1976). The weight of opinion from these sources was on the side of introducing some form of local income tax.

Irish opinion has been, on the whole, negative. The Commission on Direct Taxation (1956) rejected the idea, as did the Inter-Departmental Committee on Local Finance and Taxation, whose Third Report (1968) is referred to earlier. The Copeland-Walsh paper showed some degree of receptivity to the suggestion, and carefully balanced its merits and defects. Among the latter the most telling arguments against a local income tax in Ireland were:

First, the base of the tax is very unevenly distributed throughout the country so that the tax would seriously increase disparities in local financial resources . . . .. Second, a local income tax would imply raising the already high rate of marginal income taxation in Ireland. Finally, the amount of genuine local autonomy with regard to local income tax would probably be small: the central government would probably stipulate a fairly narrow range within which local taxes would have to lie . . . (p. 152).

The attractions of local income tax were listed: greater fairness, progressivity, and buoyancy. But 'on balance, then, we do not believe that a local income tax is an attractive option in Ireland'.

Local VAT

The third Inter-Departmental Report (1968) suggested a local addition to Turnover Tax, but before the idea could take hold, Turnover Tax was replaced by VAT and ceased to be a possibility. 'VAT does not lend itself to local administration due to the problem of measuring value added locally. (France, for example, abolished local sales taxes on the introduction of a national VAT)'. (Copeland and Walsh, p. 151).

Revenue Sharing and Block Grants

The Copeland-Walsh paper discusses some of the possibilities of boosting local tax revenues by means of a revenue sharing scheme on the lines of that operated in the USA under the State and Local Fiscal Assistance Act of 1972. The American formula, contrasted with the collective effects of the variety of specific grants operated in Ireland involved 'a totally different approach to the provision of grants to local authorities' (pp. 154–9). The shift in emphasis in many countries from specific to block grants was also discussed, with special reference to the UK Rate Support Grant, and the Netherlands Municipal Fund which receives a fixed proportion of the national tax yield.

A Working Party set up by the Institute of Public Administration reported recently (1977) in favour of introducing some form of block grant. As many as possible of the present specific grants should be channelled into an Equalisation Fund, and distributed to local authorities on the basis of a formula taking account of (1) needs and (2) resources. The formula was not worked out in detail.

Copeland-Walsh (Chapter 8) discussed various measures of needs for local services, adding that the needs element of the Rate Support Grant is calculated by a relatively elaborate regression analysis of actual expenditure patterns. The new (1971) Danish system is also described: a combination of equalisation and needs grants. The Federal German system is one, not of local authority, but of inter-state equalisation of shares of national value-added tax on the basis of population.

Layfield Committee

In Britain the problem of reconciling local freedom with some measure of macro-economic control was examined by the Layfield Committee on Local Government Finance, which reported in 1976. Proceeding on the assumption that the value of local government depended to a crucial extent on the room allowed for local manoeuvre, innovation, and discretion, the Committee said:

> The ability of local authorities to exercise discretion in carrying out their functions depends on their being able to raise their own taxes. A body operating within a fixed budget may have delegated to it a good deal of discretion over the way money is spent but the limits of that delegation are set by whoever is providing the money.

This line of argument led, perhaps inevitably, to the Committee's main recommendation:

> That a local income tax (LIT) on personal incomes, levied according to where people live, is the only serious candidate for a new source of local revenue that could give a substantial yield and at the same time maintain or enhance accountability.

This recommendation was, however, rejected by the government. The Local Government Planning and Land (No. 2) Act, 1980, is a clear sign that the government are concerned less about local discretion and accountability than restraining local expenditure as part of the struggle to control public sector spending. The Act replaces Rates Support Grant with a Block Grant calculated on a new basis involving a measure of central direction.

13

Local Finance II

Certain kinds of fixed or immoveable property are liable to rates. This property consists principally of land and buildings and includes mines, commons and rights of common, profits out of land, rights of fishery, canals, navigations and rights of navigation, railways, rights of way and other rights, tolls levied in respect of those rights and all other tolls (Poor Relief (Ireland) Act, 1838, s. 63; Valuation (Ireland) Act 1852, s. 12). Land used for advertisement hoardings is rateable under the Advertising Stations (Rating) Act, 1889.

Plant and machinery are not rateable in themselves, a point which has been highlighted in recent years by a court case involving a brewery, part of whose vats and storage tanks were not housed in buildings. The point may also come under scrutiny in the case of installations such as oil refineries and fertilisation plants, much of whose gear stands in the open. A turf bog or bank used exclusively for cutting or saving turf or making turf mould for fuel or fertiliser is rateable only if a rent or other valuable consideration is payable.

Rating Exemptions, Reliefs, and Remissions

Exemptions of fixed property from rating may be classified under two heads: exemption at common law and exemptions allowed by statute. State lands used for public purposes and lands occupied by state servants in the discharge of their duties are not liable to rating. This exemption follows from the rule that the state cannot be affected by a statute unless by special enactment. The rule does not cover quasi-state property such as that of the Electricity Supply Board. Such exemption as that Board enjoys (confined to works for generation, transmission and distribution of electricity) has been the subject of special legislation (Electricity Supply (Amendment) Act, 1930). Although state property is not rateable the practice has been, since 1874, for the government to pay a contribution, formerly called a bounty, in lieu of rates.

The second kind of exemption, that given by statute, comprises property of a public nature, churches and other places of religious worship, schools for the poor, burial grounds, lighthouses, beacons and buoys (Merchant

Shipping Act, 1894), infirmaries, hospitals and other buildings used for charitable purposes, premises used for the purposes of science, literature and the fine arts (Scientific Societies Act, 1843). Mines are not deemed to be rateable until seven years after they have been opened. Oil wells (if we had any) would be exempt for twenty years from the time of first extraction (Petroleum and Other Minerals Development Act, 1960). Farm buildings and improvements thereto are now fully exempt. Fisheries were relieved of local rates by the Fisheries Act, 1925 when they became liable to special rates imposed by boards of conservators. Dwellings, secondary schools and community halls were relieved of rates in 1978. Besides exemptions there are also provisions for remission of rates in certain cases which are referred to below.

The occupiers of certain classes of property are relieved of some of the burden of the rates. The farmer gets partial relief from rates on his land. The relief comes out of a government grant, the Agricultural Grant, particulars of which will be found below under the heading 'Grants'. In the boroughs and urban districts special treatment is given to arable land, pasture ground, market gardens, canals and land used for railways. The rate is levied only on a fraction of the valuation in these cases. The law prescribes different fractions according to the area and the class of property. This differential rating is justified on the ground that all kinds of property do not benefit equally from expenditure out of rates, particularly from expenditure on sanitary services (Local Government Act, 1946).

To encourage building projects, a remission for seven years of two-thirds of the rates on the increased valuation of new premises or premises enlarged or improved was formerly granted but this relief was phased out by the Local Government (Temporary Reduction of Valuation) Act, 1970. Rates remission on new and improved houses ceased to have effect, with the derating of domestic property, but the following may still be relevant to the calculation of the Exchequer grant which replaced domestic rates:

1. remissions up to ten years for new and improved houses under the Housing Acts, 1966 to 1970;
2. remissions up to twenty years for new houses, hostels or chalets under the Housing (Gaeltacht) Acts;
3. remissions up to ten years for improved Gaeltacht houses.

A rating authority may remit two-thirds of the rates for a period up to ten years on premises certified to have been provided for an industrial undertaking in an undeveloped area, as defined in the Undeveloped Areas Act, 1952. Such remissions may be cancelled under an amending Act of 1957. Factories built by, or with the aid of Gaeltarra Éireann, are eligible for similar relief. Industrial remissions are now given under the Industrial Development Act, 1972, section 3.

Valuation

The valuation of rateable property is carried out by the Commissioner of Valuation, who is head of the Valuation Office, a government office under the general control of the Minister for Finance. Local authorities levying rates have lists containing a description of the rateable property in their area, its annual value, and the names of the occupiers and immediate lessors. These lists are revised annually.

The procedure in connection with the annual revision begins with the rate collectors making out lists of properties requiring revision. Any rate-payer can propose a revision in a particular case. The lists are sent in due course to the Valuation Office with the opinion of the manager for the rating authority whether such revision is necessary, and officers are sent to the districts to examine the properties. On the reports of these officers the valuation lists are revised wherever necessary and are sent to the rating authorities before September every year. The lists are open to inspection and anyone aggrieved has twenty-eight days to appeal to the Commissioner who can alter the valuation. If the rates have been paid on a valuation subsequently altered, the amount can be adjusted. If a person still feels aggrieved with the valuation he can appeal to the Circuit Court and thence, if still dissatisfied, to the High Court. Generally speaking, the valuation of land cannot be altered.

This annual revision has failed to keep valuations in general up-to-date, because the Commissioner can only deal with property reported to him for revision. Provision was made by the Valuation (Ireland) Act, 1852, for a general revision every fourteen years on application of the grand jury, but no grand jury or county council, to whom the power to make application passed, has ever sought to exercise it.

Under the Local Government Act, 1898 the corporation of a county borough could ask to be revalued and the Corporations of Dublin and Waterford had revaluations made, the former in 1913 and the latter in 1926 on the basis of 1913 money values. Between 1946 and 1950 general revisions were carried out at the request of the local authorities, in Galway borough, Ballinasloe urban district and certain towns in the county health district. In 1950, Buncrana Urban District Council requested the Commissioner of Valuation to revise all valuations in the urban district. Revision resulted in an increase of over fifty per cent in aggregate valuations, with a consequent greatly increased liability to county-at-large charges. An attempt to restore the balance was made in the Local Government (Temporary Reduction of Valuation) Act, 1960.

In the absence of general revisions, apart from those cited above, it became necessary for the Commissioner of Valuation to deal with the individual cases coming before him each year (about 3 per cent of total properties) with due regard to the general level of valuations in the area. For some years following the repeal in 1946 of the Increase in Mortgage

Interest (Restrictions) Act, 1923, a rule of thumb was used by the Valuation Office which gave new and revised valuations broadly in line with the general run of figures for similar properties in the areas involved. The formula was based on various fractions of current rental and capital values. With, however, the onset of inflation from the mid-sixties producing sharp increases in rents and purchase costs, the Valuation Office was obliged to resort to pragmatic adjustments in real and notional rents of premises with the object of preserving due relativity between properties and, thus, an equitable spread of tax.

Early Valuations

The first of the general valuations for rating including houses was made under an Act of 1826; before then the only rateable property was land (with a few minor exceptions). Under this Act land was valued by reference to the general average prices for farm products and houses at two-thirds of the rent, but the valuations under the Act were made by townlands, not by separate tenements. This townland valuation did not meet the requirements of the Poor Relief Act of 1838; consequently the boards of guardians constituted under that Act were empowered to make a valuation based on the net annual value of every tenement. The valuations made by the guardians were much below the letting value of the land and as between poor law unions were by no means uniform.

When the townland valuation had been completed (except in six counties and four cities) a general tenement valuation was commenced under an Act of 1846. For a time there were two different valuations, one for county cess and the other for poor rate. This divergence was brought to an end by the Valuation (Ireland) Act of 1852, which is still in force. Under this Act one valuation was to be used for all assessments. This valuation was generally known as Griffith's valuation; it was carried out by Sir Richard Griffith, Commissioner in the Valuation Office from 1828 to 1868. It was completed in 1865 at a cost of over £300,000 (about £15 million at the present day). In Griffith's valuation a distinction was drawn between land and other property. Land was valued by an estimate of the net value with reference to a scale of prices for farm products laid down in the Act, and to all local circumstances affecting the particular piece of land assuming the tenant paid all the rates, taxes and public charges.

The valuation of houses and other buildings was made by an estimate of the rent for which, taking one year with another, the property might in its actual state be reasonably expected to be let from year to year, the probable average cost of repairs, insurance and other expenses necessary to maintain the property in its actual state and all rates, taxes and public charges being paid by the tenant. How other property is to be valued was not specifically stated but the same principles are followed as in the case of houses.

In 1931 special provision was made by statute for the railways: Railways

(Valuation for Rating) Act, 1931. Every five years the Commissioner revises the valuation of railway undertakings. The valuation is an estimate, by reference to the net receipts, of the rent, making the usual deductions, at which the undertakings might reasonably be expected to let. A minimum valuation is also made. This is the valuation of the property if it had not been adapted for use as a railway. If the valuation by way of the net rent is less than the minimum valuation then the valuation is fixed at the minimum valuation. Railway lines, in practice are valued at the minimum or land figure; normal values are given to station premises and other buildings.

At least one serious attempt was made in the 1930s to reform the valuation system. A Valuation Bill was introduced by the Minister for Finance in December 1938, with the aim of bringing the valuations of buildings and certain other properties up to date: agricultural land was not to be touched. The Bill met with so much opposition that, after surviving a second reading, it was quietly dropped. The Inter-Departmental Committee on Local Finance and Taxation, in its first Report (1966) recommended a renewed attack on the general revaluation of property, other than land. The Government, while agreeing (White Paper, 1972) proposed transferring the Valuation Office to the Minister for Local Government, who would then undertake measures of practical reform of the valuation system.

Rates and Rating

The rating system as it exists in Ireland is derived from the system that operated in England. The basis of the English rating system was the Poor Relief Act of 1601. Under that Act parish overseers were directed to raise the money they required for poor relief according to the ability of the inhabitants of the parish. In the seventeenth century it would have been a matter of great difficulty to rate personal property as well as real property and the practice was established of rating only real property, and disregarding stock-in-trade. This custom was not recognised by statute until 1840. Thus it happened that the poor rate which was at first intended to be of the nature of a local income tax became a tax on the use of a particular class of property.

The name rate derives from the fact that the expenses to be met are raised rateably, that is proportionately, according to the value of the property in respect of which it is assessed. The person liable for a rate is as a rule the occupier of the rateable property or in his default the subsequent occupier. An occupier is defined as the person who is in immediate use or enjoyment of the property. To this general rule there were a number of exceptions, e.g. a house let in separate apartments or lodgings but the only one which survived the abolition of domestic rate seems to be premises not occupied when the rate is made.

Before the poor rate was introduced in 1838 there was a county rate called grand jury cess levied by the grand juries. This cess was a charge on land or premises, unlike the poor rate which was a personal tax. Except in the case of holdings of £4 or under it was payable by the occupier, who in the case of tenancies created after 1870, had certain rights of deduction from the rate. At first the cess appears to have been assessed according to the area of land occupied, as shown in surveys made from the middle of the seventeenth century. To overcome the difficulties caused by inequalities in the value of land, allowance was made for poor land by entering a reduced number of acres on the list. It was not until the first government valuation for rating in 1826 that houses were included for assessment. The proceeds of the cess were applied towards the construction and repair of roads and to meeting expenses in connection with courthouses, lunatic asylums, county infirmaries, county fever hospitals, contributions to industrial and reformatory schools, the cost of extra police and some other purposes.

The Local Government Act of 1898, by abolishing grand jury cess and transferring the charges on that rate to the poor rate, reduced the rates in the county to one, the poor rate, which in 1946 was given the name county rate. In the period 1930–46 rates in cities and towns were consolidated. The reduction of the numerous separate rates in county boroughs and the borough of Dun Laoghaire was effected by the Acts relating to city management and in urban districts by the Local Government Act, 1946, which also abolished the town rate in towns that were not urban districts. The rates which have disappeared in towns include the borough rate, the public libraries rate and water rates together with a number of rates authorized under local Acts under such names as general purposes rate, improvement rate, harbour rate. Rates are not now made for a particular service but to meet the deficiency arising in the fund out of which all the expenses of the local authority are met. The rates abolished in towns had not all the same incidence and consequently provision was made for assessing the municipal rate on a fraction of the valuation of some herediments, including agricultural land, canals and railways.

Rates are levied by rating authorities in respect of fixed property of the kinds described above. There are now two rates, the *county rate* levied by county councils in the area of the county which is not included in any urban districts and the *municipal rate* in boroughs and urban districts. A charge for water supplied for other than domestic purposes or under contract to a person not otherwise entitled to such supply is in some towns called the *contract water rate* but this is not a rate in the true sense.

Owners (the persons entitled to occupy) are responsible for rates on vacant premises, but liability may be reduced in certain circumstances. Part or all the rates paid may be reclaimed if the owner can show that he has tried unsuccessfully to get a tenant at a reasonable rent. Recovery is limited to half the yearly rate in the county boroughs of Dublin, Cork and Limerick (City Management Acts: and Local Government Act, 1946, s. 23).

How Rates are Made

Local authorities empowered to levy rates are county councils, corporations of county boroughs and non-county boroughs and the councils of urban districts. Commissioners of a town which is not an urban district do not levy rates; they obtain funds from the county council who recoup themselves by levying an addition to the county rate on the town. Subsidiary bodies, such as vocational educational committees and the county committees of agriculture are not rating authorities. They obtain funds from the rating authorities by way of estimate and demand.

The Exchequer and Local Financial Years Act, 1974 changed the national and local financial years from April-March to the calendar year. Enactments were adapted to bring the local budgetary and accounting cycle into conformity with the new arrangement. The change was determined by the adoption of EEC standards. Subsidiary bodies now prepare their estimates and demands in the month of February for the local financial year beginning on 1 January. The estimate when adopted is sent to the rating authority concerned. County councils prepare their estimates between 1 February and 16 March, and councils of urban districts and non-county boroughs between 1 February and 31 March.

Under the City and County Management (Amendment) Act, 1955, the manager arranges for the estimate for a county council to be prepared showing the amount which will be required for each service in the following financial year. The council can, but rarely does, appoint an estimates committee (1955 Act s. 7) to assist the manager in this task. The estimate is submitted to the council for their consideration at a special meeting called the estimates meeting at which the manager must be present. The estimate must be open to public inspection at the county council office. It is considered at the estimates meeting. At least seven days before the meeting a copy of it must be sent to every member. When the estimate is adopted (deliberations, if adjourned, may not take more than twenty-one days) the council proceeds to determine the resulting rate in the pound. This is done by resolution (City and County Management (Amendment) Act, 1955, ss. 9, 10). Both the preparation and consideration of the annual estimates have been seriously affected by the intervention of the Ministers for the Environment and Finance in the process under the Local Government (Financial Provisions) Act 1978. Directions under this Act have hitherto taken the form of specifying upper limits to increases in rates.

The demands on the urban district councils for their share of the expenses are prepared and the applotment of rates in the rate book can then be put in hand. The Local Government Act, 1955 altered the basis of these demands from the relative gross valuations in urban district and county, to the relative product of a penny rate in each area. The City and County Management (Amendment) Act, 1955 has assimilated estimates procedure for other rating authorities to that for county councils.

Rate Book

The rate book is based on the valuation list which comes to hand on 1 December. It shows the assessments on the persons liable and the reliefs, if any, to which the ratepayer is entitled by reduction of the valuation, abatement of rates on agricultural land, or whatever. The book is open for inspection for fourteen days after the applotment is finished. Public notice has to be given that it is available. The Secretary certifies that it is in conformity with the valuations in force. Under the ancient procedure he submitted the certificate at a special meeting of the council and the rate was made at this meeting by affixing the seal of the council, the chairman, two members and the secretary signing the book.

The second 'rates' meeting at which the rate is formally 'made' by the elected members has been dispensed with under the Act of 1978. Procedure has been simplified by making this formal endorsement of the substantive 'estimates' decision an executive function, performable by the manager. The warrants authorising the collectors to collect the rates are then sealed and signed and public notice is given that the rate has been made. In towns the town clerk has the secretary's duty. It may happen that the rate book contains errors: changes in occupation which had taken place after the valuation list was made up and before the rate was made may not have been noted; houses that were occupied may have become vacant; the property shown in the valuation list as in the occupation of one person may have been divided among several; the amount of rates may have been incorrectly computed. Provision is made to meet contingencies of this kind. The manager may correct errors. Where property has been divided it can be provisionally valued pending a final valuation. The person affected by any amendments must be notified of the changes and has the same right of appeal as he would have on the making of the rate (Local Government Act, 1941, ss. 61, 62; Local Government Act, 1946, s.46).

A ratepayer aggrieved by the rate or having material objection to any person being included or excluded or material objection to the sum charged on any person may appeal against the rate to the Circuit Court within four calendar months. An appeal to the same Court may be made if the rate is illegal, or the rate may be brought up to the High Court to be quashed. If a rate is bad on the face of it, if the person was not in occupation, if the property is not in the rating area or is entitled to a statutory exemption, objection can be raised at the time the rate collector or rating authority sues for the rate (Street, pp 1321–2).

The 'ratepayer's' right to object in this and other cases (development plans, change of names of streets, localities etc.,) has not been affected by the abolition of domestic rates: Local Government (Financial Provisions) Act, 1978, s.17.

Collection of Rates

The rate for the year is collected in moieties or halves, the first due after the rate is made and the second on 1 July. A system of rate-paying by instalments was introduced for householders and farmers by the Local Government (Rates) Act, 1970, but has become, of course, largely unnecessary following the de-rating of domestic properties. The same fate has overtaken the rates waiver schemes operated under that Act.

For the purpose of collecting rates the area may be divided into districts with a rate collector for each. Collection from county council headquarters by a single collector is exceptional. Collection through the post office was tried in some rural areas but abandoned. The collector in addition to his warrant gets collecting books of demand notes and receipt forms. He has also an interim receipt book to be used where less than a full moiety of the rates is paid. The collector and the rating authorities have extensive powers to recover if the ratepayer fails to pay. The collector may on refusal to pay after demand, distrain and sell goods of the person refusing. He may give a six-days' notice demanding payment and, if there is still failure, summon the defaulter before the District Justice who may order payment and costs. If the order is not obeyed the justice may issue a distress warrant. The collector may proceed by civil bill in the Circuit Court up to any amount (Street, pp 1336–9). The collector has to lodge the rates collected at frequent intervals. After the close of the financial year on 31 December if he has not collected all the rates, he presents a statement of the arrears showing at the same time why he has not been able to collect them. Irrecoverable rates are struck off and temporarily uncollectable rates are carried forward to the following year unless the delay is due to the collector, when he may be directed to lodge the amount.

Criticisms of the Rating System

The rating system has been criticised on many grounds. Briefly, these are that the ratepayer is made pay for services which are national in character and should therefore be charges on the taxpayer; that poor areas have a heavier burden than rich areas: they require the same services but their ability to pay is less; that industry is penalized and trade handicapped by raising valuation on account of improvements; that persons in possession of non-rateable property are placed in a better position than those such as farmers, who require to have a relatively large amount of property; that rates are assessed wholly on occupiers although expenditure on roads, sewers and water goes to increasing the value of the property; and that local authorities have insufficient scope by being confined to one tax.

Some of these complaints have been met by changes in the relationship between taxpayer and ratepayer. The occupier of agricultural land, for instance, has had a large and increasing amount of relief granted in order to diminish the burden of rates, the increased cost of the health services and housing was largely and is now wholly met by government grants. The assumption by the state of the cost of unemployment assistance, with only a relatively small contribution from the larger urban authorities, and the introduction of widows' and orphans' pensions and supplementary benefits have transferred the bulk of former public assistance charges from the rates to the Exchequer. Health and housing charges followed in 1973–77. Finally, the de-rating of dwellings and certain other properties has removed the sharpest cause of resentment against the rating system.

Complaints about rates are as old as rating itself, and a number of suggestions and remedies have been put forward from time to time. Differential rating – modifying the rates charge on various kinds and sizes of properties in something like the way in which income tax is scaled – has been suggested, but was never taken up. A form of differential rating was however applied to the consolidated municipal rates created by the City Management Acts, and the Local Government Act, 1946 (s. 21 and Second Schedule). Another idea, recently revived, is that a rate on annual value should be replaced by a rate on site value. This was examined by the Royal Commission on Local Taxation (1902) which rejected it by a majority. Five of the Commissioners were of opinion that in urban areas site and structure ought to be valued separately and that the site when separated from the structure was capable of bearing somewhat heavier taxation. They proposed a special site value rate payable by means of deduction from the rent, thus putting part of the rate on whoever had superior interests to the interests of the occupier. This special site value rate would also be levied in respect of unoccupied property. The five Commissioners did not think the amount that could be raised in this way would be large. One of the benefits that the Commissioners saw was that an actual site value tax would show there was no large undeveloped source of taxation for local purposes.

In 1914 a departmental committee on local taxation again considered the rating of land values and were divided in their recommendations. A majority was against the proposal to substitute for the rating of annual values a system based *wholly* on the taxation of land values. They were of opinion that the present system conformed more closely to the principle of distributing the burden according to the ability to pay than the proposed system and that rating of land values would increase congestion of buildings. At that time the taxation of site values under the Finance Act, 1910 had begun and this was regarded as a more equitable method of taxation than imposing a rate. These state taxes were abolished in 1920. A minority on the committee was, however, in favour of ascertaining site values separately and putting a special rate on them which would go to relieve rates on buildings and improvements. Occupiers would pay the site value rate but deduct it from the rent. It was not intended that the site value rate would be an additional source of revenue. It was to be in lieu of portion of the annual value rate. The effect of the levy of a general rate on site value in cities and urban districts would be to shift some of the burden of rates from the occupiers of property on the outskirts to those having interests in property in the central districts.

Taxation of land values made a brief reappearance in Britain between 1931 and 1934, and there were sporadic attempts to bring in site rating as a replacement or supplement to the traditional rates system. The Simes Committee (1952) recommended against, and a study group set up by the RIPA 'New Sources of Local Revenue' (1950) followed suit. The demerits of the scheme were that its administrative difficulties, as they saw them, outweighed the relatively insignificant yield of the tax. Rating of site values was also examined at some length, and rejected, by the Inter-Departmental Committee on Local Finance and Taxation (Third Report, 1968). Their objections may be summarised:

1. owners of land are not obliged, and may not be able, to realise its full potential profit;

2. the future value of land, on the basis of full permitted development, cannot be determined with certainty for tax purposes;

3. adoption as a supplement to existing rates would produce two separate rating systems, based on different principles.

The ESRI Report No. 84 (Copeland and Walsh, 1975) took a more positive line, citing the operation of the system in a number of countries including New Zealand, Denmark, Canada, South Africa and the USA. 'The main benefit of site valuing is the penalty it imposes on a failure to put land to its most efficient use' (p. 90). The Inter-Departmental Committee's philosophical argument about an owner's right to withhold land from optimum development was all very well, but the economic as well as the social advantages, especially in urban conditions, of penalising derelict and under-used sites were compelling.

The Committee urged examination, by an expert body, of taking full account of site value as a factor in revaluation. Their suggestion was adopted in the White Paper on Local Finance and Taxation.

Grants and Subsidies

The state comes to the aid of the ratepayer in various ways: in the form of general grants in relief of rates, and by way of contributions towards the cost of specified services which are made out of grants provided annually by the Oireachtas. Grants were formerly made from special funds, but these have now disappeared and grants are paid directly from the Exchequer.

Government grants have a long and involved history. In the eighteenth century the Irish parliament made grants to hospitals in Dublin and to county infirmaries. Grants towards meeting poor law expenditure on medical and educational services began in 1868. In 1875 grants were first made towards the maintenance of patients in asylums. To assist sanitary authorities in the administration of the Public Health Act of 1878 grants were made towards the salaries of sanitary officers. Some details were given in the preceding Chapter of the creation and demise of the Local Taxation Account, through which were channelled a number of 'local' taxes such as estate and probate duties and certain licence duties, (liquor licences, game licences etc), together with a grant under the Purchase of Land Act, 1891, called the Exchequer Contribution.

Agricultural Grant

The largest grant going to local authorities out of the Local Taxation Account was the Agricultural Grant. This grant had its origin in the Local Government Act of 1898. Two years earlier the occupiers of agricultural land in England had been relieved of half the rates on land. To meet the deficiency thus caused in the revenue of the local authorities a fixed yearly grant was made, nominally from the proceeds of the Estate Duty. At the same time it was proposed that 9/80ths of the sum payable to English local authorities should be paid out of the proceeds of the same duty to the Irish Local Taxation Account. A sum calculated in this way would not have been sufficient to meet half the rates on land in Ireland. In 1898 a larger grant charged on the Consolidated Fund (now the Central Fund) was substituted. The first grant amounted to slightly less than £600,000 (for all Ireland £727,655) but has since been much increased.

The occupier of land in Ireland was not relieved of half the rates, although the amount of the grant was equal to half the rates in the standard year (1896–7). As a rule the occupier before 1898 bore the whole of the county cess and only half the poor rate, the other half being transferred to the landlord by means of a deduction from the rent. The Act of 1898 placed the whole of the new poor rate (in which the old poor rate and county cess were merged) on the occupier, who was deprived of any right of deducting any part of the rate from the rent. Thus the benefit of the grant to the occupier was in respect of the county cess only. The landlord got the benefit as regards half the old poor rate.

The arrangements of 1898 in regard to the grant remained undisturbed for more than a quarter of a century. In 1925 a series of changes began which altered the grant in amount, in the method of allocating it to county councils and in applying it to the relief of rates. The question of large-scale relief of rates on agricultural land, industry, railways etc. was examined by the De-Rating Commission of 1929. The majority report recommended against de-rating agricultural land, factories, railways and canals. Nor did it favour the transfer of major services from local authorities to the state. The majority stood firmly for the status quo between central and local government. Any concession to demands for lessening local burdens would lead to the gradual but inevitable decay of local patriotism and enterprise which 'could not fail to have far-reaching effects on the social and political life of the country' (para. 69).

Table 1: Agricultural Grant

Allowances	Primary	Employment	Supplementary
1939	On holdings up to £20 valuation	On holdings over £20 valuation	On holdings over £20 valuation
1946	Three fifths of general rate	50p in each £ of valuation over £20 to a maximum of £6.50 for each male worker	One fifth of general rate
1953	Three fifths of general rate	£17 for each male worker, total not to exceed rates on land over £20	Suspended
1962	Seventy percent general rate	As 1953	One fourth of general rate
1964	Eighty percent of general rate	As 1953	Thirty percent of general rate
1967	One hundred percent-total de-rating-of rates on first £20 of holdings under £33 valuation. Eighty percent on first £20 of holdings over £33	As 1953	Thirty percent of general rate on portion over £20 of holdings of £33 and over
1976	As 1967	Discontinued	As 1967
1978	As 1976 but no relief for holdings over income tax threshold (£75 in 1978 and £60 in 1979)		
1980	As 1978: ceiling of entitlement to relief lowered to £40 (see note)		

Note: In 1980 further relief amounting to 50 per cent of rates payable was granted in the case of holdings between £40 and £50 valuation. This has not yet (September, 1981) been validated by legislation.

Originally there was a flat rate of relief for every rated occupier of agricultural land proportionate to valuation. In 1932 for the first time a differential system was introduced in favour of occupiers of low valuation. The legal basis of the grant at present is the Rates on Agricultural Land (Relief) Act, 1939 which provides for relief by way of three allowances, a *primary allowance* on valuations up to £20 and the first £20 of higher valuations, an *employment allowance* for men at work on the land which goes only to occupiers of land over £20 in valuation and a *supplementary allowance* on the valuation above £20. In 1946 the primary allowance was fixed at three-fifths of the general rate, the supplementary allowance at one-fifth and the employment allowance of ten shillings (50p) in the pound on the part of the valuation above £20 but not exceeding £6.10s.0d. (£6.50) for each man at work. Many modifications of the 1939 scheme have since been introduced (see Table 1).

During the period 1967–77 the Agricultural Grant rose very substantially but since then has tended to decline.

Table 2: Agricultural Grant

Year	£m
1975	30,091
1976	36,231
1977	40,732
1978	38,341
1979	39,800
1980	43,725

The Employment Allowance was discontinued after 1975. As announced in the 1978 budget, farmers with valuations over £75 became ineligible for rates relief. The upper limit was reduced to £60 in 1979, and to £40 in 1980.

Towards the close of 1980 there were signs of a change of attitude to the Agricultural Grant, when the government notified county councils that the second moiety of rates for that year should be remitted in the case of farmers who had suffered from the reduction of the ceiling from £60 to £40 valuation. Further remissions were announced in the 1981 Budget and embodied in the Rates on Agricultural Land (Relief) Bill, 1981, which lapsed, after a brief appearance in the Dáil, with the General Election of June of that year. Among the bill's objectives were:

1. total de-rating of holdings below £50 valuation; and 50 per cent relief for holdings valued between £50 and £70.
2. extension of reliefs to land in urban areas.

3. inclusion of separate charges, such as special rates for malicious injuries, in the scheme of relief.

Full rates would be payable on holdings over £70 valuation. Under the Finance Act, 1978, rates on farm land could be set off against any liability to income tax.

The 1981 Bill would have fully de-rated 94 per cent of all holdings and given partial relief to a further 3 per cent. The Agricultural Grant would have risen to £62 million. During the parliamentary debate the point inevitably came up that total derating of all farm land was the obvious next step — small for government, a giant stride for the farming community. The new administration which took over towards the end of June 1981, have in fact included in their *Programme for Government 1981 - 1986* following this passage: 'Agricultural rates will be abolished on all full time farmers who draw up an agreed 5-year expansion programme with their ACOT adviser or other authorised agency.'

Guarantee Fund

Two of the grants mentioned, the Agricultural Grant and the Exchequer Contribution, were paid first into a fund called the Guarantee Fund, created in 1891 in order to meet any deficiencies that might arise from failure of tenant purchasers to pay land purchase annuities. The Agricultural Grant is still so paid. Arrears of repayments under the Land Reclamantion Act, 1949 are also brought into account. The Guarantee Fund is cleared once a year and every county is debited with arrears accrued and credited with the amount recovered in respect of old arrears. Any cash standing to the credit of the Fund, except what is required to meet the arrears, is paid to the local authorities. Thus it may happen that the agricultural grant paid to a county is less than the amount of the full grant. The occupiers of agricultural land do not get less rate relief on that account. The deficiency has to be made good out of the county fund. If in future years the arrears of annuities etc. are paid an equivalent amount is released from the Guarantee Fund and ultimately goes to the credit of the county fund.

Domestic Rates Relief

A new grant analogous to the Agricultural Grant was introduced in 1977. It was a grant in relief of rates on domestic property — houses, flats and dwellings generally. Relief of 25 per cent was given in 1977, a further 25 per cent intended for 1978, until the domestic rate was eventually phased out. The mid-1977 change of government led however to the total abolition of domestic rates from January 1978. Secondary schools, community halls and farm buildings were also de-rated. The new grant 'in relief of rates on domestic and certain other hereditaments' amounted to about £81 million in 1978 and £92 million in 1979.

Government and diplomatic properties

The state makes an annual *ex gratia* payment (formerly known as bounty-in-lieu) to rating authorities, equivalent to the amounts which would have been payable on offices and other government property if occupied by non-exempt owners or tenants. The state also contributes towards rates on premises occupied by diplomatic missions of external governments. The total due in 1979 was £4.7 million. Embassies are exempt, by convention, from national and local taxes, and are thus rate-free, or largely so. They pay, in accordance with international practice, those portions of rates attributable to 'beneficial' services such as water supply, domestic refuse collection etc.: service charges, rather than taxes in the strict sense. The balance is paid by the Exchequer.

Grants for roads, road safety etc.

The winding-up of the Road Fund was announced in the 1978 budget statement. State support for road improvement and up-keep is now a direct charge on the Exchequer. Estimates provision in 1978 for road works, road safety and related services was £35m; the figure for 1979 was £43m. Some account of the Road Fund will be found in Chapter 17. Grants amounting in the aggregate to over £0.5 million are made to the National Road Safety Association, the Medical Bureau of Road Safety and for signposting on the national roads network.

Housing Subsidies

Some account has been given in the preceding Chapter of the transfer of housing charges from local rates to the state. Aggregate subsidies (central taxation and rates) to local authority tenants have risen sharply in recent years — from £20m in 1974 to £45m in 1978. The estimates provision for 1979 was £55m. This sum includes subsidy of $33\frac{1}{3}$ per cent of loan charges on sites for private building and an annual grant to the National Association of Building Cooperatives.

Water Supply and Sewerage Subsidies

These subsidies, in the form of state contributions towards the repayment of loans raised by local authorities, amounted to £8.7m in 1978 and something over £10m in 1979. Swimming pools and sanitary conveniences are also subsidised from this source. Average contributions amount in total to some 53 per cent of loan charges.

Environmental Improvement Schemes

Grants for environmental improvement were introduced in 1977 as part of the government's job creation programme, with emphasis on employment for young people. The grants were designed to cover the full cost of works undertaken by local authorities. The project is now being phased out: £3.1m was provided in 1978; the amount for 1979 was £1.7m.

Local improvement grants provided by Department of the Environment are a continuation of the aid formerly given by the Special Employment Schemes Office under the Commissioners of Public Works. The grants are paid towards the cost of accommodation and bog roads, drains etc. A sum of £2.75m was provided in 1979; Local Government (Roads and Drainage) Act, 1968.

Gaeltacht. Roinn na Gaeltachta gives grants to certain county councils for the improvement of services in Gaeltacht areas: £275,000 was spent on roads, £155,000 on water and sewerage, £275,000 on marine works. The total provision for 1979 was thus £0.705m.

Motor Licensing and Registration. Recompense formerly paid from the Road Fund, is now made from the Exchequer to county councils and county borough corporations to meet the expenses of licensing and registering mechanically propelled vehicles and the issue of drivers' licences. Provision of £1.6m made for 1979.

Libraries. Grants for the improvement of local library services are channelled through An Chomhairle Leabharlanna. The total for 1979 was £0.27m, a figure which also covers the expenses of An Chomhairle. The grant meets 50 per cent of the cost of repaying loans borrowed for library purposes.

Malicious Injuries. State aid is now forthcoming to local authorities against whom compensation awards are given in cases arising from the disturbances in Northern Ireland, and other cases. The state recoups 100 per cent of local charges arising from the Northern troubles. In other cases recoupment covers amounts in excess of a rate of 20p in the pound in any rating area. The amounts payable have diminished in recent years. The provision for 1979 was £0.5m.

Other Grants

Other state grants to local authorities include: **1979**
                                                                      £m
Recoupment to county and county borough councils
of 50% of cost of preparing Register of Electors
Electoral Act, 1963, s. 7   0.26

Grants for rehabilitation of itinerants: 100 per cent of housing charges; 60 per cent of cost of caravans and 90 per cent of expenses of social workers	0.46
Grants to maritime local authorities and harbours for anti-oil pollution measures	0.08
Local schemes to encourage apprentice employment in construction industry	0.01
Grants to Regional Development Organisations and to local planning authorities	0.04
Grants to county borough corporations etc for school meals	0.52
Grants to local authorities for fuel schemes	1.52
Grants to Public Assistance Authorities for footwear schemes	0.02
Recoupment to local authorities of expenditure on Higher Education Grants	3.09
Subsidy to local authorities of 50 per cent of loan charges for vocational schools: Vocational Education Act, 1930, s. 51	0.42
Recoupment to local authorities of 50 per cent of pensions and gratuities of officers and servants of Vocational Education Committees	1.02
Compensation to local authorities for de-rating of fisheries: Fisheries Consolidation Act, 1959, s. 55.	0.21
Grants to local authorities for civil defence	0.51

A grant-in-aid of £1 million was voted for the Dublin Inner City Group Fund in 1980.

Department of Agriculture gives grants to county councils for the construction of sheep dipping baths. The amount provided for 1979 was £12,000. Grants for allotments are still made to local authorities under the Acquisition of Land (Allotments) Act, 1934, but the provision for 1979 was a mere £500.

Grants in support of local administration

A number of grants, not made directly to local authorities, operate to sustain the system of local and regional administration. Certain of them are of major significance. Grants to and on behalf of Regional Health Boards, for example, exceed in amount the sum of state grants to local authorities.

		1979
		£m
Grants to and on behalf of Health Boards		431.00
Grants to Vocational Education Committees		49.00
Capital grants to Harbour Authorities		4.30
Grants to County Committees of Agriculture		4.60
Expenses of County Development Teams		0.13
Grant to An Bord Pleanala		0.15
Grants to promotional and advisory bodies:		
	£	
Irish Water Safety Association	34,000	
Fire Prevention Council	30,000	
Water Pollution Advisory Council	20,000	
UN Environment Fund	13,000	.097

Grants totalling £60,000 were provided by the Minister for the Environment in 1979 for cats' and dogs' homes.

Arterial Drainage and Coast Protection. These works involve, paradoxically, local authority aid to two state services. Capital outlay on arterial drainage projects is met by the Commissioners of Public Works, with costs of maintenance charged on county councils. Much the same arrangements apply to coast protection works. In 1979 the amount recoverable from county councils was £1.89 million.

Income from Local Services

The third major source of revenue available to local authorities is the service charge, whose number and variety elevate their significance to a point not now far below rates as a money earner. They amount in the aggregate to £80 million (1979). Of this sum more than two thirds consist of house rents, loan repayments and a proportion of the proceeds of sales of homes. Next in earning ability were charges for water supply and sewerage and after them a long list headed by receipts from driving licences and parking meters and comprising burial ground fees, tolls for markets, abattoirs and weighbridges. Also included are income from libraries and museums, rents for allotments, harbour dues and charges for swimming pools, public conveniences, pounds and sheep dipping baths. Some income is derived from fire brigades, but it is mainly from other local authorities for agency work. Numerous licences and certificates carry charges, usually at controlled and very modest rates, but adding up to an appreciable amount.

A growing item is sales of developed sites for private building, but the most important source of cash, from a potential viewpoint, is development charges leviable from developers under the Local Government (Planning and Development) Act, 1963, s. 26. This provision should enable local authorities to recoup themselves for some part of the heavy public outlay on roads, water mains, sewers etc. which opens land to further development by speculative builders.

Despite rejection of the idea by the Inter-Departmental Committee on Local Finance and Taxation (Third Report, 1968) the Oireachtas has authorised the construction of toll bridges and roads and these may in due course prove a valuable source of additional revenue. The White Paper on Local Finance and Taxation (1972) contained a proposal, not yet implemented, to confer on local authorities a general power to charge for services, undertake trading services ancillary to their normal functions and review rates of charge at regular intervals.

Capital Expenditure

Most local authorities, particularly housing and sanitary authorities, have from time to time to undertake schemes, execute permanent works and purchase land, buildings or expensive equipment. Expenditure of this nature comes under the head of capital expenditure and is, as a rule, met by loans to be repaid with interest over a number of years. Whilst borrowing makes it possible to carry out large scale works which could not be financed out of current revenue it adds to the cost of these works; where repayment is spread over a long period the addition of interest may add considerably to the total cost.

Not all capital expenditure is met by borrowing. The heavy expenditure incurred in the early post-war years in building hospitals was for the most part met out of the Hospitals Trust Fund. For some years it was the practice to give state assistance out of money earmarked for employment schemes by way of a proportion of the capital cost of water supply and sewerage works. This practice was altered and state assistance now takes the form of recouping a portion of the loan repayment charges, which is the method of giving assistance in the case of housing loans.

Borrowing Powers

Before a local authority can borrow it must have the power to do so. This power was usually derived from particular statutes. County councils and county borough corporations had a general power (Application of Enactments Order, 1898, Art. 22) to borrow for capital purposes, including the consolidation of their debts on capital account, but this power was not extensively used. In practice these authorities availed themselves of particular powers given for specific purposes. Borough corporations could borrow on the security of their corporate property (Municipal Corporations Mortgages Act, 1860). In general, it may be said that when a local authority was authorized to do anything the cost of which ought to be spread over a number of years there was power to borrow. Commissioners of towns not urban districts had such power, but since the abolition of the town rate in 1946 they had no rate on which the loans could be secured. The commissioners could get loans from county councils who were authorized to borrow for the purpose of relending to them.

The Local Government (No. 2) Act, 1960 has substituted a single general power of borrowing for the multitude of specific statutory provisions which were previously operative. A general power to lend to other local authorities has also been conferred on local authorities. Local authorities were authorized by the Public Health Acts Amendment Act, 1890 and by Art. 22 of the Application of Enactment Order, 1898 to raise money for capital schemes by the creation and issue of stock. Such issues are subject to regulations governing the payment of the dividends, the redemption fund, the application of the money and other matters. The raising of loans in this way was practically confined to the larger urban authorities and even these have not resorted to stock issues for a number of years past; most local authorities borrow either from the Local Loans Fund under the control of the Minister for Finance, or in the case of small loans for short terms, from the banks. Occasionally loans have been obtained from insurance companies, trade unions, societies and even individuals. The security on which local authorities borrow is usually the fund out of which they are authorized to defray their expenses or all their revenues and in the case of a rating authority the rates.

Borrowing is controlled by being made subject to the sanction of the central authority. In applying for sanction the local authority submits details of the proposed work. The Minister has professional and technical staff who examine the proposals. If there is no technical objection and the Minister is satisfied that the project is one for which borrowing should be permitted, that the local authority has power to borrow for the purpose and the ability to repay, sanction is given. By this the Minister does not assume any responsibility for the plans or schemes put forward. If the loan is sought from the Local Loans Fund the Minister will recommend the issue from the Fund.

Local Loans Fund

The Local Loans Fund in its present form was established by an Act of 1935. The Minister for Finance has assigned the management of the Fund to the Commissioners of Public Works. He borrows on behalf of the Fund or makes advances out of the Central Fund. If a local authority fails to make repayments within thirty-one days of their falling due, penal interest may be charged on the unpaid sum. If necessary recovery of sums due to the Fund can be effected by deduction from any grant or other money payable by a Department to the local authority.

The period for which loans are made varies according to the purpose for which the money is borrowed. Maximum periods of repayments were fixed in the statutes but loans are not necessarily advanced for the full period. Loans for housing and major water and sewerage schemes were made for periods of fifty years but the terms have been shortened to thirty-five years for new loans.

Various limits were formerly placed on the amount an authority might borrow. These limits were fixed in relation to the annual value of the premises assessable within the county, city, town or other district. Borrowing by sanitary authorities under the Local Government (Sanitary Services) Acts was limited to twice the net valuation, by county councils to one-tenth and by public assistance authorities to one-fourth. These limits were partly nullified by numerous exceptions to which they did not apply. Loans for housing, courthouses, bridges and vocational schools were excluded from the limit that would otherwise apply. All remaining statutory limits that would otherwise apply were removed by the Local Government (No. 2) Act, 1960.

When a loan has been sanctioned and before the formalities have been completed temporary borrowing from a bank is sometimes resorted to in order to obtain money for work that has been commenced. These temporary loans are paid off out of the long term loan when it is issued.

Temporary borrowing which is not for capital purposes but in anticipation of current revenue is permitted. After the 1914—18 war there was much disturbance of local finances which was aggravated by trade depression. It was found necessary to authorise by statute temporary borrowing on current account. This was done by the Local Authorities (Financial Provision) Act of 1921 which also relaxed the limit of borrowing for employment schemes. This power was availed of by rating authorities that had not enough money during the early part of the financial year before the rates began to come in or whilst waiting for grants. An overdraft is obtained from the treasurer. The overdraft is paid off when the rates have been collected or the grants paid. This borrowing also requires the sanction of the Minister. The Local Authorities (Financial Provisions) Act, 1921 s. 3, was replaced by the Local Government Act, 1955 s. 42, which was in turn supplanted by the Act of 1960.

Funds and Accounts

Local authorities are required to keep proper accounts of their receipts and expenditure and to ensure so far as reasonably possible by means of internal check that this is carefully and punctually done. Registers of lands acquired, leased or mortgaged, charges on property and insurance must also be kept (Public Bodies Order, 1946, Art. 6 et seq.). County councils have a general fund called the county fund to which all receipts must go and from which all payments are made (Local Government Act 1946, s. 7). Where gifts have been received and placed in a voluntary civic improvement fund, this fund is kept separately from the general fund. Where special expenses are charged on areas less than a county or county health district ('separate charges') accounts must be kept in such a manner as will prevent the larger area from being charged with expenses payable by a portion only and will ensure that sums raised in the smaller part are not applied in reduction of expenditure payable by the larger (Application of Enactments Order, 1898, Art. 17).

Areas of Charge. Expenses of a county council are (unless otherwise provided by law) chargeable over the whole county, including boroughs and urban districts. The principal items so levied are main roads, harbour charges, libraries (with some exceptions) coroners and contributions towards expenses of combined purchasing and the Local Appointments Commission. County-at-large charges are apportioned between the county council and urban authorities in accordance with the produce of a rate of one penny in the pound in the different areas (Local Government Act, 1955, s. 50).

Funds. The general fund in boroughs and urban districts is called the municipal fund. In towns under town commissioners the expression town fund is used as a name for the general fund but it appears to have no statutory recognition. County and urban district councils, borough corporations, town commissioners, committees of vocational education and committees of agriculture may adopt schemes for administering gifts of property made to the authority for civic improvement. Under these schemes separate funds (civic improvement funds) are established under the control of the local authority. Sums paid to the local authority for the purposes of a voluntary civic improvement fund do not go to the county, municipal or other general fund as the case may be of the local authority and, therefore, cannot be used to meet the ordinary expenses of the authority.

The Local Authority (Acceptance of Gifts) Act, 1945, was, although framed in general terms, passed in response to the wish of G. Bernard Shaw to present his late wife's property in Carlow to the Urban District Council for the benefit of the town.

Public Bodies Orders

The Order that governs the keeping of accounts and records is the Public Bodies Order, 1946. This basic Order was amended on numerous occasions to take account of changes in local government law affecting finance and structure.

The application of programme budgeting to local services resulted in the segregation of local government activities into the eight programme groups already described. The Public Bodies (Amendment) Order, 1975 prescribed a revised format of estimates for these programmes. The question of radical further revision of the 1946 Order is being pursued and has been extended to an examination of the audit and general financial procedures of local authorities. An amending Order of 1977 prescribed a new form of Abstract of Accounts for County Councils and Urban District Councils.

Audit

After the close of the financial year a summary of the accounts in prescribed form, called the abstract of accounts, is prepared and laid before the authority. When it has been considered it is forwarded to the Minister for the Environment. The accounts are audited by a local government auditor who certifies the abstract and reports on the audit. The Minister sends the report and the certified abstract to the local authority for their consideration. Cost accounts must be kept of every work of construction or improvement. All money received by officers on behalf of the local authority must be lodged forthwith or within the time specified. The accounts of every officer receiving money, such as rate collectors, rent collectors, etc., are checked by some other officer. Authorizations to the treasurer for the payment of money are made over the signature of the manager on a treasurer's advice note countersigned by a nominated officer.

The centralized system of audit by local government auditors appointed by the Minister had its origin in the poor law. From the beginning the accounts of the poor law unions were subject to the audit of persons appointed for the purpose by the central authority. For some years a different system obtained in the boroughs and other municipal towns. In the boroughs there were three auditors, two elected by the burgesses and one a member of the council nominated by the mayor. In towns under the Act of 1854 the ratepayers present at the annual meeting appointed the auditors. Pursuant to the Local Government (Ireland) Act, 1871 the auditors of the poor law union accounts became auditors for the borough and town, with few exceptions. When county and district councils were constituted their accounts were brought under the auditors of the poor law unions and the exemptions from this audit which had been allowed in 1871 were abolished. Thus the system established for the poor law authorities in 1838 has been extended to all local authorities as well as to Health Boards, Vocational Education Committees, Committees of Agriculture and certain other bodies. The title 'local government auditors' was not given to the auditors until 1941. A detailed account of the legal framework may be found in Street, Appendix A, pp. 1253–1285.

Duties of Auditor. The local government auditor has statutory duties to perform for which he is solely responsible. His authority to inquire into the validity of payments extends into the legal and administrative background, and he must be supplied, on demand, with the information, documents etc., he requires. A request by an auditor to see papers relating to staff appointments was resisted by a Health Board but the auditor's power to do so was vindicated by the Supreme Court (Phelan v. Western Health Board, 1981). He must disallow every payment contrary to law or unfounded in fact. A person responsible for an illegal or unfounded payment is made liable for the amount by means of surcharge. A deficiency or loss incurred by reason of the negligence or misconduct of any member or officer (including, since 1955, consultant) can be charged on such person. Sums due by reason of these charges or surcharges have to be paid within six weeks unless there is an appeal. The Devlin Group (1969) recommended dispensing with the surcharge procedure as outmoded and of little present-day utility (25.3.10).

Apart from his general accounting responsibility an obligation rests on the manager, and in his absence on the county secretary or town clerk, to warn the members of a local authority in relation to any decision arising out of their reserved functions which lacks legal foundation or could result in a loss to or deficiency in local funds (City and County Management (Amendment) Act, 1955, s. 16).

Appeals. A person aggrieved by the action of the auditor may apply to the High Court and the auditor is bound to appear as defendant, his costs coming out of the rates unless the Court decides to the contrary. In lieu of making an appeal to the High Court an appeal may be made to the Minister who can determine the question at issue after inquiry. Very few appeals are now made to the High Court. An aggrieved person who appeals to the High Court and loses his appeal may, with a view to having the charge or surcharge remitted, make a subsequent appeal to the Minister.

The accounts are, as a rule, audited for the period they are made up, that is, yearly or half-yearly as ordered by the Minister. It may occasionally be necessary to hold special audits, called extraordinary audits, for any period. The cost of audit is met in the first instance by the Exchequer and subsequently recovered in part from the local authorities whose accounts have been audited.

Insurance. A local authority may insure against damage to their property or loss to their funds. At the instance of the General Council of County Councils local authorities were empowered by the Local Authorities (Mutual Assurance) Act 1926 to join in promoting a company complying with certain statutory conditions and having for its objects the mutual insurance of its members against damage to its property by fire and also mutual insurance against certain other risks. The Irish Public Bodies Mutual Insurances Limited was accordingly established.

14

Physical Planning

The first Irish town planning legislation in modern times arrived comparatively late, in 1934. There were, of course, elements of town planning in the Public Health Acts and in the early Housing Acts, in the sense of building regulations, control of living conditions and the like. And earlier still the Dublin Wide Streets Commissioners commenced in 1757 their extraordinary career of civic improvement and design. The Commissioners ceased work in 1840 leaving Dublin, though no longer a capital city, with much of the dignity and beauty which served as a reminder of its former status.

A Town Planning Exhibition was organised by the Royal Dublin Society in 1907, but despite this show of interest the Housing, Town Planning Act, 1909 which contained elementary planning powers did not apply to Ireland, nor did the somewhat more elaborate Housing and Town Planning Act of 1919. Between these dates ideas for a better Dublin were being canvassed and a prize of £500 offered in connection with the Civics Exhibition of 1913 was won by the young Patrick (later Sir Patrick) Abercrombie for a set of proposals called 'The Dublin of the Future'. None of those involved, of course, foresaw that within a few years a considerable part of the city centre would be in ruins following the 1916 Insurrection. The task of restoration was started promptly and the Dublin Reconstruction (Emergency Provisions) Act, 1916 contained some elements of re-planning. The same measures were invoked in the Dublin Reconstruction (Emergency Provisions) Act, 1924 after the Civil War with the aim of rebuilding 'destroyed areas in accordance with a harmonious general scheme' (First Report DLGPH p. 145). Meanwhile support for the idea of a renewed town planning effort was building up and the Greater Dublin Commission (1924–6) heard evidence on the subject. Senator Thomas Johnson introduced a Town Planning Bill in the Seanad on 2 May, 1929, which received a Second Reading but subsequently disappeared.

The Town and Regional Planning Act, 1934, was modelled on the English Town and Country Planning Act of 1932. These Acts embodied a planning mechanism operating the classic early sequence: survey – analysis – plan. The Act of 1934 was an adoptive measure. The passing of a planning resolution conferred powers of development control on the authority concerned. Before the resolution stage the practice was to survey the area, assess its requirements and prepare a report. In fact, only one authority (Dublin Corporation, under pressure of a Court Order secured in 1959 by Modern Homes (Ireland) Ltd.), got to the further point of making a statutory scheme or plan which never came into force. If it had come into effect it would have had the force of law and the scheme would have rigidly controlled the future development of the area.

The term regional planning in these Acts meant simply planning on the scale of a city with its surrounding rural hinterland. There was provision for a number of planning authorities to combine into a planning region under a joint committee and special regions were designated for Dublin and Cork but these provisions were never used. Regional planning did not carry the meaning it now commonly conveys, of economic planning and development by regions.

The virtual failure of the 1934 Act (an amending Act of 1939 tried to improve matters by introducing some flexibility) created a post-war demand, not very well articulated, for new and better legislation. The evolution of planning thought exposed the theoretical defects of pre-war legislation with its emphasis on the blue-print or detailed statement of an imagined end-state. This concept had come to be discarded in favour of a continuous process starting with the definition of goals and objectives for the development of an area, a constantly updated information system, evaluation of alternative methods of furthering growth or change, choice and monitoring results. In its new guise planning has been defined as a general activity, 'the making of an orderly sequence of action that will lead to the achievement of a stated goal or goals'.

Another aspect of the new thinking was the multi-dimensional nature of spatial planning. Physical planning was not merely a summation of road and sewer plans, housing schemes, shopping centres and so on. It involved many difficult decisions about economic and social development and though physical planners could not determine particular economic and social problems their decisions in environmental affairs must, nevertheless, accord with and possibly assist towards economic and social objectives. The Local Government (Planning and Development) Act, 1963 was the product of this intellectual climate and exhibits many characteristics of the new planning. It also laid heavy emphasis on the development role of local authorities; it gave statutory recognition to this role and while the conversion of local councils into development corporations was, perhaps, overstating the case in practical terms the new powers conferred by the Act of 1963 were remarkably comprehensive.

Local Government (Planning and Development) Acts, 1963 and 1976

The main objects of the 1963 Act were:
1. to set up a new and more flexible local planning system;
2. to enable local authorities to facilitate industrial and commercial

development and to secure the re-development of congested or obsolescent built-up areas;

3. to preserve and improve amenities of town and countryside; and

4. to modify the compensation liabilities of planning authorities.

Planning authorities, as in the 1934 legislation, comprised county councils, county borough and borough corporations and urban district councils but the duties and powers of the new Act were not optional. They were conferred uniformly on all planning authorities. As the Act came into operation in October 1964 this meant that each local authority was obliged to make a development plan within three years and review and vary the plan at least every five years thereafter. Making and altering plans were reserved functions under the Management Acts. The amending Act of 1976 made a number of changes in the law.

The new development plans provided a framework within which decisions might be taken by planning authorities on development projects in their areas. The plan indicates the objectives of the authority for the future development of their area. Draft plans and any variations following review are open to public inspection and the views of the public are invited before the final plans are adopted. A rate-payer has the right to make objections to a person or persons appointed by the planning authority.

The plans are in the form of a written statement, supplemented by maps. The plans for cities, boroughs, urban districts and scheduled towns (towns with 1,000 inhabitants or upwards) must show:

1. the different zones, residential, commercial, industrial and so on to which the available land might best be allocated;

2. proposals for dealing with traffic needs, both present and future, including pedestrian needs;

3. the proposed re-development of areas which have become obsolete by reason of economic or social changes;

4. amenities such as parks and open spaces and buildings or features of historic or artistic interest which should be preserved or developed.

County councils must prepare and revise plans for their areas, including plans for scheduled towns where the towns are not themselves planning authorities. The plans must specify the council's objectives for the development and improvement of the county and the special features which should be preserved and improved. Section 19(2) (b) requires objectives under three heads:

1. for development and renewal of obsolete areas;

2. for preserving, improving and extending amenities;

3. for the provision or extension of water supplies and sewerage services.

Traffic and zoning objectives in scheduled towns must also be indicated. The Third Schedule to the 1963 Act contains a list of purposes for which optional objectives may be indicated in development plans. The categories include roads and traffic, regulation of structures, community planning and amenities. Under community planning an objective may determine the provision and siting of schools, churches, meeting halls and other community facilities. In the section on amenities the objectives may include land reservation for open spaces, caravan or camping sites, game and bird sanctuaries, preservation of scenic views and prospects, prohibition or restriction of advertisements and the preservation of public rights of way giving access to seashore, mountain, lakeshore, riverbank or other places of natural beauty or recreational utility.

Objectives for the preservation of interiors of buildings may be included in development plans (Act 1976, s. 43). If a plan lists a structure or any internal feature for preservation the owner and occupier must be specially notified. A planning authority may now make a new development plan in lieu of amending their existing plan (Act 1976, s. 43).

Public Consultation

Public notice must be given of draft development plans or variations of plans and arrangements must be made for public inspection (Act 1963, s. 21). Copies of the plans and variations must be sent to the Minister and to certain prescribed bodies: these are contiguous planning authorities, local authorities in the area, An Chomhairle Ealaion, Bord Fáilte Éireann, An Taisce, National Monuments Advisory Council; the Minister for the Gaeltacht must get a copy if any part of the Gaeltacht is included. Special notifications must also be sent to owners and occupiers of buildings of artistic, historic or architectural interest listed for preservation in the draft plan. Planning authorities must take into consideration any objections or representations made to them within the time (at least three months) when the plan is open to public view.

The draft plan may but need not necessarily be altered in the light of public reaction. If they made any material alteration to the draft, planning authorities were formerly obliged to repeat the whole procedure but the 1976 Act (s. 37) enables finality to be reached, after public notice. Where the draft plan includes preservation of an existing public right of way to the seashore, etc., the owner and occupier of the land affected must be specially notified. He or they may, in addition to making objections or representations to the planning authority, appeal to the Circuit Court. If the Court is satisfied that no public right of way exists, it must be excluded from the development plan. Copies of the final plan must be kept available for public inspection or purchase.

The Minister's approval to plans is not required but he has power to have model plans prepared and to ensure that local plans are amended or that they are co-ordinated in the interests of regional planning (Act 1963, s. 22). The Act does not expressly provide otherwise for planning by regions.

Planning Control

Part IV of the 1963 Act deals with the control of development.

Subject to a number of exemptions the undertaking of any development without the prior permission of the planning authority is an offence. 'Development' is defined as 'the carrying out of any works on, in or under land or the making of any material change in the use of any structures or other land' (s. 3). Fixing advertisements to structures or trees on land, or using land for caravans or tents, or keeping old car batteries or rubble constitutes a change of use.

Section 26 does not place any express limitations on applicants and until the decision in the Frescati case (1975 IR 177) it was assumed that any person could seek and be granted development permission, whether or not he or she had an interest in the land in question. The Supreme Court, however, decided in that case that an application for development permission, to be valid, must be made either by, or with, the approval of a person who is able to assert sufficient legal estate or interest to enable him or her to carry out the proposed development or so much of it as relates to the property in question. A planning permission does not authorise a developer to carry out works which he is not entitled otherwise to do (s. 28).

Exemptions from control include the use of land for agriculture or forestry, development by local authorities in their areas, roadworks and the operations of local authorities or statutory undertakers in maintaining or renewing sewers, mains, pipes, cables and overhead wires (s. 4). Also exempted are works of maintenance or improvement of structures which do not alter their character by changing their external appearance. The Minister made Exempted Development Regulations in 1964 specifying in detail a number of additional developments which are not subject to planning control: these have been replaced by Part III and the Third Schedule of the Local Government (Planning and Development) Regulations of 1977. Any question about what is or is not 'development' is decided by An Bord Pleanála on a reference to them. An appeal may be taken to the High Court within three months of the Board's decision.

Notice of intention to apply for planning permission must be given either in a newspaper circulating in the area or by way of a notice 'erected or fixed on the land or structure'. The code of permission regulations made by the Minister pursuant to s. 25 of the Act in 1964 – now Part IV of the 1977 Regulations – specifies a two-stage procedure. The first step is an outline application merely identifying the location and nature of the project, with evidence of public notice having been given. If outline permission is granted, approval must then be sought for the full project, supported by detailed documents.

An applicant must now give particulars of his interest in the property he proposes to develop. The plans must show the name and address of the person who prepared them. A new regulation, introduced in 1977, requires a planning authority to submit weekly lists of planning applications to councillors, display the lists in the Council offices and if the authority so decides publish the lists in a newspaper circulating in the area. An application for an industrial development costing over £5 million may have to be supported by a study of its likely effects on the environment (Act of 1976, s. 39).

Applications for planning permission are decided by the planning authority (i.e. the manager – acting in an executive capacity) who may attach conditions to the grant of permission. The authority has power to carry out works to secure compliance with the permission or conditions and recover any expenses incurred (s. 26). Conditions may relate to a wide variety of factors, including:

1. development or use of adjoining land under the applicant's control;
2. required landscaping, planting, provision of open space and car parks (Act 1976, s. 25);
3. contributions from applicant towards cost of works carried out by a local authority;
4. security for satisfactory completion of a development: (Act 1976, s. 25);
5. noise or vibration: (Act, 1976, s. 39).

In dealing with applications, the planning authority is restricted to considering the proper planning and development of their area (including the preservation and improvement of its amenities). Regard must also be had to the development plan and to any special amenity area order under s. 42 of the 1963 Act. Under the Act of 1976 (s. 24) account must also be taken of development outside the area and the probable effect of the permission on adjacent planning areas.

A permission for development which would materially contravene the development plan or a special amenity area order could formerly not be given without the Minister's consent. The Minister's approval is no longer necessary and the decision now rests with the elected members (Act of 1976, s. 39). Prior public notice must be given and any objection or representation must be considered by the council before the decision (by a majority of the members present and voting, those in favour numbering at least one third of total membership) is affirmed. The time limit in such cases runs from the date of public notice.

Planning applications are normally dealt with by city and county managers; decisions are an executive function. Councils can, however, exercise their reserved powers in certain cases, as noted above. They can also revoke or modify a permission already granted (Act 1963, s. 30). This power has been used in the past to restore a local decision where the planning authority's refusal or permission has been reversed on appeal by the Minister. The Act of 1976 (s. 39) restricts the power of revoking or modifying permissions to cases in which 'there has been a change in circumstances relating to the proper planning and development of the area concerned'.

The powers of elected members have also been used in the past – some would say misused – in planning cases by requiring a manager, by resolution under section 4 of the City and County Management (Amendment) Act, 1955 to decide a planning application in a particular way – usually by granting the permission sought. The Act of 1976 seeks to restrain councillors so minded by complicating the procedure (hitherto simple and speedy) and introducing an element of publicity. Where notice is given that section 4 is to be used for the grant of permission, the manager if he is of the opinion that the permission would contravene the development plan or any special amenity area order, may make an order requiring the councillors to embark on the same elaborate ritual as applies to contraventions of development plans or amenity area orders.

Planning application must if properly made be decided within a period of two months, which does not commence to run until requirements about notices, further information or the like have been complied with (Act 1963, s. 26). The two month time limit may be extended if the applicant gives written consent (Act 1976, s. 39). The 1976 Act also limits the life of a permission to five years but extensions may be allowed by planning authorities in certain circumstances (s. 29).

State Authorities

The planning Acts apply indirectly to works done by Departments of State, the Commissioners of Public Works or by the Land Commission. These authorities must consult the planning authority and if any objections raised are not resolved consult the Minister for the Environment (Act 1963, s. 84).

Enforcement of Planning Controls

Where development is carried out without permission or without compliance with a permission or the attached conditions, the planning authority can serve enforcement notices requiring the land to be restored to its former state, or the permission or conditions to be complied with. Under sections 36 and 37 of the Act of 1963 a planning authority can require the removal or alteration of any structure or the discontinuance of any use of land if it is necessary for planning reasons. Section 38 enables a planning authority to make an agreement with a person interested in land for the purpose of regulating the development or use of the land and the agreement may be enforced against those deriving title from that person.

The Act of 1976 (s. 25) reinforces the powers of planning authorities to secure completion of housing estates. It enables them to take action where open space has not been provided in accordance with the planning permission or attached conditions. Action may involve the acquisition of the land from recalcitrant developers.

Section 26 of the 1976 Act provides a quick procedure for countering unauthorised development. A warning notice may be served on developers requiring compliance with the terms of a permission, subject to heavy penalties for failure to observe the notices. Under section 27 the High Court may prohibit the continuance of any unauthorised development or use. Where development does not comply with the terms of a planning permission the Court may direct that it should be so carried out. The Court may act on the application of a planning authority or any person, whether or not the person has an interest in the land.

Planning Appeals

Any person may appeal (formerly to the Minister, now to An Bord Pleanála) against a local decision on a planning application; the applicant within one month of getting the decision, others within twenty-one days. A deposit of £10, refundable with the decision, must accompany each appeal. Procedure for dealing with appeals and references is set out in regulations made by the Minister. A party to the appeal may demand an oral hearing and the hearing formerly had to be granted. But under the 1976 Act an oral hearing is discretionary; it may be allowed or refused by the Board as it sees fit, subject to appeal to the Minister. The appellate system furnishes a corrective against unreasonable decisions by planning authorities and introduces a degree of uniformity and consistency into a devolved decision-making process. It gave an opportunity to the Minister to indicate and influence planning and development policy for the guidance of local authorities.

In a Circular Letter PI 210/8 of 12 November 1973 the Minister, alarmed by the increasing volume of planning appeals, urged planning authorities to:

approach applications for permission in a far less restrictive way and grant permission unless there are serious objections on important planning grounds such as traffic safety, public health, or amenity. In particular, proposals for residential development in rural areas (one house or a small group) should be granted if at all possible.

The Circular went on to develop this idea as it applied in particular cases. The Minister and his Department were thus acting as initiators of planning policy. They also operated in a quasi-judicial capacity and it was this combination of roles which caused many difficulties and a great deal of controversy in appeal cases. Conflict was inevitable where a permission refused by a planning authority was conceded on appeal by the Minister. The local decision was taken for administrative and technical reasons. Reversal is a question of planning policy but in the clash of debate the fine distinction between policy and politics became obscured. In the words of Baroness Sharp: 'Planning policies depend more on political than on technical objectives; and they are always in a state of evolution. Planning is essentially a service rather than a science in its own right.'

In Ireland people have tended to regard the idea of the political nature of the planning process with suspicion. Development became associated in the public mind with property interests. During the sixties pressures began to build up in favour of some form of administrative tribunal which would isolate the quasi-judicial from the developmental function. In September 1967 the annual conference of the Association of Municipal Authorities suggested that appeals should be heard by the judiciary. In January and February 1968 a private members' Bill was debated in the Dáil which proposed to transfer the Minister's appellate powers to a Planning Appeals Board, chaired by a judge of the Circuit Court, High Court or Supreme Court. This Bill did not succeed but a year later a government bill was introduced, the Local Government (Planning and Development) Bill 1969, whose object was to set up an appeals tribunal, An Bord Achomharc Pleanála. The Bill, however, was not proceeded with and lapsed when the Dáil was dissolved before the General Election of 1973.

Judicial Decisions

Shortly afterwards a number of legal decisions profoundly altered the performance of quasi-judicial functions. The cases dealt with two kinds of contentious issues: compulsory acquisition of land and planning appeals. The vital judgment, delivered by the Supreme Court in July 1975 *(Susan Geraghty* v. *Minister for Local Government)*, related to planning, but the Court made it clear that the principles laid down were equally applicable to compulsory acquisition of land. The following excerpt from the planning case gives the essence of the Court's view of the proper conduct of inquiries or hearings precedent to decision-making.

> Under each of the Acts, there are certain fundamental matters or principles which are unalterable. The first is that the Minister is the deciding authority. He cannot in any way be treated simply as an authority whose function is to review the recommendations or the opinions, if any such are made or offered, of the person holding or conducting the inquiry. The second is that if the Minister comes to a conclusion or makes a decision which is not supportable upon the evidence properly before him he is acting *ultra vires*. Thirdly, neither the Minister nor the person holding or conducting the inquiry can come to a conclusion of fact unless there is evidence upon which such a conclusion could be formed. Fourthly, if the person holding or con-ducting the inquiry should come to a conclusion of fact and should express it, the Minister is not bound to come to the same conclusion of fact and is quite free to form a contrary conclusion if there is evidence and materials properly before him from which he could come to such a conclusion. Fifthly, to enable the Minister to come to any decision, the person holding or conducting the inquiry must transmit

to the Minister a report which fairly and accurately informs the Minister of the substance of the evidence and the arguments for or against the issues raised at the inquiry by those represented at the inquiry. Ordinarily the Minister can only look at what is in the report. He cannot avail himself of other testimony, expert or otherwise, or of other material from within his Department or elsewhere without informing the persons concerned and giving them an opportunity to deal with that evidence or material.

The *Geraghty* and *Murphy* judgments (see below), while actually re-inforcing the Minister's authority as sole decider of planning appeals, laid down strict procedural rules for hearing and deciding such cases. But a new situation has been created by the Oireachtas.

An Bord Pleanála

When the 1969 Bill lapsed with the dissolution of the Dáil in February 1973 a fresh Bill was introduced in the Senate and became law three years later. By the Local Government (Planning and Development) Act, 1976 the appellate function was transferred to a new body called An Bord Pleanála. The Board consists of a chairman (a judge of the High Court or a former judge) and from four to ten ordinary members. The chairman-ship of the Board is a government appointment, and wholetime; ordinary members are appointed by the Minister for Local Government (now the Environment), for terms up to three years and may be part-time. Dáil Deputies and Senators, or local councillors, may not serve as ordinary members.

The Board is required to keep itself informed of the policies and objec-tives of public authorities and in particular of the Minister for the Environ-ment and planning authorities. For his part the Minister must give general policy directives to the Board from time to time but he may not intervene in any particular case coming before the Board. The Board may decide to grant permission even if the proposed development is at variance with the development plan or a special amenity area order (Act 1976, s. 14).

As to oral hearings the 1963 right (s. 82) of any party to an appeal to demand a hearing has been modified. The Board now has an absolute discretion except where the Minister directs the holding of an oral hearing. Application may be made to the Minister within fourteen days of refusal by the Board (Act 1976, s. 16).

Apart from transferring appeal functions to the Board the Act of 1976 makes a number of minor changes in procedure. Section 23 requires that reports of oral hearings and inspections should, for consideration by the Board, or in certain cases by the Minister, include the inspector's recom-mendation on the question at issue.

Appeals must now be accompanied with a £10 lodgement. The deposit is refundable unless the appeal has been adjudged to be vexatious (1976 Act, ss. 15 and 18). Such appeals may be dealt with by the Board in summary fashion.

The Board must report annually to the Minister and their reports must be laid before each House of the Oireachtas (s. 9). The Board may also make submissions to the Minister on matters of planning practice and procedure (s. 31).

The Board's procedure in dealing with appeals or references is spelt out in regulations made by the Minister (s. 20). These — in Part V of the consolidated 1977 Regulations already referred to — replace the Appeals and References Regulations of 1964 made under the 1963 Act (ss. 10 and 82) and allow rather more flexibility. In considering an appeal, for example, the Board may invite an applicant to modify his proposals and grant their permission accordingly.

The Board may also direct a planning authority to pay the expenses of an appeal to the appellant or the Board. This power is similar to that given to the Minister by the 1963 Act (s. 18) except that provision is now made for payments by appellants to other parties to the appeal. An Bord Pleanála in addition to deciding appeals in planning cases, has the duty of adjudicating in a range of other items arising under the 1963 Act.

They include:

1. References on questions of exempted development, s. 5.
2. Demands to remove or alter hedges, s. 44.
3. Tree preservation orders, s. 45;
4. Conservation orders, s. 46;
5. Creation of public rights of way, s. 48;
6. Running cables, wires and pipelines over private land, s. 85;
7. Licensing petrol and oil pumps, vending machines, advertisement signs etc. on or along public roads.

The last-mentioned power has been extended by the 1977 Regulations to include cellars and other underground structures, private tunnels under roads etc. An Bord Pleanála is also the appeals body for the licensing system operated under the Local Government (Water Pollution) Act, 1977.

Declaration of Interests

The Act of 1976 (s. 32) requires members of the Planning Board and of planning authorities together with officers and employees involved in the planning process, to make written declarations of their interests in land or any business, profession or occupation relating to the development of land. Obligation to declare extends to prescribed employees or agents of the Board and to prescribed officers of planning authorities. The categories of officers, etc. to which the section applies may be prescribed by Ministerial regulations. The present position is set out in the 1977 Regulations, Article 69. Broadly, the requirement to disclose any interest applies to all professional and technical personnel of Bord Pleanála, and to administrative staff from executive officers upwards. In the case of planning authorities, the obligation is wide-ranging, from City and County Manager to Town Clerk, City, County, Borough and Town Engineers, Planning Officers and Assistants, and all other officers whose duties 'relate to the performance of any functions of a planning authority under the Acts'.

The Board and each planning authority must keep a register of interests. A member, officer or agent having a pecuniary or beneficial interest in land affected by an appeal or dispute must disclose the nature of his interest and take no part in the discussion or decision of the issue.

Amenities

Part V of the Act of 1963 as amended by section 40 of the 1976 Act gives a wide range of powers to planning authorities for the preservation and improvement of amenities. They may make special amenity area orders for the protection and enhancement of areas of outstanding natural beauty, recreational value, or in need of nature conservation. Where necessary, the Minister may step in to direct a planning authority to take action. Planning authorities may also make conservation orders to safeguard fauna or flora in areas of special amenity. These latter orders must be preceded by consultation with 'prescribed' authorities listed in Part IX of the 1977 Regulations as: the Minister for Fisheries, the Royal Irish Academy, Bord Fáilte and An Taisce. Notice of special amenity area orders must be given in the press and require confirmation by the Minister. Making them is a reserved function. Conservation orders on the other hand may be made by managers. They also must be publicised and appeals by objectors, if any, are for determination by An Bord Pleanála.

The Act of 1963 also has provisions designed to minimise injury to amenities from noise (s. 51), litter (s. 52) and poster advertisements (ss. 53, 54). Planning authorities may enhance land by planting trees, shrubs or other plants and contribute money or plants to private persons and local development associations.

Development

The Act of 1963 greatly enlarged the scope of local capability in development. Planning authorities were empowered by s. 77 of the Act to 'develop or secure the development of land' and this sweeping declaration is spelt out in a variety of ways:

1. road works and other services and works needed for development;
2. redevelopment and renewal of obsolete areas;
3. preserving views and prospects, structures and natural physical features and sites of geological, ecological and archaeological interest, etc.

Planning authorities may also provide premises for industry, business and recreation: factories, offices, shops, dwellings, amusement parks, structures for the purpose of entertainment and caravan parks. They can put up buildings for use as restaurants, hostels and the like and may maintain and manage them. They may also construct 'buildings for providing trade and professional services and advertisement structures'.

Planning authorities can also provide industrial estates, factory sites, sites for businesses such as hotels, motels and guesthouses and sites for dwellings, offices, shops, schools and other community facilities. The Act of 1976, s. 43, adds cats' and dogs' homes to the list. They can also provide any ancillary services required for the buildings and sites listed above. They can maintain and manage sites, buildings and services and make charges for the facilities provided.

Planning authorities are thus enabled, in the language of the 1971 White Paper 'to provide sites and services for all sorts of public and private development and . . . themselves undertake virtually any kind of development (including industrial and commercial development) and engage in promotional activities. . . . Local authorities therefore must now regard themselves and be regarded as development corporations for their areas' (p. 14). The potentialities inherent in the 1963 Act, however, have remained to a large extent dormant in the absence of resources for new investment. Available capital for new works has been pre-empted by the traditional infrastructural services: housing, sanitary services and roads.

Land Acquisition and Disposal

Planning authorities are obliged (s. 22) to take action to secure the objectives of their development plans. For this purpose they are empowered to appropriate land already in their possession (s. 74) and to acquire land compulsorily or by agreement. The latter power is conferred not by the Planning Acts but by Section 11 of the Local Government (No. 2) Act, 1960. They may sell, lease, or exchange any land acquired or appropriated by them for the purpose of securing the proper planning and development of their area (s. 75). The Minister's consent is not necessary unless the price or rent is not the best reasonably obtainable or the development proposed would materially contravene the development plan.

A planning authority may, with the Minister's consent, make an order extinguishing a public right of way (s. 76). The Minister's decision must be preceded by publication of the order and in the event of an objection the holding of an oral hearing. This method of handling objections was substituted for public inquiry by the 1976 Act, s. 43.

Regional Planning

The Local Government (Planning and Development) Act, 1963 made no provision for regional planning but the intention to construct a regional framework was part of ministerial thinking while the Bill was still on its way through the Dáil and Seanad. During the Seanad debate the Minister said:

> It is my aim that, following on the passage of this Bill, regional studies should be made with strong support and guidance from my Department in order that the economic objectives of planning that I have outlined will be pressed forward vigorously. Other countries in Europe are using physical planning to advance their economic development and we cannot afford to ignore their example. Indeed, I regard this as probably the most important long-term task facing the local authorities in this country . . . (Debates Vol 56, 1692–3, 31 July 1963).

Senator Dooge commented in his reply on the absence of any mechanism in the Bill for an expression of regional opinion on development plans:

> Just as public involvement is important at the local level – and I agree heartily with the Minister in what he has done in making the authorities under this Bill as local as possible – public involvement is equally necessary at the regional and national level.

But the idea was not taken up and when the Bill became law a few days later the Minister, with the aid of An Foras Forbartha, designated a number of planning regions and set about commissioning planning consultants to prepare advisory reports on their development. Professor Myles Wright of Liverpool was engaged for the Dublin region, Nathaniel Lichfield and Associates for the Limerick region and Colin Buchanan and Partners (commissioned by the United Nations) for the rest of the country.

The consultants' reports – Wright and Lichfield in 1966 and Buchanan in 1969 – were of considerable value in guiding local planning authorities but their more general proposals, in particular those dealing with regional organisation, were received with some reservations. Wright suggested a Regional Planning Agency for Dublin – a small planning and advisory body with a full-time chairman and representatives of government departments and local authorities. Lichfield put forward a number of ideas including an Inter-Departmental Committee while Buchanan recommended joint planning authorities in the regions with statutory responsibility for all significant planning decisions.

But in fact the government had already made up its mind. A statement of government policy on 31 August 1965 said:

> The 1963 Act provides for the co-ordination of the development plans and, for this purpose the country has been divided into nine planning regions. A regional co-ordinating body has already been established in

the Limerick Region, and the Government propose that co-ordinating groups should now be established in all regions. The main function of these groups will be to co-ordinate the programmes of regional development in each region. The purpose of the programmes will be, principally, to identify the potential in each area, including the factors which make for economic expansion (such as growth centres) and the factors which impede expansion. It is not intended that the regional groups will assume any executive functions. (*Regional Policy in Ireland: A Review* NESC, Report, No. 4, Appendix IV)

This stance was held in the face of the consultants' advice and reiterated in a government statement of May 1969 on the Buchanan Report. The regional groups, called Regional Development Organisations (RDO) generally followed the pioneering Limerick model 'which has brought together elective and official representatives of the planning authorities, the Shannon Free Airport Development Company, the Regional Tourism Organisation and the harbour authorities' (White Paper, 1971, 7.3.2.). The RDOs were asked in 1969 to prepare reports on their regions and the government, in the light of these reports, delivered their decisions on the Buchanan proposals. The statement 'Review of Regional Policy' can be found in Appendix IV of the NESC Report referred to above, dated 4 May 1972.

The most recent authoritative pronouncement on regional organisation was contained in NESC Report No. 22 on *Institutional Arrangements for Regional Economic Development* (1976) which criticised the RDOs for their uneven performance and recommended giving them statutory recognition and assigning specific functions to them. The Report also pointed to certain weaknesses at the centre and recommended: (1) that a Minister should be assigned responsibility for regional policy and (2) the establishment of a Central Committee for Regional Economic Development. Raising the question of Ministerial responsibility recalled the idea pressed by the Devlin Group (1969) that the scope of the Department of Local Government should be extended to enable it to lead co-ordination of all aspects of development in local areas — under the title of Department of Regional Development. The NESC Report did not come down on the side of Devlin, or any particular Minister and when in 1977 it was decided to create a new Department of Economic Planning and Development, the job of providing and monitoring regional planning was included in its remit. This job has now passed to the Department of Finance.

Planning and Compensation

Where land is acquired compulsorily compensation is, in default of agreement, assessed in accordance with the rules laid down in the Acquisition of Land (Assessment of Compensation) Act, 1919. The method is arbitration and the basis of compensation is market value. This basis is preserved in land transactions by planning authorities but the 1963 Act recognises that comprehensive planning is a factor which has to be taken into account in assessing market value. The Act (s. 69 and Fourth Schedule) requires that regard be made to planning considerations but that no account shall be taken of any increase or decrease in value attributable to provisions of a development plan or a special amenity. order. This amendment of the Act of 1919 applies not only to land acquisition for planning but to compulsory acquisition generally. Compensation payable in respect of planning restrictions is assessed on the same basis and where the amount is disputed the dispute is also settled by arbitration under the Act of 1919 as amended by the Property Values (Arbitrations and Appeals) Act, 1960.

The principle of compensating land owners for losses caused by planning operations has always been inherent in the system. It has been carried from the Town and Regional Planning Acts of 1934 and 1939 into the Acts of 1963 and 1976, with the difference that questions of compensation are now related to individual planning decisions or orders and not development plans. Under the 1934 Act compensation did not come into play until a planning scheme was adopted; there was thus an irresistible premium on remaining safely in the interim control stage. The general provision (s. 55) is that compensation is payable by a planning authority for any reduction in land values resulting from a refusal of planning permission or a grant of permission subject to conditions. Claims for compensation must normally be made within six months of the decision. Compensation is also payable to an occupier of land for any damage to his trade or business occasioned by planning restriction.

There are many exceptions to the general provision about compensation. The most important is a prohibition on compensation for refusal of permission where permission is available for an alternative development of the land for residential, industrial or commercial purposes (Act 1963, s. 57). Liability for compensation is thus removed for turning down an application for erection of a factory in, say, a residential area. Compensation is not payable for the refusal of permission for a material change in the use of buildings or land (s. 56). Neither is it payable for refusing permission for the display of advertisements or: where development would endanger public safety by reason of traffic hazard; or would impair any view or prospect of special amenity value or interest; or is located in an area included in a special amenity order, and would conflict with the development permitted by the order; or where the land is not adequately served with water or sewerage.

Where planning restrictions render property incapable of reasonably beneficial use in its existing state the owner may (by serving a purchase notice) require the planning authority to buy the property and subject to confirmation by the Minister the planning authority must do so (s. 29). Compensation is not payable for conditions relating to air pollution or noise.

Betterment

There are no provisions about betterment in the present planning code. The provisions in the 1934 Act never came into operation and experience elsewhere was not encouraging. The Act of 1963 does, however, provide for contributions to planning authorities from developers for benefits derived from public services (s. 26).

Building Regulations

The Minister is empowered to make building regulations to be applied by planning authorities throughout the country (s. 86 and Fifth Schedule). These regulations replace the byelaws formerly made by local authorities pursuant to s. 41 of the Public Health (Ireland) Act, 1878, and s. 23 of the Public Health Acts Amendment Act, 1890. The 1976 Act enables a regulation to take account of the special needs of disabled persons. A code of building regulations is currently in preparation.

Derelict Sites

Derelict sites disfigure the townscape with neglected, ruinous buildings or they may be unused patches of land which invite dumping and thus become health hazards. An Act of 1940 attempted to cope with them but had only partial success for legal reasons — it was difficult and troublesome for local authorities to bring the machinery of the Act into play. The Derelict Sites Act, 1961 replaced the earlier statute with a clearer definition of what constituted a derelict site and a more effective procedure. Business picked up and the Department encouraged action with a scheme of grants payable to local authorities, voluntary bodies and private individuals. The state paid half the cost of improvement — demolition, clearance, fencing etc. — up to £100 per site. The scheme terminated from 1972 when resources were concentrated on work of positive amenity.

Amenity Grants Scheme

Promotion of works of public amenity was stepped up by the decision in 1971 to terminate the Derelict Sites Scheme and expand the amenities programme. Grants of 50 per cent of cost were paid to local authorities and voluntary bodies for parks, open spaces, playing fields, river walks, boating, fishing and swimming facilities, beach works, car and caravan parks, local museums and community centres. The state grants scheme was terminated in 1974.

European Regional Development Fund

The Fund, which came into operation in 1975, does not normally assist specific projects. Assistance is paid directly to the Exchequer where it is used to expand the Public Capital Programme and finance additional industrial and infrastructural projects in areas of greatest need. Commitments on the Fund are calculated and grants allocated by reference to the aggregate of schemes recommended by Ministers. In the case of the Minister for the Environment these include road, water and sewerage schemes, mainly in western counties.

A specific commitment of £2m. was made in 1976 for the Cork City and Harbour Joint Water Supply Scheme. A loan of £10m. from the European Investment Bank was approved.

Acquisition of Land

Local authorities need land for many purposes and so it has been necessary to give them power to acquire it. Prior to 1960 they had, however, no general power and whenever a statute was passed imposing new duties or functions which in their exercise involved the acquisition of land fresh power to acquire was given. Section 11 of the Local Government (No. 2) Act, 1960, broadened section 10 of the Local Government (Ireland) Act, 1898, to give all local authorities the same general powers of land acquisition as exercisable by county councils.

If local authorities could get all the land they require in the same way as the private citizen has to get it, that is, by agreement with the owner, the matter would be simple. Very little legislation would be necessary beyond giving the power to acquire and perhaps enabling owners, who were not under any legal disability, to sell. But local authorities are not always able to acquire suitable land by agreement for roads, housing and public works and therefore power of taking land compulsorily, subject of course to the owner being properly compensated, has been given to them.

The taking of lands compulsorily has been hedged round with many safeguards and is subject to a code of legislation consisting now of seven Acts passed in the period 1845 to 1919 to which the collective title Lands Clauses Acts has been given. The Lands Clauses Consolidation Act of 1845 is the foundation of the compulsory acquisition procedure. This Act was found unsuitable to Ireland and was largely replaced in 1864 by the provisions of the Railways Act, 1851. When towards the end of last century the need was felt for more satisfactory provisons to cover compulsory acquisition for housing the law was varied for that purpose by the second schedule to the Housing of the Working Classes Act, 1890 and for public health purposes this schedule was in 1896 substituted for the compulsory clauses of the Act of 1845. In some modern statutory provisions relating to compulsory purchase of land (e.g. Health Act, 1947 Part VIII) it will be found that seven Land Clauses Acts including Railways Acts as amended by the second schedule referred to above are incorporated with the new enabling power and that there are some additional modifications contained in the statute itself. The Local Government (No. 2) Act, 1960 conferred a general power on local authorities to acquire land for the purposes of their existing or future powers and duties.

Procedures

There are several acquisition procedures and the particular one to be followed in any case depended on the statute authorizing acquisition. Up to 1960 the procedure was by provisional order if land was taken for sanitary purposes, roads, allotments, vocational education, courthouses, fire stations and some other purposes; by compulsory purchase or acquisition order for housing, public assistance purposes, mental hospitals and health institutions and by preliminary notice and vesting order for derelict sites.

The provisional order procedure began with a petition presented to the Minister to allow the appropriate parts of the Lands Clauses Acts to be put in force. The Minister could dismiss the petition or order a local inquiry. After the inquiry the Minister could make the provisional order. Formerly a provisional order had to be confirmed by an Act of Parliament but in 1925 the Minister was authorized to confirm orders made under the Public Health Acts (now the Local Government (Sanitary Services) Acts) and the Local Government Act, 1898. Any person interested could appeal to the Minister or to the Circuit Court. A compulsory purchase or acquisition order is made by the local authority and is subject to confirmation by the Minister. It may be questioned in the High Court by an aggrieved person.

Compulsory acquisition has now been largely standardised. The Local Government (No. 2) Act, 1960, s. 10, superseded the provisional order procedure by substituting for all purposes the compulsory purchase order powers exercisable originally under the Housing (Miscellaneous Provisions) Act, 1931 and now under the Housing Act, 1966.

Section 86 of the 1966 Act replaces section 10 of the 1960 Act referred to above, a move required by the repeal of almost all the provisions of the Housing of the Working Classes Acts relating to compulsory land acquisition. A modern code re-stating the compulsory purchase order procedure was substituted, which can now be used for all local government purposes, including multiple purposes.

The Local Government Act 1946, s. 82, expanded the land acquisition powers of local authorities to include land for future use, even though 'they have not determined the manner in which or the purpose for which they will use the land'. Despite the wide terms in which the acquisition provisions of the 1960 and 1966 Acts were drawn the Courts have tended towards a rather narrow view of local authority capabilities in the matter of the compulsory taking of land. A recent (1979) High Court decision obliges a local authority, before availing themselves of compulsory powers, to state precisely how they propose to use the land and to specify the relevant statutory sections.

Judicial Interventions

A recent series of judgments throws light on other aspects of the quasi-judicial process. In *Murphy's* case, 1972, it was decided that:

> The function which is given to the Minister by Article 5 of the Third Schedule of the 1966 (Housing) Act is not an executive power of the State assigned to his Department or a power which is vested in the Government as an executive power from the State. He is *persona designata* in that the holder of the office of the Minister for Local Government is the person designated for that function. The Act, if the Oireachtas has so enacted, could just as easily have assigned the function to the Chairman of CIE or the Chairman of the ESB or the head of any other State-controlled or semi-State corporation, and if it had done so there could be no question of such person seeking or being granted the executive privilege of non-production of the document in question.

The effect of this part of the judgment was to nullify the Minister's executive privilege in withholding copies of the inspector's reports in cases of compulsory acquisition and planning appeals. Such reports must now be produced if requested by parties to the objections or appeals. The role and functions of inspectors were also examined. *Murphy's* case proceeds:

> No direct assistance is obtainable from the statute (1966) as to the precise functions of the inspector or of his powers. It is clear, however, that in so far as the conduct of the inquiry is concerned he is acting as recorder for the Minister. He may regulate the procedure within the permissible limits of the inquiry over which he presides. In as much as he is there for the purpose of reporting to the Minister his function is to carry to the Minister, if not a verbatim account of the entire course of the proceedings before him, at least a fair and accurate account of what transpired, and one which gives accurately to the Minister the evidence and the submissions of each party because it is upon this material the Minister must make his decision and on no other. The inspector has no advisory function nor has he any function to arrive at a preliminary judgement which may or may not be confirmed or varied by the Minister. If his report takes the form of a document then it must contain an account of all the essentials of the proceedings over which he presided. In my view, it is no part of his function to arrive at any conclusion. If the Minister is influenced in his decision by the opinions of the inspector or the conclusions of the inspector the Minister's decision will be open to review. It may be quashed and set aside if shown to be based on materials other than those disclosed at the public hearing.

Acquisition of Derelict Sites

In order to acquire a derelict site compulsorily under the Derelict Sites Act, 1961 a local authority must publish, post up and serve notice of their proposal. Acquisition is then effected, after a due interval, by a vesting order made by local authority which, in disputed cases, required the prior consent of the Minister for the Environment. The local authority acquires the site free from all encumbrances but compensation is payable. The procedure is a simple and rapid one.

Compensation

In 1919 the law with regard to the assessment of compensation for land acquired compulsorily was altered by the Acquisition of Land (Assessment of Compensation) Act, 1919. Questions in dispute are referred to an official arbitrator taken from a panel appointed by a Reference Committee consisting of the Chief Justice, the President of the High Court and the Chairman of the Surveyors' Institution (Irish Branch) or his nominee. The rules in the Act for the assessment of compensation are set out in section 2. The main effect is that compensation is assessed on the market value, assuming a willing seller. A further ten rules were added by the Fourth Schedule to the Planning Act, 1963.

Building Land

Local authorities are encouraged to build up 'land-banks' in advance of requirements and to develop sites for private house building. State subsidy is available, both as a stimulus to local action and in order to moderate costs. By the late 1960s pressures on building land in the Dublin area and elsewhere had driven up prices to the point that major problems had developed or were clearly in sight. An expert committee was set up in 1971 to examine building land prices and make suggestions.

The committee, which was chaired by Mr Justice John Kenny, submitted majority and minority reports in 1973, the majority favouring the idea of the High Court, on the application of local authorities, designating areas likely to come under development within ten years. Land in such areas could be purchased by local authorities at its 'existing use' value plus 25 per cent. The price, in cases of disagreement, would be determined by a Lands Tribunal chaired by a judge of the High Court, sitting with two assessors, one with planning experience and the other a qualified valuer. The minority report, signed by two members from the then Department of Local Government, proposed that the power of designating areas of urban expansion should be exercised, not by the High Court, but by city and county managers acting for the local authorities concerned. Land in the designated areas would be subject to pre-emption (first choice, or refusal) by local authorities. Compensation would, however, be reckoned on the basis of market values.

The government announced its acceptance in principle of the majority report scheme in January 1974, but official proposals for legislation have not appeared. A Private Members' Bill based on ideas from both majority and minority reports was introduced in the Dáil in 1980 by the Labour Party but failed to gain acceptance. The Bill went some way with the minority report in entrusting local authorities with the power to designate areas, but the power was reserved to the elected members. The Bill then changed sides to the majority plan of assessing compensation on 'existing use' value. A five member Lands Tribunal headed by a High Court judge, would determine the amounts. Designated area orders would be subject to confirmation by the Minister for the Environment, but no statutory obligation would lie on local authorities to initiate action. In this the Bill diverged sharply from the majority proposals which made it mandatory for local authorities to apply to the High Court for designation. The Local Government (Building Land) Bill, 1980 was opposed by the Government and Fine Gael and was defeated on second reading.

Water and Water Rights

The term 'land' in section 10 of the Local Government (Ireland) Act, 1898 includes rights to water, while the powers of land acquisition in the Public Health (Ireland) Act, 1878, comprise, for water supply purposes, 'land covered with water or any water or right to take or convey water'. In cases of compulsory acquisition, compensation is assessed under the 1919 Act, whose ambit extends to 'water and any interests in land or water'.

Despite what might have seemed the adequacy of these provisions, the Water Supplies Act, 1942 was found necessary to settle doubts about the rights of riparian owners affected by taking water upstream of their lands. Under the Act a local authority makes a proposal to take a supply of water from a source such as a lake and, if objections are forthcoming from people who might be at loss, the local authority applies to the Minister for the Environment for a provisional order authorising the project. After local inquiry at which the objectors are heard, the Minister may (or may not) make the provisional order, and give notice accordingly. In the case of the order having been made, any person aggrieved can petition either the Minister or the Circuit Court for redress. On due hearing and consideration the Minister or Court, as the case may be, can confirm, amend or disallow the provisional order.

15

Urbanisation

Ireland is still in many minds a mainly rural country, but Irish society is rapidly changing in colour and character. Some observers are in fact convinced that the process of change has progressed to the point of transformation.

We have *already* passed from the kind of society that is traditional to another kind of society altogether — the urbanised, industrialised society which has emerged from the several technological revolutions that have transformed large parts of the earth in the past two centuries and have affected every corner of the globe (Dr L. de Paor, 'Ireland's Identities' 1979).

The national urban population has grown steadily since 1891 and, sometime after 1961, the balance between town and country shifted finally away from the immemorial rural preponderance. The Census of 1966 was the first to show a majority of urban dwellers. The following table gives an idea of the relationship:

Table 1: Urban/Rural Population

Year	Urban '000	Rural '000	Total '000	Urban Proportion %
1951	1272	1688	2960	42
1956	1287	1611	2898	44
1961	1307	1512	2818	46
1966	1445	1439	2884	50
1971	1556	1423	2979	52
1979	2020*	1348*	3368	60*

*Estimated

The term 'rural' included, in addition to country people as ordinarily understood, the inhabitants of villages and small towns up to 1500 population. If dwellers in open country only are taken into account the 1951 figure of rural population falls to 1.57 million, equal to 53 per cent of the national propulation. In 1971 these figures were, respectively, 1.22 million, or 41 per cent of the total.

In this respect, as in others, there is a strong regional imbalance. The 1971 Census showed, in each of the nine planning regions, a predominantly rural population – with one exception. This was the Eastern or Dublin region, though in the South-West region, which includes Cork City and County, urban dwellers were rapidly overtaking rural. In every region, rural population is on the decline, urban on the increase. All regions thus show varying rates and degrees of urbanisation. And the process is accelerating. W. K. Downey (1980) says: 'Moreover, urbanisation seems to be gaining momentum in Ireland. The increase over the ten-year period since 1970 in the percentage of the Irish population living in towns and cities is roughly equivalent to the total over the previous twenty years.'

Dublin deserves special attention. There was a steady growth up to 1966 in the proportion of national population living in the Dublin conurbation, but the proportion levelled off between 1966 and 1971 and fell slightly thereafter. It appeared to be stabilised at 0.778 millions. The rest of the Eastern region, however, continued to grow rapidly. The partial census of 1979 returned a population of 1.26 million for the Eastern region, or 38 per cent of the national population. The relative stabilisation of the Dublin area is only a statistical concept, since much of the expansion in Dublin County (154 thousand or 64 per cent between 1971 and 1979) amounts to the creation of new suburbs (or new towns) adjacent to the city, Dun Laoghaire and the other older suburbs.

The growth of Dublin and its surrounding territories has, in Professor Walsh's words (1978) 'vast social and political, as well as economic implications.' If, for instance, Dublin expansionist tendencies were to be constricted by some means, it would be necessary (if emigration is to be avoided) for other towns and cities throughout the country to expand rapidly, to accommodate the Dublin overspill.

Two factors should be noted in this context. One is the upsurge in town population that began in 1961, 'closely co-inciding with the economic take-off', noted by Curtin, Geary and others in their ESRI paper (1976). This paper was a study of 97 towns in the population range 1,500 to 10,000, ranking them in order of 'goodness', a shorthand term covering high standards of housing, employment, and amenities. Most of the 'good' towns were in the Eastern part of the country. One of the conclusions emerging from this paper is that municipal government, or the absence of it, seems to have little effect. An inspection of the population figures in Appendix 2 bears this out, if one equates numerical expansion with 'goodness'.

The second factor was the 'dramatic narrowing of the gap in living standards between Dublin and the rest of the country revealed by the County Incomes Data for the years 1965–73' as Walsh put it. The dissemination of prosperity which the figures reflect would ease the problem of absorbing surplus population, if some means were adopted of stabilising the Eastern region, or, more specially, the metropolitan part of it. In any event it is estimated that between 1971 and 1991 the urban population will grow by upwards of one million wherever accommodation facilities and jobs may be found.

Urban Problems

A recent policy statement on urban affairs (Fine Gael, 1979) prefaces its list of specific problems — city centre renewal, transport, traffic and the rest — with the statement that the process of urbanisation is itself 'a very major political and sociological problem.' Urbanisation presents in a heightened form such issues as the conflict between economic growth and environmental quality, to say nothing of the conservation of natural resources. It presents also the choice — if one can call it that where the process seems irreversible — between the traditional life and culture of our society and new forms which are in some way alien and foreign. These are issues transcending local government, of course; they call for attention and policy-making by the community as a whole through the national institutions of parliament and government. But a number, admittedly not the majority of the specific problems, are susceptible of treatment at local or sub-national level.

Urbanisation, normally linked with industrial development, creates a series of problems and demands which fall to local authorities. They include water supplies and water resource management, the remedy and control of water and air pollution, waste disposal, retrieval and recycling of waste materials and grappling with the environmental health hazards associated with urban living. Then there is the growing pressure of motor traffic on roads and streets, noise levels and the constant concern with sustaining and renewing the urban fabric. All these are found in their most acute form in the larger cities, where, in the old city centres, there are new manifestations of urban malaise.

The most intractable problems affecting many inner cities are the rundown condition, amounting to decay, of the physical environment and the underlying causes of this condition — the economic and social decline of the communities which once gave the inner city its vitality, colour and life. The programmes of slum clearance which marked the earlier decades of this century began the process of depopulation by transferring large numbers of inner city dwellers to new housing estates at the periphery. Industry and employment tended to follow the outflow of population. Those who remained behind suffered in consequence from various social disabilities — high unemployment, sub-standard housing, poor amenities, the virtual absence of facilities for outdoor recreation and so on. The impact on youth was particularly damaging; the scarcity of jobs for school-leavers meant idleness, alienation, violence, crime and vandalism.

The effects were particularly severe in Dublin, where the Corporation established a Permanent Development Team in 1977 with the object of attracting industry to city centre locations. In the following year the government set up an Inter-Departmental Committee on Dublin Inner City problems whose report (1979) they backed with a grant of £1 million and by appointing an Inner City Group to further the Committee's proposals and develop a programme of action by the various Departments and public agencies operating in the centre city. The Committee's view was that the general objective of inner city policy should be to create a resident population capable of sustaining itself, economically and socially. A series of measures to this end was outlined covering job opportunities, (particularly in service industries), environmental improvement programmes (in consultation with local communities), relief of traffic congestion and social development through better housing, education and training, sports, recreation and youth activities, health and community care and community development projects. In the meantime Dublin Corporation had made progress with a Central City Housing Programme for the re-development of a number of sites in traditionally residential areas.

Administration

Urban government has (as outlined in earlier chapters) a largely nineteenth century basis; the twentieth century superstructure consists of city management and its variations, in particular the ingenious combination of administrations in counties under unified management in the hands of county managers.

City management in Ireland has been a success story but not an unqualified success. The story began in Cork where the ability and personality of its first manager, Philip Monahan, gave the system an excellent start — so good indeed that the government of the time became unshakably convinced that city management on the Cork pattern was the answer to most, if not all, municipal problems. There were complaints from the councillors about Monahan's authoritarian style of business but in the 1920s that is what the term 'management' was assumed to imply. During the ten years 1929 to 1939, city management was applied to all four county boroughs. Limerick and Waterford reported, on the whole, satisfactory results. The story in Dublin was somewhat different.

The first Dublin city manager was Gerald Sherlock, who had been Town Clerk and accepted his new job on the understanding that decisions on most matters remained with the council. The next incumbent was P. J. Hernon who, after some years as one of the city commissioners, spent the years between 1931 and 1937 as borough manager in Dun Laoghaire. Shortly after taking over in Dublin the job was up-graded and Hernon became a metropolitan manager, with responsibility for Dublin city, Dublin county, Dun Laoghaire borough and Balbriggan town. He had, in addition, to concern himself with three boards of assistance and certain other joint authorities.

It is not surprising, perhaps, that the 1942 experiment of a municipal supremo in the person of the Dublin City and County Manager was a failure at first. The job was too big and Hernon proved unable to pull the various administrations together. In fairness the question may be asked: Was city management the answer to the Dublin situation? The American experience has been that city management is most successful in cities of small to medium sizes: it is, on the whole, unsuitable for big city governments.

The Dublin situation has improved but is still unsatisfactory. The administrations in Dublin city, county and Dun Laoghaire have been unified or streamlined in such services as roads, planning, housing, water supply and drainage but the local government re-organisation plan of 1971 proposed, nevertheless, to abolish the city, county and borough councils and replace the lot with a Metropolitan Council — an idea first put forward in 1938 by the Local Government (Dublin) Tribunal. The official reason was that despite all that had been done at the administrative level, perfect co-ordination still eluded the City—County Manager.

Neither the Lord Mayor of Dublin nor his congeners in the county and borough councils have much political muscle or any executive authority. There is therefore little prospect that a political overlord might emerge from a metropolitan council who, at the head of a million citizens, would lead the forces of order and progress in the battle for civic conservation, renewal and a better life. Irish local government has no such thing as the American strong mayor and our system is unlikely to evolve in that direction. We cannot therefore look forward with any confidence to a future leader of the forces of right with weight and force enough to prevail against the property speculators and developers, the land manipulators and commercial interests, the automobile lobby and other enemies of the planned city.

The only organisational change in contemplation at present appears, however, to be the metropolitan authority, with a second tier of district councils to lend a neighbourhood element, a chance to participate. But the Dublin problem, according to some, is more deep-seated than a new pattern of councils could cure, A recent assessment, under the title 'A City Powerless to Save Itself' has the following:

> The root cause of Dublin's problems is easy to find. It lies in the tangled maze of bureaucratic undergrowth which passes for local government in the city. There is no single authority in charge, just a series of competing forces, none of which has sufficient power to make any real impact . . . [Dublin] is divided by a totally artificial border separating the Corporation area from the area controlled by the County Council, and within the county area there's the fiercely independent borough of Dun Laoghaire . . . But if the division of Dublin into city and county

is unreal, the division of responsibility on important policy issues is positively bizarre. Take the crucial question of transportation for example . . . (Frank McDonald, *The Irish Times*, 15 November 1979).

This is one view, strongly held by many. But there are others. In the same issue of the *Irish Times* the City and County Manager, under the heading 'Everything will work out' spoke confidently of the future, insofar as the local authorities he managed were capable of influencing living conditions in the metropolis.

Other County Boroughs

Dublin is not, of course, the only city with problems. The White Paper on *Local Government Reorganisation* (1971) referred to Cork's 'particular difficulties' but did not propose a definite solution. The *Discussion Document* (1973) contained a statement (para. 14) that 'the previous government had decided in principle on a merger of the City and County' but that solution was considered too extreme by the Coalition Minister concerned. Problems of co-ordination were also said (Discussion Document, 15) to exist in Limerick and Waterford. Both the White Paper and Document seemed to accept the case for amalgamating city and county management in Waterford.

Boroughs, Urban Districts and Towns

The County Management Act, 1940 imposed a system of unified management on the majority of local bodies in each county and urban authorities were expected to benefit in large measure from the reform. They undoubtedly did and the administration of smaller urban districts and towns which was notoriously weak got a badly-needed boost. But the management plan, which promised so much, did not perhaps have all the success hoped for it. County managers were expected to moderate the traditional antagonisms between town and country, as well as building up urban effectiveness in economic and social development. They did these things in varying degrees but certain deficiencies remained. The White Paper (1971) reviewed the effectiveness of urban authorities and concluded that all town commissioners and the majority of urban district councils should be merged in county councils, on the ground that 'a small urban authority cannot hope to provide the resources, equipment and staff required to discharge their functions effectively in modern times and so develop the town to its full potential'.

There was considerable political opposition to this proposal and despite support from consultants (McKinsey & Co. *Strengthening the Local Government Service,* 1972), it was not put into action before the change of government in 1973. The *Discussion Document* (1973) withdrew the abolition plan, substituting the idea that while all existing elected bodies should survive there should be a radical re-arrangement of functions involving transfer of planning, housing, roads and environmental functions to county councils. This idea also proved politically unwelcome. The Discussion Document suggested the creation of new municipal authorities, with limited functions, in existing non-municipal towns, built-up communities, and suburbs. These bodies would have representative but not executive functions. The chairman could, where appropriate, carry the title of mayor.

Town and Country

The White Paper (1971) cited, as an argument in favour of the proposed merger of urban and county authorities, the illogicality of confining administrative areas to strictly urban areas. The case for town-hinterland authorities was dealt with in an earlier part of the Paper and rejected in favour of the strengthened county:

> The establishment of such a system would mean the breaking up of most county council organisations into smaller units, and, most important of all, perhaps, would lessen the prospects of working out a strategy of development on a county and regional basis.

The foregoing touches on one of the main themes of the reform movement which developed during the 1960s — the social and economic interdependence of town and country and the consequent need to turn away from the Victorian division of urban from rural administration towards areas of combined urban-rural character. The majority report of the Redcliffe-Maud Commission (1969) has the following:

> The division between town and country in the present system has been very bad for local government. With the passage of time, it bears less and less relation to the changing distribution of population or to modern patterns of living, and it prevents problems from being considered over the areas necessary for their solution . . . Our own researches confirmed the community of social and economic interest joining towns of various sizes with the countryside in a mutually advantageous relationship which the present pattern of local authorities fails to reflect. . . . Each local authority should be responsible for a continuous area that makes, so far as practicable, a coherent social and economic whole, matching the way of life of a mobile society and giving the authority the space it needs to assess and tackle its problems.

This idea was generally adopted and became part of the thinking underlying the reform plans in England, Wales, Scotland and Northern Ireland.

The district system which it embodied was developed in some detail in the Institute of Public Administration response to the White Paper of 1971, *More Local Government* (1971). This report urged the adoption of District Administration as an escape from the political dilemma inherent in the White Paper project of cutting down drastically the number of urban authorities. But the District plan, though persuasively presented, did not attract either official or political favour.

New Towns

There is nothing in our legislation similar to the New Towns Act, 1965, for England and Wales and its counterparts the New Towns Act (Northern Ireland) 1965 and the New Towns (Scotland) Act 1968. These Acts enable the central authorities, whether Secretaries of State or Ministers, to designate land for development as new towns and to appoint development corporations (or development commissions in Northern Ireland) to carry the projects through. Development corporations or commissions are compact bodies comprising chairman, deputy chairman and not more than seven ordinary members. They are chosen for their capabilities, experience and expertise and may include a businessman, an industrialist, an academic with knowledge of the social services and one or more local councillors.

The development corporations are not representative in the democratic sense. They are a form of business board or directorate with extensive powers of land acquisition and development. They are funded by the state.

A considerable number of new towns were created under this legislation: some twenty in England, three in Wales, six in Scotland and one (Craigavon) in Northern Ireland, where an additional three further development commissions were charged with responsibilities in the established towns or city of Antrim, Ballymena and Derry. Not all these towns have been successful: Craigavon, for example, was reported to have failed to attract and keep population and industries and many new towns in Britain failed, initially at any rate, to provide the kind of environment and living conditions in which the inhabitants felt at ease.

Shannon

The new town at Shannon, Co Clare is our only example of a town comparable with those mentioned above. The role of development corporation was taken by the Shannon Free Airport Development Company (SFADCo) and no separate corporation or commission was set up. The company, which dates from 1957, began work in 1958 on a new industrial estate and the first instalment of the new town (an apartment block and community hall) was constructed in 1960. The town has grown to about 8,000 inhabitants and there is a local move to acquire municipal status.

Dublin Area

The rapid growth in recent decades of population in Dublin city and county had the effect of focusing attention on the crucial question of whether the spread of the city should or could be contained and if containment were decided on, how could it be achieved? How, in fact, could the inevitable city overspill be accommodated? Professor Myles Wright, whose advice on planning the Dublin area had been commissioned by the Minister for Local Government in April 1964 submitted his report and advisory plan in December 1966. He recommended the creation of a cluster of four new towns to the west of the city, under the aegis of a Regional Planning Agency under an independent chairman with two government representatives, one elected member from each of the six major local authorities in the region and the four county managers, one of them being also Dublin City Manager. The proposed new towns would take the form of linear development fingers separated by green spaces.

The suggestion of a special agency has not been accepted by the government: the Minister had, it appears, decided that the new powers conferred on planning authorities would make the creation of separate development corporations unneccessary. It would, moreover, involve more direct state intervention, and more demands for state investment than were desirable.

The projected new towns were therefore assigned for development to the city-county planning authorities which, as housing authorities, could undertake a share of public housing and amenities; and to private enterprise, which took on the remainder of housing, with shopping facilities etc., in accordance with the County Development Plan. The new towns were initiated by the Dublin Corporation which took the lead in acquiring land for satellite development with their own needs in view. The County Development Plan (1972) envisaged the units as largely self-contained in accommodation, employment and amenities — towns rather than suburbs, with their own industries, offices and other job opportunities, so that migration from home to work would be kept on a minimum.

The new towns which emerged from the County Plan differed in a number of ways from the Wright plan. The proposed linear design was dropped in favour of three more compact town units at Blanchardstown, Ronanstown (Clondalkin—Lucan) and Tallaght. The reasons for this modification were twofold. In the first place the drainage catchments in the area did not suit linear development. Secondly, the preservation of green spaces between the 'fingers' could only be secured either by acquiring the land, a move which would have attracted much opposition, or by zoning the land under the Planning Act and meeting heavy demands for compensation.

As Zimmerman pointed out:

Although the city and county acquired some land by compulsory acquisition, the development policy has been primarily a *laissez-faire* one with heavy reliance placed upon private developers because of the inadequacy of available public funds. The general approach of the two local authorities was to install sewers, construct major roads, facilitate construction of homes by private developers and acquire open space. Construction of churches and private schools by appropriate authorities also was given a high priority. The Dublin County Planning Department co-ordinated school site planning with Diocesan officials and Education Department officials, and plans for schools were based upon assumption that each house on average would be the residence of four persons.

(New Town Development, 1978)

In a recent (1980) statement the Dublin City and County Manager said that the three growth areas to the west of the city were well advanced. The aim was to create 'three vibrant towns, with their own well-developed town centres, their own industrial areas, their own neighbourhood centres, schools, parks and recreational facilities'.

Is Dublin Too Big?

There is no simple answer to this question. When the problem was looked at in 1954 (it seemed to bulk as a problem even then) greater Dublin, with a population of 634,000, constituted 21.4 per cent of the national total. The weakness then discerned by Dr McCarthy was not that Dublin's size of rate of growth was abnormal but its bulk relative to the rest of the town population of the country: 'the town population outside the capital is too small'. This condition seems to have corrected itself since the 1950s, but the relative size of greater Dublin has become more pronounced and is now definitely a problem of national concern.

Dublin, in the absolute sense, is not impossibly large: there are many bigger cities that are better managed, better planned and where living is, in some ways at least, pleasanter. The trouble is that the population of the metropolitan area, the conurbation, is growing too fast. If it continues to grow at a rate of 2 per cent per annum, the population will double in thirty-five years, and it is impossible for any city to double its infrastructure, the facilities essential for good living, in that period.

Is there an even deeper cause affecting not only Dublin, but other metropolitan areas? Donnison, in the third Sean Lemass Memorial lecture, (1977) noted that 'many people are profoundly disillusioned about the capacity of urban industrial societies to plan their cities, to solve social problems or to give effective help to their most deprived people'. His prescription for remedial action is a combination of planning, urban development and priorities for social development. The strategies he outlines are far wider than the British Urban Aid Programme, launched in 1968 'to provide larger resources for housing, health and welfare services, day nurseries, education and other services in "areas of special social need"'. The range of English local government services is of course more comprehensive than the Irish and their urban aid programme is based largely on local council and community effort. The White Paper 'Policy for the Inner Cities' (1977) projected a much expanded programme with heightened emphasis on the problems of deprivation and decay at the centre of a number of metropolitan counties.

The question of optimal city size is discussed by the National Economic and Social Council whose report (No. 45, 1980) concludes that: 'The crucial issue is not whether Dublin is too big or smaller towns in the provinces too small, but whether the changes in the spatial structure of the Irish urban system and, in particular, the increasing concentration of population in the Greater Dublin area, are in harmony with the goals of the Community' (p. 49). The report goes on to draw attention to the general issue of urbanisation, to the absence of any coherent statement from government to replace the outdated document of May, 1972, on urban and regional issues, and to urge the case for an urban strategy with, as its principal aim, moderating the magnetic attraction of the Eastern region. 'The tendency towards spatial concentration of employment (especially services) and population in the Greater Dublin area is so strong that the only policy with any realistic chance of stabilising the East region's share of national population is to accelerate the process of polarisation elsewhere, possibly in one or two counter-magnet cities' (pp. 97–8).

A recent report issued by NESC on *Urbanisation: Problems of Growth and Decay in Dublin* (1981) examines the complex of troubles besetting the capital in the context of developments in Britain, Europe and America, and recommends a number of possible lines of advance. It revives the plan for a Greater Dublin Council first projected (on a much smaller scale, of course) in 1926 and elaborated by the Local Government Tribunal of 1938. The new GDC would be assigned a territory fanning out from the city, covering Dun Laoghaire and the built-up county, and stretching to the adjacent urbanised parts of north and east Wicklow, east Kildare, south Meath and possibly south Louth. Other proposals dealt with housing, new-built and refurbished; employment; and the redirection of social policies towards a Community Development approach. These measures would improve conditions in the deprived inner city, but the consultants also included an integrated package of proposals designed specifically for that problem. Among them were: planning for a more compact and attractive city centre; a shift away from private transport in the centre; a wide range of inner city housing and provision of more land for industry; priority education policies involving school, home and community; and the creation of an Inner City Fund supported by local business, government and the European Community.

16

Housing

In the public mind housing stands in the forefront of local services. There are cogent reasons for this — its strong social and community significance, an economic importance deriving from the heavy capital investment it involves and its prominence in the building industry and as an employer of labour, skilled and unskilled. With its abiding visual element it can impose a character, good or bad, on a townscape and even in some degree on a countryside. It is hardly surprising then that housing performance and shortcomings have been a constant issue in local and even national politics. On 12 July 1966 Northern Ireland commemorated the Battle of the Boyne. In the Republic it was, less emotively, the day when the Housing Bill, 1965 became the Housing Act 1966. The Act replaced three codes of law with a single comprehensive and more comprehensible Act.

Before dealing with this Act and the current situation the historical background may be filled in with an account of the earlier codes. The housing of urban workers was governed by a code entitled the Housing of the Working Classes Acts, the housing of rural workers by another entitled the Labourers Acts and the help given to private enterprise was determined by the Small Dwellings Acquisition Acts and a number of Housing Acts. For historical and social reasons these codes pursued separate lines of development for the best part of a century. The Labourers Acts, for example, were linked closely with the land struggle and carried with them some of the characteristics of the legislation under which ownership of agricultural land passed to the former tenants.

Urban Housing

Legislation authorising intervention by local authorities in housing began in the third quarter of the nineteenth century with two Acts promoted by Lord Shaftesbury. The Common Lodging Houses Act, 1851 made the licensing and inspection of all common lodging-houses compulsory and was operated to some effect. A second Act, the Labouring Classes Lodging Houses Act, 1851 empowered urban authorities to build and let houses for workers. It was a failure but over the following four decades the initial impetus gathered momentum and the ideas of house improvement — the Artisans and Labourers Dwellings Act, 1868 — and of slum clearance —

220

the Artisans and Labourers Dwellings Improvement Acts of 1875 and 1879 – gained ground. The movement culminated in a Royal Commission on the Housing of the Working Classes whose report (1885) formed the basis of the Housing of the Working Classes Act, 1890.

The Act of 1890 applied equally to cities and towns in Britain and Ireland and operations – clearance of unhealthy areas, dealing with unhealthy individual houses or building new houses for workers – depended wholly on local rate resources. The special needs of Ireland found a modest response in the Housing of the Working Classes (Ireland) Act, 1908 which established the Irish Housing Fund to give some financial aid to Irish urban authorities. The need for action was underlined by the 1914 report of a Departmental Committee on Housing in Dublin which has supplied a generation of writers, speakers and readers with material on the appalling slum conditions in the city before the British departed. The Housing (Ireland) Act, 1919 offered more substantial state subsidies to local housing authorities and state aid to private persons and public utility societies building houses. About 9,000 houses were built by urban authorities before 1922.

Rural Housing

Rural conditions began to claim public attention at much the same time as the problem in towns. The earliest approach to action was to give landlords the opportunity to borrow from the Public Works Loans Commissioners for the purpose of building cottages for their tenants. But the plan, given form in the Dwellings for the Labouring Classes (Ireland) Act, 1860 inspired little or no interest. Thus successive censuses commenting on rural housing reported deplorable conditions everywhere except in a few north eastern counties. The census of 1881 returned a total of 215,000 cottiers most of whom lived in one-room mud-walled cabins roofed with thatch. There were, in addition, some 60,000 agricultural labourers equally poorly housed. The Irish Party, led by Parnell, introduced a Private Members Bill which became the Labourers (Ireland) Act, 1883, the foundation stone of the rural housing code.

The Act of 1883 passed the initiative to local ratepayers, twelve or more of whom could apply to the rural sanitary authority (then the board of guardians) to undertake a scheme of cottage building. The original procedure was unnecessarily cumbersome but successive amending Acts smoothed out difficulties and much good work was done with the stimulus of a small state subsidy. Provided under the Purchase of Land (Ireland) Act, 1891 the Exchequer contribution was paid from 1896 onwards. Further state aid was forthcoming from the Labourers Cottages Fund, established by the Labourers (Ireland) Act, 1906. This Act applied to labourers' cottage schemes the very favourable financial terms inaugurated in 1903 for land purchase. Loans were advanced by the Land Commission repayable over 68½ years by means of annuities of £3.25 per £100. In addition, 20 per cent of the annuity was borne by a new fund called the Ireland Development Fund. The combined result of these measures was that between 1883 and 1920 some 42,000 cottages were built under the Labourers Acts.

Private Housing

The Building Societies Act, 1874 marked the emergence of a (mainly English and Scottish) movement to channel savings and investment into house ownership. In the majority of early cases, society members bought house property not for ownership but for investment and letting. The Small Dwellings Acquisition Act, 1899 was designed to aid occupants to buy out the landlords' interest but potential borrowers from local authorities (county councils and urban authorities) were hampered by landlords' reluctance to sell. Comparatively few loans were made during the period up to the 1914 War.

After the war, the Housing (Ireland) Act 1919, under the pressure of post-war demand, inaugurated the making of state grants direct to persons building houses for their own or others' occupation. Only some 350 houses were built under this scheme before the new government took over.

Independence

The housing shortage in towns was the most urgent social problem that faced the new government in 1922. The virtual suspension of building from 1918 resulted in a dearth of houses for families for whom the speculative builder would have catered had the war not brought his activities to a standstill and aggravated the deficiency of houses for the working classes that had existed in pre-war years.

The new administration was faced, in short, with a housing crisis and sought to meet it by launching a crash programme. This was known as the Million Pound Scheme. The plan envisaged the immediate raising of a shilling rate by housing authorities, estimated to produce about £125,000. To this would be added three times that amount, £375,000 by means of short-term bank loans, making a total of £500,000. The government undertook to give double the amount so raised – the million pounds which gave its name to the scheme. It was an imaginative stroke and found a ready response – 71 out of a possible 94 housing authorities adopted schemes. The target of two thousand houses was substantially met. Most of the new houses were built in the Dublin area, followed by the other county boroughs and the bulk of them sold to tenant-purchasers.

The government made it clear that they could not commit the new state to the kind of long-term subsidies which had marked the Labourers

Act schemes in the early years of the century and the handful of projects under the Housing (Ireland) Act, 1919. Slum-clearance was a slow and expensive process and the re-housing of poor badly-housed tenants could only be done with the aid of long-term loans and equally long-term state contributions towards loan charges. The new administration turned away, therefore, from the problem of the worst-housed and looked for quick returns from grants to the middle range of house-seekers. This was not entirely a narrow class approach. It was reasonable to expect that a re-vitalised building industry would give, directly or indirectly, badly-needed jobs and that the activity promoted at middle level would result in good or not-so-bad housing filtering downwards to the lower stratum.

The Housing (Building Facilities) Act, 1924, reflected the government's openly middle-class orientation — going so far as to allow civil servants to build their grant houses up to 1500 sq.ft floor area, while all others were kept within 520-1000 sq.ft limits. The grants were substantial; up to £100 was payable for a serviced house and £90 for unserviced. This meant that the state paid about one sixth of the building cost. Grants of two thirds of these amounts were payable for reconstructed houses. Local authorities were authorised to help with loans, free or cheap sites and by remitting rates on the new houses on a sliding scale over twenty years. The Department of Local Government and Public Health prepared sets of plans and sold them to prospective grant-winners. The scheme was successful; the grants were eagerly taken up and houses were built, improved or reconstructed in large numbers, particularly in rural areas.

Local authorities were not overlooked. The Million Pound scheme, completed before the end of 1924, had created a momentum which it was important to keep up. Accordingly the Housing (Building Facilities) (Amendment) Act, 1924 offered amounts similar to private grants to urban authorities deciding to operate under the Housing of the Working Classes Act. In the following year the Housing Act 1925 tilted the balance in favour of local authorities by reducing private grants to a maximum of £75 while continuing the standard grants (up to £100 a house) to urban authorities and public utility societies. The 1925 Act also extended the grants to the new county boards of health providing cottages under the Labourers Acts.

Local authorities, however, were inhibited from undertaking large-scale operations by difficulties in raising loans — the best terms available were bank loans at 4½ per cent repayable over 15 years. Although house costs were falling during the decade these borrowing terms meant that high rents had to be charged. Local authorities remained therefore relatively inactive and the bulk of house building and reconstruction was done by the private sector. In 1929, however, the government decided to restore the practice, suspended since 1922, of helping local authorities with state capital. The Local Loans Fund was revived by the Minister for Finance and loans made available at 5¾ per cent over a maximum of 35 years.

Later in the same year housing surveys were put in train in urban areas to get some measure of further house needs if an attack were to be made on the elimination of unhealthy areas and dwellings. Total estimated needs topped 40,000 houses, 30,000 to replace unfit houses and even allowing for some over-estimation it was clear that a serious problem existed in our cities and towns. And this despite vigorous action: some 26,000 houses were built with state and local aid between 1922 and 1932; in round figures 9,000 by urban authorities, 5,000 by private efforts in cities and towns and almost 11,500 privately built in rural areas. The Labourers Acts were virtually dormant. The tally of cottages built by boards of health in the ten years was a mere 500.

Pre-War Decade

The government's housing plan took the form of the Housing (Miscellaneous Provisions) Act, 1931. The Act was closely modelled on the Housing Act, 1930 a fairly radical measure put through by Britain's second Labour government of 1929–1931. It replaced Parts 1 and 11 (unhealthy areas and houses) of the Housing of the Working Classes Act, 1890 with new, more effective machinery. For land acquisition in urban areas it substituted procedure by Compulsory Purchase Order for the slower, more elaborate provisional order method carried over from the nineteenth century. The Act terminated, for local authorities, state assistance by way of lump-sum grants in favour of annual subsidies towards loan charges. The rates of subsidy were generous for those depression times but not enough to satisfy growing political demands, rising to a clamour as the general election drew nearer. They were:

> 40 per cent of loan charges for houses replacing slums and unfit houses;
> 20 per cent for houses for other urban workers;
> 20 per cent for labourers' cottages in rural areas.

Private building was encouraged by continuing the £45 grant for self-help houses and by enlarging the scope of the Small Dwellings Acquisition Acts to enable local authorities to lend to persons intending to build; loans were formerly confined to purchasers of houses already occupied. The cost-limit of houses financed under the Acts was raised to £1,000.

The 1931 Act was in large measure the basis from which the great housing drive of the 1930s took off, but its financial scheme never came into effect. It was superseded by more generous terms. The new government had their own ideas which emerged as the Housing (Financial and Miscellaneous Provisions) Act, 1932 and offered the following subsidies:

> 1. 66⅔ per cent on houses for families displaced under the Housing Acts;

2. 33⅓ per cent on houses for other workers;
3. 60 per cent on labourers' cottages.

Certain limits were set to the capital outlay on which these subsidies were payable. They were realistic enough for the time ranging from £500 per flat in county boroughs down to £300 per cottage in rural areas. The 1932 Act also extended to boards of health the compulsory purchase procedure introduced for urban housing by the Act of 1931. Increased grants were offered to private individuals and public utility societies in rural areas; for agricultural workers the maximum grant was raised to £80. The system of rates remission was also changed from the twenty-year descending scale to a seven-year two-thirds remission.

A few provisions of the 1932 Act were radical carry-overs from the new government's opposition days. Labour party influence could also be traced in the condition that trade union rates of wages must be observed in housing schemes. The Minister was empowered to purchase or manufacture building materials and machines — a power never directly exercised. Neither did he use the power given in the Act to assume the housing functions of a recalcitrant local authority — though there was no hesitation during the 1930s in dissolving a number of councils which did not come up to scratch in such essentials as rate collection. Finally the 1932 Act was followed by the establishment of a non-statutory three-man Housing Board with advisory and research functions; it was never significant enough to overshadow the very active and colourful Sean T. Ó Ceallaigh, Deputy President, Tanaiste and Minister from 1932–39.

The housing drive was one of the successes of the first Fianna Fail government: a total of 81,000 houses were built with state and local aid in the ten years from 1933 to 1942; a further 29,000 were reconstructed. Difficulties about capital money began to surface towards the close of the 1930s. The Banking Commission (1934–38) was critical of the amounts spent and of the state aid towards repayment of the amounts borrowed. The majority report (paras 518–520) commented sternly: 'An item of growing importance in the dead-weight debt of the state is attributable to subsidising by the government of various housing schemes.' Despite the protest of a member (James Hurson, Secretary of the Department of Local Government and Public Health, Reservation No. 2) the commission recommended discontinuance of long-term fixed subsidies in favour of annual disbursements in the light of each year's budgetary circumstances. Dublin Corporation, whose titanic exertions in slum-clearance and rehousing had been very costly, was denied the full co-operation of the banks and investors in the floating of stock issues for capital purposes. The crisis thus threatened led to the setting up by the Minister of the Dublin Housing Inquiry in 1939, headed by M.P. Colivet, chairman of the Housing Board. Its report, delayed by war conditions, appeared in 1943. One of its recommendations on the isssue of over-spending was to criticize centre-city flats schemes as both expensive to build and financially un-productive and to favour suburban house development (report, paras 330– 339). The tribunal's second principal recommendation was on rents policy. It urged the general application of the differential rents system inaugurated by the Cork City Manager in 1934 (report, paras 172–214).

Rural Housing

The revival of operations under the Labourers Acts which followed the Acts of 1931 and 1932 led to renewed pressure for tenant-purchase on favourable terms. This had been a political issue of some years' standing and the old link between Labourers Acts and land re-asserted itself as a demand for something equivalent to land-purchase terms for cottages, with the boards of health in the incongruous role of landlord. The govern-ment sought a solution from a commission representing the interests con-cerned – tenants, county councils and state. The Commission on the Sale of Labourers' Cottages reported with exemplary speed in April 1933; all but one of the eight members were in favour of a scheme of universal sale on an annuity basis. The sole dissenter was John Collins, a senior officer in the Department of Local Government and Public Health whose memorandum of dissent argued with admirable courage the case against sale. The government sided with the majority. Right or wrong? Collins's dispassionate but impressive assemblage of facts and figures was a plea for the *bona fide* agricultural worker, a class already in decline. Was his protest merely an expression of nostalgia for a vanishing feature of rural society? Collins was a townsman.

The Labourers Act, 1936 followed after some delay. It placed an obligation on boards of health to prepare sale schemes covering all their cottages, the annuities to be set in general at 75 per cent of the rent, exclusive of rates. The period of each terminable annuity was also, in general, the period of the loan, less the age of the cottage. Before vesting a cottage in the tenant-purchaser the board of health was obliged to put the cottage in good repair and sanitary condition. The annuity could be consolidated with any land purchase annuity payable by the tenant. Cottage purchase schemes were subject to the Minister's approval and subsequently to scrutiny by the Dáil. There was a good deal of agitation by tenants in favour of reducing annuities and in 1951 the Minister con-ceded the point; the basis of calculation thence forward was 50% of the rent.

Post-War Period

Despite the energetic attack on the housing problem in the 1930s, the situation outlined in the White Paper 'Housing – A Review of Past Opera-tions and Immediate Requirements' (1948) gave no grounds for complacency. The task facing the country was bigger than ever. One hundred thousand new dwellings were needed, sixty thousand to be built by local authorities and forty thousand by the private sector.

Local Authorities

It was not found necessary to change the rates of subsidy fixed in 1932 — 66⅔, 60 and 33⅓ per cent but the Housing (Amendment) Act, 1948 extended loan repayment and subsidy periods from 35 to 50 years. Capital grants were given from the Transition Development Fund to compensate for the increase in building costs, together with special grants to maintain the effective interest rate on housing loans at 2½ per cent. Both urban and rural authorities were required, in making lettings, to have regard to the character, industry, occupation, family circumstances and existing housing conditions of applicants and subject to these to give, where practicable, preference to certain defined categories. In rural areas for example priority was to be given to genuine agricultural labourers. Certain houses could be reserved for newly-wed couples.

For private building the 1948 Act offered increased grants up to £275 per house (£285 if paid through a public utility society) for owner-occupation and grants up to £400 per house built for letting payable over ten years. The upper limit of value for loans under the Small Dwellings Acquisition Acts was raised in stages from £1,000 to reach £2,000 in 1962. There was an immediate and vigorous response to the new financial measures. House completion more than doubled between 1948 and 1949, from 1600 to 3,400. The same dramatic increase occurred in the following year and output continued to rise until it reached a peak of 14,000 in 1953. About this time the international balance of payments crisis led to an economy drive in public spending which restricted house building; this was coupled with evidence that housing demand had been wholly or largely met in most areas and Dublin Corporation had vacant houses on hand. There was a sharp drop in output in 1958, from 11,000 to 7,500 and a further steep fall in 1959 to a total of some 4,900 houses. During this period the share of total output contributed by local authorities tended to fall. The contraction persisted from 1960 onwards when there was a revival in house building; private builders were quicker to recover. The result was that in 1964 when local authorities had reached the target of 60,000 set in 1948, private builders had achieved almost twice their share — 40,000 — of the national task. The respective figures were: local authorities 63,000 and private builders 74,000.

Private Building. Since 1960 the lead role in house production has been taken by the private sector and the 1948 predictions have been to that extent belied. This reversal in roles (the change was from the 1930s experience, but not from that in the 1920s) was largely a consequence of a series of Housing Acts offering ever more attractive terms to private builders. The Housing (Amendment) Act 1950 introduced the idea of local grants in addition to state housing grants and admitted larger houses to eligibility for state and supplementary grants. The maximum floor area was raised from 1,250 to 1,400 square feet. The Act also authorised county councils to operate the Small Dwellings Acquisition Acts in urban areas where the urban councils were unable or unwilling to exercise their lending powers.

The Housing (Amendment) Act, 1952 made further progress. A scheme of state grants for private water supplies and sanitation payable by the Department of Local Government was inaugurated. The maximum grant for house reconstruction was raised to £120. The system of local supplementary grants was elaborated, the amounts being graded according to the applicant's family income or, in the case of farmers, valuation of holding. The provision for local supplementary grants was extended to reconstruction, water supply and sewerage grants and to grants given by the Minister for the Gaeltacht under the Housing (Gaeltacht) Acts.

The Housing (Amendment) Act 1958 carried inducements still further by increasing maximum grants for serviced houses (in unserviced areas) to £300 and for reconstructed houses to £140. The Act offered private grants of £75 for combined water and sewerage facilities – £50 for water and £25 for sanitation. The Housing (Loans and Grants) Act, 1962 is significant not for the innovations it brought to the private grants scheme but because it was the first step in the rationalisation of housing law which culminated in the Housing Act, 1966. The 1962 Act consolidated the law relating to grants and loans for private housing. It made some changes in the grants system: a new scheme of special grants to assist essential preservation work on houses in rural areas; the amounts payable being two-thirds of outlay, up to £80. A new grant was also introduced for housing old people: up to £300 per house built by an approved society or other approved body. Supplementary grants of equal amounts were payable by local authorities. A scheme of grants was also inaugurated to encourage experimental designs in low-cost housing; a grant amounting to half the agreed cost was payable for a proto-type dwelling.

Local Authorities

As noted above, the 1950s were marked by a decline in the relative size of local authority housing output. This trend persisted through the following decades and is the current norm. The numerous Housing Acts of the 1950s made improvements in the legal and financial provisions relating to local authority building and after the recession of the mid-fifties capital for housing ceased for a time to be an acute problem but the dominance of private sector building seemed and still seems irreversible. This position is, of course, the norm in most market economies.

The general effect of the legal changes from 1950 onwards was towards phasing out the old separate code dealing with rural housing and the evolution of a single code, based on urban conditions, to cope with both urban and rural needs. The 1964 White Paper 'Housing – Progress and Prospects' outlined the steps in this process of convergence, the most significant being the application by the Housing (Amendment) Act, 1958 of urban financial arrangements to operations under the Labourers Acts. At the time of publication the White Paper gave the following outline of subsidies paid by the state towards loan charges incurred by local authorities in borrowing for house building:

1. $66\frac{2}{3}$ where the dwellings are provided to accommodate persons displaced from unfit or overcrowded houses, left homeless through the collapse or destruction of their dwellings, or in need of rehousing on medical, compassionate or other similar grounds where their circumstances would not permit them to be rehoused otherwise;
2. $33\frac{1}{3}$ in other cases.

These subsidies were payable only on the cost of a dwelling up to the following limits: £2,200 for a flat, £1,650 for a house with piped water and sanitation, £1,100 for an unserviced house.

The merging of the Labourers Acts and the Housing of the Working Classes Acts was a symptom of creeping urbanisation, of a gradual breakdown of the old differences between urban and rural standards. The 1964 White Paper identified the chief remaining distinction of any significance as the special sale arrangements applicable to labourers' cottages which, deriving from the Land Purchase Acts, had nothing of a corresponding nature in urban housing law. Urban authorities had powers of sale conferred by the Housing (Ireland) Act, 1919, s.11 which had been used extensively during the housing campaign of the 1920s but not more than occasionally thereafter. In July, 1953 the Minister for Local Government circularised urban authorities suggesting the advisability of selling houses to tenants at figures not less than the outstanding balance of the loan or a suitable multiple of the rent, exclusive of rates. The multiples depended on the age of the houses, ranging from a factor of 10 for pre-1922 houses to a factor of 30 for houses built after 1946. There was a moderate response.

The 1964 White Paper proposed to simplify procedure for cottage sales in rural areas. In addition, both urban and rural housing authorities would be obliged, before sale, to ensure that the dwelling was in good structural condition – this represented a less onerous obligation on county councils which had been compelled by the Labourers Act 1936 to put cottages, before vesting in the tenants, into 'good repair and sanitary condition'. The same right of appeal against a condition of sale would apply to both urban and rural tenants.

Housing Act, 1966

This Act replaced more than fifty earlier housing Acts and re-stated, with improvements, as much of the old code as was thought necessary in present day conditions. Emphasis was placed on modernisation. A number of time-worn cliches were dropped: the venerable duality of rural and urban housing codes; the careful definition of agricultural labourer and his eligibility for benefit under the Labourers Acts and the elaborate qualifications for membership of the working class. All these were consigned to the dustbin and replaced by a straightforward statement of powers enabling housing authorities (county councils, corporations of boroughs and county boroughs, urban district councils and town commissioners) to build, manage, let and sell houses for people who are unable for one reason or another to build or rent for themselves. The older powers of dealing with sub-standard areas and dwellings were re-enacted. The housing functions of town commissioners were placed under certain limits.

Apart from modernisation, improvements in the housing code included:
1. special provision for re-housing elderly people and persons displaced by planning and dangerous buildings operations;
2. special provision for housing farmers with land valuations of £5 or less;
3. encouraging housing authorities and approved bodies to provide developed sites;
4. a new range of grants for private housing of farmers under £60 valuation and certain other persons; dower houses; improvement of local authority houses etc.; private house grants became payable for houses up to 1500 sq. ft;
5. special loans for reconstruction work.

The Act made provision for additional state subsidy to housing authorities constructing blocks of flats or maisonettes in high-rise (six or more storeys) buildings. This provision was inspired by the Ballymun experiment, undertaken by Dublin Corporation at the instance of the Department of Local Government, work on which commenced in March, 1965. These high-rise flats did not however prove attractive to tenants and the project was not repeated in Ireland.

The Act empowered the Minister to make housing subsidy conditional on, *inter alia*, letting the houses on a system of differential rents, or rents varying with the financial circumstances of the tenants. A strong case for the general adoption of such a system was made in the 1964 White Paper (pp 19–20) and all new local authority dwellings have been, since 1967, let on approved schemes of income-related rents. In 1973 a further step towards uniformity was taken when the practice of leaving many of the details of differential rents schemes to individual housing authorities was abandoned in favour of a national system worked out by the Department of the Environment in consultation with the people and bodies involved.

The 1966 Act also provided a common power of sale of dwellings by both urban and rural authorities, in replacement of section 11 of the Housing (Ireland) Act, 1919 and of the Labourers Act, 1936. It was no longer necessary for the Minister to give specific consent to individual sales. Ministerial consent was confined to laying down minimum terms of sale for subsidy and audit purposes.

Further Legislation

The Housing Act, 1966 was followed by two minor enactments in 1969 and 1970. The Housing Act, 1969 provided a control procedure to restrain the demolition of dwellings or their diversion to other uses. The 1970 Act recast the private grants scheme in favour of houses of moderate size. It was, in addition, an anti-squatting measure.

The Housing (Miscellaneous Provision) Act, 1979, was a more important piece of legislation. Its principal objects were to validate the accumulated changes in housing practice since 1972 and to introduce a flexible method of giving statutory cover to these and any future changes in grants, loans and subsidies under the Housing Acts. The Act also strengthened ministerial powers of control over new house prices by extending the system of certificates of reasonable value and applied certain optional arrangements to the letting and sale of local authority houses. In the matter of house sales the Minister was enabled to direct housing authorities to sell, or not to sell, houses of a specified category, e.g. to retain for letting purpose-built houses or flats for elderly people or other special groups. The Act, in addition, made provision for devolving the administration of certain grant schemes to housing authorities.

With a view to cutting down the need for frequent recourse to the Oireachtas the scheme of the 1979 Act was to confer, in very broad terms, powers on both the Minister and housing authorities in relation to grants, loans, subsidies and so on. Details of amounts and conditions would then be set out in regulations. The first produce of this scheme has been the Housing Regulations, 1980 (S.I. No. 296 of 1980) a comprehensive range of provisions dealing with new house and other grants, subsidies, loans, certificates of reasonable value, letting and house sales by local authorities.

Gaeltacht Housing. There is a separate code, beginning with the Housing (Gaeltacht) Act, 1929 dealing with the erection and improvement of houses in the Gaeltacht. This code is administered by the Department of the Gaeltacht. In 1952 housing authorities were empowered to supplement improvement and building grants made under the Act of 1929 but supplementary grants were terminated in 1977.

The Housing (Gaeltacht) Acts, 1929–79 provide grants of sufficient amount to make up for the loss of supplementary grants. The maximum new house grant is £2,000 for a fully serviced house. Home improvement grants continue to be paid to Gaeltacht applicants, currently (1980) at 75 per cent of cost up to £750. Grants of special amounts are also paid for private water supplies and sanitation – up to £360 for piped water and £300 for sanitation. An additional grant of £600 for provision of a bathroom with hot water supply is available. Further grants are available to residents in the Gaeltacht providing additional rooms for visitors and holiday chalets. Loans for house building or improvement are also available from Roinn na Gaeltachta.

Private enterprise housing. There were considerable fluctuations of policy during the 1970s regarding grants for private housing. From January 1976 new house grants were limited to applicants who were eligible for supplementary grants viz, those in a specified income bracket or (in the case of farmers) whose land valuation did not exceed £60. In January, 1977, reconstruction grants were limited by reference to house valuation. This arrangement was, however, superseded later in 1977, when the new Government announced a scheme of £1,000 grants for first time owner-occupiers, two-thirds grants up to £600 for house improvements (since largely discontinued) and the termination of local supplementary grants. Grants of two-thirds of cost up to £200 for individual water supplies and £150 for sewage facilities were also announced; where the services were installed as part of a group scheme the limits were raised to £300 and £250 respectively. The grants for individual installations have since been discontinued, but those for group schemes are still in operation.

Reconstruction and Improvement Grants

The first grants for reconstruction were given under the Housing (Building Facilities) Acts, 1924. The scheme was limited to certain types of houses but eligibility was extended by the Housing (Financial and Miscellaneous Provisions) Act, 1932 and subsequent legislation. Grants were increased to meet rising costs, and from 1952 local supplementary grants were paid. In November 1977, following a change of Government, state grants were raised to £600 maximum and supplementary grants discontinued except in Gaeltacht areas. Reconstruction grants were, however, terminated from January 1980 with the decision to confine State aid to new houses. The scheme of loans for reconstruction and improvement which could be advanced by local authorities under the Housing (Loan and Grants) Act, 1962 and later under the Housing Act, 1966 continued to operate. The amounts of loans and income limits for borrowers were increased following the discontinuance of most of the improvements grants.

Details of the current position on improvement grants are set out in Parts III and IV of the Housing Regulations, 1980. Special improvements grants may be paid to householders in certain off-shore islands. Grants continue to be available for the private installation of piped water and sanitation on a group scheme basis. Housing authorities are enabled under Part IV of the 1980 Regulations to give what are known as essential repairs grants to people in rural areas (mainly of advanced years) who may wish to prolong the life of their houses without the expense of full-scale improvement. The grant is limited to the cost of repairs; the Minister may recoup 50 per cent of the grant, up to £300.

County councils and the corporations of county boroughs can assist people to carry out structural work, erect additional rooms or provide chalets to meet the needs of the physically or mentally handicapped, or of the mentally ill. Grants are generally two thirds of cost and the Minister may contribute 50% of the outlay, up to £1,200.

Voluntary Housing Associations. In 1978 a scheme of special assistance was introduced for voluntary associations undertaking housing for the elderly. Housing authorities could give loans to approved bodies up to 75 per cent (and 90 per cent in certain circumstances) of cost of a project and subsidise the rents. In addition State grants of £1,000 were available for each dwelling, plus £200 a room up to £1,000, for caretaker – welfare accommodation. The grant aspect of the scheme is dealt with in Part V of the Housing Regulations, 1980.

Co-operative Housing. Housing co-operatives have certain clear advantages in securing economies – in building materials, sites etc. – and in providing information and advice to members. With the aim of encouraging the movement the Minister makes an annual grant to the National Association of Building Co-operatives, under section 3 of the Housing (Miscellaneous Provisions) Act, 1979. The Association was established in 1970 as a promotional body for co-operative effort in building. Housing authorities may allocate subsidised sites to co-operative societies whose members include a reasonable proportion of people in a low-income category.

Sites for Private Housing. The Housing Act, 1966 introduced a new subsidy of $33\frac{1}{3}$ per cent of loan charges for housing authorities providing developed sites for private housing. The subsidy was continued by section 9 of the Housing (Miscellaneous Provisions) Act, 1979, and Part VIII of the Housing Regulations, 1980. It is limited to one third of loan charges on the capital cost up to £500 per site. The sites must be sold for not less than cost of acquisition and development, less subsidy. Allocation of sites is confined to persons eligible either for local authority housing, or house-purchase loans. A site subsidy is also available on similar terms to approved bodies.

House Loans

Mortgage finance was a continuing problem during the decade from 1969. The principal suppliers were the building societies. Other sources were housing authorities, banks and assurance companies. In 1969 ministerial responsibility for building societies was transferred to the Minister for Local Government and shortly afterwards the Department in consultation with the Irish Building Societies Association commenced a review of the legislation which resulted in a consolidated and modernised law: the Building Societies Act, 1976. But the Act did little to relieve the difficulty of finding enough capital for lending, on satisfactory terms.

In 1973 the Minister had sought a solution in a special subsidy to building societies with the purpose of keeping lending rates down without diminishing the attractions of the societies to investors. The subsidy was terminated in 1976 but the problem reappeared in 1978 when sharp rises occurred in both house prices and interest rates. The Minister asked the building societies to divert the bulk of their mortgage finance towards lower price houses, at least 40 per cent of total mortgage finance towards the purchase of new houses and to stipulate certificates of reasonable value as a condition of new house loans. In June 1980 the subsidy was re-introduced in order to stabilise interest rates but was terminated from October 1980 in line with their general downward movement at that time.

Housing authorities are the next most important source of home loans. Dating back to the Small Dwellings Acquisition Act, 1899 local authority lending functions have been progressively expanded to cover house construction as well as purchase and the reconstruction and improvement of older dwellings. The various enactments from 1899 onwards were consolidated in the Housing (Loans and Grants) Act, 1962 since replaced by the Housing Act, 1966. Under Part VI of the Housing Regulations, 1980 loans are generally limited to £12,000, £13,000 in certain islands off the West coast or 95 per cent of the value; borrowers must belong to certain income categories. The upper limits are £5,500 for non-farmers and in the case of farmers a land and buildings valuation of £44, or £66 where a borrower is employed on the parental holding.

Provision for house improvement loans is now contained in section 8 of the Housing (Miscellaneous Provisions) Act, 1979 which replaced section 40 of the Housing Act, 1966. Part VII of the Housing Regulations, 1980 sets an upper limit of £4,000 to loans (£4,500 in offshore islands) and applies the same income limits on borrowers as for house purchase loans.

Towards the close of 1976 a special scheme of 'low-rise' mortgages was initiated by the Minister for tenants of council houses, or tenant purchasers who wished to surrender their houses to the local authority and buy private houses. Certain families eligible for re-housing could also benefit from the new scheme. The upper loan limit was £7,500. Mortgage repayments were subsidisable both by the state and by the local authority. Section 11 of the Housing (Miscellaneous Provisions) Act, 1979 gave statutory backing to these subsidies. Part X of the Housing Regulations, 1980, specifies amounts of subsidy. Loans up to £12,000 or 98 per cent of value (£13,000 in offshore islands) may normally be advanced.

House Prices. Building costs rose steeply in the decade from 1970 and house prices responded. Between early 1973 and September 1980 building costs had more than trebled (3.7) and house prices had quadrupled (4.2). In the same period consumer prices had increased by a factor of 2.9, and earnings by 3.5. In 1975 the Minister had inaugurated a House Building Cost Index based on information supplied by Dublin Corporation which is widely publicised and serves as a guide to house buyers, builders and the general public.

In February 1973 a system of certificates of reasonable value (CRV) was introduced under section 35 of the Housing Act, 1966 as a condition of state grants for new houses. The 1966 provision was replaced by section 18 of the Housing (Miscellaneous Provisions) Act, 1979, giving wider powers of control. Part XII of the Housing Regulations, 1980 has extended the CRV requirement to all new house loans. Flats and maisonettes in blocks of two or more storeys are excepted from this general application. By arrangement with the Construction Industry Federation, a guarantee scheme for new houses was put into operation in 1978. Registered builders will, under the scheme, give six-year guarantees against major structural defects.

Local Authority Housing

The first stage of the local housing process is a survey of needs. Section 53 of the Housing Act, 1966 requires each housing authority to make a regular assessment (at least once every five years) of the position in its area — substandard houses, unhealthy pockets of accommodation, and emerging demands. This requirement goes back to the Housing (Ireland) Act, 1919 and the Housing (Miscellaneous Provisions) Act, 1931. The next step is a five-year building programme, adoption of which is a reserved function. The programme has two aspects — dealing with overcrowded and unfit houses, (Part IV of the Housing Act, 1966) and (Part III) provision of new dwellings. In addition to re-housing people living in unfit and over-crowded conditions local authorities may also build for special categories of need — the aged, the handicapped and newly-weds. Under section 60 of the 1966 Act it is for the local authority to draw up and review their scheme of letting priorities, subject to the approval of the Minister. Some devolution of responsibility was applied in 1973 to the planning and construction of local housing schemes of 60 dwellings or less. Larger projects must have ministerial approval. Loan charges on local authority houses provided for letting are generally met in full by the state.

Over the last three years the number of tenants and prospective tenants of council houses who have either qualified for a low-rise mortgage or obtained a new council house on a tenancy basis ranged from 6,700 to 7,000. When the number of casual vacancies in council houses is taken into account, the total number of persons qualifying for such houses or mortgages has been about nine thousand in each of the last few years. The numbers of approved applicants on waiting lists add up to some twenty seven thousand, two thirds of whom represent families of three persons or less. The acute pressure on housing authorities has, in general, diminished somewhat in recent years.

Management. The management of houses, flats etc, provided under the Housing of the Working Classes Acts, the Labourers Acts and now under the Housing Acts 1966–79 is vested in housing authorities. The gradual extension of state subsidies carried with it certain controls. Lettings had to be made according to a prescribed order of priorities and since the Housing Act of 1932 subsidy has been conditional on houses etc, being let at rents approved by the Minister. This control was maintained with the introduction of differential or graded rents. The Minister's consent had to be sought for each income-related rents scheme which operated within approved upper and lower limits. Part II of the Housing Act 1966 empowered the Minister to attach various conditions to subsidy payments, including adoption of systems of renting which take account of the financial circumstances of the tenants. Under regulations made in April, 1967 all new houses must be let at rents taking account both of a tenant's household income and the standard of accommodation and amenity of the dwellings.

Each housing authority operated its own scheme of differential rents although a measure of uniformity was achieved by the issue in 1969 of a Departmental circular letter containing general guidelines. But dissatisfaction was widespread, principally on the issue of deductions from household income which varied from one housing authority to another. Rent strikes, headed by the National Association of Tenant's Organisation, led in 1973 to the replacement of all existing schemes of differential rents by a national scheme, applying uniformly throughout the country.

Imposition of a national scheme followed from the troubles experienced by housing authorities but was mainly a consequence of the decision taken by the Coalition government of 1973–77 to phase out local rates subsidies for housing and transfer the entire deficit to the state. In the 1973 national scheme overtime, shift allowances and bonus payments were no longer taken into account in assessing household income. Revised schemes were introduced annually since 1976, but the emphasis remains on the basic income of the principal earner, after deduction of income-tax and social welfare contributions. Income from subsidiary earners is reckoned for rent purposes, within certain limits.

The rent is calculated on a proportion of the assessable income of the principal earner ranging from one seventh to one twentieth in accordance with a graded scale which includes allowances for the principal earner and dependent children. Of a total of 103,000 local authority rented dwellings at the end of 1979, 91,000 are on differential rents. The remainder have fixed rents, which are revised annually to meet increased maintenance and management costs.

Finance

Capital

Housing absorbs over 60 per cent of the capital resources of local authorities, as well as making heavy demands on private sector capital. Gross capital formation in housing in 1979 amounted to £523 million, of which local authority capital expenditure (about £143m) represented something over one quarter.

Housing occupies a prominent position in the Public Capital Programme; in size it comes second only to industry in the eighteen items listed. It takes about 16 per cent of the total in recent years (1979–80); the proportion has been falling since the peak year of 1975, when it was 25%. The accompanying table shows the figures for the decade ending 1980.

Table 1: Public Capital Expenditure on Housing (£ millions)

Year	House Purchase Improvement Loans	Private Housing Supplementary Grants	Grants from Department of the Environment	Local Authority Housing	Other	Total
1971–72	8.96	2.37	4.49	24.79	1.96	42.57
1972–73	10.99	3.48	6.50	28.78	2.08	51.83
1973–74	21.77	3.88	7.82	35.48	2.77	71.72
1974 (Apr-Dec)	30.35	3.79	5.35	40.08	3.77	83.34
1975	42.51	5.13	7.49	55.60	4.41	115.14
1976	25.80	4.17	6.47	65.30	3.61	105.35
1977†	17.66	3.16	4.28	72.58	2.25	99.93
1978†	27.79	2.12	14.48	81.24	2.80	128.43
1979†	46.13	1.39	24.60	95.08	1.84	169.04
1980†	64.27	0.50	27.00	106.75	2.85	201.37
1981*	95.35	0.80	28.50	114.00	3.75	242.40

†Provisional outturn
*Allocation

Source: Quarterly Bulletin of Housing Statistics, Department of the Environment.

Note: The figures in column 6 represent expenditure by the Industrial Development Authority, Shannon Free Airport Development Company, Department of Defence, Roinn na Gaeltachta, and the National Building Agency.

The great bulk of local authority capital requirements for housing is raised by means of borrowings from the Local Loans Fund. Up to about 1950 some of the larger urban authorities floated stock issues to meet their capital needs but about 1952 the Department of Finance decided that all major local borrowing should be channelled through the Local Loans Fund in order to curtail market competition for scarce funds.

Between 1948 and 1972 repayment of loans for housing, water supply and sewerage schemes and other major projects was spread over fifty years. With the steep rise in interest rates, particularly since 1970, the attraction of very long-term loans faded and in 1972 the maximum loan period was shortened to thirty-five years.

Subsidy

The Housing Act, 1966 consolidated the various provisions dealing with subsidy. The higher rate of subsidy — $66\frac{2}{3}$ per cent of loan charges contributions — remained payable for housing for people displaced by operations under the Housing Acts, Planning Acts and the Dangerous Building code. Other categories were added: elderly persons and (from 1969) key workers in new or expanded industries. Before the old subsidy system was superseded in 1973 virtually all local authority houses earned subsidy at the higher rate.

Following transfer to the Exchequer, on a phased basis from 1973 to 1976, of the rates subsidy towards housing, the state generally recoups in full the repayment charges on loans in respect of local authority houses provided for letting. From January 1977 housing authorities retained all rents and miscellaneous receipts together with 60 per cent of proceeds from tenant-purchase schemes. They are responsible for maintenance, improvement and management of their rented housing estates. In 1979 the proportion of sales receipts credited to current revenue was reduced to 50 per cent, in 1980 to 45 per cent and in 1981 to 40 per cent. The balance of the receipts was applied to housing loans or other approved capital purposes.

Provisional figures for 1979 are detailed in Table 2:

Table 2: Housing Authority Finances

Receipts		£million
Rents		16.39
Net proceeds of sales		7.47
State subsidies		53.06
Contribution from rates		8.21
Miscellaneous		0.20
	Total:	85.33
Expenditure		
Loan charges		55.43
Maintenance and Management		29.90
	Total:	85.33

Tenant-purchase

Following enactment of the Housing Act, 1966 the Minister for the Environment made regulations prescribing the general lines which sales schemes should follow. The 1967 regulations stipulated terms of sale based on the market value, or cost of replacement of the house, less certain discounts according to the length of tenancy. The Labourers Act 1936 would not apply to cottages built from 1966 onwards. Sale would be effected by simple transfer order, in a prescribed form.

Selling arrangements were the subject of much discussion and some agitation and in 1973 a major change was made in the method of calculating the sale price. Instead of market value or replacement cost the sale figure was determined by up-dating (in current money values) the original all-in cost of the dwelling. Under the 1980 tenant purchase scheme, settled by the Minister in consultation with local authorities and following representation from the National Association of Tenants' Organisations, the gross price is an updating of the original cost to November, 1979 money values less £1,300 (£1,000 for a new house grant and a maximum £300 for notional rates remission). The rates factor is made up of £30 for each year of tenancy before 1 January 1978, up to £300. A further discount of 3 per cent a year is allowed for length of tenancy, subject to a maximum of 30 per cent in built-up areas and 45 per cent elsewhere. Minimum sale price is £1,000.

While there are cogent arguments against the principle behind tenant purchase the national leaning in favour of owner-occupancy has hitherto sufficed to overbear them. This prejudice, partly emotional and partly traditional, is reinforced by reasons of respectable backing and weight – the distributive argument in favour of multiplying small property-owners; the civic philosphy which sees in property a stable foundation for society, and others. The ESRI broadsheet No 17 (Baker and O'Brien, 1979) sharply criticised tenant-purchase schemes, with their heavy weighting in favour of the tenant: 'From the point of view of equity, this heavy subsidy . . . is impossible to justify. Although there may seem to be some attractive arguments in efficiency terms in reducing public expenditure on maintenance and lowering the future subsidy flow to the particular house in question, the benefits to the system as a whole are highly problematical. If there is a continuing need for houses to rent, then the houses sold must be replaced by new schemes, which, in the nature of local authority financing and rent-fixing, will in fact incur far higher levels of subsidy than the dwellings they replace' (p.241). This, it should be realised, is a criticism of methods rather than aims. The authors, under the heading 'Policy Recommendation' say (pp. 258–9) that 'owner-occupation should be further encouraged as the most suitable basic tenure form especially for family households'. Their opinion coincides with that of the US Commission on Urban Problems (1968) on the social advantages of house-ownership. With an estimated 75 per cent of owner-occupied houses, the Irish figure is the highest in Europe. The most recent figures of tenant buyers, however, do not show a steady trend towards purchase and away from renting. After a decline in the early 1970's, the stock of rented local authority houses has been increasing since 1977. The annual numbers of purchases fell steeply between 1975 and 1978.

Housing Needs

Successive governments have vainly pursued, in housing terms, what George O'Brien called the phantom of plenty. Goals are set, programmes confidently launched and energetically pushed along but the end is still distant. Demand is a receding horizon. When the targets fixed in 1948 had been reached and passed the 1964 White Paper estimated that fifty thousand houses were still needed to replace unfit and overcrowded dwellings while a further eight thousand houses were required each year to cope with population changes, rising marriage rate, industrial development and finally, obsolescence of the housing stock. The aggregate need meant that housing output would have to be raised to between 12,000 and 13,000 houses a year. In fact between 1964 and 1970 some 68,000 houses were built, an average of 11,000 a year. The demographic turn-about which occurred about 1960 has of course radically changed the position. It is now accepted that the rate of household formation is such that there is no foreseeable prospect of any 'final solution' to the housing problem.

A further White Paper issued in 1969, 'Housing in the Seventies' estimated accumulated need — to remedy unfit houses and overcrowded dwellings — at 59,000. This figure emerged from housing surveys conducted by local authorities during 1967 in discharge of a duty imposed on them by Part III of the Housing Act 1966 which showed a need for 35,000 houses to replace sub-standard dwellings; and from local surveys, combined with 1966 census data, showing some 24,000 required to relieve overcrowding. In addition to accumulated need the White Paper estimated that some 9,000 houses a year must be built to meet prospective needs — to replace obsolescent dwellings, accommodate new households, and cope with immigration to urban areas. Aggregate needs were seen, on the basis of these figures, as rising to 15,000 – 17,000 a year by the mid-seventies.

Actual performance, however, exceeded the forecast. Housing output, buoyed up by a carry-over from the expansionist 1960s, rose from less than 14,000 in 1970 to 21,600 in 1972. The Coalition government which took office in 1973 announced their intention of building 25,000 houses a year and this target was reached and passed in 1974 and 1975. There was some falling back in the two following years but the 25,000 mark was again exceeded in 1978, 1979 and 1980. The great bulk of new house building was done by the private sector: from 1975 to 1977 there was a decline in local authority output. Since 1977 the number of local authority house completions has remained within the range of 6,000 to 6,300 a year.

In 1976 the National Economic and Social Council essayed in Report No. 14 a long-term forecast of housing needs up to 1986. Their conclusion was that 'projected total dwelling needs over the period 1971–1986 are in a range between 314,000 and 372,000' (p.35). The partial census of 1979 returned an unexpectedly high increase in population for the period since 1971. Total population increased at an annual rate of 1.6 per cent in the period, the highest rate of expansion in Europe. This was the national average but in the Eastern region population growth was as high as 2 per cent per annum. This extraordinary rate of expansion places heavy burdens on both local authorities and the private sector whose task it is to house the spreading metropolis.

The last assessment by housing authorities of the supply and condition of housing in their areas was carried out in 1976 for the period up to 1981. Housing authorities were asked in 1980 to assess accumulated and prospective needs for a further five years. A manual on 'Housing Needs Assessment' was prepared by An Foras Forbartha in conjunction with the Department of the Environment for the guidance of local officers and elected bodies towards a standardised approach to surveys. Statistics of house building and reconstruction over the century since 1879 will be found in Appendix 5.

The National Building Agency. Housing for industrial workers, particularly for key workers in new and expanding factories, began to present problems early in the 1960s. Local authorities operating under old codes lacked the flexibility to respond adequately to the developing needs of new industry. The Minister accordingly formed the National Building Agency, a private company financed by the state, which commenced operations shortly after 1960. The Agency, in addition to industrial housing, undertook housing for other Departments, e.g., Garda requirements for the Department of Justice. In 1965 its functions were extended to enable it to provide houses for local authorities at their request and in 1979 this aspect of the agency's operations accounted for about 95 per cent of its annual turnover. Since 1976, the capital for industrial housing is channelled through the Industrial Development Authority. More recently, the authority makes capital monies available to the agency to give house purchase loans to approved applicants instead of the previous arrangement which involved the actual construction of schemes by the agency.

The NBA also administers a scheme of loans from the European Coal and Steel Community for housing workers in the coal and steel industries. Loans at specially low rates are made through the NBA to eligible workers for new houses or for improvement works.

Building Industry. In recent years the Department's traditional concern with housing has broadened to encompass most aspects of the building industry. The National Building Advisory Council, set up in 1963 to survey the volume of work in progress and in prospect, came within the ambit of the Minister for Local Government in 1966 — it had been with the Minister for Industry and Commerce — and soon afterwards the Council was merged with An Foras Forbartha. The Minister issues in consultation with other interests an 'Annual Review and Outlook' relating to output and employment in the building and construction industry. An Foras Forbartha has also undertaken work on the change to the metric system in building and on modular co-ordination, in metric terms, in the industry. A national code of building regulations is in preparation under the Local Government (Planning and Development) Act 1963, s.86. These regulations will replace local bye-laws and will of course incorporate metrication. An Foras Forbartha has monitored the technical aspects of the new rules.

Travelling People

The growing number of itinerants on the roads thrust itself insistently on public attention through the 1950s. Farmers complained about straying animals, allegations by householders about petty thievery mingled with the voices of a small minority of sympathisers to create a demand for action of some kind. The Minister for Justice decided in 1960 to set up a commission to study the problem.

The Commission on Itinerancy chaired by Mr Justice Brian Walsh reported in 1963. Recommendations were: an advisory committee, financial aid for voluntary groups and for employing professional social workers and a subsidy for new camping sites. Special health, educational and social welfare measures for itinerants should be put in hand. The government accepted these proposals in 1964 and designated the Minister for the Environment as co-ordinator. The Minister appointed an advisory committee soon afterwards and announced a two-thirds subsidy for local authorities providing serviced camping sites. Local progress was however disappointingly slow. There was on the other hand rapid growth in the number of voluntary groups and in 1968 they formed a national council for itinerant settlement.

In 1970 subsidies were increased and diversified:

100 per cent for serviced sites and chalets;
100 per cent for renovated houses;
90% for expenses of employing social workers and youth leaders who work with itinerants.

Progress was accelerated, despite continuing difficulties in finding sites and integrating travelling people in settled communities. A number of houses were allocated to travelling families but there were outbreaks of resistance in a few areas. A survey in 1976 showed that out of 1,900 itinerant families, 1,034 had been given accommodation, in standard housing, serviced sites, in trailers or in mobile homes. Over £2 million had been spent on normal housing with £1 million going on serviced sites, chalets and mobile homes.

Subsidies at 50 per cent rate for caravans allotted to tent-dwelling families and 100 per cent for halting places were added to the scheme of state aid. Local authorities could also recoup two-thirds of the cost incurred by voluntary groups providing accommodation, half of which was repayable by the state.

Mr V. E. H. Bewley, Vice Chairman of the National Council for Travelling People was appointed Adviser to the Minister for the Environment in 1974. The National Council employs a whole-time National Co-Ordinator for work with voluntary groups. About fifty social workers and youth leaders are engaged, whole or part-time, on the programme. A recent development has been the opening of training centres for the rehabilitation of travellers. The Ministers for the Environment and Health have (1980) set up a joint Review Body to examine the present position of travelling people and suggest whatever legal and administrative innovations they consider might be introduced.

A Supreme Court judgment delivered by Chief Justice O'Higgins on 23 July 1980, *(McDonald v. Feely, City and County Manager and the Chairman and Councillors of the County of Dublin)* supported council action in removing an itinerant family from council property. The decision hinged on the council's discharge of its duty under s. 60 of the Housing Act, 1966, subsection (3) (c) of which requires 'the provision of suitable housing for those in need and unable to provide for themselves.' The Chief Justice added, in reference to itinerant families occupying unauthorised sites:

Nothing is solved merely by moving such families from place to place. By doing so, not only is the problem perpetuated but the claims and rights of the children to any possibility of education and a settled life and future are ignored. Pending a special programme for settlement, based if necessary on special legislation, serviced halts and camping sites should at least be provided.

17

Roads and Road Traffic

A road is a passage open to everyone, a part of the surface of the land dedicated to the public in order that they may pass and repass along it. Although most of our roads may never have been formally dedicated, uninterrupted use by the public over a long period is taken to imply dedication and public acceptance. A road may be created otherwise than by dedication and acceptance. A county or urban district council or a borough corporation, each of which is a road authority, has power to acquire land to make new roads where necessary and may declare a road a public road if they are satisfied it is of general public utility and if there is a public right of way over it. The purpose of declaring a road a public road is to allow the road authority to maintain it. A public road which ceases to be of any use to the public does not cease to be a public road until it has been legally abandoned (Local Government Act, 1925, s.26). The road authority can acquire ownership in the soil of a disused road for the purpose of extinguishing a right of way (Local Government Act, 1946, s.84).

A road authority has the duty of keeping every road under its control fit for the ordinary traffic that passes along it and this duty may be enforced by the courts. If the traffic changes, as it did when mechanically propelled vehicles carrying heavy loads came on to the roads, the road must be made suitable to serve the new traffic passing along it (Vanston I, p.340). The road authority may recover from the person responsible any expenses incurred in repairing damage to a road from exceptional traffic (Public Roads (Ireland) Act, 1911). The road authority cannot at present be made liable for injuries due to their not repairing the road but if injuries are due to some positive act the road authority has done they may be made liable. Section 60 of the Civil Liability Act, 1961 which alters the law of liability for failure to maintain, has not so far been brought into operation.

Early Roads

The oldest roads in Ireland have their origin in prehistoric times. They probably had their beginning in tracks followed by men and animals moving from one place to another. Short stretches of ancient paved roads have been found, from which it would appear that in the first centuries of the Christian era Roman methods of road construction were known in Ireland. The ancient road system (such as it was — there cannot have been a developed national system) fanned out not from Tara but from Dublin. A northern road went through Armagh to the coast. Western roads went through Rath Croghan in Roscommon to Galway and the road to Galway crossed the Shannon at Clonmacnoise. A road along the east coast was carried over the Liffey by a hurdle bridge and went southwards through Bray. The main highway through Leinster branched from this road and went on to Cashel. Another road went on to Limerick through Naas, Roscrea and Nenagh. Much of the traffic went of course by river and sea and stone bridges do not appear to have been built before the twelfth century.

Early Legislation

Early in the seventeenth century an unsuccessful attempt (the Highways Act, 1614) was made to introduce a system of statute labour that had been tried in England for maintaining roads. The inhabitants of every parish were required to furnish free labour, tools and materials for road work. This system was abolished in 1765 but more than a century earlier the roads had been placed under the grand juries by an Act of 1634 who could vote money for them and levy it by means of the county cess.

The number of Acts, many of them of a local character, relating to roads which were passed in the eighteenth century by the Irish Parliament showed that the increase in population and traffic was causing greater use of the roads. The canal system relieved the roads of much heavy traffic but horse and foot passengers, carts, coaches and carriages grew in numbers. Experiments in road-making went on in order to raise the standard of the roads and enable them to cope with heavier usage. The first to use a layer of small broken stones to make a foundation for a road was John Metcalf (1717–1802), a road contractor of Yorkshire. The vehicles on the road forced the broken stones into the soil; round stones which before that time had been used were easily pushed aside by the passage of wheels. Metcalf's work was carried forward by Telford (b.1757) and McAdam (b.1756). The necessity for good post roads to carry the mails and the turnpike system were also factors in road improvement.

To improve the post roads the Commissioners of Public Works were given power to repair these roads if asked to do so by the Post Office. The money for the work came in the first instance from state funds and improvement was carried out under the superintendence of a surveyor appointed by the Commissioners. When the repair of the road was completed the expenditure was certified to the grand jury who were bound to refund the sum required to defray the cost. Half the cost of repairing and improving the post roads was levied off the county and half off the relevant barony. Obviously it was much better for the grand juries to improve the post roads themselves than allow the Commissioners to do it at their expense.

The first of numerous Irish turnpike Acts was passed in 1729, to improve the road from Dublin to Kildare. The law permitted turnpike trusts to be formed to maintain stretches of road and levy tolls on certain kinds of traffic. The user of the road was thus compelled to pay for his use of it. The name turnpike comes from the bars which revolved on a pillar and were used as toll gates. The coming of the railways made the turnpikes no longer profitable; they were abolished in 1857 and all existing turnpike roads became public roads. Toll bridges and ferries also existed. The owner of a ferry outside a town was given the power by the Grand Jury Act, 1836, to erect a bridge in place of the ferry and charge the same toll as he was entitled to charge for the use of the ferry. Toll roads and bridges have become a possibility again with the enactment of the Local Government (Toll Roads) Act, 1979.

Public works including the making or maintenance of roads were carried out up to 1899 in the counties by the grand juries. All road works were put up to tender and done by contract. The grand jury was not, like the county council a permanent body. It could not itself purchase the equipment needed for repairing roads that were defective and consequently the contract system became the normal system of road making and repair. If no one came forward with a tender the county surveyor had to execute the works within whatever amount was allowed.

The cost of road maintenance, improvement and repair incurred by the grand juries was met out of the county cess levied off the occupiers of rateable property. It was not until the year 1888 that some relief was given to the ratepayers in respect of road expenditure. A proportion of the probate duty, for which part of the estate duty was afterwards substituted, was assigned for that purpose and distributed to councils in proportion to their road expenditure in the year 1887.

The development of the railways had an effect on the roads. The railways, wherever they extended, put an end to all long distance passenger traffic by horse, coach, long car or carriage. The fly boats on the canals ceased to run, as well as river steamboats to towns to which railways extended. The transfer of much of the road traffic to the railways enabled road authorities to keep road expenditure within bounds but the coming of the railways merely postponed the road crisis. In the present century the roads have been growing rapidly in importance as through traffic routes. The full circle of the revolution away from the road to the railway and back again was completed in less than a hundred years.

Local Government (Ireland) Act, 1898

Although the first motor cars had appeared on the roads a few years before the Local Government Act of 1898 created county and district councils and made them road authorities, the framers of the Act could not have foreseen the effects the motor car, bus and lorry were going to have, not only on road administration but on the whole structure of local government. The Act is characterised by a nineteenth rather than a twentieth century outlook. So far as roads were concerned the Act raised some obstacles to improvement where none had existed before.

The grand jury had a convenient method of taking land for new roads. If they did not propose to go through an enclosed deer park or run the road through a house or its out-offices all they needed to do was to give notice to the owners before the application for a vote of money for the road that was considered. This simple procedure was not made available to the county councils because county councils in England did not happen to have that power at the time and the expensive procedure of the acquisition of land by provisional order was substituted.

The fear that the new councils might be extravagant in regard to roads also found expression in the Act which prohibited expenditure on roads exceeding by more than one quarter the average for the three years before the passing of the Act, unless by consent of the Local Government Board. Against these defects must be set the provision which gave the county council power to purchase steam rollers and other machinery and take quarries. The councils were enabled to place both the machinery and materials at the disposal of contractors.

Main Roads

The county councils were given power to declare which roads were to be main roads. The effect of declaring a road a main road was to transfer from the county district to the county half of the expenses of maintaining it. Fourteen councils made no declarations and consequently, in these counties there were no roads of that class. The power to originate and determine expenditure on roads rested primarily with the rural district councils which were not abolished until 1925. The occupiers of land were strongly represented on these councils. The anomalous position of the county council in regard to the main roads soon became apparent when motorists came on to the roads with their machines raising dust, scattering mud or disintegrating the surface. The county councils were offered grants but they were not free to enter into commitments regarding future maintenance because the district councils had the whip hand.

Motor Traffic

Bicycles with pneumatic tyres appeared on the roads in great numbers about the middle of the 1890's and cyclists began to complain of the state of the surfaces, but their complaints had little effect. The safety of the roads was threatened and the roads themselves were being subjected to unusual wear and tear by the weight and speed of the new motor traffic. The question, not by any means new, then arose whether it was the duty of the ratepayers to make roads to suit every new form of traffic. Although motorists were relatively few in number they had considerable influence. The Locomotives Act of 1865, which required every locomotive propelled by other than animal power to have a man with a red flag sixty yards ahead to warn all drivers of horses that the engine was coming, was repealed in 1896. The Motor Car Act, 1903 required motor cars to be registered and licensed, to carry identification marks, to be driven by a licensed driver, to have a horn or alarm and lights and a speed limit was fixed for them.

The demand that the motorist should be made pay something towards the maintenance of the roads was conceded in the Budget of 1909. The Finance Act, 1909 put a licence duty on motor cars and a tax on petrol. The government did not adopt the established device of making grants out of the produce of these duties to local authorities. If they had done so the money might have gone merely in relief of rates. Instead of making such grants they set up, under the Development and Road Improvement Funds Act, 1909, a Road Board which was to devote funds derived from the new taxation to road improvements that might take the form of new roads, or straighter or wider roads, or better surfaces, particularly a dust-free surface. This was not the kind of relief ratepayers were looking for because it left them with all their existing liabilities. The Road Board lasted until 1919 when its functions were merged with those of the Ministry of Transport established in that year. In 1922 the functions of the Roads Department of the Ministry of Transport passed to the Provisional Government and are now functions of the Minister for the Environment.

Road Fund. The Roads Act, 1920 made county and county borough councils the authorities for registering and collecting duties on motor cars and also constituted the Road Fund into which the duties levied by the councils found their way, together with fees for driving licences and petrol pumps and certain other receipts. Neither excise duties on imported motor spirit nor customs duties on imported car parts went to the Fund. County and county borough councils were paid their expenses of levying the duties and collecting fees and the expenses of government departments and the Commissioner of the Garda Síochána in administering the Act were met out of the Fund. The Fund lasted until 1978 when the government decided to terminate the arrangement and substitute other forms of finance.

Local Government Act, 1925

The first steps towards implementing a new road policy taken by the new government were embodied in the Local Government Act, 1925. Under that Act roads were divided into main roads, county roads and urban roads. Main roads are those declared to be such by order of the Minister. This removed from the county councils the power to determine which were main roads. All expenses in regard to these roads fell on the whole county including the urban districts. The county roads were constructed and maintained at the cost of the county excluding the urban districts and the cost of urban roads fell on the urban districts. Power was given to transfer the responsibility for urban roads to the county councils or to put all roads in an urban district under the urban district council. This, however, would not alter the incidence of the charge.

For the purposes of administration the chief roads were divided into trunk roads, which were the most important arteries, and link roads. It was decided to improve the worst portions of the trunk roads of which there were about 1,500 miles. This was done without waiting for the necessary revenue to accrue to the Road Fund. A scheme was adopted by which the Exchequer would advance the money which would be repaid over a period out of the revenue from motor taxation.

In the years before 1925 motor buses outside Dublin were few in number but from that year the number of such vehicles on the roads began to rise and compete with the railways. Under the Railways (Road Motor Services) Act of 1927 the railway companies received powers to run passenger and goods services on the public roads along approved routes. The Local Government Act, 1925 contained a number of minor amendments to the law relating to roads, such as the power to have buildings removed that obstructed the view on roads and to have trees and hedges trimmed; as well as the improvement of signposts and control of the erection of petrol pumps on roads.

Road Improvements

The roads in 1922 consisted for the most part of unrolled water-bound macadam, the surface of which was not dressed. With the revenues of the Road Fund increasing it was possible to make substantial improvement grants. On the main roads the waterbound macadam was given a waterproof and dust-proof surface. Up to 1926–7 all grants were confined to improvement works but from 1927 contributions were given towards the upkeep of main roads. The grant from the Road Fund was used as a lever to induce county councils to provide more money from the rates. In little over a decade the surfaces of the main roads had all been improved and attention could then be given to widening and improving alignment. At this stage money became available for relieving unemployment by putting men to work on roads. Grants out of the Employment Schemes Vote were offered on condition the road authority made a small contribution and took on men who were in receipt of unemployment assistance.

The second world war practically suspended road improvements as tar and bitumen were no longer available in sufficient quantities. At the same time turf had to be brought to the towns. Under these conditions many roads deteriorated. When the war was over the immediate business was to restore these roads and a new system of grants increasing with the rate of expenditure from local funds was devised. For the first time the county roads became eligible for grants. This system of restoration grants continued for three years. When it came to an end the normal system of improvement and maintenance grants for main roads was restored and an improvement grant for county roads was provided. The effect of all these measures was a marked improvement in both main and county roads; many dangerous corners have been removed and the principal roads have been strengthened and made more suitable for the ever increasing volume of traffic. Grants to urban district councils were instituted to deal with the problem of urban roads.

Bridges

The term 'roads' includes 'bridges' and in general the law on the construction and maintenance of roads applies to bridges. Where a bridge is to span a river separating two administrative areas, or will be of particular service to a number of areas, the question who should build, pay for and maintain it, arises. The Minister for Local Government may, under Part IV of the Local Government Act, 1946 make a bridge order setting out the authority to build and maintain the bridge, the authorities to pay for it and their respective contributions. Such an order will also determine the site of the bridge and whether or not it is to have an opening span, matters frequently the subject of contention. A bridge over navigable water cannot be built without the consent of the Minister for Transport. Again, bridge work over any watercourse cannot be undertaken without the consent of the Commissioners of Public Works under the Arterial Drainage Act, 1945. In the case of an important bridge work a substantial Exchequer grant is generally made available.

Special provisions, either in general or in local Acts, deal with particular bridges or particular classes of bridge. For example, in the case of road bridges over railways and canals the general position is that the transport company is responsible for maintaining the bridge in its original condition. When such a bridge is being replaced by an improved structure the transport company pays a proportion corresponding to the cost of replacing the original structure and the local authority pays the balance.

Post-War Developments

The process of *aggiornamento* undergone by virtually all local services in the post-war period began for roads and road traffic with the Road Traffic Act, 1961. This Act substituted a wider and more up-to-date battery of powers for the rather faded provisions of the Road Traffic Act, 1933. The traffic position in the early 1960s was that there were something over 400,000 licensed drivers using 300,000 motor vehicles on 52,000 miles of road. There are now about 810,000 licensed drivers and 750,000 vehicles on roughly the same mileage of (somewhat improved) roads. Annual expenditure on road improvement and maintenance has risen dramatically from about £13 million to an estimated £75 million in 1978; but much of the drama is due to inflation and the later figure must be discounted by at least two-thirds.

The Annual Report of the Department of Local Government for 1962–3 contains an excellent account of roads administration, problems and strategies at the time. Road Fund assistance for arterial roads was being doubled and certain limited research projects were in progress in UCD, financed by the Department. In 1964, however, with the establishment of An Foras Forbartha (the National Institute for Physical Planning and Construction Research) major studies began in road planning, with special focus on arterial roads. A report on *Administration of the Arterial Roads Programme* (1969) recommended the transfer of responsibility for arterial roads to the Minister for Local Government. A further study of *Highway Construction and Maintenance Management* pointed towards a reclassification of the roads system, suggesting three grades: national routes, primary and secondary, regional roads, primary and secondary and county roads.

These reports and the discussions which followed them provided the groundwork for the Local Government (Roads and Motorways) Act, 1974. This, the first important revision of roads law since 1925, gave road authorities power to construct motorways and reinforced local powers to construct dual carriageways, central medians and flyovers and to provide traffic route lighting. The Minister was empowered at the same time to declare roads to be national routes. He could also, after consultation with the road authorities concerned, direct the planning and execution of work on national roads and motorways. The Act diverged somewhat from an earlier government decision (July 1969) that the prospective legislation should transfer the national route system to the Minister, the work of construction etc. to be done by local authorities on an agency basis. Under the 1974 Act local authorities retained responsibility for the entire road system but were subject to strong ministerial direction and control in relation to arterial routes. The Act empowers the Minister to declare a public road to be a motorway or national road and, after consultation with the road authorities concerned, to direct the planning and execution of works on national roads and motorways in the interests of efficiency and uniformity of standards.

National primary and secondary roads were also designated and from 1974 their improvement and upkeep became wholly a charge on, firstly the Road Fund and later the Exchequer. At the same time the separate grants to road authorities for main and county roads, tourist roads, county

borough and urban roads were replaced by general or block grants for
roads purposes. A formal order under the 1974 Act identifying the
national road system was made by the Minister in June 1977.

The public road system comprises (1979) a total of 57,000 miles
(92,000 kms) of roadway.

Table 1: Public Road System

Level	Miles
National Primary	1,630
National Secondary	1,630
Main	6,660
County Borough	820
Urban	620
County	46,000
Total	57,360

Responsibility for the maintenance and improvement of national roads
rests with county councils, county borough corporations and borough
corporations (other than Kilkenny and Wexford). They get 100 per cent
state grants for maintenance, improvement and bridge works on these
roads. Responsibility for main roads (including those sections of main
roads in boroughs and urban districts) rests with county councils and
expenditure — so far as it is not met from general road grants — is a county-
at-large charge. Roads in county boroughs are the concern of the corporations, assisted by general grant. Urban roads which are not main roads are
looked after by the urban council, or in boroughs by the corporations.
County roads are a matter for the county council, net expenditure being
a charge on the county health district.

The foregoing is taken from the recent Government paper (May 1979)
'Road Development Plan for the 1980s', outlining a ten-year roads programme with the principal aim of:

— providing an adequate inter-urban road system connecting the
principal towns, seaports and airports;
— bringing the national route network up to a minimum two-lane
standard, with higher standards for particular sections;
— meeting special needs for new river crossings, ring roads and relief
routes in county boroughs and other major urban centres.

A number of towns on national routes would be bypassed and dual carriageways would be constructed on radial roads in the Dublin and Cork regions
and at Limerick, Waterford and Galway cities. As regards motorways

(dual-carriage highways with limited access, grade separation and elimination of crossings by means of fly-overs, underpasses etc.), the plan does not envisage development of a motorway network, despite its economic advantages and the fact that Ireland is the only member country of the EEC that does not have motorways. But the heavy expenses, far above ordinary road costs, of land acquisition, design, construction and maintenance combined to put large-scale projects out of bounds, at least in the short term. A motorway scheme under the 1974 Act was made by Kildare County Council in 1978 for a proposed bypass at Naas.

The roads programme 1980—89 is estimated to cost £684.5 million in direct state investment, at constant 1978 prices of which £240 million or 35 per cent would be spent on maintenance and normal improvements of national routes and £282 million (40 per cent) on major improvement works in the Dublin region and other critical areas. The bulk of the investment would be financed from the Public Capital Programme, with support coming, in addition, in the form of loans from the European Investment Bank and grants from the European Regional Development Fund.

Toll Roads

The possibility of supplementing public resources for road purposes emerged towards the close of the 1970s. As the Plan (8.5) stated: 'The accepted principle of toll roads and bridges is that the facility to be provided offers an alternative route to road users who may choose to pay for the convenience of using the toll facility. In the UK special legislation was enacted for this purpose in respect of a number of major bridges and tunnels. In France, Italy, Spain and other countries, toll motorways have been provided, financed and managed by private enterprises at locations chosen by central government and offered publicly for contract to private enterprise consortia.' In Ireland the Local Government (Toll Roads) Act, 1979 empowers local authorities to enter into agreements with private interests for the construction, maintenance and management of toll roads and bridges. The road authority must make a formal toll scheme after public notice and if there are objections a public inquiry must be held. Decisions to make arrangements with private enterprise and to draw up toll schemes are reserved to elected members of local authorities.

The Plan (8.7) expresses the government's 'hope that the private sector will respond to this opportunity to participate in the development of the country's road system.' Similar invitations have been issued by government speakers in regard to other aspects of the infrastructure.

Transportation and Traffic

With the multiplication of motor vehicles, traffic has become a problem of more or less intensity in many cities and towns. Symptoms of approaching crisis began to appear in Dublin as early as 1970 and in the 'Dublin Transportation Study' (1972) An Foras Forbartha presented 'a co-ordinated transport and planning exercise undertaken jointly by Dublin Corporation, Dublin County Council, Dun Laoghaire Borough Corporation, Wicklow County Council, Bray Urban District Council, the Department of Local Government and An Foras Forbartha' (Hall, 1980). The proposals which included some seventy miles of motorway in the Dublin region were however slow in materialising. In 1978 the Minister for Transport set up the Transport Consultative Commission to advise on measures necessary to deal with goods and passenger traffic generally, giving priority to urban passenger services. The Commission's first report on 'Passenger Transport Services in the Dublin Area' (1980) recommended the establishment of a new Dublin Transportation Authority with the main object of securing effective co-ordination and policy integration between local authorities, Garda Siochana and the Departments of the Environment and Transport. This recommendation has been accepted by the government. The National Economic and Social Council Report No. 48 (1980) on 'Transport Policy' stresses the need for increased investment in the inter-urban road network, diverting, if necessary, cash from minor county and urban roads. The Road Development Plan (1979), of course, predicted heavier spending on the improvement of major inter-urban routes.

Road Workers

The work force employed on roads has declined in the post-war period owing mainly to increasing mechanisation. Increased road grants were made in 1977 as part of the government's job creation programme and these had the effect of raising the monthly average employed from 9,540 in 1976 to about 11,000 in 1978. In addition to road workers directly employed, considerable indirect employment results in the form of jobs in road materials production and related activities. A certain number of jobs are also generated as a spin-off from road investment – what is called 'induced employment'.

Motor Taxation

The government decided in 1977 to abolish road tax on private cars up to 16 h.p. and on all motor cycles. Annual registration is still a requirement, with a licence fee of £5 for cars and £1 for motor cycles. With this abolition, the Road Fund lost much of its original purpose and the government decided to terminate it from January 1978: Section 50 of the Finance Act, 1978. Road grants are now made from voted capital for road improvement, and from voted revenue monies for road maintenance. As noted above, grants and loans are available from EEC sources for road subjects – grants from the European regional development Fund, and loans from the

European Investment Bank. Registration now costs £20 for cars, and road taxes have been restored from 1 September, 1981.

Road Safety Regulations

Regulations in 1964 made the issue of new driving licences conditional on passing a competence test. The Minister became the issuing authority for certificates of competence. This involved the recruitment of a corps of testers and the organisation of some 40 test centres throughout the country. Some 70,000 successful candidates are now licensed every year. The pass rate is about 50 per cent.

Following the report (1963) of a Commission on Driving while under the influence of drink or a drug, the Road Traffic Act, 1968 introduced a procedure by which driver-incapacity would be assessed by reference to blood-alcohol level. A Medical Bureau of Road Safety was set up for the analysis of blood and urine samples. Enforcement of the Act was hampered by legal difficulties and despite an effort — Road Traffic (Amendment) Act, 1973, — to improve matters the Director of Public Prosecutions decided in 1977 to suspend prosecutions. The Road Traffic (Amendment) Act, 1978 has given the campaign a new lease of life. In addition road traffic regulations made by the Minister in December 1978 made it obligatory for drivers and front passengers of private cars to wear safety belts. The regulations also require crash helmets to be worn by drivers and pillion passengers of motorcycles.

Traffic Management

The regulation of traffic must for obvious reasons be organised on a nation-wide basis but local authorities have an essential function in the application of general rules. The Act of 1961 vested authority for making national rules and local bye-laws in the Garda Commissioner after consultation with the Minister for Local Government and the local authority. Part VIII of the Act of 1968 transferred the power to make general rules — in effect the Rules of the Road — from the Commissioner to the Minister for Local Government. It was thought that Rules so important and universally applicable should be made by a Minister answerable to the Dáil.

On the local scene Part VIII enabled traffic management functions (except enforcement) for a particular area to be concentrated in one local authority. The Minister must be satisfied before making an order to this effect that the local authority has the necessary resources and staff for the task.

The Road Traffic Act 1968 authorised the Garda Commissioner to recruit traffic wardens as auxiliaries to the Garda in certain traffic matters. Some progress was made, but it was clear that a local concern of this kind would benefit from local initiative. The Local Authorities (Traffic Wardens)

Act 1975 transferred the employing functions to local authorities. Consultation with the Garda Commissioner is required before local action can be taken. The movement towards local management has lost momentum in recent times. In Dublin City for instance the Gardai have taken over responsibility for the traffic warden service; Cork Corporation followed suit.

Road safety campaigns were launched by the Department in 1965, with the aid of a Road Safety Propaganda Consultative Committee. Publicity and information work had begun at an earlier date: a 1962 version of *Rules of the Road* was circulated widely. Films, posters, leaflets etc. were made from the early 1960s onwards and television shots appeared soon after RTE commenced to broadcast. The Department, in consultation with the Department of Education and the INTO distributed visual aids to primary schools. Stands were set up at the yearly Spring and Horse Shows of the RDS.

In 1973 the Minister set up the National Road Safety Association to take over the Department's work in publicity and education. The Association, a corporate body, is financed by an annual grant, formerly from the Road Fund, now from the Department's vote.

Public Works

County and district councils must keep all public works maintainable by them in good repair. A large number of marine works (quays, piers, etc.) are now in the control of county councils. The Local Authorities (Works) Act, 1949 extended the powers of the councils and corporations to execute works to afford relief from flooding. Substantial grants were voted by the Oireachtas to meet the cost of works carried out under that Act in the years from 1950 to 1957.

The Air Navigation and Transport Act, 1936 enabled road authorities to provide and operate airports, but the opportunity was not availed of to any extent. There was some question in 1937 of Dublin Corporation contributing jointly with Dublin County Council towards the capital cost of the airport at Collinstown; it was not pursued. Recent developments in providing regional air facilities have, however, been marked by more positive measures of local aid.

18

Water Supply and Sewerage

County councils, county borough and borough corporations, and urban district councils are, as sanitary authorities, responsible for the construction and maintenance of public water supply and sewerage schemes. The Local Government (Sanitary Services) Acts, 1878 to 1964 although just past their centenary, provide a reasonably adequate range of powers for both domestic and non-domestic water and sewerage and since 1962 for private installations, individual and group.

Adequate water supplies and sewerage are an essential part of the infrastructure for industrial, tourist and commercial development and piped water makes a significant contribution towards raising standards in agriculture, especially market gardening and milk production. The need for these facilities is expanding as the pace of industrialisation increases and has reached the point in many areas where industrial demand predominates. Industrial requirements are equally if not more important in the case of sewerage since industrial effluents are greater in quantity and more difficult to treat and dispose of than domestic wastes.

Up to 1959 the emphasis was largely on the provision of water and sewerage services in urbanised and built-up areas: the census of 1946 returned almost 92 per cent of dwellings in urban districts and towns with over 1,500 inhabitants as having piped water but in smaller villages and the countryside the figure was only 8.6 per cent. Of farm dwellings, a mere 5 per cent had piped water. In 1959 the government launched a major drive with the twin objectives of spreading the benefits of piped water and sanitation to rural Ireland and improving the facilities already available in urban areas which were unable to cope with rising population, higher living standards and growing industries. The programme involved large schemes of a 'regional' type and the promotion of group schemes — essentially a collective use of the private grants which had become available some years earlier under the Department of Agriculture's farm water supplies scheme and under the Housing Acts.

The campaign gradually gathered momentum assisted by publicity in the form of films, literature and stands at national and local shows and by mobilising the energies of rural organisations like Muintir na Tire and the Irish Countrywomen's Association. The success of the drive was demonstrated by the figures from successive censuses. In 1961 97 per cent of urban dwellings and 25 per cent of those in rural areas had piped water supplies. By 1971 the rural tally had risen to 60 per cent for piped water and 42 per cent with flush toilets; there have been substantial advances since then.

Increasing industrialisation and the demands of urban housing and tourism have, in recent years, claimed a major share of the water and sewerage programme, so that group schemes have had to shoulder much of the burden of rural piped water and sanitation. In this they have had substantial help from local authorities, before 1977 in the form of supplementary grants to match state grants, but also by facilitating group endeavour. Councils have, as part of the public programme, constructed headworks, reservoirs and trunk main extensions from which groups could develop local distribution networks. In 1977 supplementary grants were discontinued and state grants became payable at two-thirds cost subject to the following maxima:

Group water supply	£300 per house
Individual water supply	£200 per house
Group sewerage	£250 per house
Individual sewerage	£150 per house

Additional grants are payable for farm water supplies.

At the end of 1979, over 2,500 group water schemes had been completed, serving nearly 78,500 houses. Work was in progress on schemes serving a further 8,400 houses. Expenditure in 1979 from public and private sources amounted to £7 million. Public water and sewerage schemes are designed largely by consulting engineers and executed by contractors. The capital is raised by borrowing, repayable over 30 years, from the Local Loans Fund. State subsidy is paid by way of contributions towards loan charges at the following rates:

Dublin County Borough	40 per cent
Other areas, except those below	50 per cent
Former congested districts, Counties Cavan, Longford and Monaghan and urban districts with valuation under £25,000	60 per cent
Gaeltacht areas	85 per cent

Capital expenditure by local authorities has risen from less than £2m. in 1962–63 to £39m. in 1979. Grants amounting to about £6m. have been paid by the European Commission from FEOGA (European Agricultural Guidance and Guarantee Fund) for a number of rural water supply schemes undertaken by county councils and voluntary groups.

Water Charges

Sanitary authorities have a general power under the Sanitary Services Acts — particularly the 1962 Act — to charge for water supplied. In urban areas no charge may be made for a domestic supply but water supplied to business or trade premises, clubs, hospitals and other institutions is subject to special charge and may be metered. The running costs of sewerage and drainage usually falls entirely on the local authority even in the case of industrial and trade wastes. Contributions may be required from developers towards the cost of new water and sewerage schemes.

The Health (Fluoridation of Water Supplies) Act, 1960 provides for the compulsory addition of a minute proportion of fluorine to public piped water supplies, in accordance with regulations made by the Minister for Health. The object of the measure is to combat tooth decay.

Sanitary authorities can build public conveniences where they are needed. Loans may be raised and state subsidy is paid at the rate of 40 per cent to 60 per cent of repayment charges.

19

Environment: Protection and Services

The Minister for Local Government became the Minister for the Environment in July, 1977. In February 1978 the government decided that the re-named Minister and Department should have general responsibility for promoting, protecting and improving the physical environment, with the following specific tasks:

1. to prepare a national environment policy for government approval and to keep it under review;
2. to examine the state of the environment and report on it to the government from time to time;
3. to promote specific programmes or projects for the protection and improvement of the environment;
4. to promote co-ordination in environmental policies and programmes; to designate areas as national parks or regional parks.

It had been increasingly clear for some time that positive measures to protect the environment had become a necessity. In the words of a Minister for the Environment:

The development programmes which have been undertaken in this country, and the huge tasks before us in the provision of houses and factories, in increasing employment and production and in developing natural resources, must lead to big changes. The environment will be affected by these changes but . . . those engaged in the development process must come to terms with the need to work within a stringent system of environmental protection.

Some years before the 1977–8 moves the government had decided (April 1974) to set up an Inter-Departmental Environment Committee under the aegis of the Department of Local Government with the object of preparing a provisional statement of policy and programme of action. The committee issued a report on 'Control of Pollution' (1978) in which they reviewed existing arrangements in regard to water, air, waste, noise and nuisance and made a number of recommendations. The Committee continues to operate but its terms of reference, revised following the creation of the Environment Council, have shifted emphasis towards the exchange of information, co-ordination and collaboration between Departments.

In consonance with the assumption of environmental responsibilities the Minister established an eighteen member Environment Council with representatives from industry, agriculture, trade unions, education, science, health and administration. The Council's first report, 'Towards an Environment Policy' (1979) outlined major pressures on the environment and the issues which should govern the approach to an environment policy. Urbanisation drew special comment: 'The consequences of increased urbanisation have not received adequate consideration.' This statement was supported by another report which came out in 1979 — the annual report of the Water Pollution Advisory Council. The report criticised various aspects of the working of the Local Government (Water Pollution) Act, 1977 including the failure to provide sufficient capital for the treatment of town sewage.

A scheme of grants for works of environmental value was introduced in 1977 as part of the government's job creation programme. Allocations amounting to £500,000 were notified to local authorities on the basis of their unemployment figures. Grants covered total recoupment of labour costs and 50 per cent of other expenses. On the suggestion of the Employment Action Team part of the special allocation of £5 million provided in the 1978 Budget for youth employment was applied to environmental projects.

International Perspectives

International organisations are coming to play an increasingly prominent role in environmental affairs. The United Nations, with its offshoot the Economic Commission for Europe (ECE) and the EEC have developed programmes or activities which overlap to some extent but, broadly speaking, complement each other. The organisation having the most immediate effects on national concerns is the EEC, many of whose decisions deal with practical matters of detail in such areas as levels of air and water pollution.

The European Economic Communities adopted a Programme of Action in 1973 towards working out a European environmental policy. The Programme includes the following measures:
1. reduction of pollution and nuisance;
2. improvement of the physical environment;
3. international action.

A Second Action Programme for the period 1977—81 included a number of new provisions, such as:
1. a Community mapping system identifying regional characteristics;
2. measures against air pollution, noise and waste discharge;
3. and environmental problems relevant to developing countries.

Major decisions in furtherance of these objectives are taken by a council of Ministers for the Environment, aided by a Working Party on the Environment. The Commission prepares and puts proposals forward to the Council of Ministers which are processed by the Working Party and then adopted, modified or rejected. Ireland, in common with other members, has a representative on the Working Party.

The United Nations Environment Programme (UNEP) was inaugurated following the UN conference held in Stockholm in 1972. The functions of UNEP, whose headquarters are in Nairobi, Kenya are to promote and co-ordinate international cooperation in the field of the human environment and to keep the world environmental situation under review. Ireland makes an annual contribution to the UNEP Fund.

The Economic Commission for Europe also takes action in environmental matters. At a meeting of Environment Ministers organised by ECE in 1979 an International Convention on Long-Range Transboundary Air Pollution was adopted and signed.

Water Pollution

The Local Government (Water Pollution) Act, 1977 is the most recent example of a control system for conserving an essential part of the environment. The licensing of effluent discharges into water courses is administered by county councils and the corporations of county boroughs. Appeals against local decisions are decided by the Planning Appeals Board. The Act augments the power of sanitary authorities to provide adequate sewerage systems for the disposal of trade effluents and those of planning authorities to control, under the 1963 Act, the quality and quantity of effluents from new factories and other installations. The 1977 Act is based on the recommendations of an inter-Departmental committee in, 'Report on Water Pollution' (1973). A statutory Water Pollution Advisory Council has been appointed by the Minister. In its 1979 annual report the Council commented on the failure of local authorities, as licensing agents, to control the spread of pollution of water resources and expressed concern about the continuing degradation of our rivers and lakes. An Foras Forbartha provides a water quality information service for local authorities and other bodies.

Air Pollution

Controls are exercisable under the Alkali etc. Works Regulation Act, 1906 for certain potentially noxious industries and under the Planning Act, 1963 for new development. The Control of Atmospheric Pollution Regulations, 1970 (made under the Sanitary Services Act, 1962) enables sanitary authorities to deal with offensive emissions of smoke, dust, grit, gas or fumes from premises other than dwellings. More than thirty monitoring stations have been set up to enable a watch to be kept on air conditions and more are planned. More stringent control measures may be required in the light of test measurements. Records are forwarded periodically to the EEC Commission.

Oil Pollution

The clearance of oil pollution in coastal areas is now the responsibility of maritime local authorities. Contingency plans have been prepared and stocks of dispersants laid in. The cost is met in large part by the state.

Fire Service

Under the Fire Brigades Act, 1940 each county borough corporation operates its own fire service. In the rest of the country, county councils have taken over from most urban authorities and unified county services have been formed. Dublin city and county services were amalgamated in 1970 but Dun Laoghaire still maintains its own fire brigade. City and county services are organised under Chief Fire Officers. Fire Officers are also concerned with fire prevention measures, inspection of buildings and the issue of fire precautions notices.

A Fire Protection Association was set up by the Minister in 1965 for advisory work in fire prevention. The Association was replaced in 1978 by a Fire Prevention Council established under the Local Government (Corporate Bodies) Act, 1971 whose duties include publicity and education about fire hazards and the promotion of fire safety in the design, control and use of buildings. Four of the eight members of the Council are from insurance companies, the others represent the Departments of the Environment and Labour and the County and City Managers' Association. The Council is financed jointly by the Environment Department and the Federation of Insurers in Ireland.

A Working Party formed in 1972 to review the fire service reported in 1975. The report urged a general improvement in the service, the merging of remaining urban (excluding city) brigades in county services and a state subsidy for new fire stations and appliances. Training should be stepped up and a National Training Centre created. The Local Government Manpower Committee appointed a sub-committee to comment on the training proposals and following its report, submitted in 1977, the Department organised an expanded programme of central training. A training centre for fire service personnel provided by Wexford County Council at Castlebridge is used as a central training centre by the Department which contributed a grant to its establishment and equipment.

While the Fire Brigades Act, 1940, was effective enough, it had been realised for some time that its provisions were in need of updating. New legislation was in preparation, and its appearance was accelerated by the 'Stardust' fire disaster of February, 1981, in which nearly fifty lives were lost. The Fire Services Bill, 1981, proposes:

- to designate county councils and county borough corporations as fire authorities, together with Dun Laoghaire and Drogheda boroughs and Athlone and Dundalk urban district councils (which currently maintain fire brigades).
- to introduce a more comprehensive system of fire safety control of potentially dangerous buildings.
- to place a general obligation on persons in charge of certain premises to guard against fire risk.
- to enable the Minister to make fire safety regulations for certain premises.
- to allow a fire authority to apply to the High Court for an order for the immediate closure of a premises where necessary.
- to give fire authorities wider powers of inspection.
- to strengthen arrangements for training fire brigade staffs.
- to enable the Minister to provide training facilities and courses, and to establish a Fire Service Training Council.
- to bring penalties up to present day money values.
- to empower the Minister to pay subsidies to fire authorities.

The Bill when enacted would replace the Act of 1940 and, in addition, the Cinematograph Act, 1909, now regarded as obsolete.

Civil Defence

The Minister for Defence is responsible for civil defence planning and organisation. Detailed planning of the casualty and fire-fighting services has been undertaken by the Departments of Health and Local Government respectively under the general direction of the Department of Defence. County and district councils and borough corporations are, under the Air Raid Precautions Act, 1939 the local authorities responsible for giving effect to approved civil defence plans and receive from state authorities technical advice, special equipment and financial assistance to the tune of 75 per cent. In practice, however, civil defence functions are exercised only by county councils and the corporations of county boroughs.

Regulations made under the Air Raid Precautions Act, 1939 to 1946 deal with public shelters, storage of equipment, compensation to personnel for injuries incurred on service in peace time, lighting restrictions, evacuation of civil population and other matters. Officers responsible for organizing civil defence measures have been appointed by all local authorities and have taken courses of instruction in the Civil Defence School in Dublin. Civil defence covers the preparation of local plans, the recruitment of large numbers of voluntary workers, the provision of control centres and shelters and the adaptation of buildings as fire stations, rescue depots and food and rest centres. The Department of Defence is, of course, responsible for national planning. Regional Officers, drawn from Army personnel, have been designated, and a regional organisation provisionally worked out.

Water Safety

Local authorities have the duty of taking measures for water safety in their areas: warning notices, safety equipment such as life belts, and employment of life guards on beaches etc. The Minister set up An Comhlachas Snámha is Tárrthála (Irish Water Safety Association) in 1971 to undertake a national programme of instruction in basic swimming and life saving and to promote water safety generally. The Department pays an annual grant (£34,000 in 1977) and sanitary authorities also contribute.

Dangerous Buildings and Places. Local authorities were enabled by the Local Government (Sanitary Services) Act, 1964 to deal with dangerous places such as disused quarries and dangerous structures. Fences and warning notices can be up up at rivers, cliffs etc. Dangerous buildings can be closed off, demolished, or otherwise made safe. A state subsidy of 50 per cent is paid for works on dangerous places.

Nuisances. Nuisances in the legal sense have been defined in ten categories by the Public Health Acts. In general they are all those conditions which are injurious to health but they also include such things as diminish the comfort of life although not actually injurious to health. It is the duty of the sanitary authority to detect nuisances and see that they are abated, if necessary getting an order of court for the purpose and abating the nuisance itself if the order is disobeyed.

Factories, Offices and Shops

The Factories Act, 1955 contains a comprehensive range of provisions to secure the health and safety of workers during working hours. Sanitary authorities and fire brigade authorities (the same people, more or less, wearing different hats, or helmets) are charged with keeping a special eye on factories, and seeing that they are properly equipped with sanitation, fire escapes and so on. The Minister for Labour can make special regulations about fire precautions and factory inspectors must report deficiencies in sanitation to sanitary authorities for remedial action.

The Office Premises Act, 1958 applies something like the same procedure to offices but here the Minister for Labour is enabled to make regulations and set standards for a wide range of working conditions: cleanliness, overcrowding, temperature, ventilation, lighting, welfare and sanitation. Enforcement is the work of sanitary authorities but state offices and certain others come directly under the Minister for Labour and his officers.

Shop workers are cared for under an earlier code which goes back to the Shops (Condition of Employment) Act, 1938. Sanitary authorities are charged with looking after and enforcing the health requirements of the law.

Waste and Litter

Local authorities provide domestic refuse collection and disposal services. They may, if they so wish, collect and dump trade wastes. The Department began in the 1970s to interest itself in local arrangements and a series of Circular Letters from 1971 onwards gave suggestions about organisation and methods in the service. Waste disposal plans are in preparation, under Departmental guidance. An Foras Forbartha set up a working party on the disposal of solid waste. The possibility of re-cycling wastes drew increasing attention and a Steering Committee was formed to oversee an investigation. The problem of finding suitable dumping sites began to surface in several areas. Pursuant to EEC Directives of 1975–6, European communities' (Waste) Regulations have been made, dealing with toxic and other materials.

The Local Government Planning and Development Act 1963 prohibited throwing litter about or otherwise depositing waste material on streets, road sides or open spaces. City and other authorities can provide litter bins and Dublin Corporation, with other authorities, has worked hard and spent a good deal of money on publicity and education. The rapid increase in recent years in the volume of packaging and other disposable materials has created a most intractable problem. Sanitary authorities have lacked the resources in people, cash and equipment and possibly the enforcement capacity, to cope.

The Department has from 1973 onwards issued to local authorities a series of circulars on environmental cleanliness and tidiness, removal of graffiti, slogans and so on but the problem continues to grow. The national temper is not oriented to tidiness and civic pride is not offended by litter-strewn streets. Local authorities have been asked to call residents and community groups to aid the effort but a long-term educational programme is possibly the only alternative to a national or civic campaign of draconic enforcement which public opinion would hardly tolerate. Dublin Corporation has made Anti-Litter Bye-laws and employs a corps of Litter Wardens. A 'Keep Dublin Tidy' Campaign is run with poster and media publicity, Tidy School Committees, Tidy Road Clubs, lectures in schools and youth clubs and the circulation of a School Newsletter. Beach clean-ups are also organised.

The Litter Bill, 1981 proposes a series of measures designed to cope with the litter problem. Duties to prevent or remove litter will be placed on sanitary authorities and occupiers of land and sanitary authorities will be given enlarged powers of making bye-laws dealing with abandoned cars and generally disposing of litter. On-the-spot £5 fines may be imposed by litter wardens, while increased penalties up to £500 will apply in other cases. The Bill replaces s. 52 of the Local Government (Planning and Development) Act, 1963.

The annual 'Tidy Towns' Competition sponsored by Bord Fáilte, which now has a virtually nationwide coverage, has done much to inculcate some notion of civic housekeeping into the public consciousness, at least in small towns and villages. Local authorities are closely associated with Tidy Towns committees in their improvement work.

Flood Relief. Works are undertaken by local authorities where the need is serious enough, the necessary powers being supplied by the Local Authorities (Works) Act, 1949. Local, mainly urban, authorities became involved in works of minor extent while arterial drainage is the responsibility of the Office of Public Works. Work to combat serious coast erosion can be undertaken by cooperation between local authorities and the Office of Public Works under the Coast Protection Act, 1963.

Burial Grounds. The provisions of the Act of 1878 regarding burial grounds have been supplemented by those of the Local Government (Sanitary Services) Act of 1948. Sanitary authorities are as a rule burial boards and can provide burial grounds. It is the business of the sanitary authority to see these burial grounds are fenced and kept in order. The Act of 1948 prohibits burials in places that are not burial grounds but clergymen may be buried in or adjacent to a church.

The Minister for the Environment can make regulations for the disposal of bodies otherwise than by burial; but cremation which is the most widely used alternative to burial in other countries is not practised here. There are currently no crematoria in the Republic. Proposals for at least one major project are however underway.

Dogs and Cats Homes. These are provided and managed by private groups. Local Authorities may now under the Planning Acts, assist persons or bodies with shelters for stray cats and dogs. Since 1978 the Department recoups 50 per cent of local outlay.

20

Recreation and Amenity Services

This aspect of local government activities has been overshadowed for many years by other programmes – housing, road construction, water and sewerage, for example, which have claimed priority and pre-empted most of the necessarily limited resources available to local bodies.

Parks and Pools

Sanitary authorities may provide indoor and outdoor swimming pools and other bathing facilities. They may either undertake the work themselves or contribute under the Local Government Act, 1955 towards their provision by swimming clubs, local committees or other such bodies. In either case, if a loan is raised, state assistance is available in the form of contributions to the loan charges. The usual subsidy is at the rate of 50 per cent. A programme of swimming pools built throughout the country to modern standards was launched by the Minister for the Environment in the late 1960s. Loans from the Local Loans Fund, with subsidy, were approved for over eighty projects in the ten-year period up to 1977. Work on sixty-six new pools had been completed.

Sanitary authorities in all urban and county health districts can acquire land either compulsorily or by agreement for recreation facilities; they can also lay it out, maintain it and make bye-laws to govern its use. The site of the recreation ground may be either within or, if it is convenient for the use of the inhabitants of the district, outside the district. All the authorities mentioned can acquire land by agreement for an open space and may permit the open space to be used as a recreation ground subject to the terms on which they hold the land: Open Spaces Act, 1906.

By virtue of the Public Parks (Ireland) Acts, 1869–72, borough corporations, urban district councils and commissioners of towns having a population of over six thousand can establish public parks. Special powers have been conferred on local authorities for the management and improvement of parks, pleasure grounds and recreation grounds held by them. When an estate is being sold by the Land Commission, advances may be made to local authorities or trustees for the purpose of providing sports fields, parks, pleasure grounds and playgrounds. Playing fields may be provided as part of a housing scheme. In Dublin city, where the need is most felt, spaces have been set apart as playgrounds and playcentres for young people. These centres have been supplied with play equipment. Similar facilities have been provided in a number of other areas.

Libraries

Town councils were allowed by an Act of 1855 to levy a rate not exceeding one penny for library purposes and the produce of this rate could also be used to meet the expenses of a museum or school of art and science. The council could delegate the business of managing the library to a committee. The Act did not affect any town until it had been adopted. At first it could only be adopted at a public meeting. After 1877 it was possible to ascertain the wishes of the people by plebiscite but in 1894 a resolution of the local authority, of which special notice had to be given, was sufficient for adoption. Authorities were allowed to combine in carrying the Acts into execution, a power which was extended in 1901 and 1902 to cover the exchange and hire of books. In 1902 rural district councils were empowered to adopt the Act.

Town councils were slow to adopt the Act. In the latter part of the nineteenth century a few municipal libraries came into existence, otherwise there was no public library provision at that time over the greater part of the country. Andrew Carnegie encouraged the library movement by presenting buildings and shelving if a free site was made available and a full rate levied but the absence of trained librarians and the limited rate levied made satisfactory development difficult. In 1920 the limit on the rate was raised to threepence with power to raise a further threepence in county boroughs with the consent of the central authority. In 1946 the rate limit was removed.

When the rural district councils were dissolved in 1925 the county councils were given power to adopt the Libraries Acts for the rural areas and urban district councils enabled to hand over their powers to county councils. All urban district councils except Clonmel, Dun Laoghaire and Bray have relinquished their powers to the county councils. The Carnegie United Kingdom Trust, created in 1913 by Carnegie, abandoned the policy of presenting library buildings but gave financial assistance to the county councils in establishing libraries.

Public libraries now exist in every county. The counties of Tipperary North Riding and Tipperary South Riding have joined in one scheme and likewise Westmeath and Longford. County libraries operate from a headquarters where the main book stock is kept. From this the branches and other book repositories are supplied. In all counties there are, in addition, service points where books can be exchanged. Many counties also operate mobile libraries.

In 1923 the Irish Central Library for Students was established by the Carnegie Trust in order to supply books other than fiction that may not be available locally. If a reader cannot get the book he wants through the local library the librarian can apply to the Central Library which can, if necessary, draw on other libraries including the central libraries of England and Scotland.

The Irish Central Library for Students was transferred in 1948 to An Chomhairle Leabharlanna, a body established by the Public Libraries Act, 1947. The Council is appointed by the Minister for the Environment, the members other than the Chairman being appointed on the nomination of bodies representative of the local authorities and a number of learned bodies. The functions of the Council are to supplement the local library services, to assist them to improve such services and make recommendations to the Minister. The Council receives contributions from the local authorities and an Exchequer grant and may, with the Minister's consent, give financial aid to public libraries. In 1961 the Council was empowered to recoup 50 per cent of capital outlay on buildings, mobile libraries and book stocks.

Museums, Art Galleries, Theatres, Cinemas

The power given by the Public Libraries Acts may be used by library authorities to establish museums and schools of science and art, including schools of music. There is an independent power given to borough corporations and urban councils to establish a museum and a gymnasium: Museums and Gymnasiums Act, 1891. County councils and county borough corporations were authorized in 1955 to contribute towards local museums: Local Government Act, 1955. Urban authorities can provide city or town halls with accommodation for public meetings, concerts, dances and so on. The Local Government Act, 1960 enabled city authorities to provide, or assist in providing, concert halls, theatres and opera houses. Substantial grants were voted under this Act by Cork and Dublin Corporations in aid of Cork Opera House and the Olympia Theatre, Dublin. The 1960 Act does not apply outside county boroughs, and is concerned only with buildings. An Act was to follow, however, which concerned itself with what went on inside and, thus transformed the scene.

The Arts Act, 1973 extends to all local authorities and is interested primarily in exhibitions, recitals and performances of all kinds. It is odd that the only previous enactment in this area covered band performances in public, mainly in parks and goes back to the Public Health Acts Amendment Act, 1907. It was re-enacted in slightly more liberal form as recently as 1946 but it remained a period piece recalling nostalgically the open-air concerts which were an afternoon feature of endless Edwardian seaside summers.

The Arts Act, 1973 gives to local councils the reserved function of assisting the Arts Council or any person, with money or in kind or by the provision of services or facilities (including the services of staff) . . . organising an exhibition or other event the effect of which . . . would . . . stimulate public interest in the arts, promote the knowledge, appreciation and practice of the arts, or assist in improving the standards of the arts (s. 12).

This language opens up an entire new range of activities and patronage to local government, and a number of councils have responded to the opportunity. Dublin Corporation has made grants to the Dublin Theatre Festival, the Royal Irish Academy of Music, musical events, stage performances, picture exhibitions, grand opera and other artistic activities. Cork Corporation and many other local councils have also exercised new powers. The capability is spread very wide and covers painting, sculpture, architecture, music, drama, literature, design in industry, the cinema and the fine arts and applied arts generally.

Local authorities can help local groups to build community centres and halls for various communal activities. Artistic and cultural, as well as recreational and sporting ventures depend heavily on physical accommodation. The Chairman of the Arts Council said (1977), 'There is a desperate need for new buildings to house the arts, particularly at local level' and went on to urge a partnership between the Arts Council and local authorities. The need and desirability of local leadership had already been accepted by the government (White Paper, 1971).

A number of local councils are participating in community work. Dublin County Council's scheme of grants for community and recreational projects supports halls, etc., up to £5,000 in each case, playing fields, play schemes, festival and community weeks, garden competitions and numerous cultural activities. A number of councils operate development funds on much the same lines. There are many other examples of the nationwide effort to meet developing leisure needs.

Cinematograph exhibitions cannot be lawfully given unless the statutory regulations for securing safety are observed. The building in which an exhibition is given must be licensed unless it is used occasionally or exceptionally only and for not more than six days in the year. The occupier must notify the authorities of his intention to use the premises and comply with the regulations and any conditions imposed by the local authority. The licensing authorities are county councils, borough corporations, urban councils and town commissioners. These authorities cannot attach any condition or restriction as to the character or nature of the pictures to be exhibited (Cinematograph Act, 1909; Censorship of Films Act, 1923, s. 10). The licensing of dance halls rests with the District Court and the licensing of places used for music or other public entertainment of the like rests with the Circuit Court.

Licensing of theatrical performances in the city and county of Dublin is governed by an Irish Act of 1786 under which patents are issued to certain theatres but on the application of the corporation of the county borough or the county the Taoiseach grants occasional licences for theatrical performances for charitable objects. Dublin Corporation has power to grant provisional licences in the city under a local Act and Cork Corporation also has powers under a local Act of licensing and regulating theatres in Cork city.

Caravans, Camping etc. Local authorities were given power by the Local Government (Planning and Development) Act, 1963 to provide caravan parks but this type of enterprise is generally left to private developers. Dublin County Council, however, operates two caravan parks and others have also provided these facilities. The local council can provide sites for development. Temporary dwellings include tents, caravans, huts and houseboats. Sanitary authorities are empowered by Part IV of the Local Government (Sanitary Services) Act, 1948 to control the erection or retention of these forms of dwelling in their areas. They may make bye-laws regulating them and their owners, or prohibit them altogether in certain areas. Alternatively they may license caravan sites and other land on which huts, tents, etc., are pitched. The hiring of pleasure boats is controlled by a licensing system operated by county councils and other councils to which the Public Health Acts (Amendment) Act 1907 (s. 94) applies.

National Monuments

Authority to protect ancient monuments (as they were then called) was vested in county councils by the Local Government Act 1898 (s. 19). The National Monuments Act, 1930 went farther by enabling local authorities, urban and rural, to take on the guardianship or ownership of national monuments which were defined at some length. Local advisory committees could be appointed. Local authority concern with national monuments was not generally active and in 1954 an amending Act empowered any local authority having guardianship or ownership of a monument to transfer it to the Commissioners of Public Works.

21

Education, Agriculture, Welfare

Unlike most countries, Irish local authorities are not charged with the administration of primary or secondary education. They provide higher education grants, enforce the School Attendance Acts in county boroughs and contribute to the maintenance of boys and girls in industrial and reformatory schools but their main educational involvement is with technical or vocational schooling. They are responsible through Vocational Education Committees for the provision of vocational and continuation education and have up to recently been concerned with providing winter agricultural classes for young men engaged in farm work. The public libraries, under the control of local authorities, have a partly educational purpose although largely availed of for recreational reading.

Vocational and Continuation Education

For the purpose of vocational education the country is divided into vocational education areas. For every area a vocational education committee must be appointed by the county, borough, or district council as the case may be. The areas and the constitution of these committees have been described in Chapter 7 above. Every committee must appoint a chief executive officer and any other officers that may be necessary.

A committee's duty is to provide vocational education and continuation education for their area. Vocational education includes education for trades and business, in science and art and in agricultural subjects; continuation education is intended to continue and supplement the work of the elementary schools in the period between the school leaving age and the age when employment may be expected to begin. The courses of study vary according to the district. A committee may prepare a general scheme showing its policy and how it proposes to give effect to it, establish schools and contribute to the expenses of residents in obtaining vocational education. A committee that is not making adequate provision having regard to its resources may be required by the Minister for Education to make good the deficiency. Examinations are held by the Department of Education and certificates issued. In recent years adult education diploma courses in social and economic science have been organised by some committees in conjunction with university colleges.

Every year an estimate of expenses for the next financial year is prepared in the autumn. Although the greater part of the expenses is met out of grants voted annually by the Oireachtas, the main grant being in aid of expenditure under the annual schemes, rating authorities can contribute up to 10p in the £ from the rate. The Minister for Education, when he has considered the estimate, gives the committee a certificate which authorizes a demand from the rating authority. The contributions from the rates are limited to a maximum fixed by statute. Administration is now carried on under the Vocational Education Act, 1930 and amending Acts. The Act of 1930 repealed the statutes in relation to technical instruction passed in the period 1889 to 1924.

Regional Technical Colleges

Colleges have been built and staffed by the Department of Education at Athlone, Carlow, Cork, Dundalk, Galway, Letterkenny, Limerick, Sligo and Waterford. They offer education for trade and industry up to professional level and include scientific, management, commercial, linguistic and other specialities. The colleges operate under the aegis of the Vocational Education Committees for the various locations.

Vocational Technological Colleges

Five colleges developed in Dublin by the City Vocational Education Committee provide degree and diploma courses in engineering, architecture, building, business studies, catering, etc. The colleges, which include the Municipal College of Music, together constitute the Dublin Institute of Technology. The Cork City VEC has established a College of Art, and Limerick a College of Art, Commerce and Technology.

Residential Houses and Special Schools

Industrial schools were originally established by charitable bodies for children who through want, neglect or lack of control, might drift into crime. Renamed residential houses, children are now sent there mainly by health authorities, and, in declining numbers, by the Courts. Special schools, formerly reformatories, where the courts intervene, are for young offenders, and committal is through the Courts.

County councils and county borough corporations contribute to the maintenance of boys and girls in both types of schools. The amount to be contributed in respect of each boy or girl is fixed by regulations made by the Minister for Education under the Children Act, 1941. The state also makes an equivalent contribution towards maintenance. If a health board is the agent, the whole cost is met by the board.

School Attendance

The enforcement of school attendance is a matter for the Garda Síochána except in county boroughs and Dun Laoghaire where school attendance committees have been appointed. The constitution of these committees has been described in Chapter 7. The committees appoint attendance officers for the areas mentioned.

Higher Education Grants

County councils and county borough corporations assist students who are ordinarily resident in the county or borough by means of grants, exhibitions, busaries, payment of fees or otherwise. The students must be qualified to profit by university or other third level instruction, and comply with prescribed conditions as to age, means, etc. The Local Authorities (Higher Education Grants) Act, 1968 limits the amount payable by a local authority each year to expenditure in 1968-69 under older Acts. Costs in excess of that limit are met by the state. The council or corporation prepares a grants scheme for the approval of the Minister for Education. The Minister for Education prescribes the examination tests and age limits and his approval is required to the award of scholarships.

School Meals

School meals provided by public authorities had their origin in the Education (Provision of Meals) Acts, 1914 to 1917, which authorized borough and urban district councils to make provision for meals for children attending national schools in their districts. In 1930 similar power was given to town commissioners. If any school children in the area of these authorities are unable by reason of lack of food to take full advantage of the education provided for them, and there are no other funds available to defray the cost, the local authority can be authorised by the Minister for Social Welfare to expend from the rates an amount that will meet the cost of food. Half the actual expenditure on food may be recouped out of a state grant. In 1930 the scheme was extended to rural national schools in the Gaeltacht. This is the only part played by county councils in school meals. Expenditure on the scheme is about £700,000 a year.

Agricultural Services

Every county council must establish a committee of agriculture the composition of which has already been described in Chapter 7 above. The committee gave assistance and instruction in agriculture, horticulture, bee-keeping, poultry-keeping and butter-making, under the general supervision of the Department of Agriculture. Under the Agriculture Act, 1979, amending the National Agricultural Advisory and Research Authority Act, 1977, the agricultural advisory service became the responsibility of a new body entitled An Comhairle Oiliuna Talmhaiochta, or ACOT.

Committees of Agriculture will not disappear, but their functions will be largely consultative. They will be expected to form and express opinions on the working of the new advisory service, and on certain other aspects of agriculture.

The committee will continue to be financed by contributions from rates and from grants. The county council must raise a rate each year for the committee and the Department of Agriculture supplements the local product. The committees are the successors of bodies that were first constituted under an Act of 1899. They function under the Agriculture Act, 1931, and amending Acts.

Diseases of Animals

County councils and the corporations of county boroughs have had certain functions under the Diseases of Animals Acts since 1898. The Minister for Agriculture is the central authority. The functions of local authorities are now confined to (1) the appointment of veterinary inspectors; (2) the administration of the Bovine Tuberculosis Order, 1926; and (3) the enforcement of sheep dipping regulations. The Order of 1926 deals with clinical or open cases of bovine tuberculosis and is not connected with the general bovine tuberculosis eradication scheme, although the need for it is diminishing as the general scheme takes effect. About half of the expenses of local authorities under the Acts was formerly recouped from the General Cattle Diseases Fund, a capital fund which was established under the Contagious Diseases (Animals) Act, 1878, and fed by means of levies made from time to time on local authorities. The intention was that the cost of dealing with outbreaks of animal disease, which might bear unduly on one or two local authorities should be met in part from the Fund. The Fund was, however, by the Diseases of Animals Act, 1960, wound up with effect from March 1963. The law was modernised and consolidated in the Diseases of Animals Act 1966, which left the functions of local authorities more or less as they were.

Sheep Dipping

Under the Sheep Dipping Order, 1966 it is the business of the local authority to secure the compliance of sheep owners with the obligation to have sheep dipped during the prescribed period (August, September, and October). Sheep dipping stations on approved sites and baths have been provided by local authorities. County councils and county borough corporations are the authorities for licensing persons to sell poisonous substances (sheep dips, weed killers etc.,) and the granting of such licences is governed by regulations.

Seeds and Fertilisers

County councils have been authorized to provide and sell seeds (wheat, barley and oats), seed potatoes and fertilisers or to undertake to guarantee payment to seed merchants who supply seed or fertilisers or both to an occupier or cultivator approved by the council. The recipient is required to refund the cost with interest to the council who can, if necessary, recover it from him by a special rate to be levied and collected with the county rate. The scheme is operated in very few counties, and the number of participants has fallen sharply.

Slaughter of Animals

The slaughtering of animals is regulated both in urban and rural districts. Early legislation which applied to towns was directed towards ensuring that slaughter houses were kept in a proper state, and preventing cruelty to animals. New slaughter houses had to be licensed and every slaughter house registered. Carcases not fit for use could be seized by officers of the local authority who had a right of entry. Later, sanitary authorities were given power to provide slaughter houses; and Dublin and Limerick Corporations are examples of authorities operating municipal abattoirs. Bye-laws could be made for the decent conveyance of meat through the streets. In 1935 further provision was made towards securing the humane treatment of animals in slaughter houses, and the use of approved instruments for slaughter was made compulsory.

Arterial Drainage

Drainage districts were constituted under early drainage Acts (1842-66). When drainage works were executed by the Commissioners of Public Works in these districts they were handed over for maintenance to drainage boards. These bodies were expected to keep the districts in good repair and had power to levy a rate on benefited proprietors. Drainage schemes were prepared on receipt of memorials from proprietors whose lands were injuriously affected by floods. Many drainage works were carried out but the system did not prove successful.

The Local Government Act of 1898 made it possible to transfer drainage districts to the county councils and a number of districts were so transferred.

In the first quarter of the present century very little drainage work was done and districts fell into disrepair. In 1924 the Commissioners of Public Works were empowered to carry out repair work. The Exchequer and county councils could assist such work with free grants, and loans could be advanced by the Commissioners of Public Works. The loans were charged on the benefited lands and the county funds. When works were completed they were transferred to the county councils concerned, who could levy a drainage rate on the benefited occupiers. The legislation of 1924 did not have the results anticipated. Many districts had deteriorated to the point that reconstruction was necessary and the demand for new works could not be met.

In 1925 fresh legislation provided for the formation of new drainage districts and laid down a procedure for dealing with petitions to the county council to have drainage works carried out. The county council was required to give an undertaking to maintain a drainage district if formed, and to accept responsibility for the collection and repayment to the Commissioners of Public Works of such portion of the cost as was charged on the benefited lands. The councils were empowered to appoint drainage committees. The Act, by giving any six ratepayers power to initiate schemes, was a hindrance to dealing with the drainage of river basins as a whole and considering drainage problems comprehensively. Some councils made a satisfactory effort to maintain their districts but the majority failed to achieve a reasonable standard of maintenance. In 1928 a temporary Act was passed with the object of helping small local drainage works costing less than £1,000 each. Under this Act minor schemes were carried out by seven county councils. Contributions towards the cost of the schemes were made by the state and the county councils concerned, and the remainder of the expenses were charged on the land that was drained. The Act expired after five years.

The Arterial Drainage Act of 1945 made a fresh start. The provisions of the Act followed in the main the recommendations of the Drainage Commission of 1938-40. The Act dissolved existing drainage boards and transferred their functions to county councils. The Commissioners of Public Works are responsible for preparing schemes. When a scheme is prepared a copy is sent to the county council and the occupiers of the lands that would be affected, and other persons having interests are notified. If it is confirmed by the Minister for Finance it is carried out by the Commissioners who are responsible for maintenance. The Commissioners may take over existing districts but they are not obliged to maintain them in a better state than at the time of transfer. Until these districts are taken over they remain with the existing drainage authorities. The Act apparently contemplates their gradual transfer. The county council must meet costs of maintenance of drainage districts and the Commissioners are empowered to send an estimate and demand to the council annually. The council in the financial year following the receipt of the demand raises the money required over the whole county by means of the county rate and pays it in moieties.

Allotments

Borough corporations, urban councils and town commissioners may take land for allotments by agreement or, if unable to get it by agreement, may take it compulsorily. Land acquired compulsorily cannot be taken for more than five years. The local authority may let an allotment to one or two persons or to a number of persons working on an approved co-operative system or to an allotment association. The rents should meet the expenses but if the plots are let to the unemployed, merely nominal rents may be charged and seeds, manures, etc., provided free. A grant is made to recoup local authorities the loss of rent when nominal rents are fixed, and the cost of free seeds, manures and implements supplied to the unemployed is borne by the Exchequer. The county council can provide allotments for workers in the rural districts. Interest in the scheme has declined greatly in recent years, and very few councils operate the service.

Fairs and Markets

These also are a declining service, particularly on the fairs side. Fairs were at one time an indispensable part of the agricultural economy, but they began during the 1950s to be replaced by the modern and much more organised and convenient system of cattle marts. Fairs, with their colour and bustle, have virtually disappeared. Some urban markets still survive. Dublin City operates markets for wholesale food stuffs; retail fruit, vegetables, meat and fish; and secondhand clothes and furniture. What follows is of mainly historical interest.

A fair is a market and may be something more, but every market is not a fair. Fairs and markets have existed in Ireland from the earliest times. After the introduction of English law the Crown, following the practice in England, made grants of markets and fairs to individuals and corporations. Such rights, including the right to collect tolls, usually carried with them the obligation to provide a convenient place for the market and to maintain order in it. Legal markets which owe their origin to royal charters or letters patent still exist; and, in addition, there are markets that have been established under Acts of Parliament, either local or general. The Public Health Act of 1878 contains important provisions relating to markets. Section 103 gives any urban sanitary authority, that is, any borough corporation or urban district council, power to establish a market and make byelaws for it, but the sanitary authority cannot interfere with any existing rights without the consent of the person having these rights. In order to enable the urban authority to establish and regulate the market, section 103 incorporated the Markets and Fairs Clauses Act of 1847 so far as that Act related to markets. This Act of 1847 contained a set of model clauses that could be applied to every type of market and its protection, the weighing of goods and carts and the levying of rents and tolls. Tolls have to be approved by the central authority, now the Minister for the Environment. In addition to providing a market place and doing everything that was necessary for its convenient use urban sanitary authorities were empowered to purchase or lease public or private rights in markets and tolls. Some charter markets have passed into the hands of the local authorities in exercise of these powers. In 1896 the central authority was enabled to invest the rural sanitary authority (now the county council) with the powers of the urban sanitary authority as regards markets. Town commissioners got these powers under the 1978 Act (s. 103).

The time or place at which a fair is held may be altered by the Minister for the Environment at the request of the owner, but the new place for the fair must be within half a mile of the old. In some cases where the power to alter the conditions for holding a fair has been given in the original grant the Minister for the Environment may make an alteration.

Public Assistance

The term 'public assistance' formerly covered a wide variety of services, most of which, in somewhat altered form, are now classed as health services. It is one of the ironies of administrative history that public assistance should have shrunk to comparative insignificance before its final disappearance in 1977. Under its earlier title of poor relief, it first revitalized and then dominated the machinery of nineteenth century local government in Ireland, gradually imposing its distinctive marks on the entire organisation: strong central control and direction; subordination of local bodies; and uniformity of services. The comprehensive system of general and medical reliefs which once operated under the Poor Relief Acts has been eroded on the one hand by social insurance and assistance measures, and on the other by the health services, until virtually nothing now remains.

Home assistance survived until 1977, and each county and county borough operated its own scheme of allowances, more or less as it saw fit. The Social Welfare (Supplementary Welfare Allowances) Act 1975 substituted a uniform national scheme administered by the Department of Social Welfare. The Department makes grants amounting to about £2.5 million to Health Boards, which handle the local administration. County and city councils, however, still contribute towards the cost.

Footwear

The supply of footwear for necessitous children comes under the general oversight of the Minister for Social Welfare. The scheme is now operated as part of the Supplementary Welfare Allowances Scheme.

Fuel

During the Emergency local authorities in cities and in towns situated in areas that were not producing turf made regular supplies of fuel available for necessitous households with the aid of government subsidies. Winter schemes have been continued with the aid of a state grant amounting at present to about £1.5 million. In some areas free supplies of fuel are distributed, but most authorities issue vouchers exchangeable for various types of fuel, or used to pay gas and electricity bills.

Unemployment Assistance

The county boroughs and all urban districts with populations over 7,000 are required to make a contribution towards the cost of unemployment assistance administered by the Department of Social Welfare. The county boroughs and Dun Laoghaire pay the equivalent of eight new pence in the pound on the rateable value which for this purpose has been given a special interpretation. In the other urban districts the contribution is equivalent to a rate of ninepence in the pound. The introduction of unemployment assistance in 1933 relieved public assistance authorities of part of the cost of relief arising because of unemployment and on that ground it was considered equitable that there should be a local contribution towards the new charges falling on the Exchequer. The local contribution amounts to about £0.5 million a year.

Pension Committees

Under Section 8 of the Old Age Pensions Act, 1908, old age pensions committees must be appointed by every county council and county borough corporation and by borough corporations and urban councils if the population of the area exceeds 10,000. These committees are statutorily responsible for deciding claims for old age (non-contributory) pensions.

Miscellaneous Services

Local authorities operate a number of services difficult to classify under the somewhat arbitrary scheme adopted in this work. Some, but not all, have survived from another era, like Oisin after the Fianna. They are remnants of once impressive systems operated as part of local government. This is particularly true of the items collated below under the heading of justice, which are a carry-over from the apparatus of local courts administered by grand juries and the old municipal corporations.

Register of Electors

County councils and county borough corporations compile the registers of voters for European, Dáil and local government elections. The registers are revised and brought up to date annually. Draft registers are put on public display on 1 December each year, and can be examined at post offices, public libraries, garda stations, etc. Claims for corrections, insertions, etc., can be made up to 15 January. Objections and claims are adjudicated by county registrars. The new registers come into force on the 15 April. The cost is shared equally by state and local authorities. Residents in Ireland, eighteen years of age and over, can be registered as local (but not Dáil) electors even where they are not Irish citizens.

Rate Collection

Despite recent radical changes in rating, rate collection is still an important local function. Valuation appeals are channelled through rating authorities.

Administration of Justice

Juries The Juries Act, 1927 limited liability to jury service to male electors who occupied a certain minimum rateable property. Women could, however, be included in the jury lists at their own request, if otherwise qualified. In December 1975 the Supreme Court ruled (*Mairin de Burca and Mary Anderson* v. *Attorney-General*) that the restriction of jury service to rate payers, and the partial exemption of women, were unconstitutional. The Juries Act, 1976 now provides that, with a few exceptions, all persons between 18 and 70 on the register of Dáil electors are liable to jury service. County councils and county borough corporations must deliver copies of current registers annually to county registrars, whose business it is to summon and empanel jurors. Certain functions of the sheriffs in Dublin and Cork relating to empanelling juries have transferred to the county registrars.

Coroners County councils and county borough corporations are obliged to appoint coroners, and meet the expenses of inquests (Coroners Act, 1962).

Courthouses The county borough corporations and county councils are bound to provide such courthouse accommodation as the Minister for Justice directs. The custody of a courthouse that is used only as a district court is vested in the district court clerk and of other courthouses in the county registrar. The letting out on hire of a part of a courthouse is a matter for the registrar or district clerk as the case may be (Courthouses (Provision and Maintenance) Act, 1935).

Pounds The corporations of boroughs and county and urban district councils are bound to provide and maintain in their respective areas such pounds as the county registrar, with the approval of the Minister for Justice, directs them to provide. The control of the pound rests in the county registrar. The poundkeepers are appointed by the local authority to the number required by the county registrar. The Minister for Justice regulates the management of pounds (Pounds (Provision and Maintenance) Act, 1936).

Police etc. Local authorities are not concerned in the organisation of police forces or the maintenance of prisons. The police rate of eightpence in the pound, which the Dublin police district had to contribute towards the expenses of the metropolitan police, was gradually reduced after that force was amalgamated with the Garda Síochána in 1925, and is not now levied. All ordinary local prisons were transferred to government control in 1877.

Malicious Injuries Compensation for malicious injuries is one of the oldest liabilities of local authorities. Claims for compensation may be made to the Circuit Court, and awards may be levied off the county or some part of it, or off the county borough.

An Inter-Departmental Committee on Malicious Injuries was set up by the Minister for Justice in 1960. Their report (1963) recommended that the system of compensation by means of local levies should be retained, subject to some revisions. The government decided in 1974 to recoup local authorities the full cost of malicious damage awards attributable to the disturbances in Northern Ireland. A further decision relieved rate payers of compensation awards in excess of 20p in the £ on the rates.

The Malicious Injuries Act, 1981, consolidated the numerous earlier enactments, commencing with the Grand Juries (Ireland) Act, 1836, and made a number of amendments in the code. The principal changes were:
  – claims under £2,500 can now be dealt with by the District Court;
  – compensation is not payable for the first £100 of any claim;
  – compensation is allowable for damage occurring in coastal waters;
  – the Act provides a statutory basis for payment by the state of portion of a claim involving a local rate in excess of 20 pence in the pound.

Transport: Energy

Ferries A few local authorities operate ferries. Dublin Corporation has run ferries across the river Liffey since 1665. Under the Ferries (Acquisition by Local Authorities) Act, 1919 a road authority may acquire and operate a ferry. Or contribute to the enterprise (Local Government Act, 1955).

Gas Supply A fair number of urban authorities were formerly gas undertakers, taking powers by means of provisional orders under the Gas and Water Works Facilities Act, 1870. The number has declined steeply in recent years. The Limerick undertaking, one of the last of the municipal businesses, is (1980) under threat of closure. Where, as in Dublin, the public utility is not in municipal hands, the local authority can appoint a gas examiner to supervise the undertaking in certain limited respects.

Regulatory Functions

Lodging Houses   Common lodging houses must be registered and are subject to regulation. The sanitary authority may make byelaws for the registration, inspection, drainage, provision of water closet accommodation, lighting, safety and fire protection of or for such houses.

Street Trading   Street trading in county boroughs and urban districts was regulated under the Street Trading Act of 1926. In Dublin, street trading was prohibited without a Garda certificate for sale of goods in a street, or in the case of stall trading, a licence. The Corporation granted licences for stall trading and made byelaws with respect to it. In county boroughs other than Dublin, and in urban county districts, the Act was adoptive.

Following a report (1976) by the Restrictive Practices Commission, the Casual Trading Act, 1980, replaced the 1926 Act in large measure by enabling local authorities (county councils, county borough corporations, and urban district councils) to designate particular areas as casual trading areas, and to license traders. Casual trading means selling goods by retail at a place (including a public road) to which the public have right of access, or in a casual trading area designated as such.

Weights and Measures   In Dublin city and Dun Laoghaire where a separate metropolitan police force existed up to 1925, inspectors of weights and measures are appointed by the municipal corporations. Elsewhere, members of the Garda Síochána, selected by the Commissioner for this duty, are ex-officio inspectors, and their expenses are met by the county councils or borough corporations. The central authority is the Minister for Trade, Commerce and Tourism.

Consumer Protection

The Weights and Measures service developed in Britain to become a wide-ranging consumer protection service. In Ireland, where the weights and measures service was (and still is) locally administered in only two areas, consumer protection is largely a state service, although local authorities have certain enforcement functions. Suggestions that the limited local authority concern should be promoted to become a leading role have not found acceptance. The recent Consumer Information Act, 1978 authorises county councils and the corporations of county and other boroughs to take proceedings, but the primary enforcement function clearly rests with the Minister for Trade, Commerce and Tourism, and the new Director of Consumer Affairs.

Information Service   Citizens' Advice Bureaux successfully fill a much
felt need in Britain and Northern Ireland. They supply advice, information
and guidance to the public in coping with the mass of official material and
problems, thrown up by all developed and highly governed societies. The
bureaux originated during the 1939-45 war in response to the disorientation
and confusion of wartime conditions. They survived into peacetime, and
the English Local Government Act, 1948 gave them a local base of support.
There is no similar system here, but some local associations and community councils operate information services.

The National Social Service Council, which was established in 1971 by
the Minister for Health, has organised a network of voluntary Community
Information Centres. It gives modest grants to get new Centres going, and
issues a monthly information bulletin focused on social service and welfare
concerns.

22

Northern Ireland

Up to 1921 local government in Northern Ireland was on precisely the same footing, legal and administrative, as local government in the south. Both were directed and controlled by the Local Government Board in Dublin. Under the Government of Ireland Act, 1920, control of local bodies in six north-eastern counties – Antrim, Armagh, Londonderry, Down, Fermanagh and Tyrone – passed to the Stormont government, which began to operate in June 1921. Conflicts soon arose with a number of local councils having nationalist-Sinn Féin majorities following the local elections of January 1920. Fermanagh and Tyrone county councils refused to recognise the 'partition parliament' and pledged allegiance to Dáil Éireann. In December 1921, the Northern Parliament rushed through an Emergency Powers Act under which the councils were disbanded and replaced by commissioners appointed by the Minister of Home Affairs. Other recalcitrant councils were similarly dealt with.

In the following months the Local Government (NI) Act, 1922 withdrew proportional representation for local elections, reverting to single-member constituencies and election by simple majority. The reasons for the move were obvious – minority views were unwelcome but certain others were cited in support: proportional representation was complicated and costly, and it 'weakened the sense of responsibility of councillors who were, in effect, elected *en bloc*'. The doubts of the British cabinet, and the protests of the Free State government, which delayed the Royal Assent for some months, were eventually overcome. The outcome of these manoeuvres was a massive shift of local political power in marginal areas. In Fermanagh, for example, where the nationalists controlled five of the seven local councils, the entire local government apparatus fell into Unionist hands within a year. And power was inevitably followed by patronage.

A curious aspect of the brief local resistance to Belfast was a threat of financial support by the Free State government to councils whose Exchequer grants were cut off by the Northern government. The plan, urged by Collins in February 1922, was scotched by Blythe, then Minister for Trade and Commerce.

In 1922, the Ministry of Home Affairs administered six county councils, two county borough corporations, twenty-nine urban district councils and five towns under town commissioners. In addition, there were twenty-seven boards of guardians, and thirty-one rural district councils. The contrast between north and south was as marked in local government as in other ways. The enthusiasm with which boards of guardians were swept away by the southern government found no official echo in the north where these venerable relics were preserved, and continued to operate as 'a highly successful aspect of government' (Oliver 1978, p. 28).

Satisfaction with the unchanged pre-1920 system was however by no means universal. A Departmental Commission on Local Government Administration (1927) recommended something on the lines of development on the southern side of the border — the abolition of boards of guardians and the creation of county authorities for health and public assistance. But these proposals were rejected by the government, on the plea that they would place too heavy a burden of business on county councils and county committees. The northern plan, of course, lacked the vital ingredient of professional county management, which was the formula followed in the south: it would have meant yielding up to (presumably) non-political administrators decision-making in such vital areas as staff appointments and housing.

The first sign of an approaching thaw was the establishment of a new Ministry of Health and Local Government in June 1944. This was followed by the Northern Ireland Housing Trust (1945) and the Northern Ireland Tuberculosis Authority (1946), both bodies charged with the task of supplementing the inadequate efforts of local elected bodies. The Northern Ireland Fire Authority had already (1944) taken over all local fire brigades with the exception of Belfast Corporation. On the local government side structural reform took the shape of the Public Health and Local Government Act (NI), 1946, under which county and county borough councils became health and welfare authorities which assumed both the work of boards of guardians and the health functions of urban and rural district councils. On the health services side the position was overtaken and completely transformed within a year or two by the extension to Northern Ireland of the British National Health Service. The Northern Ireland General Health Services Board and the Hospitals Authority both date from 1948.

In the matter of local administration the disappearance of boards of guardians, while the most significant of the immediate post-war changes, was by no means the only one. There had been a certain amount of tidying-up on the urban front. Ten of the larger urban districts (apart from Belfast and Derry) had become boroughs. The towns under town commissioners had been promoted to urban council status, making a total of twenty-four urban district councils, some of them quite small. The second tier was completed by thirty-one rural district councils. With the first-tier authorities — six county councils and two county borough corporations — they made a combined total of seventy-three local bodies. This was the position in 1965, just before the process of reform began.

Local Government Franchise

The government, for reasons of their own, preserved the nineteenth century bias in favour of property long after it had been phased out elsewhere in these islands. The local franchise was restricted to householders (and spouses) together with occupiers of other land or premises of £10 value and over. In addition a company could nominate up to six electors — one for every £10 of value of the premises it occupied. In the civil rights agitation which began in 1968 reform of the local franchise was a prominent theme.

Table 1: Local finances in N. Ireland 1921—67

Date	Rates		Grants		Other Income		Total	
	£m	%	£m	%	£m	%	£m	%
1921/2	29.5	74.4	5.0	12.6	5.2	13.0	39.7	100.0
1936/7	24.2	45.2	20.7	38.8	8.5	16.0	53.4	100.0
1945/6	29.7	41.0	28.4	39.2	14.3	19.8	72.4	100.0
1956/7	67.2	33.9	109.1	55.1	21.7	11.0	198.0	100.0
1966/7	184.9	28.7	399.3	61.9	60.6	9.4	644.8	100.0

Revenue Sources

Source: M. N. Hayes 'Some aspects of local government in Northern Ireland' in *Public Administration in Northern Ireland*, 1967.

As in the south, local finances in the north in 1921 were heavily reliant on local taxation. The position began to alter almost at once, following the general pattern of change in these islands of steadily shrinking rates contribution balanced by growing Exchequer aid to local expenditure. The process was hastened in the north by certain factors one of which (not duplicated in the south) was the transfer in 1923 of primary education to county and county borough committees. In this the north followed the lines of an All-Ireland Education Bill (the McPherson Bill, 1919) which had met vigorous opposition from Catholic interests. From 1929 onwards, moreover, there was total de-rating of agricultural land and buildings, and 75 per cent rates relief for industrial premises. A General Exchequer Contribution was introduced in 1948 which absorbed the de-rating grants, together with an equalisation element for poorer areas on a formula compounded of population, road mileage and valuation. Specific grants continued for education, welfare, roads and some other services.

Local finances were reviewed in 1955—7 by a committee chaired by Sir Ronald Nugent, without however finding any solution to the problem of local government's increasing dependence on state support. Revaluation of property (including land) was recommended, as well as some modification of the de-rating of land and industry, but the government flinched from the unpopular decisions involved.

In the matter of revaluation, Northern Ireland did rather better than the south – not from greater determination to modernise the rating system, but under sustained pressure from Westminister to refurbish the income tax base for Schedule A purposes. In response to a British threat to insert a clause in the Finance Bill, 1930 Stormont reluctantly passed the Valuation Acts Amendment Act (NI), 1930 which produced in 1936 a general revaluation of rateable property, other than land. A similar tussle led to another revaluation in 1957 – house values being revised to 1939 levels, and other premises at current values. Land was not touched. As a matter of interest, the comparative productivity of rating systems, north and south were in round figures (1962–3, per capita):

north £9, south £8, England & Wales £18.

A further revaluation took place following the 1972 reforms. The new updated valuations came into effect from 1 April 1976.

Reform

The prelude to local government reform in the north was the creation in 1964 of the Ministry of Development which was 'to bring together a wide range of physical services in planning, roads, transport, airports, housing in all its forms, water, sewerage, nature conservation, amenity lands, new towns and local government' (Oliver, 1978, p. 85). New towns had recently come in prospect – the New Towns Act of 1965 had been passed, following the publication of Robert Matthew's *Belfast Regional Plan* in 1963.

Early in 1966 the new ministry set about what they felt to be a long-needed re-structuring of local government. After much local consultation they composed a document which was issued as a White Paper in 1967, under the title *Reshaping of Local Government: Statement of Aims*. The plan envisaged absorption of boroughs, and urban and rural district councils in from twelve to eighteen administrative areas with a combined urban-rural coverage. County and county borough councils would continue to administer such services as education and health. These proposals were argued over and discussed and finally issued in revised form in a further White Paper: *The Reshaping of Local Government: further proposals* (1969). This more radical document reflected in some measure the storms which had already begun to whirl about the northern administration, in which local government figured as a prime target. County councils were to be swept away with the rest of the old local apparatus, and the whole replaced by sixteen area councils, leaving Belfast City as it stood. Derry Corporation and its contiguous rural district council had already been replaced, in exercise of powers under New Towns Act, 1965, by the Londonderry Development Commission. It was also decided in 1969 to remove housing altogether from local government, and to create a Central Housing Executive which would absorb the Northern Ireland Housing Trust. Education was divorced from local government, while the somewhat tattered remnant was to be re-examined by an independent review body chaired by a prominent businessman, Patrick MacRory.

These dramatic developments came about because the orderly process of reform, master-minded by the Ministry of Development, was caught up in the civil rights movement which was the immediate occasion of the Northern troubles. A patently sectarian decision in a housing tenancy case ignited the powder-keg, but there was apart from this particular instance a mounting sense of grievance about discrimination against the minority in housing, jobs, and such other patronage as lay in local hands. Much of this was brought to light by the Cameron Commission whose report in 1969 on *Disturbances in Northern Ireland* commented on the 'manipulation of electoral boundaries to achieve and maintain party control of local government'. Countermeasures were quickly introduced – a Complaints Act (NI), 1969 which established an ombudsman for local maladministration and, most important of all, the reform of local franchise on the basis of one man (or woman) one vote.

The MacRory review body reported in 1970. Major services were to be dealt with on a regional basis – education, personal health, welfare and child care, planning, roads, water and sewerage. Housing had already been centralised. The narrow range of functions left to local government could be handled by smaller and more numerous district councils than were in mind when the Ministry of Development set out on the road to reform. Twenty-six district councils were recommended, each with a borough or town as centre, and this plan was the basis of the Local Government Act (NI) 1972. Proportional representation was restored after an absence of fifty years. Local functions comprise domestic and trade refuse collection, street cleaning, litter, clean air; public toilets, rodent and pest control, caravan sites and site licences; entertainment, culture and recreation, public parks and open spaces, local museums, swimming pools and sports centres, licensing of pleasure boats, cinemas etc.; burial grounds, crematoria; building regulations; local tourist development; and a number of others.

Four regional Health and Social Services Boards, and five Education and Libraries Boards are largely nominated but have a certain representative element. About one-third of the members are district councillors. Planning, roads, water and sewerage are the direct responsibility of the Ministry of the Environment, which has replaced the Ministry of Development. Appeals from the Ministry's planning decisions are decided by an Independent Planning Appeals Commission.

Rates have survived. They are levied and collected by the Ministry of Finance. They have two components: a regional rate for the centralised or regional services, and a district rate. The regional rate is levied uniformly over the whole six counties area on the basis of parity with a comparable area in Britain – Humberside was chosen for this purpose. The district rate is determined by the council, taking into account the general support grant, and any specific grants. In 1980 the regional rate was 60.8p; district rate varied from 16p to 32p.

A Local Government Staff Commission, established under the Act of 1972, is limited to advisory functions. It advises District Councils on the recruitment, training and terms and conditions of staff, and has drawn up a code of Employment and Promotions Procedures for use by councils. Its remit was extended in 1976 to the Northern Ireland Housing Executive.

23

What Next?

In the foregoing chapters an attempt has been made to give a coherent account of the origin of local government as we know it today, to trace the way it has grown and to describe in some detail the stage of its development that has now been reached. The narrative has been confined to local government in its formal aspects. Local government can be looked at from other angles. It has a function in the education of the citizen, and may be the means of associating with the conduct of public business many who would otherwise have no opportunity of public service. Its tendencies and shortcomings might have been examined or the role the political parties play in sustaining public interest in it. These aspects of the subject have, however, been regarded as outside the immediate aim, which is to give the student of administration, the local officer, the candidate for employment under a local authority or anyone interested in this field of public activity a concise account of the structure and modes of operation of local government and to present its main features as they are at the moment. Local government is not static — for upwards of a century its activities have been expanding. It has changed and is changing; our theme is local government in transition.

Extension of Franchise — And Controls

At the base of the system are the local government electors with whom rests the choice of persons to constitute the main bodies. When representative local bodies were coming into existence the electors were persons qualified as occupiers or owners of property or as rate-payers, women being excluded. By stages the whole body of adult citizens, men and women, has been enfranchized. So far, therefore, as representation is concerned there can be no further major advance in making the electorate more democratic. The extension of the franchise has been accompanied by an increase in the power of central authorities of government to intervene in local administration. These authorities are not confined to advising, criticising and drawing attention to default or inefficiency. Their control over local government has been tightened and extended. It operates by requiring sanction to important decisions before they can take effect, regulating the appointment of the principal officers, by centralised audit, control of loans, inspection and enforcing the law, if necessary by superseding the elected body. The wide autonomy which most of the elected bodies enjoyed at one time is thus qualified and is further affected by entrusting a manager with the discharge of the executive functions of the principal authorities. Local government here has been moving away from the British pattern, of which it was an adaptation, and approximating to those American and Continental models in which there are separate executives. The Oireachtas in assimilating the method of recruitment and superannuation to that of the civil service has unified the local service and increased its mobility.

Wider Areas

The enlargement of the areas of administration has in the last thirty years or so become a conspicuous feature of the changes that have taken place. The areas formed after 1838 for poor law administration collapsed under the new demands for more and better services. The unions and rural districts were too limited in their resources for the new institutions and the new roads that were required, and moreover they had by the improved mode of transport been rendered unnecessary from the point of view of convenience. Small town authorities have lost many of the powers they originally had and it is noteworthy that a few towns have passed under the direct administration of the county councils. This trend towards larger areas and the larger councils has affected the urban district councils. Four of these have dropped back into the rural areas giving up their powers as sanitary authorities. When in 1947 health authorities were created the health functions of all the urban districts passed to county councils; the movement was carried a step further by the formation of regional health boards in 1972.

From the point of view of economy and efficiency this trend was regarded as inevitable, but it removes the elector further from his representative. A danger to local government here as elsewhere is the indifference and apathy of the electors. It does not follow from the extension of the franchise to all adults that the new electors exercise their power. Where a large proportion does not vote it cannot be said that local bodies are fully representative. The education of the electorate in a wider understanding of, and interest in, local government is a problem of the future.

Functions and Finance

It has been said in criticism of local government that it is neither local nor government. This criticism is not wholly invalid. Many of the activities of local authorities are in the strict sense not local at all. They are national. The assignment of functions to local authorities does not accord with any general principle; it has been largely a matter of expediency or convenience. In many matters the local bodies are little more than the agents or auxiliaries of the central government but in others they are still real organs of local government exercising their powers without outside control or direction and subject only to the law.

The earlier chapters afford convincing evidence of the important role the central authorities are now playing in local government. In most of the post-war years the aggregate of the sums contributed by means of grants and other subventions to local authorities has exceeded the amount raised by rates. It is little use to call for autonomy for local bodies if the general taxpayer is contributing the major part of the money to sustain local services. This fact has prompted some reformers to ask for a clean cut which would detach certain services altogether from local control in the same way as police and prisons were detached in the nineteenth century, and health services in recent times.

The law for the last hundred years or so has regarded local authorities as having no more than the powers given to them and the local body has, therefore, been under an obligation to show authority for its actions. They have no general power to act as they think fit in the public interest. At one time local authorities were hampered in taking the initiative in improvements by lack of power and, where they were active enough, they got these powers individually by private legislation; now, when general legislation has enlarged their powers, it is more often lack of money that cramps their action. It is not an uncommon experience when something costing much money needs to be done, the first thought is to send a deputation to the minister to ask for a grant. This, no doubt, is inevitable when a single tax on an obsolete valuation of immovable property is the main resource of the local authority, and when the freedom to fix the tax level is securely constrained. As the state is not likely to increase the taxing powers of local authorities and as expenditure will not fall below its present levels but rather go beyond them the prospect is that, in the administration of local government, central and local authorities will remain very closely linked.

A new pattern may in time emerge. In 1923 the Oireachtas in the preamble to its first local government statute declared its intention to effect a comprehensive re-organisation. That work was substantially accomplished during the following three decades. In laying the foundations of a representative system more than a century ago parliament was not prepared to treat the question as a whole or to apply any one principle, and in consequence produced an unco-ordinated structure of representative and unrepresentative bodies. The initial flaws in the foundation were mended. By the creation of a system of related bodies, elected on a broad franchise, having enlarged responsibilities and working under the general supervision and in close contact with the central departments of state, local government was made more responsive to public needs and better able to discharge its responsibilities.

Since 1950 other major changes have been made: physical planning and other environmental aids towards a better life have been refurbished;

health services withdrawn from local government; and, on the financial side, housing has become largely an exchequer charge, while, most significant of all, domestic rates have also been shifted from the local to the general taxpayer. These convulsions (if that is not too strong a term) have been succeeded by a time of reorganisational calm, but institutions cannot or should not remain static in a changing world. If they do, they lay themselves open to the very real threat of take-over by more dynamic forces, and of being superseded by organisms better adapted to developing conditions. Institutions which have not some principle of self-renewal become the discards of history, left behind by the inexorable movement of society towards a new age. Fortunately, local government has shown some evidence of self-criticism and regeneration. An almost worldwide impulse towards re-assessment and re-equipment has characterised the 1960s and 1970s. What follows deals, necessarily in outline, with what has happened in these islands.

Re-organisation of Local Government

In September 1965, Richard Crossman set in motion the wave of reform which swept over England, then Scotland, and finally reached Ireland. He did not, of course, originate the notion of reform: it had been in the air for many years. But his strong desire to start something new with which his name would be associated acted as catalyst for a cloud of ideas, desires and partial remedies which had hovered in suspension during the post-war period. His diaries tell the tale for posterity.

> Last Thursday (27 January 1966) I got the Cabinet decision in favour of my local government reform, and I have been tracing its history this weekend. When I first became Minister of Housing I started with the usual ideas that were taught me . . . the one thing one couldn't possibly have was the reform of local government because no sane politician would touch it . . . then as I travelled round the country I became more and more aware . . . that what I was told by local government politicans and civil servants was untrue. In sober fact the time was ripe for a total and radical reform of local government . . . . So last September I had the idea of introducing the theme of a radical reform in my speech to the Association of Municipal Corporations at Torquay and I told them that the dinosaurs would have to give way to modern animals; and I had an enormous success. (Volume III pp. 439—41).

Dame Evelyn Sharp, his Permanent Secretary, was not consulted. When she read the announcement (she was on holiday) she was appalled. Incidentally, Crossman also claimed credit for de-rating the domestic ratepayer. 'This is my own bright idea' he records under 22 December 1965, and goes on to describe how the annual degree of rate relief could be tailored to the aggregate amount, whatever it was, conceded by the Treasury.

The Redcliffe-Maud Commission which emerged from this flurry of low cunning and high politics reported in 1969. There was unanimous agreement that local government in England needed a new structure and a new map, but the Commission was divided about solutions. The majority (ten members out of eleven) favoured an extension of the county borough or unitary authority in 'coherent areas which made good units for planning and transportation, and also contained a population of about 250,000 to about 1,000,000.' In such areas responsibility for all local services would be combined in a single-tier authority. Where larger areas required unified planning (in effect an urban concentration with some rural enclaves with from two to three million inhabitants) two operational tiers were felt to be necessary. These ideas gave the result of fifty-eight unitary authorities with comprehensive responsibility for all local services; and three metropolitan areas (apart from London) with a two-tier structure involving a total of twenty metropolitan districts. The existing local government network in England was made up of:

> 45 counties
> 79 county boroughs
> 227 boroughs
> 449 urban districts
> 410 rural districts
> ————
> 1210

The Redcliffe-Maud plan would have cut this figure down to a total of eighty-one authorities — sixty-one at top level and twenty at second level in the three metropolitan areas of Merseyside, SE Lancashire and NE Cheshire, and west Midlands. These three areas contained a total of twenty-five county boroughs, together with numerous urban and rural districts. In each of the three a large metropolitan authority would handle comprehensive planning, transportation and major developments; while a number of metropolitan districts, like London boroughs, would look after education, personal social services, environmental health and housing.

Above and below the network of big all-purpose authorities would be eight provincial councils; and at 'grass-roots' or community level a large number of local councils without administrative functions but holding watching briefs for their localities, to promote and watch over their interests, urge their needs, and defend their well-being.

The minority Report was a one-man effort in the form of a massive memorandum of dissent by Derek Senior. It was a closely argued case against the unitary town-and-country authorities favoured by the majority, and presenting instead a flexible pattern of two-tier government throughout most of the country, founded on the city-region concept. The city region emerged from the spread and general use of motor-vehicles, which transformed the city as a social unit from the physical entity, the actual built-up area, to include 'the society of people who have effective access to the city centre. . . . It embraces the people living in neighbouring towns and villages and even in isolated farmsteads twenty or thirty miles away.' Senior went on to pursue this thinking to what he saw as its logical conclusion. 'When one thinks of the social unit based on a city centre as a city region, one realises that the size of the population of the brick-and-mortar city is no longer important. What matters now is whether or not the number (and the wealth) of the people, wherever they live, who have easy motorised access to a centre is big enough to sustain 'city' standard of diversity in the opportunities the centre can offer.' (Memorandum of Dissent, para 186). Senior's analysis yielded thirty-five regions ranging in size from Carlisle (312,000 pop, 1822 sq. miles) to Birmingham (3,993,000 pop, 2799 sq. miles). Four of these regions were too small in area and population to need sub-division into districts. The remaining thirty-one regions required second-level administration through some 150 'town-districts'. There would be a re-drawn map with enlarged counties or city regions which would be the catchment areas for such major services as planning and transport. At second level there would be from two to twelve districts in each new county for personal services and services appropriate to smaller areas, and population, than the counties.

As things turned out, it was the one-man minority view which had a greater influence on the outcome. The Labour government broadly accepted the majority view, but the Conservative government which took over in 1970 detected some Labour advantage in the unitary plan and favoured the two-tier arrangement, without however following Senior in his thinking or his practical suggestions. Their White Paper *Local Government in England* (1971) projected a two-tier system of enlarged counties and county districts of a combined urban-rural character. There were no real city-regions, but their six metropolitan counties had some echoes of the city-region concept. The Local Government Act 1972 produced a structure consisting of six metropolitan and thirty-nine other counties; thirty-six metropolitan and 299 other districts. The results have not given universal satisfaction.

Wales

Welsh local government started on the road to reform from the same point as England, and ended in much the same position. The only difference lay in the paths they travelled. No royal commission sat on Welsh problems. A Local Government Boundary Commission reported in 1961 and met such resistance that its modest proposals were dropped. An Inter-Departmental Working Party took up the task in 1965, with the result that Wales was excluded from the deliberations of the Redcliffe-Maud Commission. The Working Party, going their own way, produced a document which was published as a White Paper *Local Government in Wales* in 1967. It contained little that was new, proposing five counties in the place of the existing thirteen; three county boroughs instead of the existing four; and a reduction in county districts from 164 to thirty-six. When however the Royal Commission reported in 1969 in favour of ending the old division between town and country and setting up a network of unitary authorities with administrative areas of a mixed urban-rural composition, the Welsh Office decided to follow suit. But with the accession of the Conservatives to government in 1970, there was an about face in the direction of a two-level system: *The Reform of Local Government in Wales: Consultative Document* (1971). The Local Government Act 1972 gave Wales eight county councils and thirty-seven county districts, with functions following, more or less, those of non-metropolitan counties and districts in England.

Scotland

The Wheatley Commission (1966–9) had a different problem, or set of problems, to cope with. The Scottish population is unevenly distributed but in general much more dispersed than elsewhere in Britain. The same defects were, however, observable in Scottish as in English and Welsh local governments: shifts of population had resulted in the failure of many boundaries to correspond with the natural movements of people between homes and work. Centres of population were divided from hinterlands with which they had close connections. Many authorities were too small to provide the staff and resources necessary for the tasks imposed on them, and there were anomalies in the allocation of functions between one type of local authority and another.

The new structure proposed by the Commission was at two levels, regional and district. The particular needs and circumstances of Scotland required a two-tier arrangement. The country was divided into seven regions, in each of which an elected regional council would be responsible for major or strategic planning: roads; water and sewerage; education; social work; regional housing; police; fire; coast protection; community centres; parks and recreation; cultural services and a number of other services. At the district level, thirty-seven councils would handle local planning; housing; building control; community centres; parks and recreation; museums and art galleries; libraries; environmental health and regulatory or licensing functions. Certain functions — recreational and cultural — would be exercised concurrently by regional and district authorities. The Commission's plan was accepted, with some alterations, and became the basis for the Local Government (Scotland) Act, 1973. As it emerged from the parliamentary process the Act gave Scotland nine regions, fifty-three districts and three all purpose (unitary, in Redcliffe-Maud language) areas in the islands: Shetland, Orkneys and Hebrides.

Northern Ireland

Thoughts on re-organisation (or re-shaping, to use the preferred term) began to emerge from the Department of Development in the mid-1960s, probably under the Crossman influence. These have been dealt with in the preceding Chapter.

Re-Organisation in the Republic

The White Paper on Local Government Re-organisation appeared in February 1971. It was not preceded by a commission of inquiry, as in England and Scotland, nor by a review committee, as in Northern Ireland. Nor were there any formal consultations with local authorities. The White Paper was prepared in the Department of Local Government on the basis of a study of local government problems as they came under departmental notice; and also, it was clear, a close reading of developments abroad, particularly in Britain.

The aims were to combine the two functions of local government — its representative, democratic role, and its work as dispenser of services — to the best advantage. On the first count the unit of representation should not be so large that the council would be remote from the electors. On the second, the unit should not be too small to support modern services, thus sacrificing efficiency for a kind of cosy neighbourliness. The refurbished system should be one-tier so far as possible. The best solution was to concentrate effective local government at the county level, subject to some changes in the existing county pattern.

County boundaries would be left largely unchanged, but some modification might be called for where a major town lay too close to a county boundary. In small contiguous counties some offices could be amalgamated, and a case might even be made for establishing single councils for some pairs of counties. Second-tier governments — urban councils and towns — would be absorbed in the county apparatus, but a small number of the larger urban authorities would survive, with considerably extended boundaries.

The county boroughs of Cork, Dublin, Limerick and Waterford would be dealt with in a variety of ways, as circumstances required. Limerick was left largely untouched. In Waterford the offices of city and county managers would be merged as opportunity arose. The idea of a unified authority for Cork City and County was rejected, but special steps would be necessary for harmonising local services in city and the adjacent county area. Similar arrangements would be made for Limerick. The most drastic proposal was that for Dublin, where the project of a metropolitan authority, first put forward in 1938 by the Local Government (Dublin) Tribunal was revived in answer to the growing urbanisation of the county, and the need for building land felt by both Dublin and Dun Laoghaire Corporations. Integration at management level, effected in 1942, was no longer adequate to cope with cross-boundary problems. A single authority would therefore replace Dublin Corporation and County Council, Dun Laoghaire Corporation, and Balbriggan Town Commissioners. The magnitude of the unified body might, it was suggested, call for the creation of committees to deal with 'local services'.

At 'grass-roots' level area committees of county councils would be established, based normally on towns and their hinterlands, having a mixed membership of elected councillors and local community representatives. The formation of community councils would be encouraged. These organisations would not be a formal element in local government but would function mainly as channels of opinion and information. Special arrangements would be worked out to give Gaeltacht people a voice in local government. Separate authorities would be abolished for smaller harbours: county councils would take over. The co-ordinating role of regional development organisations would be fostered. Widening their role would be welcomed by the government.

The Debate

The arguments in support of the White Paper's plan were eloquently deployed, in language demonstrating familiarity with such modern concepts as the need to secure and encourage popular participation in the processes of local decision-making, the desirability of breaking down the boundaries between urban and rural population, and so on. It was less reassuring however to realise that none of the individual ingredients of the plan was particularly novel, with the exception perhaps of the mixed area committees of county councils.

In fact the plan as a whole, apart from a few minor items, was a resumption of the march towards county government commenced in the 1920s and marked on the way by the absorption of rural district councils, boards of health, and a few towns and urban districts. Now an indefinite number of urban councils, together with the commissioners of towns, would follow the way to extinction.

Another of the major proposals, the metropolitan authority for Dublin, revived an idea which had been floating about the Custom House, in one form or another, since the Greater Dublin Commission of 1926. Its most elaborate formulation was in the report (1938) of the Greater Dublin Tribunal. The section on the regions introduced little that was new. Chapter 7 stressed the role of the new regional organisations in planning, cooperation and joint action by local authorities, adding that a wider, possibly statutory, role would require initiatives on the part of local authorities themselves. Such initiatives have not in fact emerged in the years since 1971. Part III dealt with the operation of the system and, while informative and exhibiting an enlightened, liberal approach, was hardly revolutionary.

In general, it would not be unfair to characterise the document as a bureaucratic rather than a political product. And predictably it had certain weaknesses on the political side which condemned it to sterility. The proposition to effect what seemed like a wholesale liquidation of small urban councils attracted heavy fire from local councillors; while the modest proposal about regionalism, innocuous though it seemed, was unanimously rejected by county councils. The local authority associations – County Councils, General Council and Association of Municipal Authorities – were disappointingly negative. The three Dublin councils also threw out the metropolitan plan.

There was much opposition also to the idea of mixed area committees. Councillors, on the whole, resented the notion of sitting on equal terms with representatives of voluntary associations. Facing the local electorate, and coming out on or near the top, conferred a special status not enjoyed by the non-elect, or, worse still, 'self-elected' nominees of community groups.

More Local Government

A number of interested bodies offered comments on the White Paper, notably the ICTU, the Confederation of Irish Industry, Muintir na Tíre, the Community Consultative Council, the Irish Local Government and Public Services Union, and others. The most elaborate submission was however that of a Study Group set up by the Institute of Public Administration under the chairmanship of Professor Basil Chubb, which comprised representatives of local administration and management, the universities, research institutes, trade unions and state-sponsored bodies. It was a small expert group taking the minority side in a debate attracting little popular interest. A band of Webb-minded brothers – web-footed too from sustained swimming against the tide. The group's report was published in 1971.

The central theme of the report was one of administrative decentralisation over a wide front. In Professor Chubb's words:

> the local administration of most of our public services should be re-organised into a single system – that is, as much as possible of the government and administration of these services should be carried out in the localities at the appropriate level. The corollary of this, and a very important one too, is that the central administration would shrink drastically, since most of the business now done in the departments would be done locally.

The volume of work devolved, or dispersed, to local agencies would require decision-making at three sub-national levels – region, county and district. The argument in favour of this multi-tier system was one from simple observation. The group found that a survey of how a number of services are actually administered showed some at regional level, some at county and others at sub-county or district level. This had not been planned in a collective way, but was the result of a series of empirical decisions, each taken in relation to individual services.

The scope of local government should therefore be broadened progressively to cover as wide a range as possible of public services. A move in this direction would, as well as decentralising government, facilitate access by citizens to information, and encourage popular participation. There should be many more local representative bodies, not less. The trend since 1922 towards fewer and larger local authorities should be reversed. The group were in favour of associating nominees of voluntary bodies with elected members at one level of authority.

The nationwide formation of district councils would create town-county units roughly similar to the present county electoral districts. Towns and small urban districts would, instead of being abolished, find their status, areas and resources enhanced.

More Local Government, though recognised as a serious and noteworthy contribution to the debate, was not greeted, on the whole, with acclamation. Curiously, the prospect of more local councillors did not cause rejoicing in political circles, and in their eyes the district plan was discredited from the start by association with regionalism and, worse still, with the idea of being linked with 'voluntary' nominees, unconsecrated by election.

From the administrative viewpoint, the intimidating problem of getting a wide variety of people and organisations, each with their own peculiar needs and difficulties, ranged into one comprehensive system, was enough to repel all but the most stout-hearted. *More Local Government* remained an interesting idea, an ideal which would have required an inspired political reformer to bring to life and push through.

The McKinsey Report

This report, *Strengthening the Local Government Service* (1972), dealt mainly with the development of staff structures. It gave some attention, however, to the viability of local authorities, and recommended a unitary system based on counties alone. Some urban authorities might be retained 'for reasons that go beyond simple economy and administrative efficiency', but a population of at least 12,000 should be required for survival. The smaller counties should be paired, and staffs amalgamated under one manager.

The Discussion Document

The change of government early in 1973 put an end to any practical debate about the White Paper. The new Minister for Local Government announced that he did not intend to proceed with the 1971 plan, and would put forward his own ideas as soon as possible. The National Coalition Programme included the following among its Fourteen Points:

> *Local Democracy:* The National Coalition Government will hold it as a priority at all times that power must be vested in the people and that local government must be made truly democratic and relevant to their needs.

In December 1973, the Minister, James Tully, published his *Discussion Document on Local Government Reorganisation.* If the White Paper was in great degree an administrative prescription in the mainstream departmental tradition, the Discussion Document was a political rejoinder. The following extract summarises the basic approach:

> The Minister accepts that the present system needs improvement but considers that the defects which exist are such as to require for their solution a selective and measured response. He is opposed to the abolition of a large number of smaller local authorities (as proposed by the previous Government) and would favour instead a series of measures aimed at promoting a more effective system of local administration while preserving the democratic character of local government. His approach would in principle have the following key elements:
> (a) county councils to be the principal local authorities;
> (b) existing urban district councils and boards of town commissioners to be retained;
> (c) functions to be redistributed as between the different classes of local authorities and other practical changes to be made in the working of the system.

The Discussion Document's main proposals may be summarised as follows:

> *Smaller Urban Districts:* Planning and development functions would be transferred to the county councils which would consult the urban councils on appropriate matters; responsibility for sanitary services would also be transferred as would functions related to the construction of local authority houses.
> *Town Commissioners:* Housing functions would be transferred to the county councils.
> *Dublin Area:* A large and complicated system of authorities on the lines proposed by the previous government was rejected; consideration was to be given to (1) the need for boundary changes and (2) methods of securing better co-ordination between the existing authorities.
> *Cork:* Instead of a 'merger' between city and county various ways in which better co-ordination may be achieved were to be attempted.
> *Boundary Extensions:* The process of urban boundary extensions was to be speeded up by new legislation.
> *Community Councils:* The proposals of the previous government 'that

representatives of community councils should be placed on committees of local authorities' were rejected. However, community councils have an important and valuable function in their own sphere and the Minister hoped that local authorities would give every assistance possible to such bodies.

New Local Authorities: A simple procedure to enable new authorities to be set up (e.g. in existing non-municipal towns and built-up communities in country areas and in suburbs of large conurbations) will also be considered. The new authorities would have limited functions. They would provide an effective means through which 'grass-roots' opinions could be channelled, in an orderly fashion through representatives elected by statutory elections. The chairman could have the title of mayor.

The Discussion Document did not give universal satisfaction to the politicians. It was debated in the Senate on 20 February 1975, and attacked by many Senators, who saw little advantage to urban councils in escaping abolition at the price of losing virtually all their powers. The Minister countered this criticism, which tended towards accusations of Machiavellian subtlety, by repeating a previous assurance to the Association of Municipal Authorities that 'It was never intended that functions of smaller urban authorities would be taken from them *contrary to their wishes*.' The proposals in the Document had not been put into Bill form before the change of government in June 1977.

No further re-organisation plans have been announced, from official sources at least. But the picture would be incomplete without mention of an important collection of papers written at various times, and for a variety of audiences or readers by T. J. Barrington and published under the title *From Big Government to Local Government* (1976). The author represents and speaks eloquently for one side of the rather muted dialogue about local government. If it is not an exaggeration to say that there are two schools of thought on the subject, the author represents one of them. The other is the Department's corporate opinion, view, attitude. This tradition changes slowly, and in some respects does not change at all. Departments are very tenacious of their collective notions, called policies.

The two conceptions of local government can be clearly distinguished. They are sharply different. The picture of ideal local government presented in greatest detail in *More Local Government* is taken with a wide-angle lens. Local government according to this report should be, but is not, government in a local context. Government is a term of broad application, many-sided, pervasive — possibly, nowadays too pervasive — but that seems to be an irreversible condition of modern societies. The geographical part of government to which local government contributes has economic, social, educational, cultural and political elements which, correctly mixed together, generate a process called development.

Local government could best contribute by:

(1) accepting or remodelling the county unit, and re-establishing a district unit, in the light of the whole range of governmental services at these levels; and

(2) under-pinning the unit by using the county manager as local administrator

   (a) for all local services with popular participation;

   (b) for co-ordinating local services for the purpose of regional development;

   (c) as agents for, and co-ordinator with other public services at county level, of all other public services in relation to his county.

The foregoing, taken from an Addendum contributed by Barrington to the Devlin Report (1969), has a strong administrative emphasis. Public participation, the representative or political part of local government, 'is basically that of representing the consumers of the various services supplied.' The problems of local resources, local taxation, and the cognate problem of local discretion or 'autonomy' are not (understandably) gone into in any depth.

The departmental view finds its best expression in the White Paper of 1971, followed by *Local Finance and Taxation* (1972). The Department's attitude was, as it had been for many decades, influenced by the problem of resources. The limited possibilities of rates as a local tax have already been touched on, and pressure on this source — the only tax available to local authorities — was intensified in the 1960s by the onset of rapid inflation. The Department's answer was to narrow down the responsibilities of local authorities to a coherent set of functions which could be carried without disproportionate reliance on the Exchequer. This would allow room for manoeuvre — there would be some reality in local government as an essential element of democracy. As the White Paper put it: 'Under such a system, local affairs can be settled by the local citizens themselves or their representatives, local services can be locally controlled and local communities can participate in the process and responsibilities of government'.

Hence the emphatic dissent from the Devlin thesis which regarded local authorities simply as 'executive agencies, with elected boards, reporting to the Minister for Local Government'. This thesis derived from the doctrine of the Single Public Service on which the Devlin philosophy was founded, and as an administrative unitarian Barrington was inclined to play down the 'independence and freedom of choice' of local government. The Department, as sturdy trinitarians, were correspondingly disposed to assert the existence of local liberties, despite much evidence to the contrary. All disputes, as Chesterton said about war, are ultimately theological.

One of the earliest assaults on the theory of the single public service was by Michael P. Fogarty (*Hibernia,* 23 Jan 1970), then Director of the ESRI, who defended eloquently the traditional freedom (relatively speaking) of local government. He was speaking in Anglo-Saxon terms. Local self-government according to W. J. M. Mackenzie (*Theories of Local Government*, 1961) is part of the English constitution. It is not, as we know, an article of our Bunreacht, but can we not claim some part of the immemorial tradition which stretches back on the one hand to the forests of Germany, and on the other to the *tuatha* and *ri-tuatha* of the Gaelic polity?

Organisation of the Public Service at Sub-National Levels

Differences of theory fail to attract public interest until they are translated into action. There is little prospect therefore of a political contest between parties divided on ideological lines in the battle-ground of our subject. But something is stirring in the politico-administrative undergrowth, the outcome of which may give some idea of the balance of forces. An Inter-Departmental Committee, convened by the Department of the Public Service, has been studying sub-national organisations. Their terms of reference require them to examine and report on the appropriate structures for the planning, co-ordination and discharge of the functions of government at sub-national levels.

This enquiry is proceeding. The re-naming of the Department of Local Government as the Department of the Environment and the assignment of concern with regional planning to the Department of Planning and Economic Development — its brief life ended in 1979 — might have meant some re-appraisal. But the outcome cannot fail to have effects on thinking and, one hopes, action about local government and other forms of local administration.

And Now?

There have been signs of renewed stirrings in the reform movement. The Minister for the Environment in a public statement (February 1981) has pointed to the need for re-examination of local government problems in the Dublin region. He intended to inaugurate the process by asking the three major local authorities, as well as community, voluntary and other interested bodies, for their views. Administration of the Greater Dublin area is, without doubt, the most pressing and contentious item on the reform agenda, and a logical first priority. 'Dublin is now a sprawling mass of over one million people ruled by a Victorian local government system which is so archaic that it is of very limited benefit to the people it is supposed to be serving.' ('Greater Dublin Nightmare', *Irish Times* 23 October 1980). The reality is, of course, — as the writer goes on to explain — that a whole series of improvements have been made in our Victorian heritage: the restructuring of Dublin government in 1930, the simultaneous introduction of city management in Dublin and Dun Laoghaire, and the amalgamation of

Dublin city and county management in 1942, followed by the creation of combined services at official level in recent years – planning, fire brigades, libraries, roads and others.

At the representative level, an informal joint committee of the three councils meets regularly to discuss developments. But the ghost of the metropolitan council refuses to go away. In its more recent visitations, it has taken the form of a two-tier organisation – at the top a Greater Dublin Council for city and county to deal with planning and development, water supply, main drainage transportation, major roads and integrated fire services. At second level a number of local councils – five were suggested, each with a population of between 200,000 and 300,000 – would handle housing, libraries, parks and playing fields, community affairs and the like. As a metropolis, Dublin is not unmanageably large, nor is the problem unique. But neither is it simple. 'One of the most puzzling structural problems of local government is how metropolitan areas should be governed' (Rowat, 1980).

There are, in essence, three solutions or, more accurately, three compromise balancings of merits and demerits. The first is that proposed in 1938 and again in 1971, the unitary metropolitan council, but 'the government of a city with a million or more inhabitants could be as far away from its citizens as a state or national government' (Rowat). Moreover, the submerging of a number of constituent councils, each with its local interests and loyalties, arouses stubborn opposition. The answer in many areas – London, Toronto etc – has been the two-tier system, but it is not always successful. Winnipeg, after a brief trial, reverted to a single council, with citizen participation through a network of community committees with supervisory functions. The third possibility is the 'ecumenical' or co-operative approach whereby, as in the USA, 'councils of governments' (COGS) are formed in a voluntary spirit as agencies to facilitate flexible responses to cross-boundary problems. Where, as in New York, a unified city government operates, various measures of citizen involvement have been tried or suggested – community boards, neighbourhood governments, 'little city halls' and the like. In large American cities political leadership is usually combined with administrative or executive management through the medium of an elected or 'strong' mayor.

A fourth solution is the one persuasively argued in *More Local Government* by an IPA Working Party in 1971: 'that certain functions which require a wider base than the county borough or county council should be assigned to a statutory regional body and dealt with by specialist staff with regional terms of reference. These functions include strategic or major planning; water resources management, and water supply (head works and trunk mains) for the region; pollution control; major surface water and waste disposal works; and large scale development projects of a new town character . . .' The region has the advantage of including, in addition to Dublin city and county, the counties of Kildare, Meath and Wicklow, which have already begun to form part of the metropolitan catchment area. The Working Party Proposal envisaged the retention of the present Dublin city and Dun Laoghaire borough corporation and Dublin county council, underlined as required by a network of district councils with population ranging from 100,000 to 200,000.

Discussion of local government re-organisation in a wider context has not been resumed; as a major issue it has been dormant for some years. A few comments may be hazarded. Regional government is still alive as an idea, but as a practical proposition for re-drawing local boundaries it is a non-starter – a political untouchable. That leaves county government. But clearly the 1971 project of elevating county councils to the status of unitary authorities for most areas will no longer wash. It would mean the wiping out of a flock of small and medium sized urban authorities – the unacceptable face (in Ireland) of reform. One is left then with some version of the two-tier system, with county councils at the top and urban or combined urban-rural authorities at second level. Since it would hardly be defensible to retain town commissioners and urban district councils in an unreconstructed condition, one seems to be driven towards a pattern of urban-cum-rural districts – an adaptation, in short, of the post-1972 English, Welsh and Scottish systems.

Is there an alternative? Can one seek a solution in any other direction? In the early years of the state, as we have seen, reforming ideas were imported boldly from America and (to a lesser extent) from some continental European countries. Although we have retained much of the language and law of the Victorian (and in some cases pre-Victorian) local government, the system we now operate is no longer British in essentials. The conclusion emerging may well be that our national temper, an amalgam of origins, history, religion and doubtless many other ingredients, is not congenial to the system we have inherited. Social organisation should and must influence our administrative development, and two aspects have frequently attracted comment: personalism, and a tendency towards authoritarianism. 'Thus, to alter the structure of local government . . . under the assumption that most citizens would actively participate might lead to unexpected consequences such as greater power being concentrated in the hands of local elites' (Schmitt, 1970).

Authoritarianism, and our clear leaning towards strong executive leadership (expressed in local government terms in city and county management), has sometimes been interpreted as an argument for adopting the French prefectoral and town mayor system, as the best-known and most widely adopted alternative to British local government. But would the prefectoral system, with its undoubted advantages, be compatible with the version of British parliamentary government that has become naturalised here since 1922? When the Kilbrandon Commission came, in its search for methods of decentralising government, to look at the French system, they had to conclude that the differences in political philosophy between Britain and

France, as reflected in their constitutional arrangements, were so fundamental that no part of either system could be readily transposed to the other. What then can we do?

A research paper prepared for the Kilbrandon Commission on the Constitution (*The French Prefectoral System: An Example of Integrated Administrative Decentralisation* F. F. Ridley 1973) demonstrated the possibilities of adjusting the prefectoral system to any required extent. All you need is to determine what you want. The author's opening sentence is rather sobering: 'It is almost impossible to say whether one administrative device is better than another.' But if you are convinced that change is needed, the assumption is that you are equally persuaded that some alternative arrangement must give better results. The research paper concludes:

'Though answers are bound to depend on more concrete factors, it is useful to have a framework of possibilities. The French experience shows one solution that is not merely possible but actually works. Some lessons can be drawn from this but, just as it is well to remember that "other things are not equal", so it may be remembered that models other than the French should be considered.'

But the last word on the French system remains yet to be spoken. The Socialist president and parliament which took power from the 1981 elections have announced their intention of introducing a decentralised administration to France. The prefectoral apparatus, so long a feature of Gallic local government, is to be dismantled. The very name of perfect will pass away, after almost two centuries of occupying the administrative foreground. The prefects will become commissioners and be diminished in power and status. With the threatened dislocation of these pillars of the state, can one still draw confident comparisons between the French local dispensation and those others which go to make up the aggregate of modern local government?

Appendix I

Central Authorities and Ministers

Central Authorities

Poor Law Commissioners (English)	1838–1847
Poor Law Commissioners (Ireland)	1847–1872
Local Government Board for Ireland	1872–1922

Ministers for Local Government

W. T. Cosgrave	2 April 1919–30 August 1922
Earnán de Blaghd	30 August 1922–15 October 1923

Ministers for Local Government and Public Health

Seamus de Búrca	15 October 1923–23 June 1927
Richard Mulcahy	23 June 1927–9 March 1932
Seán T. Ó Ceallaigh	9 March 1932–8 September 1939
Patrick Ruttledge	8 September 1939–14 August 1941
Eamon de Valera	14 August 1941–18 August 1941
Seán McEntee	18 August 1941–18 February 1948

Ministers for Local Government

Timothy J. Murphy	18 February 1948–29 April 1949
William Norton	3 May 1949–11 May 1949
Michael Keyes	11 May 1949–14 June 1951
Patrick Smith	14 June 1951 – 2 June 1954
Patrick O'Donnell	2 June 1954–20 March 1957
Patrick Smith	20 March 1957–27 November 1957
Neil T. Blaney	27 November 1957–16 November 1966
Caoimhghín Ó Beoláin	16 November 1966–7 May 1970

Robert Molloy   9 May 1970–14 March 1973
James Tully   14 March 1973–5 July 1977

Ministers of the Environment

Sylvester Barrett   5 July 1977–15 October 1980
Ray Burke   15 October 1980–29 June 1981
Peter Barry   30 June 1981 –

Appendix II

Members in each local electoral area and the electorate of each area.

Electoral Area	Members	Electorate 1974/5	1979/80
County Electoral Areas			
Carlow			
1 Borris	4	4,091	4,429
2 Carlow	7	8,715	9,824
3 Muinebeag	5	4,891	5,135
4 Tullow	5	5,099	5,626
	21	22,796	25,014
Cavan			
1 Bailieborough	7	10,090	10,403
2 Ballyjamesduff	6	8,831	9,049
3 Belturbet	5	7,315	7,166
4 Cavan	7	11,209	11,586
	25	37,445	38,204
Clare			
1 Ennis	8	18,428	20,968
2 Ennistimon	5	8,216	7,669
3 Killaloe	6	9,504	10,369
4 Kilrush	6	9,628	9,428
5 Miltown Malbay	6	9,606	9,704
	31	55,382	58,138
Cork			
1 Bandon	7	22,656	23,906
2 Cork	8	28,582	36,097
3 Kanturk	6	20,803	21,376
4 Mallow	7	26,773	28,042
5 Midleton	6	22,303	24,445
6 Skibbereen	7	21,156	21,567
7 Skull	5	12,811	13,360
	46	155,084	168,793

Electoral Area	Members	Electorate	
		1974/5	1979/80

Donegal

	Electoral Area	Members	1974/5	1979/80
1	Buncrana	6	16,729	17,987
2	Donegal	6	15,408	16,519
3	Glenties	6	16,603	16,684
4	Letterkenny	6	18,267	20,479
5	Milford	4	10,535	10,789
		28	77,542	82,458

Dublin

	Electoral Area	Members	1974/5	1979/80
1	Ballybrack	4	30,487	28,978
2	Dundrum	4	30,358	27,612
3	Dun Laoghaire	3	37,119	39,084
4	Lucan	5	22,628	33,885
5	Swords	4	35,307	24,282
6	Tallaght	4	39,810	22,642
7	Malahide	4	–	28,405
8	Terenure	4	–	29,303
9	Whitechurch	4	–	23,262
		36	195,709	257,453

Galway

	Electoral Area	Members	1974/5	1979/80
1	Ballinasloe	5	14,265	14,861
2	Galway	9	36,687	43,087
3	Loughrea	6	19,907	20,629
4	Connemara	4	12,784	13,956
5	Tuam	7	19,717	20,427
		31	103,360	112,960

Kerry

	Electoral Area	Members	1974/5	1979/80
1	Killarney	6	17,645	18,656
2	Killorglin	6	16,538	16,620
3	Listowel	6	19,169	19,867
4	Tralee	8	26,516	29,352
		26	79,868	84,495

Kildare

	Electoral Area	Members	1974/5	1979/80
1	Athy	4	8,819	9,296
2	Clane	7	17,234	20,587
3	Kildare	5	11,186	12,631
4	Naas	5	14,328	17,201
		21	51,567	59,715

Electoral Area	Members	Electorate 1974/5	Electorate 1979/80
Kilkenny			
1 Ballyragget	5	7,770	8,165
2 Kilkenny	8	14,631	16,547
3 Pilltown	7	10,351	10,993
4 Thomastown	6	8,523	9,174
	26	41,275	44,879
Laois			
1 Borris-in-Ossory	7	7,382	7,874
2 Luggacurren	4	4,834	5,236
3 Portlaoise	9	11,577	12,892
4 Tinnahinch	5	5,670	5,805
	25	29,463	31,807
Leitrim			
1 Ballinamore	6	5,707	5,500
2 Carrick-on-Shannon	6	5,878	6,160
3 Dromahaire	5	4,717	4,710
4 Manorhamilton	5	4,275	4,346
	22	20,577	20,716
Limerick			
1 Bruff	5	11,322	13,371
2 Castleconnell	6	13,827	15,481
3 Kilmallock	5	10,230	10,475
4 Newcastle	6	13,086	13,151
5 Rathkeale	5	10,926	11,399
	27	59,391	63,877
Longford			
1 Ballinalee	4	3,468	3,620
2 Ballymahon	6	5,584	5,683
3 Drumlish	3	2,931	2,951
4 Granard	3	2,509	2,535
5 Longford	5	5,566	5,996
	21	20,058	20,785

Electoral Area	Members	Electorate 1974/5	1979/80
Louth			
1 Ardee	5	7,381	8,027
2 Carlingford	3	4,456	4,651
3 Drogheda	8	16,624	18,736
4 Dundalk	10	21,759	23,885
	26	50,220	55,299
Mayo			
1 Ballina	6	13,459	15,527
2 Castlebar	5	13,183	14,863
3 Claremorris	7	18,360	18,827
4 Killala	4	9,109	9,395
5 Swinford	4	9,547	9,673
6 Westport	5	13,178	13,676
	31	76,836	81,961
Meath			
1 Ceanannus Mór	7	10,566	11,631
2 Dunshaughlin	5	9,701	11,976
3 Navan	7	12,475	14,740
4 Slane	5	9,331	10,289
5 Trim	5	8,422	9,257
	29	50,495	57,893
Monaghan			
1 Carrickmacross	5	8,304	8,508
2 Castleblayney	5	7,051	8,087
3 Clones	4	6,021	6,370
4 Monaghan	6	10,191	11,179
	20	31,567	34,144
Offaly			
1 Birr	5	6,416	7,057
2 Edenderry	5	8,349	9,187
3 Ferbane	5	7,474	7,927
4 Tullamore	6	11,027	12,390
	21	33,266	36,561

Electoral Area	Members	Electorate	
		1974/5	1979/80
Roscommon			
1 Athlone	4	5,486	5,638
2 Boyle	5	7,163	7,055
3 Castlereagh	8	11,241	11,052
4 Roscommon	9	13,018	13,398
	26	36,908	37,143
Sligo			
1 Ballymote	7	9,144	9,355
2 Dromore	4	5,410	5,574
3 Sligo (incl. Urban)	9	15,682	17,495
4 Tubbercurry	4	4,973	4,945
	24	35,209	37,369
Tipperary, North Riding			
1 Borrisokane	4	6,203	6,334
2 Nenagh	7	12,685	13,130
3 Templemore	5	8,711	9,200
4 Thurles	5	9,184	10,030
	21	36,783	38,694
Tipperary, South Riding			
1 Caher	5	7,351	7,942
2 Cashel	5	8,575	8,857
3 Clonmel	5	9,660	11,005
4 Fethard	6	10,720	11,740
5 Tipperary	5	9,572	9,999
	26	45,878	49,543
Waterford			
1 Dungarvan	7	9,327	9,797
2 Kilmacthomas	5	7,051	7,448
3 Lismore	4	5,328	5,450
4 Tramore	7	10,365	12,801
	23	32,071	35,496
Westmeath			
1 Athlone	7	12,154	14,049
2 Coole	4	5,654	5,788
3 Kilbeggan	4	6,302	6,673
4 Mullingar	8	10,986	12,117
	23	35,096	38,627

| Electoral Area | Members | Electorate | |
		1974/5	1979/80
Wexford			
1 Enniscorthy	5	14,225	15,219
2 Gorey	5	13,531	14,387
3 New Ross	5	14,162	14,998
4 Wexford	6	16,652	18,405
	21	58,570	63,009
Wicklow			
1 Arklow	6	11,399	12,197
2 Baltinglass	3	6,352	7,159
3 Bray	7	18,450	22,776
4 Wicklow	5	10,166	11,682
	21	46,367	53,814

County Borough Electoral Areas

Cork City			
North-Central	5	13,343	12,903
North-East	5	13,512	14,624
North-West	5	14,413	17,044
South-Central	5	12,374	11,663
South-East	6	14,567	15,188
South-West	5	13,834	14,102
	31	82,043	85,524
Dublin			
One	4	39,546	31,883
Two	4	39,297	32,163
Three	5	36,023	40,023
Four	4	39,092	32,793
Five	4	40,353	32,732
Six	4	37,576	30,665
Seven	4	41,452	35,104
Eight	4	41,786	33,509
Nine	4	51,080	30,663
Ten	4	–	33,041
Eleven	4	–	31,367
	45	366,205	363,943

Electoral Area	Members	Electorate	
		1974/5	1979/80

Limerick

One	4	9,683	11,193
Two	5	10,087	10,245
Three	4	8,629	8,360
Four	4	8,178	8,306
	17	36,577	38,104

Waterford

One	5	5,820	5,705
Two	5	6,529	6,321
Three	5	8,186	8,351
	15	20,535	20,377

Borough Electoral Areas

Clonmel	12	6,799	7,555
Drogheda (3)	12	12,541	14,537
Dun Laoghaire (3)	15	37,119	39,084
Galway (3)	12	21,362	25,558
Kilkenny	12	6,894	6,972
Sligo (3)	12	9,431	10,877
Wexford	12	7,677	7,882

Urban Districts

Arklow	9	4,548	5,020
Athlone	9	6,255	6,620
Athy	9	2,917	3,146
Ballina	9	4,079	4,991
Ballinasloe	9	3,143	3,507
Birr	9	2,069	2,283
Bray (3)	12	10,189	13,561
Buncrana	9	2,152	2,341
Bundoran	9	950	1,200
Carlow	9	6,268	7,017
Carrickmacross	9	1,317	1,256
Carrick-on-Suir	9	3,140	3,556
Cashel	9	1,807	1,828
Castlebar	9	3,887	4,597
Castleblayney	9	1,619	1,778
Cavan	9	2,143	2,161

Electoral Area	Members	Electorate 1974/5	1979/80
Ceanannus Mór	9	1,650	1,822
Clonakilty	9	1,763	1,919
Clones	9	1,506	1,701
Cobh	9	3,931	4,248
Dundalk (4)	12	14,836	16,191
Dungarvan	9	4,014	4,361
Ennis	9	5,023	4,911
Enniscorthy	9	3,872	3,780
Fermoy	9	2,306	2,139
Killarney	9	4,232	4,675
Kilrush	9	2,021	2,049
Kinsale	9	1,270	1,301
Letterkenny	9	3,145	3,670
Listowel	9	2,233	2,486
Longford	9	2,898	2,822
Macroom	9	1,586	1,707
Mallow	9	4,126	4,354
Midleton	9	2,106	2,109
Monaghan	9	3,408	3,822
Naas	9	4,017	4,520
Navan	9	2,916	2,958
Nenagh	9	3,503	3,584
New Ross	9	3,282	3,495
Skibbereen	9	1,695	1,744
Templemore	9	1,566	1,611
Thurles	9	4,471	4,951
Tipperary	9	3,245	3,448
Tralee	12	8,737	10,450
Trim	9	1,305	1,411
Tullamore	9	4,434	5,220
Westport	9	2,099	2,279
Wicklow	9	2,736	3,201
Youghal	9	3,326	3,580
Town Commissioners			
Ardee	9	1,735	1,781
Balbriggan	9	2,610	3,067
Ballybay	9	507	521
Ballyshannon	9	1,530	1,700
Bandon	9	1,590	1,553

Electoral Area	Members	Electorate	
		1974/5	1979/80
Bantry	9	1,861	2,055
Belturbet	9	849	835
Boyle	9	1,289	1,296
Cootehill	9	928	982
Droichead Nua	9	3,001	3,489
Edenderry	9	1,827	2,211
Gorey	9	2,012	1,754
Granard	9	745	807
Kilkee	9	991	1,037
Lismore	9	574	580
Loughrea	9	2,489	2,378
Mountmellick	9	1,786	1,793
Muinebeag	9	1,444	1,508
Mullingar	9	4,479	4,479
Passage West	9	1,884	2,103
Portlaoise	9	2,423	2,647
Tramore	9	2,686	3,133
Tuam	9	2,508	2,569

Appendix III

Reserved Functions of Local Authorities

1. Financial

Function	Authority
The borrowing of money	City and County Management Acts
The demanding under any enactment of the whole or a part of the expenses of the council of a county or of an elective body from any other local authority.	County Management Act, 1940.
Adoption of annual estimate of expenses.	City and County Management (Amendment) Act, 1955, s. 10
Authorisation of expenditure or incurring liability in excess of amounts for purpose specified in estimate.	s. 11
Lending money to another local authority.	Local Government (No. 2) Act, 1960 s. 5
Agreement between planning authorities to share cost of joint performance of functions.	Local Government (Planning and Development) Act, 1963, s. 16
Scheme of guarantees for housing loans by building societies, assurance companies, banks or other such organisations.	Housing Act, 1966, s. 42
Extension of time for payment of rates on agricultural holding in order to qualify for rates relief.	Rates on Agricultural Land (Relief) Act, 1967, s. 7

Function	**Authority**
Rates remission for industrial undertakings.	Industrial Development Act, 1972, s. 3 Gaeltacht Industries (Amendment) Act, 1972, s. 3
Chargeability of certain expenses for sanitary services.	Local Government (Sanitary Services) Act, 1948, s. 50

Grants and Subsidies

Assistance of students at universities. Grants to Universities.	Irish Universities Act 1908, s. 10
Schemes of grants to students at third level institutions.	Local Authorities (Higher Education Grants) Act, 1968, s. 5
Assistance, financial or otherwise, in the promotion of public interest in the Arts.	The Arts Act, 1973, s. 12
Grants to harbour authorities.	Harbours Act, 1947, s. 7
Travelling expenses of members.	Local Government Act, 1946, s. 67
Travelling and subsistence allowances to certain members.	Local Government Act, 1955, s. 67
Swimming facilities: contribution to society, club or other body providing.	Local Government Act, 1955, s. 55
Decoration of city, borough, urban district or town on special occasions.	s. 56 See also City Management Acts.
Local museums, grants for by county or city council.	Local Government Act, 1955, s. 57
Concert halls, theatres, or opera houses in county boroughs — grants or other expenses.	Local Government Act, 1960, s. 1

Function	Authority
Planning	
Assistance to town commissioners, local development associations etc.	Local Government (Planning and Development) Act, 1963, s. 14
Grants for training and research in town and regional planning.	s. 15
Grants for planting trees, shrubs or other plants.	s. 50
Contributions towards public concerts.	Local Government Act, 1946, s. 75
Housing	
Assistance to other housing authorities or certain other bodies.	Housing Act, 1966, s. 12
Scheme of guarantees in connection with housing loans by building societies, assurance companies, banks, etc.	s. 42
Miscellaneous	
Schemes for sale of seeds and fertilisers.	Seeds and Fertilisers Supply Act, 1956, s. 2
Guarantee of repayments to suppliers of seeds and fertilisers.	s. 3

2. Legislation

Making, amending or revoking a byelaw.	City Management Acts. County Management Act, 1940
Order or resolution bringing enactment into force in city, county, borough, urban district or town.	Management Acts Gaming and Lotteries Act, 1956, s. 13

Function	Authority
Promoting or opposing legislation; prosecution or defence of legal proceedings, under Borough Funds (Ireland) Act, 1888.	Borough Funds (Ireland) Act, 1888

3. Political Matters

Parliamentary and local elections.	City and County Management Acts.
Nomination of candidate for President.	,,
Appointment or election of members of other public bodies.	,,
Grant of freedom of city or borough.	,,
Election and remuneration of Lord Mayor or Mayor of city or borough. Election of Chairman or Vice-Chairman of county or other council.	,,
Appointment of a committee, including estimates committee. Procedure of county or other council.	,,
Appointment and expenses of representatives of local authorities at conferences.	Public Health and Local Government Conferences Act, 1885.
Appointment of vocational education committee.	Vocational Education Act, 1930
Appointment of county committee of agriculture.	Agriculture Act, 1931
Appointment of members of health boards and local health committees.	Health Act, 1970, ss. 4, 7

4. Policy Decisions

Extension or alteration of boundaries	City and County Management Acts.

Function	Authority
Change of name of urban district, town, townland, street or locality	Local Government Act, 1946, ss. 77, 78, 79.
Sale or disposal of corporate property (other than leasing for less than one year) under Municipal Corporations (Ireland) Acts.	
Disposal of land other than corporate property	Local Government Act, 1946, s. 83
Application for order changing status of urban district or town.	Local Government Act, 1925, s. 74
Declaration of approved local councils, and grant of assistance and delegation of functions to such bodies	Local Government Act, 1941, ss. 72, 73, 74. Local Government Act, 1955, ss. 51, 52
Discharge of functions, on agency basis, by another local authority or by a statutory body.	Local Government Act, 1955, s. 59.
Discharge of functions of local authority by health board.	Health Act, 1970, s. 25

Planning and Development

Function	Authority
Making or varying of development plan	Local Government (Planning and Development) Act, 1963, s. 19
Application for extension of period for making development plan	s. 19(6)
Revocation or modification of planning permission	s. 30 See amending Act, 1976, s. 39
Making of special amenity area order	s. 42
Making, revocation or varying of conservation order	s. 46

Function	Authority
Notice requiring removal or alteration of hedge	s. 44
Declaration of area comprised in town specified in First Schedule, Part II	s. 2
Prohibition orders in relation to temporary dwellings	Local Government (Sanitary Services) Act, 1948, s. 31
Revocation of such orders	Local Government Act, 1955, s. 66

Roads, Traffic and Transport

Declaration of road to be public road.	Local Government Act, 1953
Application for bridge order and consent to order of any road authority concerned.	Local Government Act, 1946, ss. 46, 48
Construction etc. of cross-border bridges	Local Government Act, 1955, s. 41
Extinction of right of way over disused road	Local Government Act, 1946, s. 84
Representations to Commissioner of Garda Síochána about byelaws in relation to traffic control, parking, etc.	Road Traffic Act, 1961, ss. 84, 89 and 90
Representations to Minister in relation to orders closing roads to vehicles.	s. 94
Abandonment of railway line.	Transport Act, 1950, s. 21
Agreement by road authority to maintain bridge over Royal Canal after closure.	Transport Act, 1960.

Housing

Adoption or variation of building programme.	Housing Act, 1966, s. 55

Function	Authority
Scheme of letting priorities.	s. 60
Agreement with another housing authority to operate its own area.	s. 109
Declaration that certain tenants of labourers' cottages are eligible for vesting	s. 97

Miscellaneous

Agreements in relation to theatre, concert hall or opera house.	Local Government Act, 1960, s. 1
Acquisition by agreement of land for theatre etc.	s. 1
Consideration of arterial drainage schemes.	Arterial Drainage Act, 1945, s. 5
Consideration of matters arising out of coast protection schemes.	Coast Protection Act, 1963, ss. 2 and 5
Cinema licences.	Cinematograph Act, 1909, s. 2
Proposals for taking water supply from a source.	Water Supply Act, 1942
Schemes of acceptance and management of gifts of property for civic improvement.	Local Authorities (Acceptance of Gifts) Act, 1945
Dates of fairs.	Local Government Board (Ireland) Act, 1872, s. 10
Establishment, etc. of markets.	Public Health (Ireland) Act, 1878, s. 103
Increases in charges for market fair or abattoir, where fixed by statute.	Local Government Act, 1955, s. 52

Function	Authority

5. Control of Administration

Appointment, suspension, removal and superannuation of city or county manager.	City and County Management Acts
Grouping or de-grouping of counties for management purposes.	City and County Management (Amendment) Act, 1955, ss. 12, 13, 14
Separation of Dublin city and county for management purposes.	s. 14
Requiring county manager to submit plans, specifications and estimates of proposed works.	County Management Act, 1940, s. 17
Obtaining from city or county managers all available information on corporation council business (Mayor or Chairman is entitled to secure this information without formal action by the members).	Ditto, s. 27 and City Management Acts
Requiring manager to inform members before (a) performing a specified executive function (b) undertaking any works other than repair or maintenance, or committing the local authority to expenditure on any works.	City and County Management (Amendment) Act, 1955, s. 2
Power of veto on proposed works.	s. 3
Requiring manager to do any particular act within the local authority's competence, for which money is available. There are certain exceptions e.g. personnel, planning.	s. 4 See Planning and Development (Amendment) Act, 1976, s. 39
Power of veto of proposals to vary numbers of permanent officers, or remuneration attaching to any class, description or grade of office or employment.	s. 6

Function	Authority
Requiring manager (or estimates committee, if one exists) to furnish financial statements.	s. 7
Making regulations about seeking and dealing with tenders.	s. 15
Engagement of solicitor for local inquiry where manager separately represented.	Local Government Act, 1946, s. 90

Appendix IV

Populations of County Boroughs, Boroughs, Urban Districts and Towns:
1971–9

Municipality or Town	Population		Status
	1971	1979	
Dublin	567,866	544,586	County Borough
Cork	128,645	138,267	County Borough
Limerick	57,161	60,665	County Borough
Dun Laoghaire	53,171	54,244	Borough
Tallaght	6,174	43,833	Non-Municipal
Galway	27,726	36,917	Borough
Waterford	31,968	32,617	County Borough
Dundalk	21,672	25,240	Urban District
Drogheda	20,202	22,556	Borough
Bray	15,537	21,773	Urban District
Sligo	14,080	16,840	Borough
Tralee	12,290	15,014	Urban District
Lucan	4,245	13,570	Non-Municipal
Clonmel	11,622	12,418	Borough
Wexford	11,849	11,853	Borough
Malahide	3,834	11,618	Non-Municipal
Carlow	9,588	11,418	Urban District
Clondalkin	7,009	11,351	Non-Municipal
Blanchardstown	3,279	10,127	Non-Municipal
Kilkenny	9,838	10,079	Borough
Swords	4,133	9,950	Non-Municipal
Athlone	9,825	9,778	Urban District
Arklow	6,948	8,451	Urban District
Tullamore	6,809	7,824	Urban District
Naas	5,078	7,739	Urban District
Killarney	7,184	7,724	Urban District
Mullingar	6,790	7,470	Town
Thurles	6,840	7,439	Urban District

Municipality or Town	Population 1971	1979	Status
Shannon	3,657	7,410	Non-Municipal
Leixlip	2,402	7,317	Non-Municipal
Ballincollig-Carrigrohane	2,110	7,036	Non-Municipal
Ballina	6,063	6,960	Urban District
Greystones-Delgany	4,517	6,940	Non-Municipal
Cobh	6,076	6,668	Urban District
Mallow	5,901	6,609	Urban District
Dungarvan	5,583	6,578	Urban District
Castlebar	5,979	6,489	Urban District
Ballinasloe	5,969	6,466	Urban District
Letterkenny	4,930	6,357	Urban District
Ennis	5,972	6,279	Urban District
Monaghan	5,256	6,172	Urban District
Youghal	5,445	5,796	Urban District
Droichead Nua	5,053	5,758	Town
Nenagh	5,085	5,687	Urban District
Carrick-on-Suir	5,006	5,511	Urban District
Balbriggan	3,741	5,406	Town
Enniscorthy	5,704	5,254	Urban District
New Ross	4,775	5,238	Urban District
Tramore	3,792	5,153	Town
Portmarnock	1,726	5,000	Non-Municipal
Wicklow	3,786	4,981	Urban District
Tipperary	4,631	4,929	Urban District
Athy	4,270	4,755	Urban District
Tuam	3,808	4,507	Town
Roscrea	3,855	4,348	Non-Municipal
Portlaoise	3,902	4,346	Town
Longford	3,876	4,330	Urban District
Navan	4,605	4,305	Urban District
Skerries	3,044	4,300	Non-Municipal
Kildare	3,137	3,990	Non-Municipal
Birr	3,319	3,675	Urban District
Rush	2,633	3,641	Non-Municipal
Westport	3,023	3,474	Urban District
Listowel	3,021	3,450	Urban District
Loughrea	3,075	3,443	Town
Newcastle West	2,549	3,347	Town*
Edenderry	2,953	3,312	Town

Municipality or Town	Population 1971	1979	Status
Midleton	3,075	3,297	Urban District
Passage West	2,709	3,264	Town
Cavan	3,273	3,261	Urban District
Buncrana	2,955	3,252	Urban District
Mitchelstown	2,783	3,193	Non-Municipal
Fermoy	3,237	3,186	Urban District
Celbridge	1,568	3,054	Non-Municipal
Ardee	3,096	2,982	Town
Rathcoole	1,740	2,966	Non-Municipal
Bantry	2,579	2,963	Town
Rathluirc	2,232	2,892	Non-Municipal
Mountmellick	2,595	2,865	Town
Laytown-Bettystown	1,882	2,794	Non-Municipal
Kilrush	2,671	2,778	Urban District
Clonakilty	2,430	2,746	Urban District
Gorey	2,859	2,724	Town
Ballyshannon	2,325	2,696	Town
Ballybofey-Stranorlar	2,214	2,626	Non-Municipal
Ceanannus Mór	2,391	2,594	Urban District
Templemore	2,174	2,556	Urban District
Clara	2,156	2,547	Non-Municipal
Cashel	2,692	2,538	Urban District
Castleblayney	2,118	2,514	Urban District
Muinebeag	2,321	2,419	Town
Macroom	2,256	2,412	Urban District
Clones	2,164	2,384	Urban District
Castleisland	1,929	2,218	Non-Municipal
Tullow	1,838	2,195	Town*
Trim	1,700	2,185	Urban District
Monasterevin	1,619	2,183	Non-Municipal
Cahir	1,747	2,177	Non-Municipal
Donegal	1,725	2,141	Non-Municipal
Skibbereen	2,104	2,121	Urban District
Bandon	2,257	2,112	Town
Claremorris	1,718	2,006	Non-Municipal
Rathkeale	1,543	1,956	Town*
Kanturk	2,063	1,868	Non-Municipal
Carrickmacross	2,100	1,813	Urban District
Boyle	1,727	1,791	Town
Kinsale	1,622	1,785	Urban District

Municipality or Town	Population 1971	1979	Status
Castlerea	1,752	1,765	Non-Municipal
Roscommon	1,556	1,728	Town*
Carrick-on-Shannon	1,495	1,661	Non-Municipal
Bundoran	1,337	1,555	Urban District
Caherciveen	1,649	1,550	Non-Municipal
Callan	1,283	1,443	Town*
Cootehill	1,415	1,413	Town
Kilkee	1,287	1,309	Town
Granard	1,054	1,276	Town
Belturbet	1,092	1,154	Town
Fethard	1,064	1,013	Town*
Lismore	884	920	Town
Ballybay	754	628	Town

* Commissioners no longer elected. Administration taken over by county councils.
Note: Non-municipal towns: The partial census of 1979 did not show the population
of towns without legally defined boundaries. The figures above for non-municipal
towns have been estimated from the populations of District Electoral Divisions,
and can only be taken as approximations. They do however reflect trends. Thus the
appearance of a non-municipal town (Tallaght) at fifth place in the order of magnitude
– before Galway Borough and the County Borough of Waterford – is a not unexpected
consequence of Dublin's overspill. Malahide, Clondalkin and Blanchardstown are
also dormitory 'new towns'. In Cork the suburb of Ballincollig-Carrigrohane is the
largest town outside the city.

Appendix V

Dwellings built or reconstructed with state aid 1879 to 1979

Year ended 31 March	Private Enterprise	Local Authorities — Housing of the Working Classes Acts	Labourers Acts	Total	Grants paid for Reconstruction
Totals 1879 to 1922	348	8,861 · 41,653	50,862		–
1923 ...	–	262	–	262	–
4 ...	–	697	–	697	–
5 ...	2,593	1,505	–	5,259	105
6 ...		1,140	21		
7 ...		1,150	81		
8 ...	8,317	32		11,612	494
9 ...		1,789	243		
1930 ...		1,586	40		
1 ...	5,480	992	147	8,554	–
2 ...		309	–		
Totals 1922–32	16,390	9,462	532	26,384	599
1933 ...	803	419	83	1,305	6
4 ...	3,101	3,003	742	6,846	337
5 ...	4,777	3.943	2,912	11,632	1,742
6 ...	4,666	4,215	2,100	10,981	3,373
7 ...	3,929	3,232	2,867	10,028	4,341
8 ...	4,209	2,139	2,786	9,134	5,198
9 ...	4,692	4,064	2,867	11,623	5,393
1940 ...	2,880	3,131	2,252	8,263	3,965
1 ...	2,211	1,726	1,803	5,740	2,781
2 ...	1,429	2,445	1,144	5,018	1,466
3 ...	746	1,044	727	2,517	1,148
4 ...	364	1,395	291	2,050	430
5 ...	267	981	103	1,351	300
6 ...	286	656	41	983	330
7 ...	561	563	56	1,180	690
8 ...	873	695	34	1,602	577

Totals 1933–48	35,794	33,651	20,808	90,253	32,077
1949 ...	1,547	1,621	250	3,418	757
1950 ...	2,814	3,293	2,006	8,113	1,285
1 ...	4,518	4,820	2,967	12,305	2,121
2 ...	5,487	3,967	3,218	12,672	2,298
3 ...	6,517	5,111	2,365	13,993	2,573
4 ...	5,532	2,761	2,882	11,175	4,224
5 ...	5,223	3,074	2,193	10,490	4,889
6 ...	5,826	2,363	1,648	9,837	6,494
7 ...	6,185	3,167	1,617	10,969	8,147
8 ...	4,013	2,206	1,261	7,480	7,167
9 ...	3,082	1,164	648	4,894	7,202
1960 ...	3,578	1,684	730	5,992	8,207
1 ...	4,335	836	627	5,798	9,744
2 ...	4,388	783	455	5,626	8,989
3 ...	5,039	1,242	586	6,867	9,961
4 ...	5,575	1,371	485	7,431	10,170
Totals 1949–64	73,659	39,463	23,938	137,060	94,228

Year Ended 31 March	Private Enterprise	Housing Acts 1966–79	Total	Reconstruction
1965 ...	6,972	2,307	9,279	9,057
6 ...	7,866	2,989	10,855	9,474
7 ...	6,505	4,079	10,584	8,576
8 ...	7,522	4,045	11,567	10,290
9 ...	7,925	4,613	12,538	9,678
1970 ...	8,438	4,706	13,144	8,649
Calendar Year				
1970 ...	10,120	3,767	13,887	8,871
1 ...	10,591	4,789	15,380	8,811
2 ...	15,670	5,902	21,572	9,121
3 ...	18,588	6,072	24,660	9,610
4 ...	19,510	6,746	26,256	9,091
5 ...	18,098	8,794	26,892	10,879
6 ...	16,737	7,263	24,000	14,389
7 ...	18,215	6,333	24,548	12,209
8 ...	19,371	6,073	25,444	15,797
9 ...	20,330	6,214	26,544	30,298
Totals 1965–79	212,458	84,692	297,150	184,800
1879–1979	338,649	263,060	601,709	311,704

Estimated total housing stock (1979)	<u>867,000</u> dwellings
Owner-occupied	660,000
Local authority lettings	102,000
Private lettings	105,000

Appendix VI

Local Government: International Organisations

A number of international bodies have local government interests, most of them concerned with the exchange of information. The only organisations with legal and administrative authority over local governments are the European Communities (EEC).

European Communities

Ireland's accession to the EEC took effect from 1 January 1973. Some time beforehand the Department of Local Government circulated to city and county managers a memorandum, *Irish Membership of the European Communities: Implications for Local Authorities*, March 1972. The memorandum explained that accession meant membership of three communities, the European Economic Community (EEC), the European Atomic Energy Community (EURATOM), and the European Coal and Steel Community (ECSC), and outlined the principal institutions of the Communities – the European Parliament, the Council of Ministers, the Commission, the Court of Justice, and the Economic and Social Committee.

Accession to the Communities had certain direct effects on local administration. These included the phasing out of (1) preferences for Irish goods in public contracts, and (2) the requirement of the use of Irish materials as a condition for certain state grants. All public works contracts (other than water supplies) over a certain cost level would have to be advertised in the *Official Journal* of the Communities. A Consultative Committee for Public Works Contracts (on which each member country was represented) was set up to monitor these arrangements.

Different services are subject to varying degrees of EEC intervention and influence. Roads and traffic management attract close attention, in pursuance of the Community's aim of a common transport policy. Regulations of binding force specified the ages, qualifications and hours of work and rest of drivers of large goods and passenger vehicles. Recording equipment (the tachograph) will eventually be a mandatory requirement in such vehicles, and measures have been taken with the object of harmonising road taxation, accounts systems and statistics. Environmental matters also figure prominently – the community has been active in working out, in consultation with member states, an EEC environmental policy and programme of action.

An important feature of the EEC is its regional policy whose primary aim, never effectively realised, was to correct the imbalances in economic and social development between the central and peripheral states or regions of the community. A number of member states, including Ireland, have benefited from the Regional Development Fund, and local authorities have been helped in carrying out programmes of infrastructural works. Loans have also been advanced by the European Investment Bank for regional development projects. Less important perhaps but nevertheless significant have been grants from the European Agriculture Guidance and Guarantee Fund (FEOGA) for rural water supplies; low-interest loans from the ECSC for housing workers in the coal and steel industries; and assistance from the European Social Fund for staff training and the like.

Irish local government contacts with the European Communities are almost wholly channelled through the Department of the Environment, one of whose officers has been posted full-time to the Irish mission at Brussels. International associations of local authorities, with which some authorities here maintain connections, have sought to communicate directly with the EEC through a Consultative Committee of Local and Regional Institutions in member states. The Consultative Committee was formed jointly by the International Union of Local Authorities (IULA) and the Council of European Municipalities (CEM) to study problems of implementing community regional policy, and in general to bring collective local government influences to bear and press their interests on issues of moment to them. Another channel to the European Communities is the Local Government Liaison Group of the European Parliament, consisting of nineteen MEPs with local government experience and interests.

International Union of Local Authorities

The Union had its origin in the first International Congress of Local Authorities which was held in Ghent in 1913. The main themes of that Congress were town planning and the organisation of municipal life, and these continued for some time as the prime objects of the new body, the International Union of Local Authorities (IULA). Its aims are now stated as:

— to promote the welfare of citizens through more effective local government;

— to raise standards of local administration and services;

— to encourage the international exchange of information and personal contacts among its members;

— to foster citizens' involvement in local affairs.

IULA's membership comprises local authority associations and individual local authorities. Membership is also open to central and regional government ministries, and to institutes whose interests include local government, as well as to individuals actively concerned with local government, or with teaching or research in local affairs. IULA's range covers some seventy countries throughout the world. Membership in Ireland includes Dublin County Council, the City and County Managers Association, and the Institute of Public Administration. The General Council of County Councils was also a member for a time. Activities include large biennial congresses, with smaller regional seminars and conferences, and meetings of special interest groups. Training courses are organised for senior officers from third world countries. The headquarters of IULA are located in the Netherlands, at the Hague.

Council of European Municipalities

The council was formed in Geneva in 1951, as a contribution at local level to the ideal of a united Europe. Its aims are:

— to secure, strengthen and protect the autonomy of local authorities;

— to facilitate the operation of local authorities . . . in particular the development of inter-authority arrangements and undertakings;

— to develop the European spirit amongst local and regional communities with a view to promoting European unity founded on the autonomy of these communities;

— to provide for the participation and representation of local and regional communities and authorities in the European and international institutions;

— to achieve the establishment amongst the future European institutions of an assembly representing local and regional authorities.

The CEM is organised on a system of national sections which operate both as units and in combination with other sections. There are twelve national sections, and others are in contemplation. The central body is a European Bureau on which the national sections are represented. Every two years CEM convenes an Assembly of European Municipalities. A number of smaller meetings are also held from time to time for particular purposes.

CEM headquarters are in Paris. Ireland has no national section. Although in competition to some extent with IULA, both these organisations have in recent years joined forces in order to present a united front in local government matters to the EEC and to the Council of Europe.

Council of Europe

The Council of Europe was created in 1949 to further the cause of European unity, with Ireland as one of the original ten founding member countries. There are now twenty-one members. In spite of, or perhaps because of the emergence in 1951 of CEM, the Parliamentary Assembly of the Council decided in 1955 to convoke a conference of elected members of European local authorities. The first meeting of the European Conference of Local Authorities was held in 1957, and two-yearly meetings continued to be held until 1975. In that year the constitution and name were changed to become the Conference of Local and Regional Authorities in Europe, and meetings were convened annually. Members of the Conference are nominated either by national governments or by national associations of local authorities.

The Council of Europe has also organised, in addition to the conference of elected members, a series of committees of officials concerned with local and regional affairs. There are four 'Committees of Experts' under the guidance of a Steering Committee for Regional and Municipal Matters which deal with the following topics:

— local and regional structures;

— local and regional finance;

— management in local and regional government;

— social and economic activities.

A great deal of work has been done by these committees in the study of problems relevant to their remit, and in publishing their findings.

The third instrument created by the Council of Europe is the Conference of European Ministers Responsible for Local Government, which first met in 1975. Meetings have been held annually since then. The Conference has discussed such issues as trans-frontier co-operation, citizen participation in local government and decentralisation of government to neighbourhood level. The Council of Europe operates from Strasbourg. The Conference of Ministers, had its first meeting in Paris, and met thereafter in Athens, Lisbon, Stockholm and Madrid.

Appendix VII

A Note on Local Government in Greece

Greece became the tenth member country of the European Economic Communities, with effect from 1 January 1981.

Greek local government goes back to classical times, if one accepts the not very close parallel between the ancient city state (polis) and modern urban government. In fact the line of continuity between the two was broken by conquests enduring for over a thousand years, and Greece did not regain independence until early in the nineteenth century. Modern Greek local government dates from that period, and is modelled on the French system of prefects and communes. The Constitution bases the administrative organisation of the state on the principles of decentralisation, and local self-government.

There are some fifty provinces, corresponding to French departments, each governed by a state-appointed prefect (*nomarch*) who is the chief agent of local administration. He is assisted by an advisory council of elected and appointed members whom he consults about the provincial budget, major developments and other matters of policy. The prefect or *nomarch*, in addition to his other duties as government representative, supervises the municipal authorities in his province.

Municipal authorities, the basic level of Greek local government, are of two kinds – urban and rural. Urban authorities (*demos*) have 10,000 inhabitants or more, and rural (*koinotes*) between 500 and 10,000. Each elects a council varying in size according to population. Elections are held every four years by universal suffrage, or the list system of proportional representation. The chief executive (mayor or *demarch* in urban municipalities, and president in rural communes) is then chosen, and certain other officers. Urban authorities have, in addition to the mayor, two or four assistant mayors, depending on size. The council adopts the municipal budget, sets the level of local taxation, provides for the financing of public works, and generally assists the mayor and his aides in running the municipality. Local revenue is the product of property and other taxes, stamp duties, and income from trading enterprises. Special charges for town cleansing and public lighting are a major additional source of income. Central government grants make up the balance.

Municipalities are very numerous — 250 urban authorities and some 5,800 rural — a total in excess of 6,000 for a population of less than ten million people. In the circumstances, local government at municipal level is relatively weak and central government tends to be the dominant partner. The Ministry of the Interior, working through the prefectoral structure, provides a strong reinforcing element for the system as a whole. Central agencies, in addition, undertake a number of works and services which are within local competence but are beyond local resources in finance and staff. These include water supplies, sewerage, irrigation, power stations, roads and bridges, public beaches and playgrounds.

An elaborate structure of local (departmental) associations or unions of municipalities and communes, topped by a central association at national level, functions mainly as a communications network for the local government system. An unusual feature of the Greek polity is the recognition of Mount Athos as an autonomous community, administered by its twenty monasteries through a representative council and a small executive board.

Appendix VIII

Local Government in Irish Literature

Local government makes a rather poor showing in the sparse literature in which it happens to figure. This is perhaps to be expected. The writers whose work is mentioned in this brief note – it is confined, with one exception, to 20th century Irish literature – are literary artists taking an outsider's critical and often disparaging view of the somewhat humdrum workings of local elected boards and councils.

Irish writers have on the whole been more hostile than English to local politics: a major novel like *South Riding* (1936) by Winifred Holtby gives a remarkably sympathetic picture of local government in action. Even in France, where one would hardly expect local intrigue to escape a satirical drubbing, the *maire* who is the principal character in Gabriel Chevallier's *Clochemerle* (1936) gets off comparatively lightly.

Perhaps we may avoid bathos by mentioning before we get going, the little known or little regarded fact that the Irish Literary Theatre could only have come into being with great difficulty without section 89 of the Local Government (Ireland) Act, 1898. This section furnished a mechanism for authorising occasional stage performances in public halls in Dublin other than the three theatres – Gaiety, Royal and Queen's – licensed by the Lord Lieutenant under an Act of 1786. The Irish Literary Theatre's first session was staged in 1899 in the Antient Concert Rooms in Great Brunswick (now Pearse) Street, under permission granted, at the request of Dublin Corporation, under the 1898 Act.

George Moore, Edward Martyn

The Irish Literary Theatre's second season (1900) included a play on a local government theme: *The Bending of the Bough* by George Moore. But although Moore's name appeared as author, the idea for the play belonged to Edward Martyn, and Moore had in fact with Martyn's consent, merely adapted Martyn's original version for stage purposes. The first part of *Hail and Farewell* has as one of its more entertaining sequences, an account of Moore's condemnation of his friend's play, then in manuscript – 'muddle, gross farcical situations' – and his struggles, first to persuade

342

Martyn to improve it and (when Martyn proved obdurate but self-sacrificing) to produce his own drama on Martyn's theme, under the title *The Bending of the Bough*. Martyn's version was published as *The Tale of a Town* in 1902 and staged for the first (and possibly last) time in 1905.

It is a rather flat-footed Ibsenesque play on municipal affairs in what is obviously Galway, displaying in addition to dramatic ineptitudes only a sketchy knowledge of the realities of municipal business. According to Lennox Robinson *The Bending of the Bough*, while an improvement on *Tale of a Town,* was 'pallid' and without dramatic force, but opinions have been anything but unanimous. The acidulous Susan Mitchell who did not like Moore wrote (1913) that 'Edward Martyn's play was tortured from its original intention and became no play at all'. Una Ellis Fermor (*The Irish Dramatic Movement* 1939) said Martyn's play was a melancholy failure which Moore had turned into 'one of the most successful of the movement' and devotes a whole chapter (Chapter 6 'Martyn and Moore') to telling how. Sister Marie Therese Courtney in *Edward Martyn and the Irish Theatre* (1952) is equally emphatic but less convincing on the opposite side. In the end we can only record Yeats's verdict in *Ave* 'We couldn't produce such a play as that.'

James Joyce

James Joyce's 'Ivy Day in the Committee Room', first published in 1914 in *Dubliners*, deals with an episode occurring about ten years earlier. The Committee room in Wicklow Street was a Nationalist centre, the occasion the annual election for seats on the city council, one third of whose eighty-odd members vacated office at the end of the year. The Nationalist candidate whose canvassing literature was used as cigarette lighters was 'Mr Richard J. Tierney, Poor Law Guardian', a publican like a large proportion of city councillors. The slight element of suspense in the story hangs on the uncertainty whether the candidate will or will not send round a dozen of stout to sustain and encourage his canvassers.

Joyce re-creates the room and the people with what seems marvellous fidelity, although he was not himself present — he developed the story from a sardonic account of the episode sent to him in Paris by his brother Stanislaus. His father ('Henchy' in the story) was a pensioner of the abolished office of Dublin Collector General of Rates and a familiar figure in municipal circles. The background is presented in that style of scrupulous meanness which Joyce thought appropriate to the Dublin of the time, with echoes of past heroism and vanished nobility supplied by Joe Hynes's recitation of his deeply felt but wooden verses on the death of Parnell twelve years before. The local election and the weary canvassers are, regrettably, part of that drab background.

Joyce never lost his interest in Dublin's civic affairs and personalities. The theme re-appears several times in *Ulysses*. There are a number of ob-

scure references scattered through *Finnegans Wake* to the city's Lord
Mayor aldermen and councillors – in particular to the 1924 dissolution of
the city council, and the appointment of the three city commissioners,
Hernon, Murphy and Dwyer. These have been construed for us by Dr John
Garvin in Chapter 21 of his *James Joyce's Disunited Kingdom and the
Irish Dimension.*

William Boyle, Fred Ryan

The Irish Literary Theatre and later the Abbey created a demand for new
plays, and a number of writers followed Edward Martyn's (and Ibsen's)
example in looking to local politics for themes and situations. There is
record of a performance in 1902 in the Camden Street Hall of *The Laying
of the Foundations* by Fred Ryan, 'a drama of municipal wrongdoing and
drains, after the fashion of Ibsen'. The manuscript of this play does not
seem to have survived. A better known play was William Boyle's *The
Eloquent Dempsy* (1906), a satirical cartoon of local politics which gave
a name (now forgotten) to a generation of flatulent carry-overs from a
departed period of great political oratory. Jeremiah Dempsy, publican,
county councillor and poor law guardian, succeeds for a time, with dex-
terous and inexhaustable speechifying, in supporting both Unionist and
Nationalist factions, but he is overtaken by Nemesis at last. He loses his
seat on the county council, his publican's business is threatened with
failure and he retires to farming and a better life.

Boyle's plays, once a staple of Abbey programmes, were very popular
but valueless as literature. Dempsy was Arthur Sinclair's favourite role
when, in the words of Robert Hogan (*After the Irish Renaissance* 1968)
'he debased his talent in pursuit of laughs'.

Seamas O'Kelly

A more serious effort and one which has proved rather more durable (it
has been restaged several times by the Abbey) was *The Bribe* by Seamas
O'Kelly, first put on in 1913. It is a convincing portrayal of small-town
corruption, seen through a situation in which an honest and highminded
chairman of a Board of Guardians finds himself propelled irresistibly
into a wrong course of action. He gives his casting vote for the second
best candidate for a job as dispensary doctor, with dire results – including the death of the erring chairman's wife – for all concerned. The play
is a homily against crooked dealing in public life, but the characters are
clearly drawn and strong enough to carry the message without loss of
dramatic impact.

Edward McNulty

The Lord Mayor (1914) was another of those pieces reflecting or cari-
caturing the pre-war political scene. It was written by the not very well-

known Edward McNulty, who had an early connection with George Bernard Shaw and wrote a number of plays, most of them forgotten. The hero of *The Lord Mayor* is a dim Pooteresque character with an ambitious wife. An ironmonger, he became a Dublin city councillor, with disastrous results for his business. His election as Lord Mayor, managed by a group of councillor-creditors, rescues him from bankruptcy, and we are shown various aspects of city corruption as the hero is subjected, like St Anthony, to temptations from all sides, Unionist and Nationalist. But he survives with his conscience more or less intact, and all ends well.

Padraic Colum, Augusta Gregory

A bypath in the literature of these early years of the century led to some material on poor law subjects. Padraic Colum's play *Thomas Muskerry* (1910) gives a realistic picture of workhouse life as seen from the inside. Colum was born in one of these institutions, of which his father was superintendent or master. The central figure of his play was also a workhouse master, a worthy man, an admirable example of the profession. He is on the point of retiring – he is close to seventy – when the play opens, and looks forward to years of serenity and leisure. But owing to family failures and misfortunes he finds himself ending his days as a workhouse inmate. Lady Gregory's *Workhouse Ward* made its first appearance in the Abbey in 1907, in a version called *The Poorhouse* written jointly with Douglas Hyde, who supplied the dialogue as a contribution towards theatre in the Irish language. Lady Gregory 'thought a dramatic movement in Irish would help us as well as the Gaelic League'. The play reappeared in 1908 under its new title, re-written by Lady Gregory. It is a short piece full of human interest about two old paupers who spend most of their time enjoyably quarrelling with 'arabesques of talk'.

Lester Martin, Susanne Day

A remarkable work, of the same period although not published until 1916, was *The Amazing Philanthropists*, the highly coloured name given by the author to the Board of Guardians of which she was the first woman member. Not that the guardians were notably philanthropic: this was not presented as a piece of imaginative literature. It is a series of letters supposedly written by Mrs Lester Martin PLG and edited by Susanne R. Day, giving a lively narrative of the goings-on in a large Union in the south of Ireland, and of various happenings in the workhouse, its hospitals and in particular its children's wards. The main theme is Mrs Martin's struggles with local politicians to better the condition of the pauper children.

John McDonagh

The 1914–18 war interrupted the modest burgeoning of this type of literary work. The patriotic and idealistic emotions which fuelled plays like *The Lord Mayor* were diverted to the larger scene: it would be diffi- cult to visualise a tragic masterpiece like *The Plough and the Stars* finding a place in a municipal setting. With a single exception, it was not until the second world war that anything on local politics made a re-appearance. The exception was *The Irish Jew* by John McDonagh, brother of Thomas McDonagh, executed in 1916. The play was first shown in 1921, in what is now the Olympia. The hero is a Jewish Lord Mayor of Dublin, Ambrose Golden, who foils the machinations of a cabal of councillors engaged in a shady deal. No Jew had achieved this civic eminence when MacDonagh's play appeared. Dublin's first Jewish Lord Mayor, Robert Briscoe was not elected until 1955. In addition to this achievement, Briscoe has the rare distinction of writing a book about his political life, parliamentary and local: *For the Life of Me* 1959.

Henry Robinson

The early 1920s were also, for our purposes, marked by two works of reminiscence and anecdote by Sir Henry Robinson, last vice president of the Local Government Board. These were *Memories Wise and Other- wise*, and *Further Memories of Irish Life*, both of which appeared in 1924. Neither has much claim to rank as history or literature, but the second does occupy a niche in that voluminous corner of 'Irish' literature reserved for works of anecdotage. Although presented as a factual account of local life and politics, it is a compendium of obviously invented absurdities, and to that extent could rank as creative writing. Here is a sample, taken at random, of the goings-on at a Board of Guardians meeting. A form is being discussed, for the guidance of the Relieving Officer.

'All right so', said Mr O'Toole (the clerk). 'Column 3. "Name of sur- viving parent".' 'But suppose he's dead?' said Mr O'Loughlin. 'Ye ought to make sure about that. I knew a case of a surviving parent that was run over by a train.'

St John Ervine

After about two decades of silence on the topic of local government, the result of weightier preoccupations, St John Ervine's *William John Mac- whinney* was staged by the Abbey in March 1940. This satirical comedy about celebrating the bi-centenary of a local hero deals with episodes of small-town infighting in which councillors and town clerk figure among the belligerents. The play was not published.

Brian O'Nolan (Flann O'Brien)

Brian O'Nolan's *Faustus Kelly* was produced by the Abbey in January

1943 and ran for a fortnight. O'Nolan had been a civil servant in the Department of Local Government and Public Health since 1935, where he had been private secretary to a succession of Ministers. This, he said, involved him in 'almost daily attendance at Leinster House. Garrulity is a feeble word to describe what I encountered in Dáil Éireann. . . . The play *Faustus Kelly* arose somehow from that Leinster House gab . . .'. It is a satire on local deviousness, corruption, and verbosity; but, on the whole, not a very good play. The perennial publican, chairman of the urban council, makes his appearance as Faustian hero, with the same stupefying eloquence as *The Eloquent Dempsy*, and the same political ambition. Kelly sells his soul to the Devil in return for his help in getting elected to the Dáil, and the Devil in the guise of Mr Strange wins by nefarious means the job of rate collector, which gives him access to the electoral register. But the plan comes unstuck. Faustus Kelly tops the poll in suspicious circumstances which bring him under police investigation with the possible loss of the seat. And as a final disaster, the Department refused to sanction Mr Strange's appointment and thus 'aided by the unquestioned adherence of the Irish people to any sort of authority' (Anne Clissman *Flann O'Brien* 1975) outlaws him: he becomes an untouchable, an outcast. But even hell has its compensations. Mr Strange says goodbye thankfully to the horrors of Irish public life, gladly surrendering his claim on Kelly's soul and retreating, with relief, to his homeland.

O'Nolan wrote his play under the pen-name Myles na gCopaleen by which he is best known. He thought the alias would protect him from the resentment of the politicians whom he was satirising. At the first performance, when cries of 'author' were heard, a grotesque figure emerged from the wings in vivid green tailcoat and kneebritches, with shillelagh and the kind of hat favoured by *Punch* cartoonists for pictures of the Irish peasant. But the disguise, though effective in the short run, was not immediately necessary. O'Nolan used to say that the play's run was curtailed by political pressure, but in reality its brief career was due to its own shortcomings. There were no political assaults on the author. The Minister, Sean MacEntee, was present at the first night, and was obviously much entertained by his private secretary's shafts of humour.

Tomas Ó Súilleabháin

The only Irish language play on a local government theme was presented in the Abbey later in 1943. This was *An Comisineir* by Tomas Ó Súilleabháin, an excellent comedy which regrettably has not been published. The situation exploited by Ó Súilleabháin was much the same as that of Gogol's *The Government Inspector*, whose hero is accepted by the local community, in mistake for the real thing, as a man of authority. The fake commissioner is, for a brief period, equally omnipotent in local affairs.

Robert Collis

Before and during the Emergency housing had been a problem, varying in intensity from area to area. Dublin suffered from a chronic housing shortage, and the Corporation's effort to clear slums and unhealthy dwellings was not helped by the war. The emotions of the time found expression in Dr Robert Collis's play *Marrowbone Lane*, published in 1943 but first produced some years earlier by the Gate Theatre. It is a piece strong in sentiment, taking advantage of the abundant pathos of the slums, and packing an explosive propaganda punch. It exhibits in dramatic terms the misfortunes of a country girl, married to a Dublin man, a born loser, and trying to fight her way out of a tenement house. Her struggle brings her inevitably into confrontation with the housing authority, and this should have been the cue for local government to show its stumbling paces.

Dr Collis seems to have had only a vague idea of what constituted the bureaucracy, and one of his best scenes with the action obviously taking place in the Corporation Housing Department, is wrongly located in 'a Government Office.' We are nevertheless given a fairly authentic picture of officialdom at work, trying to cope with the impossible task of relieving innumerable cases of hardship with an inadequate supply of houses. The head official is even credited with a compassionate heart.

Mervyn Wall

A few of the more recent works with a bearing on local government took the form of novels. In *Leaves for the Burning* (1952) Mervyn Wall depicts the misadventures of a minor county council official with cultural leanings. The tone of the book is one of deep disenchantment. The events in the story took place about the time of W. B. Yeats's repatriation (1948) and burial in Drumcliffe churchyard in County Sligo. Against this cloudy background of faded literary splendour the self-seeking and farcical mismanagement which form the texture of the novel stand out in deplorable contrast. Senator Trefoil, Chairman of the County Council, and Stanislaus O'Toole, County Manager, are equally skilful in manipulating local situations, political, administrative, religious, and whatever comes to hand – including disposal of an embarrassing corpse, the by-product of a late-night drinking session – to their own advantage.

The anti-hero, Lucian Brewse Burke, of good family in decline, absurdly over-educated for his job, and burdened with artistic sensibilities, takes part in an epic pub-crawl which began with the best of intentions, as a project to attend the funeral of the returned Yeats. He never reaches Sligo and finds himself after many misdirected miles and much confused drinking, back more or less where he started. He personifies in a small way the kind of Ireland which was uprooted by the war of independence, in which Senator Trefoil bore a dubious part. The County Manager represents the type of administration and society which took over after 1922 and in which Lucian figures in a subordinate role, without significance and with no future. Local government is chosen, regrettably, as an example of the New Ireland in action.

John McCann

John McCann, Dublin City councillor and one-time Lord Mayor was a prolific playwright during the 1950s turning out a great deal of undistinguished material, most of it now forgotten. One of his best plays, *Early and Often*, was produced by the Abbey in 1956. The story is built round an election to the city council, and McCann's familiarity with electioneering and with the mechanism and tensions of local politics help to convey a better sense of reality than O'Nolan's *Faustus Kelly*. The sardonic O'Nolan touch is also absent, replaced by the interplay of McCann's soap-operatic but very human characters.

W. J. (Jack) White

The Hard Man (1958) by Jack White is about an architect who after some years in private practice spends a brief period with Dublin County Council as a planning officer. There are some revealing glimpses of political life, with diverting accounts of various characters who play a part in it — in particular a Senator Sarsfield (based on a famous real-life senator) who entertains his family, friends and followers with record recitals of classical music, conducted by himself in full evening dress under a pink spotlight. Local government is a subordinate theme in the story, but there are intriguing insights into the pressures to which the hero is subjected by ambitious and powerful developers.

G. K. Chesterton

Finally *The Napoleon of Notting Hill* (1904) by G. K. Chesterton, a book about a London suburb by a very English writer. The boundaries of the Irish literary scene would have to be impossibly elastic to accommodate this novel, despite the fact that M. J. MacManus (*So This is Dublin*, 1927) in 'The New Irish Credo' included as articles of faith 'That G. K. Chesterton is an Irishman' and 'That Mr. Bernard Shaw is not'. The reason for adding it to our list is the extraordinary regard that Michael Collins had for it. The novel was according to Christopher Hollis (*The Mind of Chesterton*) 'the favourite book of Michael Collins . . . When the Irish delegates went to meet the British Cabinet to negotiate for the Irish Treaty, Lloyd George hearing of Michael Collins' literary taste, presented a copy . . . to each member of his Cabinet in order that they might the better understand Collin's mind.'

The story is a highly-coloured romance inspired by Chesterton's passionate conviction that patriotism can attach itself to small units, and burn more intensely because of that concentration of feelings on a village, a town or even a suburb as drab as Notting Hill. It was an expression of Chesterton's revolt against Imperialism. The book is a lively fantasy about the restoration of ancient freedoms and privileges — a panoply of medieval magnificence complete with banners, bannerets, heraldry, armies and weaponry — to London suburbs. The hero, Adam Wayne, takes this improbable idea so seriously that he goes to war for it: 'Adam Wayne as a boy had for his dull streets in Notting Hill the ultimate and ancient sentiment that went out to Athens or Jerusalem.' Is it possible that Michael Collins's youthful mind might have caught fire from Chesterton's impassioned prose?

Appendix IX

The Two Tipperarys

Tipperary was divided into two ridings with effect from 10 December 1838 — 510 years after James Butler, 1st Earl of Ormond, had been endowed with the liberty of the county. The term Palatinate was applied to the territory. Ormond took the name of his Earldom from the two baronies where the Butlers had established a power base in the 13th century with Nenagh as *caput*. He set up the Palatinate court at Clonmel at the far south end of the county. When the Palatinate was extinguished in 1715, Clonmel continued its role as Assize town.

The Proclamation of 1838 tightly adapted the phrases of the enabling Grand Jury Act of 1836 in rationalising the division of the county and restoring Nenagh as a capital: 'the great extent of the said county of Tipperary and the inconvenient situation of the town of Clonmel, at which the assizes for the said county are now holden, in respect to the northern parts'.

Memorials from 'several landed proprietors and inhabitants of the northern parts' had initiated the process before the Lord Lieutenant, or viceroy/Chief governor, and Privy Council.

Tipperary was the only county to have its inhabitants pursue the provisions of the 1836 Act. In the five counties of greater extent, measured both by local acreage and greatest length-breadth, each had an Assize town relatively convenient to all of its sizeable segments: Galway (Galway), Cork (Cork), Mayo (Castlebar), Donegal (Lifford) and Kerry (Tralee). Likewise the next in order of size: Clare (Ennis) and Tyrone (Omagh). As to inconvenient situation, only Waterford and Wexford each had a namesake county town, and Louth had Dundalk somewhat analogous to Clonmel's peripheral location within Tipperary. But Louth was the smallest county and the other two could hardly be judged to be of 'great extent', their acreages being about half of Tipperary's. As to an aggravating factor, in the sense of multiplying the inconvenience — the numbers of committal for trial — Tipperary's total was just four times each of theirs: Tipperary was easily the most lawless county, having a committal rate fluctuating between three and five times the national rate in the years 1834—6.

The prize of nomination as Assize town where a Grand Jury in spring and summer would consider presentments for money for public works, that fiscal business being followed by up to a fortnight's hearing of civil and criminal cases by the presiding Judges and special juries, was contested by Thurles inhabitants and landowners from its vicinity. Before a committee of the Privy Council, two King's Counsels and a junior presented the northern/Nenagh case. It outlined Clonmel's situation on the verge of Waterford, the expense of travelling and living there for a fortnight's Assizes twice annually and that consequently there was never a good attendance of jurors from the northern baronies. These originated crown and civil bill cases in a proportion of three to the southern baronies' two. On the Nenagh versus Thurles argument, the cases also divided three : two and there was a better record of jurors' attendance at Nenagh sessions.

The Thurles KC and junior countered that Thurles Courthouse and Bridewell could be extended for £7,000, with the land offered free, against a £15,000 estimate for new buildings at Nenagh. Both sides produced witnesses as to comparative mileages from other towns; two county officials gave it as their opinion that Nenagh was the 'fittest town' and another independent witness, the Inspector of Prisons, confirmed that Clonmel gaol was insufficient and additions would be necessary to cater for a full county.

The Committee recommended the division, and Nenagh as Assize town. Six months later it presided over a compromise halving, north-south, of the barony of Kilnamanagh in the face of memorials from its inhabitants. The Lord Lieutenant and Privy Council completed the formalities which were adopted for County Councils in 1898 and, one could say, finally sealed by a Ministerial order in 1969 providing for two County Managers. The Joint Library Committee is now the only Tipperary-wide local government unit.

There are two other counties which might have shared Tipperary's distinction. Galway had east and west ridings but only for the appointment of county surveyors and management of the police force. Cork was formally divided into east and west ridings in 1823 but solely for the purpose of organising quarter sessions, and like Galway it had but a single Grand Jury.

In the Local Government (Ireland) Bill, 1898, as introduced, specific provision was made to divide Cork into two ridings within a six month period designed to gather information on the desire of its inhabitants. The provision was excised without a vote despite a difference of opinion among the Cork MPs at Committee stage. Tim Healy said that 'the west riding was so remote from the east riding that it might desire a sort of Home Rule', but explained that initial public support for a division had faded when the Chief Secretary had declared against 'equal ratings', apparently implying a heavy burden on the west in new buildings.

I am indebted principally to Desmond Roche, John McGinley and Nancy Murphy for information and discussion which influenced the above.

Sources: (Privy) Council Office Papers, State Paper Office; microfilm files of

Tipperary Constitution, Tipperary Free Press, Clonmel Advertiser, Clonmel Herald (National Library); Nenagh Guardian file; Hansard; Report to Local Government and Taxation (Ireland) Inquiry, 1878 – W. P. O'Brien, L. G. Inspector; "Disturbed Tipperary", James W. Hurst in Eire-Ireland, Fomhar, 1974.

Donal A. Murphy

Bibliography

Administration 24/3 (1976) Special issue on structures for regional development

Ahearne, P. 'The Service State and Local Government' 2 (1) *Christus Rex* (1948) pp.3-14

Alderfer, H. *Local government in developing countries* McGraw Hill, London, 1964

Alexander, Alan 'Local government in Ireland' *Administration* 27/1 pp.3-27

Allen, Herbert 'The relevance of Irish local government for today's Third World' *Administration* 22/4 (Winter 1974) pp.367-383

Baker, T.J. and O'Brien, L.M., *The Irish housing system: A critical overview* ESRI, 1979, (ESRI Broadsheet Series, no. 17)

Bannon, M.J., 'Urban Land' in *Irish Resources and Land Use* pp.250-269 D. Gillmor (Ed) IPA 1979

Barnes, Monica 'Women in local politics' *Administration* 23/1 (1975) pp.80-83

Barrington, T.J. 'The district, is there a future for it?' *Administration* 19/4 (1971) pp.299-317
'Environment and the quality of life' *Administration* 21/4 (1973) pp.424-433
'Public administration, 1927-1936' *Administration* 13/4 pp.316-323
From big government to local government: the road to decentralisation. IPA, 1975
'Can there be regional development in Ireland?' *Administration* 24/3 (1976) Special Issue
The Irish Administrative System IPA, 1980 Chapter 2

Bax, M. *Harpstrings and confessions: machine-style politics in the Irish Republic* Van Gorcum, Assen/Amsterdam, 1976

Bewley, Victor *Travelling People* Veritas Publications, Dublin, 1974

Bird, T.H. 'Municipal government of the city of Bombay, India' *Public Administration* x.1. (1932) pp.100-108 Contains comparative references to Irish system

Black, R.D. Collison *Economic thought and the Irish Question, 1817-1870* Cambridge: University Press 1960, Ch. 4, 'The Poor Law'

Blaney, N.T. 'The role and function of the councillor' *Administration* 13/2 pp.73-77

Blaney, N.T., Gill, J.F., and Meagher, G.A. 'The role and function of the councillor' *Administration* 13/2 (1965) pp.73-89

Bowles, G.F. 'Environmental sanitation, 4. The health inspector in the field of environmental sanitation and hygiene' *Administration* 8/2 (1960) pp.125-136

Bristow, J.A. and Tait, A.A. (eds) *Economic Policy in Ireland* IPA, 1968 (Chapter 12 'The Growth of Public Revenue and Expenditure in Ireland')

Bristow, S.L. 'Women councillors – an explanation of the under representation of women in local government' *Local Government Studies* 6/3 (1980)

Broe, T.F. 'Revenue and expenditure of local authorities' *Administration* 12/1 (1964) pp.1-16

Bromage, A.W. 'The council-manager plan in Ireland' *Administration* 9/4 (1961) pp.309-317

'Irish councilmen at work' *Administration* 2/1 (1954) pp.87-98

Buchanan, Colin and Partners *Regional Studies in Ireland* An Foras Forbartha, 1968

de Buitléir, Dónal *Problems of Irish local finance*, IPA, 1974

Busteed, W.A. 'The Belfast region: local government in need of change' 1 (3) *Public Affairs* (1968/9) pp.12-13

'Reshaping Belfast's local government' *Administration* 18/3 (1970) pp.256-61

Butlin, R.A. (ed) *The development of the Irish town* Croom Helm, London, 1977

Campbell, M.J. 'Towards a classification of decentralised systems' in *Comparative Local Government* 2/2 (1968)

Camblin, Gilbert 'Structures for development in Northern Ireland' *Administration* 24/3 (1976) Special Issue

Chavasse, Moirín *Terence Mac Swiney* Clonmore and Reynolds, 1961 (Ch XVI, 'As Lord Mayor')

Chubb, F. Basil *The government and politics of Ireland* Oxford University Press, London, 1970. (Ch. XI on local government.)

Coakly, J. 'Spatial units and the reporting of Irish statistical data: the evolution of regional divisions' *Administration* 27/1 (1979)

Colivet, M.P. 'The housing board, 1932-1944' *Administration* 2/3 (1954) pp.83-6

Collins, C.A. 'Local political leadership in England and Ireland' *Administration* 28/1 (1980) pp.71-96

Collins, J. *Local government*, 1954, Second edition by Desmond Roche, IPA, 1963

'Notes on local government, 1. Beginnings of county administration' *Administration* 1/1 (1953) pp.40-44

'Notes on local government, 2. Evolution of county government' *Administration* 1/2 (1953) pp.79-88

'Notes on local government, 3. Local government in municipal towns' *Administration* 1/3 (1953) pp.35-46

'Notes on local government, 4. The genesis of city and county management' *Administration* 2/2 (1954) pp.27-38

'Notes on local government, 5. The use of committees' *Administration* 3/1 pp.73-81

Comhairle na Gaeilge *Local government and development institutions for the Gaeltacht*

Commission on Technical Education Report, SO, 1927

Commission on the relief of sick and destitute poor, Report SO, 1927

Commission for Local Administration in England Your local ombudsman. Report for the year ended 31 March, 1978, HMSO, 1978

Committee of Enquiry Local government finance, London, HMSO, 1976 (Chairman: Frank Layfield)

Computers, Survey Group *The use of computers in local government* SO, 1970, Prl. 1194

Conlon, M.N. 'Local Government — Some Fundamental Principles'. *Administration* 19/4 (1971) pp.328-30

Convery, F.J. 'Concepts for environmental policy' *Administration* 22/4 (1974) pp.351-366

Copeland, J.R. & Walsh, Brendan M. *Economic aspects of local authority expenditure and finance* ESRI, 1975, (ESRI General Research Series no. 84)

Cronin, Michael 'City Administration in Ireland' *Studies* Vol XII (1923) pp.345-360

Cullen, John *Notes on Local Government* for Diploma in Administrative Science, IPA, 1979

Cullinane, M.V. 'Administrative structures for regional development: The Regional Development Authority viewpoint' *Administration* 24/3 (1976) pp.318-330

Davies, R. and Hall, P. *Issues in Urban Society* Penguin Book, 1978

Davies, Richard P. *Arthur Griffith and non-violent Sinn Féin* Anvil Books, 1974

Department of Local Government Annual Reports, 1922-, SO, 1922-

Department of Local Government and Public Health First report (1922-25), Second report (1925-27), SO

Departmental committee on the housing conditions of the working classes in the city of Dublin Report, HMSO, 1914

Departmental Committee on Valuation, Northern Ireland Reports (2), 1923 and 1924, HMSO

Desmond, T.B. 'Sub-National Organisation of the Functions of Government' *Administration* 24/3 (1976) Special Issue

Devlin, P. *Yes, we have no bananas: outdoor relief in Belfast 1920-1939* Blackstaff Press, 1981

Donnison, David 'Urban development and social policies' *Administration* 26/1 (1978) pp.5-24

Dooge, J.C.I. 'Local government from the councillor's point of view' *Public Administration* Vol III (1952) pp.217-34, Civics Institute

Downey, W.K. 'The physical environment and implications for the year 2000' in *Ireland in the year 2000* An Foras Forbartha, 1980

Drury, B. 'Regionalism—1. Local government' *Administration* 18/3 (1970) pp.211-224

Dunsire, A. 'Accountability in local government' *Administration* 4/3 (1956) pp.80-88

Early, Barry 'Dublin city commissioners at work' *Administration* 21/4 (1973) pp.450-459
'Local government reorganisation in Denmark — some comparisons with Ireland' in *Administration* 22/2 (1974) pp.128-140

Edwards, R. Dudley and Williams, T. Desmond (eds) *The Great Famine: studies in Irish history, 1845-1852* B & N, Dublin, 1962

Environment, Department of Guide to Local Government for councillors SO, March 1981
Quarterly Bulletin of Housing Statistics, 1974 —
Current trends and policies in the field of housing, building and planning. Annual, 1978-
Road development plan for the 1980's 1979
Superannuation Revision Scheme 1977
Local Elections 1979, *Election Results and Transfer of Votes,* Prl. 9322, SO
Returns of Local Taxation, Annual Prl. 8661, SO

Falkiner, C. Litton *Illustrations of Irish history and topography, mainly of the seventeenth century* Longman's Green, and Co, London, 1904

Farrell, Brian, 'The drafting of the Irish Free State Constitution' in *Irish Jurist* vol V New Series, pp.115-40 and pp. 343-56 (1970) and vol. VI, pp.111-35 and pp. 345-59 (1971)

Fennell, Desmond 'Organising Connacht for economic and social growth' *Administration* 24/3 (1976) Special Issue

Fitzpatrick, David *Politics and Irish life 1913-1921: provincial experience of war and revolution* Gill and Macmillan 1977 (Ch. 5. 'Revolutionary Administrators . . . 3 Republican Local Government', pp.184-197)

Flannery, M. *Building Land Prices* The Tribune Printing and Publishing Group, Birr, 1980
'Local finance — an outline' *Administration* 9/1 (1961) pp.65-72
Sanitation, conservation and recreation services in Ireland IPA, 1976

'Some current road problems' *Administration* 10/2 (1962) pp.97-114

'One hundred years of public health' *Administration* 26/4 pp.435-458

Foley, D. 'The public libraries' *Administration* 1/2 (1953) pp. 26-32

An Foras Forbartha *Transportation in Dublin* (report on the Dublin transportation study directed by Kevin Heanue) An Foras Forbartha, 1971 Dublin Transportation study: technical reports An Foras Forbartha, 1972

Fried, Robert, *The Italian prefects: a study in administrative politics* London, Yale University Press, 1963

Gale, Peter *An enquiry into the ancient corporate system of Ireland and suggestions for its immediate restoration and general extension* Richard Bentley, London, 1834

Gallen, Finn 'Have local authorities a future in government?' *Business and Finance:* Vol 11/26 (20 March 1975) pp.10-12; 29

Garvin, John,'Local government and its problems' *Administration* 11/3 (1963) pp.224-241

'Nature and extent of central controls over local government administration' in *Public Administration in Ireland* ed. F.C. King Vol II pp.162-173. Civics Institute (1949)

'Problems and prospects in local government' *Administration* 13/1 (1965) pp.1-10

'Public Assistance' in *Public Administration in Ireland* ed. F.C. King, Vol I, pp.163-172 Civics Institute (1944)

'Public relations in local government' *Administration* 3/1 (1955) pp.47-56

Gill, J.F. 'The role and function of the councillor' *Administration* 13/2 (1965) pp.77-82

Golden, T.P. *Local authority accounting in Ireland* IPA, 1977

Gorham, M. 'Preserving Ireland' *Administration* 9/3 (1961) pp. 241-7

Greater Dublin Commission of Inquiry Report, S.O. 1926

Gwynn, Denis *The Irish Free State 1922-1927,* Chapter XXV Local Government and Poor Law, Allen, London, 1928

HMSO *Report of the commission of enquiry into the municipal corporations* Parl. papers 1835, XXVII and 1836, XXIII, XXIV

Report of the vice-regal commission on poor law reform in Ireland 1906 CD 3202

'Review Body on Local Government in Northern Ireland, 1970'

Hall, P.A. 'Recent developments in transport policy' *Administration* 28/2 (1980) pp.184-198

Hall, Peter *Urban and Regional Planning,* Penguin, Harmondsworth, 1974

Harman, J.F. 'County Development Teams' *Administration* (1963) 11/4 pp.289-295

Harris, G. Montagu *Comparative local government* Hutchinson's University Library, 1948

Hart, Ian 'Public opinion on civil servants and the role and power of the individual in the local community' *Administration* (1970) 18/2 pp. 375-391

Hayes, C.M. 'Local Government in Northern Ireland' *Léargas* 13 (1968) pp.6-7

Hayes, M.N. 'Some aspects of local government in Northern Ireland' in *Public Administration in Northern Ireland* Edwin Rhodes (ed) Derry, Magee University College, Extra Mural Studies, 1967, pp.77-99

Hegarty, Denis A. 'An outline of local government administration' in *Public Administration in Ireland* Ed F.C. King, Vol I, pp.143-160 Civics Institute 1944

Hill, Dilys M. *Participating in local affairs,* Penguin, Harmondsworth, 1970 *Democratic Theory and Local Government* No 12 The New Local Government Series Allen & Unwin, 1974

Horgan, John J. 'City Management in America' *Studies* Vol IX (1920) pp.41-56

'Local government developments at home and abroad' *Studies* Vol. XV (1926) pp.529-541

The Cork City Management Act: its origin, provisions and application Guy and Co., Cork, 1929

Growth of the Irish manager plan *National Muncipal Review* XXXIV/6

'The development of local government in Ireland' *Journal of Social and Statistical Inquiry Society of Ireland* 17 (1942-47)

Hughes, O. 'Rates equalization' *Administration* 9/2 (1961) pp.110-119

Hughes T.J. 'Administrative divisions and their development in nineteenth-century Ireland' *University Review* 3 (6), pp.8-15

Humes, S. and Martin, E. *The structure of local government: a comparative survey of 81 countries* International Union of Local Authorities, The Hague, 1969

Humphreys, Alexander, J. *New Dubliners: urbanisation and the Irish family* Routledge and Kegan Paul, London, 1966

Hussey, M.O. 'Sir Richard Griffith — the man and his work' *Administration* 14/4 (1966) pp.314-326

Inquiry into housing of working classes in the city of Dublin, 1939-43, Report S.O. 1944

Institute of Public Administration *More Local Government: a programme for development* Report of study group, IPA, 1971

Interdepartmental Committee on Local Finance and Taxation
Report 1: Value of rating purposes 1965;
Report 2: Exemptions from and remissions of rates 1967;
Report 3: Rates and other sources of revenue for local authorities, 1968.

Interdepartmental Committee on Malicious Injuries 1960-63, Summary of report, SO, 1965

International Council of Museums (ICOM); *Directory of Local Museums and Local Societies in Ireland* Irish National Committee, 1976

IULA *Urbanization in Developing Countries,* IULA The Hague, 1968
Local government as promoter of social and economic development IULA, The Hague, 1971

Jennings, Robert 'Irish Housing Subsidies' *Administration* 28/4 (1980) pp. 409-422

Johnson, T. 'Housing' in *Public Administration in Ireland* ed. F.C. King, Vol I pp. 173-204, Civics Institute, 1944

Jones Hughes, T. 'The origin and growth of towns in Ireland', University Review II (7) (1959)

Kaim-Caudle, P.R. 'The economic and social cost of housing' *Administration* 22/3 (1974) pp.278-287
Housing in Ireland: some economic aspects ESRI, 1965

Keating, Seamus 'Administrative structures for regional development: the local authority viewpoint' *Administration* 24/3 (1976) pp.331-336

Keith-Lucas, Bryan *The English local government franchise: a short history* Blackwell, Oxford, 1952

Kelly, J.M. 'Local authority contracts, tenders and mandamus' 2 *'Irish Jurist* (1967) pp.1-9
'Judical review of administrative action: new Irish trends' in *The Irish Jurist* Vol VI New series, 1971, pp.40-49. (Deals with case of Listowel UDC v. McDonagh, an itinerant)

Keogh, C.A. *Public Library Provision in the Irish Free State* Athlone Printing Works, 1936

Killen, James, 'Urban transportation problems and issues in Dublin' *Administration* 27/2 (1979) pp.151-166

LAC *The Local Appointments Commission* 1926-1976 SO, 1976

Lawrence, R. 'Local Government in Northern Ireland: Structure, Functions and Finance' 21 *JSSISI* (119th sess) 1965-6 pp.14-23
The government of Northern Ireland: public finance and public services 1921-1946 Oxford University Press, 1965

Lewis, Norman and Gateshill, Bernard *The Commission for Local Administration* Royal Institute of Public Administration, 1978

Lichfield, Nathaniel and associates *Limerick Regional Plan: Interim Report on the Economic, Social and Technical problems of the planning of the Limerick City – South Clare – Shannon Industrial Estate Complex* SO, 1965

Local Authority Engineering Organisations Report to the Minister for Local Government, SO, December 1970

Local finance and taxation, Dublin: Stationery Office Prl. 2745, 1972. (White Paper)

Local Government and Public Health, Department of. Commission of enquiry into the sale of the cottages and plots provided under the Labourers (Ireland) Acts: final report, 1933 G.P. SO, 1933

Local Government and Public Services Union, Report to Minister for Local Government on: McKinsey Report *Local and Public Forum* 3/4 (1972) pp.3-15

Local Government, Department of. *Local Elections, 1974, Results and Statistics* SO, 1974

Local Government (Dublin) Tribunal Report, S.O. 1938

Local Government Reorganisation (1971) Prl 1572, SO, Dublin

Local Government and Taxation in United Kingdom. London, 1882. Cobden Club essays. Part VI, which relates to Ireland, is the work of Richard O'Shaughnessy, MP

Local Taxation, Royal Commission on. Minutes of Evidence, HMSO, Vol. I. Appendix C.8764. 1898. Vol. V. Appendix C.386. 1900. For changes made by the Act of 1898

Loughran, G.F. 'The problem of local government in Northern Ireland' *Administration* 13/1 (1965) pp.35-38

Lucey, M. 'Rateable valuation in Ireland' *Administration* 12/1 (1964) pp.26-34

Mac Cadáin, P.S. 'Internal auditing in local authorities' *Administration* 9/4 (1961) pp.318-325

Mac Craith, Sean *Early Irish local government 1921-1927* The Clonmel Nationalist, 1967

McDonald, Frank, 'Dublin – what went wrong', *The Irish Times,* November 12-15 1979

McDowell, R.B. *The Irish administration 1801-1914* Routledge and Kegan Paul, London 1964

McElligott, C.C. 'The problem of revaluation' *Administration* 3/1 (1955) pp.11-28

McEvoy, P.L. (ed) *Irish Local Government Year Book and Directory* McEvoy Publishing Co. 2nd Ed. 1939

McGilvray, J. 'The economics of roads' *Administration* 10/2 (1962) pp.127-138

Macken, Matthew 'City and county management and planning administration' *Leargas* (a review of public affairs – publication ceased) No. 10 June-July, 1967

Mackenzie, W.J.M. *Theories of local government* School of Economics & Political Science London, 1961

McKinsey & Co., Inc. *Strengthening the local government service: a report prepared for the Minister for Local Government* Dublin: Stationery Office, 1972

Mac Manus, Francis (ed) *The years of the great test 1926-1937* Mercier Press, 1967

McNamara, Brendan, 'Regional development: Case studies from France and Italy' *Administration* 25/1 (1977) pp.35-56

Mac Niocaill, Gearoid *Na Buirgeisi* Cló Morainn, 1964 (2 vols)

Malicious Injuries, Summary of report of Inter-departmental Committee on SO Pr. 8142, 1965

Manning, M. 'Women in Irish national and local politics 1922-27' in *Women in Irish society: The historical dimension* (ed) M. McCurtain and D. O'Corrain, The Women's Press, 1978

Mansergh, N. *The Irish Free State, its government and politics* Macmillan, London, 1934 (Ch. 13 on local government)

Marshall, A.H. *Local Government Finance* (Report) IULA, 1969

Local government administration abroad (an enquiry carried out for the Maud Committee on the management of local government) Vol. IV, HMSO, 1967

New revenues for local government Fabian Society, London, 1971 (Fabian research series 295)

Meagher, G.A. 'Housing and the taxpayer' *Administration* 2/4 (1954) pp.56-66

'Housing: Finance: *Administration* 7/2 (1959) pp. 191-202

'Planning and national development' *Administration* 13/4 (1965) pp.247-260

The role and function of the councillor *Administration* 13/2 pp.82-89

Meghen, P.J. 'The administrative work of the grand jury' in *Administration* 6/3 (1958) pp.247-264

'Building the workhouses' *Administration* 3/1 (1955) pp.40-46

'Central-local relationships in Ireland' *Administration* 13/2 (1965) pp.107-122

'City and county managers: the American viewpoint' *Administration* 8/1 (1960) pp.11-18

'The development of Irish local government' *Administration* 8/4 (1960) pp.333-346

Housing in Ireland IPA, 1963. 2nd edition, 1965

'Irish local government and the Robinson family' *Administration* 9/4 (1961) pp.291-308

'Local affairs in Sweden' *Administration* 5/2 (1957) pp.43-9

'Local government and central control' *Administration* 5/4 (1957) pp. 54-62

'Local government finance – 2' *Administration* 16/3 (1968) pp. 293-302

'Local government reform: England' *Administration* Vol 18/2 pp.99-115

'New ways of financing local government' *Administration* 9/2 (1961) pp.106-9

'Public administration in Germany' *Administration* 10/1 (1962) pp. 50-69
Roads in Ireland IPA, 1965
'Why local government?' *Administration* 12/3 (1964) pp.190-206
Local government in Ireland Fifth edition revised by D. Roche, IPA, 1975

Miley, J. and King, F.C. *Town and Regional Planning Law in Ireland* 1951
Monahan, Philip 'Housing, 1. The social background' *Administration* 7/2 (1959) pp.166-177
'Silhouette' *Administration* 2/1 (1954) pp.65-74
Mooney, T.A. *Compendium of the Irish Poor Law, and general manual for Poor Law guardians and their officers* Thom, 1887
Money, W.J., 'The need to sustain a viable system of local democracy' *Urban Studies* 10 (October 1973) pp.319-333
Muintir na Tire *Government at sub-national levels: planning, co-ordination, local participation* Muintir na Tire, Tipperary, 1977
Municipal Corporations, Report of the Commission of Inquiry into the HMSO, Par. pp.1835 XXIII and XXIV
Murphy, T. 'Environmental Sanitation: Environment and health' *Administration* 8/2 (1960) pp.93-99
Murray, C.H. 'National and physical planning' *Administration* 14/4 (1966) pp.286-297
Murray, P. 'Worker participation in local authorities' *Administration* 26/3 (1978) pp.383-391

NESC Reports:
Housing subsidies. Report No. 23 NESC, 1977
Institutional arrangements for regional economic development Report No. 22 NESC, 1976
Regional policy in Ireland: a review Report No. 4 NESC, 1975
Rural areas: change and development Report No. 41 NESC 1980 (by P. Commins, P.G. Cox, J. Curry)
Service-type employment and regional development Report No. 28, 1977 (comments by the Council; report by Michael J. Bannon, James G. Eustace and Mary Power)
Transport policy Report No. 48, NESC, 1980 (comments by the Council; report by Professor C.D. Foster, T.J. Powell and D.J. Parish; comments by P. Murphy, Irish Employers Confederation)
Urbanisation and regional development in Ireland Report No. 45, SO, 1979 (comments by the Council; report by P.N. O'Farrell)
Urbanisation: problems of growth and decay in Dublin Report No. 55 SO, 1981 (by M.J. Bannon, J.G. Eustace and M. O'Neill)
Nally, D. 'The local government grant system' *Administration* 7/4 (1959) pp.349-370

Nicholls, George *A history of the Irish poor law in connection with the condition of the people (1856)* John Murray, London

Nielsen, N. 'The Danish ombudsman' *Administration* 21/3 (1973) pp.355-364

O'Brien, George *Economic history of Ireland from the Union to the Famine* Longmans, Green and Company, London 1921 (Ch. VI)

O'Brien, W.P. *Local government and taxation (Ireland) inquiry* Special report on local government in Ireland, Par. pp. 1878 XXIII

O'Byrne, M. 'Libraries and librarianship in Ireland' *Administration* 16/2 (1968) pp.148-154

O'Ceallaigh, S.T. *Sean T.* Foinseacháin Naisiunta Teo, 1963 Caib IX, 'Comhairleoir Cathrach'

O'Connor, T.M. 'Local government and community development' *Administration* 11/4 pp.296-310
'Regional industrial planning' *Administration* 20/1 pp. 79-97

O'Donnell, James D. *How Ireland is governed,* 5th edition. Dublin: Institute of Public Administration, 1974 (Ch. 9 on local government)

O'Donoghue, F. *Tomas Mac Curtain, soldier and patriot* Anvil Books, 1955. Paperback, 1971 (Ch. XIII 'First republican Lord Mayor of Cork')

O'Farrell, P.N. 'Regional planning policy – some major issues' *Administration* 26/2 (1978) pp. 147-161

O hUiginn, P. 'Some social and economic aspects of housing – an international comparison' *Administration* 8/1 (1960) pp.43-71

Oireachtas *Administrative Justice: Report of All Party Informal Committee,* 1977

O'Keeffe, P.J. 'Economic aspects of road improvement in Ireland' *Administration* 10/2 (1962) pp.139-176
'Main roads' *Administration* 10/2 (1962) pp.183-196

O'Neill, T.P. 'The administration of relief' in R. Dudley Edwards and T.D. Williams (eds) *The great Famine* B & N, Dublin, 1962

O'Nuallain, C. 'Citizen participation and local government in Ireland (unpublished) 1971
'Training for local authorities' *Administration* 18/1 pp.31-36

O'Rourke, Felim 'The Travelling People' *Administration* 26/1 (1978) pp. 123-128

O'Sheil, Kevin, 'County councils, their powers and their possibilities' in *Irish Year Book,* Sinn Féin, 1921

Pakenham-Walsh, A.A. 'Financial controls in local government' *Administration* 12/1 (1964) pp.17-25

Pfretzschner, P.A. 'City planning and urban renewal in America' *Administration* 12/2 (1964) pp.87-101
'Development and amenity' *Administration* 12/3 (1964) pp.217-225
The dynamics of Irish housing IPA, 1965

Piekalkiewiez, Jaroslawa *Communist local government: a study of Poland*, Ohio University Press, 1975

Poor Law Reform in Ireland, Report of the Vice-regal Commission on Vol. I. 1906. Cd.3202

Poor Law, Royal Commission on the HMSO, 1910

Powell, Malachy 'The workhouses of Ireland' in *University Review* III (7) pp.3-16

Prescott, T.A.N. 'Road services for a county' *Administration* 10/2 (1962) pp.177-182

Price of Building Land, Report of the Committee on, (Kenny Report), SO, Dublin, 1974

Quinn, D. 'Anglo-Irish local government' *Irish Historical Studies I*

Raven, John and others *Political culture in Ireland: the views of two generations* IPA, 1976

Rees, I.B. *Government by community* Charles Knight London 1971

Revers, H.J.D. *The International Union of Local Authorities (IULA) 1913-63: The story of fifty years of international co-operation*, IULA, The Hague, 1963

Ridley, F.F. (ed) *Government and administration in Western Europe* Martin Robertson, Oxford, 1979

Robertson, Manning 'Town and Regional Planning' in *Public Administration in Ireland* ed F.C. King Vol I pp.205-223, Civics Institute, 1944

Robins, J.A. 'Carlow workhouse during the famine years' *Administration* 20/2 (1972) pp.63-70
  'The background to the first Irish registration acts' *Administration* 11/3 (1963) pp.267-282
  'The county in the twentieth century' *Administration* 19/2 (1961) pp. 88-94

Robinson, Sir Henry *Memories wise and otherwise* Cassell and Co, 1924
  Further memories connected with local government administration in Ireland, Cassell and Co, 1924

Roche, D. 'Local government finance' *Administration* 16/3 (1968) pp.281-292
  'The future role of Irish local government' *Administration* 13/1 (1965) pp. 26-34

Roche, D. and Christopher, R.F. *Consumer protection: A role for local government* SO, 1973 National Prices Commission, Occasional Paper No. 5

Rowat, Donald C. (ed) *International handbook on local government reorganisation: contemporary developments* Aldwych Press, London 1980

Royal Commission on the housing of the working classes. Third report, Ireland, HMSO, 1885

Royal Commission on Local Taxation, 1898-1901. Reports and minutes of evidence, HMSO, 1902

Royal Commission on Local Government in Greater London (1957-1960) Report: 2 volumes, HMSO, London, 1960. (Chairman: Sir Edwin S. Herbert)

Royal Commission on Local Government in England (1966-1969) Report: 3 volumes, HMSO, London, 1969. (Chairman: Lord Redcliffe Maud)

Sacks, P.M. *The Donegal Mafia: an Irish political machine* Yale University Press, New Haven/London, 1976

Saorstat Eireann *Commission of Inquiry into De-rating Reports,* SO 1931

Senior, Derek 'Regional Devolution — Throughout the United Kingdom' *Administration* 24/3 (1976) Special Issue

Shaffrey, Patrick *The Irish town: an approach to survival* O'Brien Press, 1975

Sheehy, E.T. 'Roads administration' *Administration* 10/2 (1962) pp. 115-126

'A study of the law on motor taxation' *Administration* 14/1 (1966) pp. 38-84

'A study of the law on public roads' *Administration* 13/2 pp. 123-154

Smiddy, T.A. 'The present system of municipal government in the Irish Free State' *Public Administration* VIII-3 (1930) pp.339-342

Smyth, T.S. 'Municipal charters of the town of Cavan' *Administration* 10/3 (1962) pp. 310-317

Stewart, D. 'Urban Form' in *Ireland in the year 2000* An Foras Forbartha, 1980

Street, H.A. *The law relating to local government* SO, on behalf of Incorp. Council of Law, Report, 1955

Sullivan, Philip *Irish planning and acquisition law* IPA, 1978

Sutcliffe, John C. 'The public image of the public servant' *Administration* 11/2 (1963) pp.101-3

Tierney, Myles *The parish pump: a study of efficiency and local government in Ireland,* Able Press, 1982

Transport Consultative Commission *Passenger transport services in the Dublin area:* (Report of the TCC to Minister for Transport, March 1980) SO, 1980

Tribunal of Inquiry, Report, *Disaster at Whiddy Island, Bantry, Co. Cork* (Ch. 22 'The Role of the Public Authorities'. Bantry Bay Harbour Commissioners, p. 330 Cork County Council, pp.332-3) SO 1980

Turpin, D. 'Local Government Service (1) Achieving a Single Service; (2) Consolidating the Service' *Administration* 2/4 (1954) pp.83-97; 3/1 pp. 82-94

'Regionalism — 2. Local government' *Administration* 18/3 (1970) pp.199-210

Walsh, Brendan M. 'National and regional demographic trends' *Administration* 26/2 (1978)

Webb, J.J. *Municipal government in Ireland: mediaeval and modern* Talbot Press, 1918
The Guilds of Dublin, Sign of the Three Candes, 1929.

Whelan, Noel 'Considerations Relevant to Central Government' *Administration* 24/3 (1976) Special Issue

Woodham-Smith, C. *The great hunger, Ireland, 1845-9* Hamilton, London, 1962

White, R.H.'Rateable Valuation' in *Public Administration in Ireland* ed F.C. King Vol III pp.248-265 Civics Institute, 1954

Wraith, Ronald, *Local government in West Africa,* Praeger New York and London 1964 (Description and comment, Irish management system pp.167-170)

Wright, Myles *The Dublin region: advisory plan and final report,* SO, 1967

Zimmerman, J.F. 'An Bord Pleanála (The Irish Planning Board)' *Administration* 28/3 (1980) pp.329-344
'Community building in large cities' *Administration* 20/2 (1972) pp. 71-87
'Council-manager government in Ireland' *Comparative Local Government* IULA Vol, 2 1972
'Council-manager government in Ireland', *Studies in Comparative Local Government:* Vol 6/1 Summer 1972 pp.61-69
'New town development in the Dublin area' *Planning and Administration,* 5/1 (1978) pp.68-80
'Role perceptions of dual office holders' *Administration* 26/1 (1978) pp.25-48
'Role perceptions of Irish city and county councillors' *Administration* 24/4 (1976) pp.482-500

Index

Acts of the Oireachtas/Parliament and Bills are listed under separate groups within the general index.

abbatoirs 74, 134; charges 148, 180; municipal 277
Abercrombie, Patrick 187
accommodation: grants 178
accountability, local 161
accounts, local authority 183-4
ACOT 78, 176, 276

Acts of the Oireachtas /Parliament: general references
City Management Acts 96, 116, 171
County Management Acts 108
Diseases of Animals Acts 80, 276; committees 109
Drainage Acts 277
Education (Provision of Meals) Acts 48, 275
Housing Acts 187, 220, 228, 231, 236, 238, 257
Housing (Gaeltacht) Acts 163, 228, 231
Housing of the Working Classes Acts 220, 229, 236
Labourers Acts 220, 222-3, 224, 226, 229, 230, 236
Land Purchase Acts 229
Lands Clauses Acts 204, 205
Libraries Acts 269
Local Government (Sanitary Services) Acts 69, 80-1, 183, 205, 257
Management Acts 72, 110, 113, 158; reserved functions 189
Municipal Corporation Acts 64, 72, 74
Nuisances Removal and Diseases Prevention Acts 41
Poor Relief Acts 280; repeal of 136
Public Health Acts 53, 187, 205, 265
Public Parks (Ireland) Acts (1869-72) 268
Sale of Food and Drugs Acts 75
Small Dwellings Acquisition Acts 220, 224, 227, 228

Acts of the Oireachtas (post-1922)
Acquisition of Land (Allotments) Act (1934) 179
Agriculture Act (1931) 60, 78, 276
Agriculture (An Chomhairle Oiliúna Talmhaíochta Act (1979) 78, 275-6
Air Navigation and Transport Act (1936) 256
Air Raid Precautions Act (1939) 264
Air Raid Precautions Act (1946) 264
Arterial Drainage Act (1925) 70
Arterial Drainage Act (1945) 250, 278
Arts Act (1973) 270
Building Societies Act (1976) 234
Casual Trading Act (1980) 284
Censorship of Films Act (1923) 271
Children Act (1941) 274
City and County Management (Amendment) Act (1955) 108, 110, 120, 124; estimates procedure 168; finance 186; planning applications 193
Civil Liability Act (1961) 244
Coast Protection Act (1963) 267
Consumer Information Act (1978) 284
Cork City Management Act (1929) 55, 102-3, 130; as Bill 113
Coroners Act (1962) 282
County Management Act (1940) 58, 77, 105, 106, 107, 214
County Management (Amendment) Act (1972) 107, 109
Courthouses (Provision and Maintenance) Act (1935) 282
Defence Act (1954) 94
Derelict Sites Act (1961) 203, 207
Dublin Reconstruction (Emergency Provisions) Act (1924) 187
Electoral Act (1923) 59
Electoral Act (1963) 93-96 *passim*, 178
Electricity Supply (Amendment) Act (1930) 162

369

Belfast 32, 34, 63, 73, 289
Belgium 4, 12, 14-15, 16, 21
Bentham, Jeremy 3, 33, 39, 40, 41, 126
betterment levies 153

Bills
County Management (Amendment) Bill
(1953) 108
Fire Services Bill (1981) 263
Litter Bill (1981) 266
Local Elections Bill (1947) 59
Local Government Bill (1940) 81
Local Government Bill (1924) 81
Local Government (Building Land) Bill
(1980) 208
Local Government (County Administra-
tion) Bill (1950) 108
Local Government (Planning and Devel-
opment) Bill (1969) 195
Rates on Agricultural Land (Relief) Bill
(1981) 175
Valuation Bill (1938) 166

boards of assistance 213
boards of fisheries conservators 70, 84,
89, 163
boards of guardians 39, 41-2, 45, 46, 47,
48, 60, 87; abolition of 51, 52;
cottage building 221
boards of health 52, 104; abolition of
105; and housing 224, 225, 226
boating; grants for 203; hire of boats
76, 272
Bord Fáilte 57, 66, 87; and conservation
orders 198; and development plans
190
An Bord Pleanála 90, 122, 191, 194;
Annual Reports 197; grant to 180;
planning practice and procedure 197;
powers of 196-7
borough corporations 35, 36, 45, 74; civil
defence 264; managers 109, 110;
museums 270; nineteenth century
126; non-county 62, 74; as planning
authorities 189; public parks 268;
roads 252; as sanitary authorities
257; seventeenth century 125
borough councils 34, 72, 74; admission
of women to 47; committees 76; disqualification for membership of 94-5;
and harbour authorities 83; meetings
117, 120
boroughs 29, 32-34, 39, 42, 44, 46, 64,
65, 66, 72, 74, 215; and Association

of Municipal Authorities of Ireland
91; and county managers 106; gymnasiums 270; museums 270; non-
county 64, 75, 168; pensions committees 79; rates remission 163 *see
also* county boroughs
boundaries: alteration of 71, 303; local
legislation 130; regional 67; town 65
bridges 30, 43, 250; Denmark 17; Italy
20; loans for 183; Netherlands 22;
stone 245; toll 181
Britain: and Constitution 4, 5; local
government reform 295-8; local
government system 24-26, 55;
National Health Service 2; *see also*
England, Northern Ireland, Scotland,
Wales, United Kingdom
Buchanan Report 85, 200
building 74, 134; industry 241-2
buildings: bye-laws 131; dangerous 74,
76, 134; in development plans 189;
municipal 74; rates on 162
building societies 233-4; interest rates
234
burial boards 45, 69, 77, 80, 109, 267;
financial statistics 146
burial grounds 42, 74, 267; bye-laws
131, 134; exemption from rates 153,
162; fees 180
bye-laws 74, 76, 128, 131; anti-litter
(Dublin) 266; land use for recreation
purposes 268; temporary dwellings
272

cables: and private land 197
camping sites 190, 272; travelling people
242
canals 245; bridges 250; rates on 162;
(relief of) 163, 173
caravans: parking, grants for 203; sites
190, 272
car parking' facilities 135; grants for
203; meters (income from) 180; and
planning application 192
cats' and dogs' homes 267; grants to 180
cattle marts 279
cellars, licensing of 197
cemetery joint committee 77
Central Fisheries Board 70, 84
central government 1, 8, 10, 11, 32, 45,
50, 54, 87-9, 109, 292, 294; controls
122-8; delegation to local authorities
132; Greece 340; and local income
tax 161; Netherlands 22; Northern
Ireland 7; reduction of powers 118;